Welfare, Modernity, and the Weimar State, 1919–1933

E D I T O R S

Sherry B. Ortner, Nicholas B. Dirks, Geoff Eley

A LIST OF TITLES

IN THIS SERIES APPEARS

AT THE BACK OF

THE BOOK

PRINCETON STUDIES IN

CULTURE / POWER / HISTORY

Welfare, Modernity, and the Weimar State, 1919–1933

YOUNG-SUN HONG

PRINCETON UNIVERSITY PRESS

PRINCETON, NEW JERSEY

Library of Congress Cataloging-in-Publication Data

Hong, Young-Sun, 1955–
Welfare, Modernity, and the Weimar State, 1919–1933 / Young-Sun Hong.
p.   cm.—(Princeton studies in culture/power/history)
Includes bibliographical references and index.
ISBN 0-691-05674-9 (cl : alk. paper).—ISBN 0-691-05793-1 (pb : alk. paper)
1. Public Welfare—Germany—History—20th century.   2. Poor—Germany—History—20th
century.   3. Germany—Social policy.   4. Germany—Social conditions—1918–1933.   5. Social
work—History.   I. Title.   II. Series.
HV275.H664   1998   362.5′8′094309041—dc21   97-34249   CIP

This book has been composed in Times Roman

Princeton University Press books are printed on acid-free paper
and meet the guidelines for permanence and durability of the
Committee on Production Guidelines for Book Longevity of the
Council on Library Resources

http://pup.princeton.edu

Printed in the United States of America

1   3   5   7   9   10   8   6   4   2

1   3   5   7   9   10   8   6   4   2
(pbk)

IN MEMORY OF
• MY GRANDMOTHER •
AND MY FATHER

• CONTENTS •

• *A C K N O W L E D G M E N T S* •

SINCE the inception of this book, I have accumulated many debts to many
different people and institutions who have had faith that my study of the German welfare system would expand our understanding of Wilhelmine and
Weimar society and, hopefully, provide a historical perspective from which to
understand the problems of the modern welfare state.

Above all, I would like to thank Geoff Eley and Michael Geyer for having
been there as friends and advisors at each stage in my intellectual development.
I don't think they'll ever know how much their support has meant to me.

This work would not have been possible without the financial support of
many institutions: the University of Michigan; the Deutscher Akademischer
Austauschdienst (for research and study visit grants in 1990 and 1995); the
German Marshall Fund; the Social Science Research Council Berlin Program;
and both California State University at Fullerton and SUNY Stony Brook,
which provided research support during the long gestation period of this book.
My gratitude to the Institut für Europäische Geschichte in Mainz can not be
reduced to the generous financial support which they provided during the early
stages of my research. The former director, Prof. Dr. Karl Otmar von Aretin,
and the entire staff of the Abteilung Universalgeschichte all made the Institut an
ideal place for exploring the arcana of German history. I would like to especially thank Dr. Martin Vogt, who constantly encouraged my work and willingly shared with me his vast store of knowledge about the Weimar Republic. I
hope that they are not disappointed with a final product which has undergone
many metamorphoses over the years and which is quite different from the dissertation upon which it is based.

This work could not have been completed without the assistance—and frequently guidance—of archivists and librarians in many cities across Germany. I
am particularly indebted to Dr. Hans-Josef Wollash, Wolfgang Strecker, Ulrike
Schiuk, and Effi Jacobs of the library-archive of the Deutscher Caritasverband
in Freiburg, who—as everyone working in this field knows—not only hold the
most important collection of material on the German welfare system, but also
go out of their way to make this material accessible. I am also grateful to their
counterparts at the Diakonisches Werk der Evangelischen Kirche in Düsseldorf
and Berlin. I would also like to thank the staff of the Bundesarchiv in both
Koblenz and Potsdam and the Archiv der Metallgesellschaft in Frankfurt, which
holds the valuable papers of the Deutscher Verein für öffentliche und private
Fürsorge. I have worked in many other archives over the past decade or so.
Unfortunately, as the focus of my work has shifted, only a small proportion of
this material has made it into the final manuscript. Still, I would like to thank
the Stadtarchive in Düsseldorf, Frankfurt, Cologne, Munich, and Nuremberg,
the (former) Geheimes Staatsarchiv Preußischer Kulturbesitz in Merseburg, the

Archiv der Hochschule für Sozialpädagogik und Sozialarbeit, the Helene-Lange-Archiv, the Bayerisches Hauptstaatsarchiv in Munich, and the Evangelisches Zentralarchiv in Berlin.

Over the years, I have exchanged ideas with many friends on both sides of the Atlantic who have contributed in their own ways to the final product: David Crew, Ross Dickinson, Elisabeth Domansky, Christiane Eifert, Gary Finder, Stacy Freeman, Michael Gross, Elizabeth Harvey, Pieter Judson, Rudy Koshar, Urusula Nienhaus, Jean Quataert, Eve Rosenhaft, Susanne Rouette, Carola Sachße, Adelheid von Saldern, George Steinmetz, and the members of my New York German women's history group. Bob Moeller deserves special thanks for having been generous and patient enough to read this manuscript at the various stages and provide copious comments displaying equal measures of insight, wit, and encouragement. Lastly, I would like to extend my thanks to someone who cannot receive them in person—Detlev Peukert. Although much of the book is critical of facets of his work, his writings have a rare quality which, unlike many others, makes it worthwhile to engage with them intellectually.

Closer to home, I would also like to thank my irreplaceable friends from Ann Arbor: Kathleen Canning, Belinda Davis, Laura Downs, Sue Juster, Susan Thorne, Lora Wildenthal, and Elizabeth Wood. They made graduate school tolerable and continue to provide a standard against which to measure both friendship and intelligence. However, since leaving the nest I have made many new friends who have been a constant reminder that there is life outside the confines of the German welfare system: Nancy Fitch, Shelley and Linda Maram, Anna-Ruth Löwenbrück, Marlene and Peter Pelzer, and my colleagues at SUNY Stony Brook, who are living proof that a department can be as pleasant as a family, especially when you are far away from home.

Now that I am back in Korea after an absence of fifteen years, I realize that I simply would not have been able to face all of the challenges—both academic and personal—without the constant support of my friends. Most of all, my husband Larry Frohman has lived with me and my book for more than a decade. Without either his unceasing encouragement or the constant flow of illuminating suggestions and critical comments from his pen, I would not have retained my sanity or finished this book. For that I will forgive him for wearing shoes in the house. Finally, although I am really quite privileged to have gained so many wonderful friends abroad, this has not come without a price, in particular, the inability to share the final moments of the lives of two people who have meant the most to me: my grandmother and my father.

Seoul
January 1, 1997

ADCV	Archiv des Deutschen Caritasverbandes
AdR	*Akten der Reichskanzlei*
ADW	Archiv des Diskonischen Werkes der Evangelischen Kirche, Berlin
ADWRh	Archiv des Diakonischen Werkes in Rheinland
AFHSS	Archiv der Fachhochschule für Sozialarbeit und Sozialpädagogik
AfS	*Archiv für Sozialgeschichte*
ARGB	*Archiv für Rassen- und Gesellschaftsbiologie*
ASS	*Archiv für Sozialwissenschaft und Sozialpolitik*
AW	*Arbeiterwohlfahrt*
BAK	Bundesarchiv Koblenz
BAP	Bundesarchiv Potsdam
BayHStaA	Bayerisches Hauptstaatsarchiv
BDF	Bund deutscher Frauenvereine
DEF	Deutscher evangelischer Frauenbund
DNVP	*Deutschnationale Volkspartei*
DV	Deutscher Verein für Armenpflege und Wohltätigkeit (German Association for Poor Relief and Charity); after 1919, the Deutscher Verein für öffentliche und private Fürsorge (German Association for Public and Private Welfare)
DVS	Deutscher Verband der Sozialbeamtinnen
DZW	*Deutsche Zeitschrift für Wohlfahrtspflege*
EZA	Evangelisches Zentralarchiv, Berlin
FW	*Freie Wohlfahrtspflege*
PrGStAM	Geheimes Staatsarchiv, Abt. Merseburg
GuG	*Geschichte und Gesellschaft*
HADV	Executive Committee of the Deutscher Verein
HAStK	Historisches Archiv der Stadt Köln
HLA	Helene Lange Archiv
IfG	Archiv des Instituts für Gemeinwohl
IM	*Die Innere Mission*
KFV	Katholischer Fürsorgeverein für Mädchen, Frauen und Kinder
Nachrichten-dienst	*Nachrichtendienst des Deutschen Vereins*
NSV	Nationalsozialistische Volkswohlfahrt
RAM	Reichsarbeitsministerium (Reich Labor Ministry)
RFV	Reichsfürsorgepflichtverordnung (National Social Welfare Law, 1924)

RGBl.	*Reichsgesetzblatt*
RGr	Reichsgrundsätze über Voraussetzung, Art und Maß der öffentlichen Fürsorge (National Guidelines for the Determination of Need, the Nature, and the Scope of Public Welfare, 1924)
RJWG	Reichsjugendwohlfahrtsgesetz (National Youth Welfare Law, 1922)
RMdI	Reichsministerium des Innern (Reich Interior Ministry)
RVG	Reichsversorgungsgesetz (National Military Pension Law, 1920)
SBA	*Soziale Berufsarbeit*
SDV	*Schriften des Deutschen Vereins für Armenpflege und Wohltätigkeit* (later *für öffentliche und private Fürsorge*)
SPr	*Soziale Praxis*
StADf	Stadtarchiv Düsseldorf
StAF	Stadtarchiv Frankfurt am Main
StAM	Stadtarchiv München
StAN	Stadtarchiv Nürnberg
VGM	Preußisches Ministerium für Volkswohlfahrt, ed., *Veröffentlichungen auf dem Gebiet der Medizinalverwaltung*
VSWG	*Vierteljahrschrift für Sozial- und Wirtschaftsgeschichte*
WuS	*Wirtschaft und Statistik*
Zentralblatt	*Zentralblatt für Jugendrecht und Jugendwohlfahrt*
ZfA	*Zeitschrift für das Armenwesen*

Welfare, Modernity, and the Weimar State, 1919–1933

SOCIAL DISCIPLINE AND THE POLITICS OF WELFARE REFORM

The history of public poor relief, voluntary charity, and welfare in Germany has been marginalized in most studies of the formation of the welfare state and treated in a niggardly manner in comparison with the vast literature devoted to both the English poor laws and the Bismarckian social insurance legislation.[1] However, the growing interest in the question of social discipline since the 1980s has pushed the development of these programs, which together form the backbone of the welfare *system*, toward the center of scholarly attention.

Since the late 1980s, scholarly debate on the significance of the welfare system has been dominated by two schools of thought—the one building on the work of Michel Foucault, the other drawing on Max Weber, the Frankfurt School, and Jürgen Habermas.[2] These two schools argue in different but complementary ways that the development of welfare states is part of a universal, yet anonymous process of social rationalization, bureaucratization, juridification, and professionalization. Both schools focus on similar themes: the development of therapeutic practices and the social-scientific discourses through which they operate, the effect of these practices on individual rights and state form, and the role of normalization and disciplinary practices in the constitution of the modern subject. Both argue that the development of therapeutic state practices has definitively blurred the classical state-society distinction and dissolved the private and familial spheres into the new intermediate "social"

---

[1] The only general study of the welfare system is Christoph Sachße/Florian Tennstedt, *Geschichte der Armenfürsorge in Deutschland*, 3 vols. (Kohlhammer, 1980–92). The history of social insurance is closely interrelated to the development of poor relief, charity, and welfare. However, the present study focuses on the latter complex of programs and treats social insurance only as it impacted the welfare system. The best survey of the social insurance system is Gerhard A. Ritter, *Social Welfare in Germany and Britain*, trans. Kim Traynor (Berg, 1983). The first steps toward the much-needed reassessment of the Bismarckian social insurance system are Martin Geyer, *Die Reichsknappschaft: Versicherungsreformen und Sozialpolitik im Bergbau 1900–1945* (C. H. Beck, 1987), and Greg Eghigian, *Making Security Social: Affliction, Insurance and the Rise of the German Social State* (forthcoming).

[2] The most important representatives of these approaches are Detlev Peukert, *Grenzen der Sozialdisziplinierung. Aufstieg und Krise der deutschen Jugendfürsorge, 1878–1929* (Bund-Verlag, 1986), Jacques Donzelot, *The Policing of Families* (Pantheon, 1979), David Garland, *Punishment and Welfare: A History of Penal Strategies* (Gower, 1985), Andrew J. Polsky, *The Rise of the Therapeutic State* (Princeton University Press, 1991), François Ewald, *L'Etat Providence* (Paris, 1986), Graham Burchell, Colin Gordon, and Peter Miller, eds., *The Foucault Effect: Studies in Governmentality* (Chicago, 1991), and Sachße/Tennstedt, eds., *Soziale Sicherheit und soziale Disziplinierung* (Suhrkamp, 1986). Geoff Eley locates Peukert's work within the broader framework of modern German historiography in "German History and the Contradictions of Modernity: The Bourgeoisie, the State, and the Mastery of Reform," in Eley, ed., *Society, Culture, and the State in Germany, 1870–1930* (University of Michigan Press, 1996), pp. 67–103.

realm, whose emergence is argued to be constitutive of the transition from the bourgeois rule of law to the interventionist, welfare, or social state.[3]

Detlev Peukert's *Limits of Social Discipline* has dominated the debate over welfare, modernity, and fascism in Germany during the past decade. In this work, Peukert argues that Progressive youth welfare reformers were the protagonists of modernity, who sought to extend both individual rights and national power through the rationalization and normalization of the sphere of working-class social reproduction. Drawing on Habermas, Peukert argues that there was a permanent contradiction between bourgeois utopias of social order, in whose name this rationalizing, normalizing process was pursued, and the expectations and experiences of urban, working-class youth, and that this contradiction was constantly being reproduced through the spread of unskilled factory labor. Consequently, inherent in the Progressive project was the danger that Progressive reformers would employ the vast apparatus of surveillance and discipline—which was originally created to extend the social rights of these children—to repress, marginalize, segregate, and ultimately annihilate those who could not be integrated into the national community through the cultural and financial resources available to them.

Although Peukert's work has already achieved the well-deserved status of a minor classic, his work is problematic in several respects. While he rightly argues that the attempt to rationalize the sphere of working-class reproduction was a contradictory undertaking which from the very beginning contained the seeds of its own crisis, his own analysis of the logic of this process led him to underestimate the importance of the many contradictions and conflicts generated by middle-class social reform initiatives and prevented him from fully understanding the implications of these counterforces for his own analytical framework. Peukert suggests that the contingent event of the Great Depression ultimately forced social reformers to abandon all attempts to balance between emancipation and discipline, as well as between the integratory and segregatory effects of these programs, and, instead, to increasingly subordinate the integrative-emancipatory aspect of Progressive pedagogy to its disciplinary-exclusionary dimension in a way which revealed fascism to be the most radical pathology latent in the Progressive project. However, despite his intentions, Peukert's argument constantly reduces the dialectic of emancipation and discipline to a one-dimensional process which bears unmistakable similarities to the bleak vision of Weber's iron cage and Horkheimer and Adorno's "dialectic of enlightenment."[4]

---

[3] Gerhard Ritter, *Der Sozialstaat. Entstehung und Entwicklung im internationalen Vergleich* (Oldenbourg, 1989). Despite Ritter's argument in favor of the term "social state," I have decided to retain the term "welfare state," while attempting to unpack the many, frequently conflicting connotations attached to this term.

[4] This tendency to subordinate the conflicts generated by social rationalization to an analysis of the logic of the process is accentuated even further in "The Genesis of the 'Final Solution' from the Spirit of Science," in Thomas Childers and Jane Caplan, eds., *Reevaluating the Third Reich* (Holmes & Meier, 1993), pp. 234–52, where what Peukert calls the logidicy and logomachy of the

Perhaps the best way to describe the intent of the present study is to say that it aims at constructively brushing the social discipline paradigm against the grain in order to shift the focus from the logic of social rationalization to the conflicts it generated and, through this, to the politics of welfare reform, the bitter struggles for control over the normalizing process and the sphere of social reproduction, and the implications of these struggles for both the structure of the Weimar state and the ultimate crisis of the Republic itself. The contradictions of this rationalizing process manifested themselves in three distinct areas:

1) Although the process of social rationalization described by Foucault and Peukert may well have been universal, it was neither anonymous nor uncontested. Instead, it led to the proliferation of welfare reform groups and social service providers whose political and religious cleavages mirrored those of German society itself and whose struggles to shape the process of social rationalization and normalization in their own image were the decisive factor in the process of state-formation in the welfare sector.

The proliferation of social reform groups was a natural part of the process of social differentiation, and the first groups active in this field regarded voluntary associations as the best vehicle for transforming the poor into responsible, providential, and hygienic individuals and solving the social question by integrating these self-disciplined subjects into that modern civil society which was taking shape in the political windstill created by the sovereign state. However, between the middle of the nineteenth century and the end of the Weimar Republic the nature of these welfare reform associations underwent a transformation from loose notable associations (*Vereine*) to rationalized, centralized organizations (*Verbände*). This process was similar to the transformation undergone by political parties in the transition from the liberal, representative system to mass, class-based parties, held together by a permanent party organization and a caucus system, and by economic interest groups in the transition from free trade to the cartellization of key industries within the framework of organized capitalism and economic nationalism. In the welfare sector, this retreat from both the liberal model of representation and the conception of political parties and voluntary associations upon which it was based set in motion a dynamic of political confrontation which, by the end of the 1920s, ultimately eroded the fragile foundations of parliamentary democracy in Germany.

Before World War I, the differences dividing these welfare reform groups were held within manageable limits by the limited degree of state intervention into the sphere of social reproduction and by the political constraints imposed by the Wilhelmine state. However, throughout the Republic, the antagonisms repelling these groups proved to be much stronger than the integrative forces of the parliamentary system. These groups were committed to antithetical religious

---

social sciences move even further into the foreground of his account of the pathologies of liberal modernity. For a critique of the accounts by both Peukert and Donzelot of the birth of fascism out of the spirit of social discipline, see Edward Ross Dickinson, *The Politics of German Child Welfare from the Empire to the Federal Republic* (Harvard University Press, 1996), pp. 286ff.

and political systems, mutually exclusive visions of both the nature and scope of public authority and the role of individal and family in civil society, and irreconcilable conceptions of social work. Consequently, instead of helping to integrate their members into the state, the polarization of these welfare organizations—like that of the political parties with which they were closely linked—intensified their desire to carve out within the broader sphere of public welfare a quasi-private domain within which they could pursue their respective visions of social rationalization free from parliamentary intrusions. In turn, this political survival strategy—which was both a defensive reaction against the expansion of state welfarist activity and an offensive attack on the very idea of the sovereign state—tended to hollow out the public sphere which had been created through the institutional modernization of the welfare sector since the 1890s. Although this tendency was contested by the Social Democrats, who remained staunch advocates of direct democratic control of public welfare, one of the main goals of the major welfare organizations—especially the umbrella organizations representing Protestant and Catholic charities—was to reprivatize this recently created domain of public activity. Although it was inevitable that the resolution of this conflict over the nature and scope of public welfare activity would directly influence the structure of the Weimar state, the compromises reached between 1919 and 1924 were intrinsically unstable, and the subsequent search for alternative forms of political organization played a pivotal role in the demise of parliamentary democracy in the welfare sector—a development which encapsulates in miniature the general crisis of the republican political system.

The contradictions of this process of social rationalization, the proliferation of competing social reform discourses and organizations, and the resulting fragmentation of the public sphere have some important methodological implications for the concept of modernization because they effectively decenter the notion of a single, universal modernizing process as a metanarrative for understanding the development of the welfare state in the nineteenth and twentieth centuries. Although Peukert's most important achievement is to have shown how these contradictions were inherent in the very idea of using social services to rationalize the sphere of working-class reproduction, in his later work this insight was increasingly pushed into the background by his relentless analysis of the latent (logical) pathologies of the Progressive project. Nevertheless, it is impossible to dispense entirely with the concept of modernization because this multiplicity of competing social reform discourses can only be understood in relation to the—logically prior—provocation of modernity. Consequently, the task should be to rethink the idea of modernization in order to understand the contradictory unity of social rationalization without, however, imposing a false homogeneity upon it or subordinating these antithetical discourses to a nonexistent telos.

2) The claim—which is closely related to the vision of social rationalization as a universal, uncontested process—that this process results in the progressive diminution of the sphere of individual rights, ultimately culminating in fascism,

is also problematic. Since the 1880s welfare reformers had articulated a new conception of social citizenship in which more extensive individual obligations to the state were linked to the expansion of the social rights of the individual vis-à-vis the state. These reformers regarded preventive, therapeutic welfare programs as the most important means of compensating for the concrete social inequalities of industrial capitalism without undermining property, family, or the freedom of individual contract. The development of a broad spectrum of "social relief" (*soziale Fürsorge*) programs during this period marked the beginning of the transition from bourgeois-Christian individualism and the rule of law to social citizenship within the welfare state, and this new approach to the social problem was ultimately codified by the major pieces of welfare legislation passed in the early years of the Republic. However, these new insights into the social nature of poverty, and the preventive, therapeutic programs established to secure the basic social rights of the individual, set in motion a dialectic of assistance and discipline which altered the conception of individual rights and responsibilities which underlay nineteenth-century poor relief and charity.

The pivotal question raised by the expansion of social relief and the subsequent codification of a preventive, therapeutic approach to poverty in the Republic was that of the relationship between social *rights* and the attendant social *duties*. Before the revolution, the subsidiarity of social relief provided by public agencies and voluntary organizations—that is, their reluctance to provide such assistance until the individual and his or her family had exhausted all of their own resources—and both the social stigma and political disabilities entailed by the receipt of such assistance had limited the effectiveness of such preventive programs. However, although welfare reformers applauded the increasing codification of these social rights after 1918, at the same time they began to worry that the increasing emphasis on prevention was undermining the personal responsibility of the recipients and upsetting the delicate balance between social rights and social duties upon which their conception of social citizenship rested. In turn, these concerns raised the complex, but politically important, question of the extent to which state power could be used to compel the needy to accept such help and the punishments which could be meted out to those who refused or subverted therapeutic assistance. By the end of the 1920s, reflections on these problems had moved to the center of the influential Progressive analysis of the contradictions of the republican welfare system. This book will explore the ambiguous relationship between the emancipatory and disciplinary dimensions of preventive, therapeutic social services by analyzing the competing visions of social citizenship articulated by the major welfare reform groups after the revolution as well as the rationale advanced on behalf of the idea of a correctional custody (*Bewahrung*) law. This analysis will show that the meaning of the simultaneous extension of both the social rights and the social obligations of the individual can only be grasped through more aleatory concepts of rights and justice than those employed by liberal-conservative jurisprudence and that, since the net impact of this transformation can only be determined in concrete, historically specific instances, it cannot be described in the categorical terms employed by Peukert.[5]

3) The third major problem complex focuses on the professionalization of social work within the process of social rationalization and the ambiguous role of social workers as both the agent and the object of this process. Although the bourgeois women's movement had argued since the 1880s that social work represented a peculiarly feminine sphere of activity and had attempted to employ this idea to legitimate their own emancipatory aspirations, the revolution destroyed the political space within which this feminist vision of social work as a vehicle for social reform had existed. At the same time, the entry of women social workers into an increasingly bureaucratized public welfare system entangled these women in intensely gendered conflicts with those same abstract, bureaucratic—ostensibly masculine—modes of thought and action against which they had originally defined their own conception of social work as nurturing and personal help.

However, the problems faced by the social work profession went far deeper and were related in a much more integral manner to the broader questions of social rationalization. In the early 1920s, the ideas of friendly visiting and social motherhood were both reinterpreted as social pedagogy in conjunction with the codification of a preventive, therapeutic approach to poverty. The problem was that the same social forces which were driving the development of the social work profession were at the same time undermining the preconditions for personal help—what the Germans called *Hilfe von Mensch zu Mensch*—which continued to underpin this idea of social pedagogy. The Social Democrats insisted that the problems which had led to the creation of a vast network of social assistance agencies could only be resolved through the transformation of the social system itself. However, the marginalization of the Social Democrats created a political space within which bourgeois feminists, male Progressives, and the confessional welfare and social worker organizations could institutionalize their own conception of social work as organized helping based upon an ethics of selfless service, which was itself underpinned by the explicit or implicit religious beliefs of these persons. However, this repression of politics was only possible at the cost of reinscribing within the structure of social pedagogical action all of the various manifestations of the contradiction between the ideal of personal help and the underlying social problems which this help was intended to correct.

While the resistance of their clientele inevitably led social workers to intensify both the integrative-pedagogical and exclusionary-disciplinary dimensions of their work, the theoretical blindness of the social work profession to the

---

[5] See Gary Finder, *"Education not Punishment": Juvenile Justice in Late Imperial and Weimar Germany* (dissertation, University of Chicago, 1997), and David Crew, *Germans on Welfare, 1919–1935* (Oxford University Press, 1998). Similarly, Marcus Gräser attributes the crisis of the republican welfare state not so much to the successes of Progressivism, but to the success of the conservative church charities in blocking Progressive reforms. Gräser, *Der blockierte Wohlfahrtsstaat. Unterschichtjugend und Jugendfürsorge in der Weimarer Republik* (Vandenhoeck & Ruprecht, 1995).

limitations of social pedagogy led them toward two complementary, yet contradictory, diagnoses of the crisis of their nascent profession. On the one hand, they argued that the root of the broad variety of motivational problems created by the resistance of their clientele lay in the personality of the social worker and could, therefore, only be solved through an increasingly intense commitment to an ethics of selfless service, whose cultivation was regarded as the *raison d'être* of the social work schools. On the other hand, the leaders of the social work profession argued that the resistance of their clientele which could not be overcome through such a commitment could only be eliminated through the comprehensive reform of the institutions through which this help was provided—a strategy which would have entailed the de facto break-up of the public welfare system and the reversal of those very developments which had originally made possible the emergence of social work as a distinct profession. As a result, by the end of the decade the crisis of the social work profession had become another central dimension of the crisis of the social welfare system and that of the Republic itself.

The analysis of these three levels of conflict will provide the three major themes of this book.

THE CONTRADICTIONS OF MODERNITY AND THE FRAGMENTATION OF THE PUBLIC SPHERE IN THE WELFARE SECTOR

The Weimar welfare state was the end product of developments reaching back to the *Vormärz*. The first stage in the proliferation of both antithetical discourses on the nature of poverty and the place of individual and family in civil society and the corresponding attempts to rationalize the sphere of social reproduction on the basis of these worldviews was the emergence of distinctly Lutheran and liberal social reform programs in the *Vormärz*. These competing visions were identified most closely with the Inner Mission, which was founded in 1848 by Johann Hinrich Wichern, and the variety of liberal reform initiatives which were ultimately gathered together under the umbrella of the Central Association for the Welfare of the Working Classes (*Centralverein für das Wohl der arbeitenden Classen*), which was founded in 1844 in Berlin by a coalition of reform-minded bureaucrats, industrialists, and intellectuals. Although both of these organizations believed that voluntary associations could provide a model for the creation of a modern civil society because they held the key to solving the "social question," they each hoped for very different things from these associations.

Wichern regarded the social distress of the pre-1848 period—and ultimately the revolution itself—as the product of the dissolution of traditional familial and communal bonds and, with this, the spread of individualism and religious rationalism, whose logic inevitably led to materialism, atheism, communism, and revolution. This view of poverty also lay at the root of the conservative Christian diagnosis of poverty and crime as the result of *Verwahrlosung*, that is, the moral endangerment or neglect resulting from the absence of patriarchal authority or other communal institutions capable of restraining the innate sinfulness of the natural will. The goal of Wichern and the Inner Mission was to solve the social question through the renewal of popular piety and the restoration of the traditional authority of the family patriarch. Wichern hoped that, by restraining both the natural sinfulness of the free will and the egoism of the isolated individual, the patriarch would teach the child to love both God and his or her fellow human beings; this display of love and authority would inculcate in the child all of those values upon which individual salvation and the existence of civil society depended (obedience, humility, self-sacrifice, and, above all, respect for authority in all its forms) and thus allow the patriarch to function as the bridge between the natural and supernatural realms.[6] The end product of this renewal of popular piety would be a Christian civil society modeled on the Lutheran doctrine of the priesthood of all believers. In such a society, the social question would be solved through "the voluntary charitable engagement of the *awakened (heilerfülltes) Volk* in order to bring about the Christian and social rebirth of the *heillses Volk*" which continued to wallow in its own sinfulness. For Wichern, this "inner mission" *of* the German people *to* the German people would be "a confession of faith through an act of redeeming love."[7]

In contrast to Wichern's modernization of Christian conservativism and his emphasis on the familial sphere as the primary object of Christian social reform, the aim of the liberal social reform movement was to give the individual the spiritual and material resources necessary to compete successfully in the dynamic, expanding sphere of civil society and the market economy. Although the various economic causes of pauperism and proletarianization—concepts which were used interchangeably through the 1840s—were visible to many, what most concerned contemporaries were the moral effects of material destitution. They feared that material need deprived these people of the economic independence, opportunity for education, and self-respect which were the defining characteristics of the members of that *Mittelstandsgesellschaft* which represented the liberal model of civil society. Paupers and proletarians were those persons who lacked the *Bildung* and material security necessary to engage in public, political activity concerning the common weal and who did not adhere to those norms through which the *Mittelstand* distinguished itself from those social groups located above and below it in the social hierarchy. Though by no means scornful of the ideas of order and authority, liberal social reformers

---

[6] Wichern presented his diagnosis of the social crisis of the *Vormärz* and his reform program in "Die innere Mission der deutschen evangelischen Kirche. Eine Denkschrift an die deutsche Nation," *Sämtliche Werke*, ed., Peter Meinhold (Lutherisches Verlagshaus, 1958ff.), I:175–363. On Wichern's social thought and social Protestantism, see Günter Brakelmann, *Kirche und Sozialismus im 19. Jahrhundert. Die Analyse des Sozialismus und Kommunismus bei Johann Hinrich Wichern und bei Rudolf Todt* (Luther Verlag, 1966), and William O. Shanahan, *German Protestants Face the Social Question* (University of Notre Dame Press, 1954).

[7] Wichern, *Werke*, I:103. Although this second motto has been passed down through the literature on the Inner Mission, I have not encountered this exact phrase in Wichern's writings.

believed that the dual goal of reducing the social insecurity of the pauperized underclasses and promoting individual independence in the dawning world of city and factory could be achieved through the combination of education, industry, and thrift. They hoped that, in addition to the material security they provided, participation in voluntary self-help associations would lead the poor beyond the sphere of their immediate material interests and open the way to both a broader understanding of the common good and participation in public, political affairs.[8]

Between the 1880s and World War I, the qualitative transformation of the nature of the social question caused by rapid urbanization and industrialization led to the formation of several other major social and welfare reform groups, each espousing their own distinct worldview. In the 1880s and 1890s, the convergence of the interests of a broad group of male social reformers (many of whom were associated with the *Verein für Sozialpolitik*), municipal poor relief officials, and bourgeois feminists gave birth to a distinctly Progressive strategy for social reform, and the reform of poor relief in particular. These policies were associated primarily with the left wing of the National Liberals, the various branches of the Progressive Party, Friedrich Naumann's national social movement, and, after 1918, the German Democratic Party (DDP). To a far greater extent than both liberals and Christian conservatives, these Progressives were willing to extend the scope of public (though not necessarily state) activity into the realm of family and social reproduction in order to enhance the welfare of the individual citizen and, in so doing, increase the economic and military strength, as well as the social unity, of the nation. The German Association for Poor Relief and Charity (*Deutscher Verein für Armenpflege und Wohltätigkeit*, DV), which was founded in 1880/81 to promote the rationalization of poor relief and charity, rapidly became the most important organization for the promotion of Progressive welfare reform ideas (though its membership embraced persons from every point along the political spectrum). Much of the practical work in the cause of Progressive reform was carried out by bourgeois women— often the wives and daughters of these male officials and social reformers— who viewed social work as the logical extension of their supposedly natural nurturing and caring powers and who hoped that social work would both provide an avenue for their own emancipation and serve as a mechanism for class reconciliation through the expiation of class guilt.[9]

---

[8] On the Central Association, see Jürgen Reulecke, *Sozialer Frieden durch soziale Reform. Der Centralverein für das Wohl der arbeitenden Klassen in der Frühindustrialisierung* (Peter Hammer, 1983).

[9] On the *Deutscher Verein*, see Hans Muthesius, ed., *Beiträge zur Entwicklung der deutschen Fürsorge: 75 Jahre Deutscher Verein* (Heymann, 1955), and Florian Tennstedt, "Fürsorgegeschichte und Vereinsgeschichte. 100 Jahre Deutscher Verein in der Geschichte der deutschen Fürsorge," *Zeitschrift für Sozialreform* 27:2 (1981), pp. 72–100. The absence of a comprehensive study of German Progressivism is a major lacuna in the existing literature. On the British discourse on poverty and social reform in this period, see Gertrude Himmelfarb, *Poverty and Compassion. The Moral Imagination of the Late Victorians* (Knopf, 1991). For the literature on social work and the women's movement in the *Kaiserreich* and the Republic, see chapter 5.

During the last decades of the century, social Catholicism began to abandon its integralist opposition to the modern world and come to terms with industrial society and the sovereign state, and in 1897 the *Deutscher Caritasverband* was formed to modernize Catholic charities and represent their interests in relation to public poor relief. Although the Caritasverband shared the social conservativism of the Inner Mission, its natural law principles and its unremitting hostility to the sovereign Protestant state gave the Catholic charity and welfare reform program a distinctly different tone than that of its Protestant counterpart. Though the organization languished in the prewar period, it was to play a dominant role in the welfare reform debates during the Weimar Republic.

The last decade before the war was characterized by increasingly intense clashes between the Progressives and both the liberals and Christian conservatives of both confessions, who believed that state intervention was undermining the religious bases of the family and who linked their hostility to the intrusion of alien worldviews into the sphere of social reproduction with a defense of personal help and the role of voluntary social engagement. These conflicts were especially intense in the area of youth welfare, whose centrality for social reproduction made it the focal point of this struggle. From the 1880s into the 1930s, the Progressives (and later Social Democrats) in the DV were the leading advocates of the modernization of public assistance from a national, social perspective, and the conflicts generated by Progressive reform strategies will be one of the leitmotifs of the story being related here.[10]

The revolution posed an existential threat to both of the confessional charities, and the politics of welfare reform were further radicalized by the creation of a Social Democratic welfare organization Workers' Welfare (*Arbeiterwohlfahrt*) in 1919.[11] While the unprecedented extension of state welfare and social policy programs during World War I accelerated the politicization of welfare reform debates, the collapse of the authoritarian Wilhelmine state burst the narrow limits which had been previously imposed upon social reform and created a vast, essentially contested space within which the major political groups struggled with each other to put their imprint upon the new Republic. At the same time, the competition of ideas within the parliamentary system compelled the various political parties and welfare reform groups to anchor their welfare reform programs in comprehensive worldviews, and the outcome of the multidimensional "cultural struggles" (*Kultur-* or *Weltanschauungskämpfe*) of the early years of the Republic played the decisive role in determining the

[10] Although the Social Democrats were to play a crucial role in the politics of welfare reform in the Republic, before 1914 their categorical rejection of the institutions of bourgeois society and their political marginalization provided them with relatively little incentive to participate in poor law and charity reform debates.

[11] I refer to the Caritasverband and the Inner Mission as "confessional" (*konfessionell*) organizations because they insisted that social work had to take place within the religious framework defined by the two positive Christian confessions (*Bekenntnis*). While the word "denominational" is more widely used in English, I have decided to retain the word "confessional" because of its greater faithfulness to the original German.

shape of the Weimar state and the way state power would be used to reshape civil society in the Republic. The reform strategies advocated by these organizations were based on very different understandings of the causes of Germany's decline and antithetical visions of the new society, and the debates over welfare reform served as a lens which focused and amplified these differences. They forced all of the major participants to articulate—on the basis of their respective worldviews—distinctive visions of social citizenship, which coupled the constitutionally guaranteed extension of social rights with the extension of the obligations of the individual toward society, but which diverged from one another in their account of the nature of these rights and the scope of these duties.

The creation of the Weimar welfare state required more than constitutional formulae, and the task of reconstruction and the need to create a viable social foundation for the new republic made it urgent to resolve the inherited tensions of urban, industrial society. This, in turn, drew into the political maelstrom of the early republic those conceptions of property, work, and family which had formed the basis of bourgeois society and which had been safeguarded by the doctrine of the rule of law. By altering the relation of individual, family, society, and the state, the debates over welfare reform forged new conceptions of citizenship, social rights, and social obligations and helped constitute a new, postliberal public space.

The history of the Weimar Republic was in many ways the history of the struggle to determine the concrete meaning of the fundamental rights enumerated in the Weimar constitution. In view of centrality of the compromise between organized labor and big business, the historiography of the Weimar welfare state has long concentrated on the changing balance between capital and labor and the relation of these organized interest groups to the state bureaucracy.[12] Though it would be wrong to ignore the role of social policy legislation in the creation of the welfare *state*, these battles were fought out in parliamentary debates over economic policy, wages, working conditions, and collective bargaining regulations. However, the debate over the welfare *system* was framed in very different terms. The collapse of the old political order and the social dislocation caused by the war accentuated a widely perceived crisis of social reproduction, which dominated the discourse of welfare reform throughout the Republic, and the historiographical focus upon the political economy of the Republic overlooks the fact that the postwar debates over welfare reform focused to a greater extent than ever before on the family and social reproduction—rather than on the needs of social classes—and were carried out primarily in a language of religion, culture, and gender.[13]

---

[12] Gerald Feldman, *The Great Disorder: Politics, Economics, and Society in the German Inflation* (Oxford University Press, 1993), and Werner Abelshauser, ed., *Die Weimarer Republik als Wohlfahrtsstaat. Zum Verhältnis von Wirtschafts- und Sozialpolitik in der Industriegesellschaft* (= *VSWG*, Beiheft 81, 1987).

[13] This insistence upon the independent dynamic of the cultural discourses underlying the welfare reform debates of the Republic and their relative autonomy from the political economy of the republican welfare state also has important implications for the ongoing rethinking of both the class

In the relatively brief period between 1914 and 1924, the welfare sector recapitulated a development which had taken place in the political and economic spheres over a much longer period: the expansion of public intervention into that sphere of social reproduction previously regarded as private; the mobilization of competing societal groups seeking to shape this sphere in accordance with their own distinct moral and religious systems; the creation of increasingly centralized and rationalized organizations to facilitate the pursuit of these goals; the countermobilization of traditionally marginal social groups who were affected by these developments; and, within the highly fragmented Republic, the intensification of political and cultural conflict among these organizations. Although this organizational modernization and rationalization had been undertaken to insure their political influence and financial survival during this turbulent period, these survival strategies ultimately brought about a fundamental transformation of the very nature of these organizations.

The societal welfare organizations which emerged from this process were increasingly concerned with creating an autonomous sphere within which they could undertake their pedagogical work in every aspect of the milieu of their clients, free from unwanted political control which threatened to limit their autonomy in the name of other, antithetical religious and political values. This tendency, as well as the increased potential for conflict among these organizations, was intensified by the postwar codification of a new approach to poverty, which regarded the many manifestations of need as symptoms of inner distress requiring remedial, therapeutic intervention. This was true for both the Progressives and the confessional welfare organizations, both of whom argued that, even though this distress might have been caused by social or economic forces which lay beyond the control of the individual, effective therapy still required personal help in addition to the alteration of the material environment. The growing consciousness that no dimension of this need could be considered as ethically indifferent provided the stimulus for the intensive and extensive rationalization of the major national welfare organizations, which felt compelled to expand their activity to address every possible aspect of the need of their clients and legitimate these new forms of social work scientifically from their own moral or religious perspective. In turn, this strategy intensified competition for influence at the local level, especially in the field of youth welfare.

This creation of a semiprivate domain within what had—especially since the war—become both a sphere of eminently public concern and the object of public, political regulation can be described as the *corporatization* of the welfare sector. Here, the concept of corporatism will be used to describe those efforts to supplement (or replace) liberal modes of political representation—

concept and the social interpretation of the welfare state. The most important contributions to this critique of the social—or social democratic—theory of the welfare state are Peter Baldwin, *The Politics of Social Solidarity: Class Bases of the European Welfare State 1875–1975* (Cambridge University Press, 1990), Gøsta Esping-Andersen, *The Three Worlds of Welfare Capitalism* (Princeton University Press, 1990), and Theda Skocpol, *Protecting Soldiers and Mothers: The Political Origins of Social Policy in the United States* (Harvard University Press, 1992).

which aimed at transcending the particular economic and cultural interests which constituted the fabric of civil society in order to represent the general interest—with a form of functional representation intended to insure the most transparent representation *of* those interests.[14] Although the concept of corporatism has been applied most frequently to describe the influence of economic interest groups on the political process, it is equally applicable to the analysis of social fragmentation along religious and cultural lines, which were the key lines of cleavage within the Weimar welfare system.

In recent literature, the concept of corporatism has been used to analyze the influence of organized interest groups upon the state. It has been employed by sociologists and political theorists in opposition to both the conservative followers of Carl Schmitt, who viewed this "societalization of the state" as the first step toward social civil war, and advocates of a pluralist theory of democracy, who recognize the legitimacy of societal influence on state policy formation, but who downplay the political dimension of this process and overlook the structural constraints imposed upon their idealized vision of corporatist mediation. In theory, such a corporatist system would depoliticize the conflicts inherent in bourgeois society—and thus stabilize the existing system—by involving organized interest groups in the formulation of state policy and, by delegating to them a limited degree of public authority, force them to accept responsibility for the implementation of those policies which they helped formulate. In turn, although state sovereignty would be limited through the delegation of public authority to these organizations, which would enjoy a quasi-public, quasi-private status, these limitations on state sovereignty would be offset by the delegation of state authority to these previously private or voluntary associations—that is, the "etatisation of society"—which would impose certain limits upon their autonomy and give the state a certain degree of oversight and control over their activity.[15]

These theories have presented corporatist representation as a hybrid form of politics which successfully transformed the problems caused by the blurring of the state-society distinction—which many commentators viewed as signs of the terminal crisis of liberal democracy—into political virtues.[16] This was, however, by no means the case in the Weimar Republic. Here, the recognition of the

[14] On the relation between these two modes of representation, see Joseph Kaiser, *Die Repräsentation organisierter Interessen* (Berlin, 1956).

[15] Suzanne Berger, ed., *Organizing Interests in Western Europe: Pluralism, Corporatism and the Transformation of Politics* (Cambridge University Press, 1981), Philippe Schmitter and Gerhard Lehmbruch, eds., *Trends Towards Corporatist Intermediation* (SAGE Publications, 1979), Ulrich von Alemann and Rolf Heinze, eds., *Verbände und Staat* (Westdeutscher Verlag, 1979), and Cornelius Mayer-Tasch, *Korporativismus und Autoritarismus. Eine Studie zur Theorie und Praxis der berufsständischen Rechts- und Staatsidee* (Athenäum Verlag, 1971).

[16] Werner Abelshauser, "The First Post-Liberal Nation: Stages in the Development of Modern Corporatism in Germany," *European History Quarterly* 14 (1984), pp. 285–318. For an interpretation of the welfare sector along these lines, see Rolf Heinze and Thomas Olk, "Die Wohlfahrtsverbände im System sozialer Dienstleistungsproduktion. Zur Entstehung und Struktur der bundesrepublikanischen Verbändewohlfahrt," *Kölner Zeitschrift* 33 (1981), pp. 94–113.

quasi-public status of the major welfare *Verbände* did not help integrate them into the state or forge a new sense of common purpose. Rather, it accelerated the fragmentation and hollowing out of the state, increased the antagonisms among these *Verbände*, and encouraged the search for authoritarian alternatives to parliamentary government in an increasingly fragmented and polarized society. The conflict among the major national welfare organizations from 1925 onward accelerated the transformation of these organizations into what Sigmund Neumann called—in contrast to classical representation parties—"integration" organizations, which embraced every aspect of the lives of their members and, correspondingly, placed greater demands upon their loyalty.[17] However, the formation of such organizations amplified, rather than mitigated, conflicts over the causes of need, the goal of the new welfare apparatus, and the social effects of the support it provided and thus undermined, rather than consolidated, the tentative compromises upon which the Republic had originally been founded. These conflicts were displaced directly into the political sphere through the close correspondence between political, economic, and religious interests within the relatively stable social milieux which had shaped the nation's political landscape since the *Kaiserreich*, and the struggle to find a new mode of political representation within the welfare sector both reflected and intensified parallel difficulties of the political system in general.[18]

The Historical Background: Poor Relief, Charity, and the Evolution of Social Welfare in Germany, 1830–1918

Like all other scholarly works, this one is the product of choices, choices which are in part imposed by the available material, but which are ultimately imposed upon this material. It is not about the German poor or the conflict-laden interaction between social workers and welfare recipients. Although this perspective often yields rich material, such subjects can only be approached through case studies because in Germany poor relief and charity were too localized and fragmented to permit generalizations about national developments. Nor is this a history of the dense network of specialized social welfare programs which constituted the infrastructure of the Weimar welfare "system"; although a knowledge of these programs is indispensable, general assistance, social hygiene, maternity and infant welfare, and youth welfare programs each developed according to their own dynamic and can only be approached through specialized studies of these fields of social engagement.

This book is about the formation of welfare policy at the national level, the conflict among the organizations which were key participants in welfare reform

---

[17] Sigmund Neumann, *Die Parteien der Weimarer Republik* (Stuttgart, 1965), pp. 18–19, 105ff.

[18] M. Rainer Lepsius, "Parteiensystem und Sozialstruktur: zum Problem der Demokratisierung der deutschen Gesellschaft," in Gerhard A. Ritter, ed., *Die deutschen Parteien vor 1918* (Köln, 1973), pp. 56–80.

debates, and the implications of these debates for the nature of the Weimar state. However, these debates did not take place in a historical vacuum. Rather, they were informed by a keen awareness of the implications of social disloca- tion and social unrest for the future of the Weimar Republic and by a historical consciousness of the transformation of public assistance over the preceding cen- tury. While the following overview of the history of poor relief, charity, and welfare in Germany from the *Vormärz* to World War I is designed to provide the reader with the background necessary to contextualize these debates, in so doing it also unfolds two theoretical issues which are crucial for understanding the politics of welfare reform in the Weimar Republic. First, it traces the trans- formation of the parameters of nineteenth-century poor relief and charity and the emergence in the 1890s of a new preventive, therapeutic approach to pov- erty. Although this logic of prevention extended the social rights and the social obligations of the individual, in so doing it inaugurated a dialectic of emancipa- tion and (social) discipline which has been the focus of recent debate over the significance of the welfare state. Second, it shows how the state regulation of poor relief and the first efforts to rationalize voluntary charity during the middle decades of the century gave birth to a conflict between state regulation and voluntary initiative. This conflict was given a new urgency, first, by the inten- sification of public intervention into the sphere of social reproduction and, later, by renewed state efforts to control organized charities during World War I, and it played a crucial catalytic role in the politics of welfare reform in the Repub- lic.

In the aftermath of the Napoleonic Wars, Prussia and the South German states initially adopted diametrically opposite approaches to poor law reform and the crisis of pauperism. Although these reform strategies reflected the dif- ferences in the economic and political structures of the two regions, they both pivoted around the same issue: the relation between the local state and the sovereign, territorial state. In the post-1815 period, poor relief in Prussia was regulated by the *Allgemeines Landrecht* (1791/94), which simply gave the sanc- tion of the sovereign state to traditional arrangements. No matter where the individual might find him- or herself at the onset of need, the destitute person received support from local institutions (the city, the parish, the manor, guilds) in his or her place of birth (or the community where the person had been explicitly admitted to the rights of citizenship). However, although the Prussian reforms had freed the subject population to leave their former residences, they did not guarantee that the newly emancipated persons would be accepted in other towns, especially if local authorities suspected that the immigrant was likely to become impoverished and a financial burden on the new community. In the 1820s and 1830s the problems created by this incongruity between the new freedoms of trade, movement, and marriage and the strictly localistic poor relief system provided the impetus for national poor law reform in Prussia.

In 1842/43, the Prussian government promulgated a set of laws regulating a tightly connected set of issues: the admission of new migrants into the commu- nity, communal responsibility for poor relief, disciplinary measures for vagabonds, beggars, and the work-shy, and the acquisition and loss of Prussian citizenship. These laws, which all reflected the impact of social change on traditional notions of citizenship, clearly established the primacy of the sovereign, territorial state in this area and the priority of national over local citizenship. To create a poor relief system which was better adapted to the problems of a more mobile market society, this legislation established guidelines for the acquisition of a relief residence (*Unterstützungswohnsitz*), which was thenceforth to be responsible for supporting the person in time of need. In this way, the law encouraged the poor to migrate in search of work. Although both conservatives and liberals initially feared that the juridification of the moral obligation of the community to support its needy members would promote the communistic illusion that the poor had an actionable right to public assistance and thus further intensify the problem of pauperism, in practice the most important problem created by the relief residence system, as it came to be known, was the constant conflict between the urban bourgeoisie in the industrial towns along the Rhine and the landed nobility in the east over the use of these regulations to redistribute the costs of poor relief.[19]

In the south, eligibility for poor relief continued to be regulated by "home law" (*Heimatrecht*: literally, right of return). Home law was an integral element of municipal citizenship because those persons who were accepted as members in the local political community, given permission to settle and marry, and granted the right to practice a trade also acquired at the same time the right to poor relief in case of need. A person's *Heimat*—which in a stable society generally meant one's place of birth—was that place where he or she enjoyed a legal right to assistance in time of need; this right could only be lost by marriage outside the community (for women) or explicit acceptance into another community (for men). The defenders of *Heimatrecht* argued this system had one overriding moral advantage over the relief residence system: since no one could lose their right to poor relief in their hometown without simultaneously gaining an equivalent right elsewhere, the *Heimatrecht* system forestalled that erosion of communal bonds which was held by many to be the cause of both moral and material impoverishment. In contrast to the more economically developed north, in the southern states it was widely believed that the nascent crisis of pauperism was due primarily to the growing disproportion between population growth and available economic resources, rather than obstacles to freedom of movement. As the pauperism crisis intensified through the *Vormärz*, the south German states responded by passing legislation to shore up the foundations of local government and further tighten local control over movement, marriage, trade, and poor relief. However, this southern alternative proved inef-

---

[19] The best account of this legislation is Michael Doege, *Armut in Preußen und Bayern, 1770–1840* (Neue Schriftenreihe des Stadtarchivs München, 1991). On the subsequent conflict over the distribution of total poor relief costs, see George Steinmetz, *Regulating the Social: The Welfare State and Local Politics in Imperial Germany* (Princeton, 1993), and Steinmetz, "The Myth of an Autonomous State: Industrialists, Junkers, and Social Policy in Imperial Germany," in Eley, ed., *Society, Culture, and the State in Germany, 1870–1930*, pp. 257–318.

fectual and was abandoned in the 1860s. The recognition of freedom of movement and trades within the North German Confederation in 1867/69 and their
extension to all of Germany after 1870 spelled the effective end of *Heimatrecht*.
In June 1870, the *Reichstag* of the North German Confederation extended the
Prussian relief residence system to all of its member states, and, after 1871, it
was soon adopted by all of the southern states except Bavaria—which retained
its *Heimatrecht* until World War I—and the *Reichsland* Alsace-Lorraine.[20]

One of the reasons for the neglect of poor relief and charity in most
studies of the development of the welfare state has been the perception that
they retained their traditional forms and thus perpetuated their anachronistic
existence until they were rendered superfluous by social insurance and social
welfare systems during the 20th century. However, the reforms of poor relief
and charity across the middle decades of the 1800s were, in fact, an integral
element in the creation of an industrial market economy, and both the
achievements and the limitations of the poor relief system are intimately related to the ideas and interests of the liberal middle classes who came to
dominate local government during this period. By the 1850s, economic and
demographic developments had made it increasingly necessary to reform public poor relief (*Armenpflege*, literally, "caring for the poor," a phrase which
carries strong paternalistic connotations and implies the permanent existence
of a stratum of dependent persons) and charity (*Wohltätigkeit, Liebestätigkeit*)
in the growing industrial centers.

In the 1850s and 1860s, the most influential model for the reform of poor
relief and friendly visiting was that adopted in 1853 by the new industrial town
of Elberfeld (now Wuppertal).[21] The essence of the Elberfeld system was the
division of the city into districts and quarters and the requirement that the honorary and voluntary (*ehrenamtlich*) poor guardians reside in the same quarter
for which they were responsible, that they visit each household at least once
every two weeks, and that they personally distribute benefits to the recipients.
Since these *ehrenamtlich* poor guardians were representatives of the same economic and political class which levied the taxes necessary to pay the costs of
public poor relief, in the second half of the century the fusion of public authority and private initiative which resulted from the "decentralization" of poor
relief onto district and quarter poor relief commissions provided a widely-
accepted model for liberal self-government, while service as an *ehrenamtlich* poor

---

[20] On the development of poor relief legislation and practice in the south, see Doege, *Armut in
Preußen und Bayern*, Peter Blum, *Staatliche Armenfürsorge im Herzogtum Nassau 1806–1866*
(Historische Kommission für Nassau, 1987), and Klaus-Jürgen Matz, *Pauperismus und Bevöl-
kerung. Die gesetzlichen Ehebeschränkungen in den süddeutschen Staaten während des 19. Jahrhunderts* (Klett-Cotta, 1980).

[21] On the crisis which provided the impetus for these reforms in Elberfeld, see Bernd Weisbrod,
"Wohltätigkeit und 'symbolische Gewalt' in der Frühindustrialisierung," in Hans Mommsen and
Winfried Schulze, eds., *Vom Elend der Handarbeit* (Klett, 1981), pp. 334–57. The most recent
account is Steinmetz, *Regulating the Social*, who also cites the vast contemporary literature on the
Elberfeld system.

guardian was increasingly recognized as the first rung on the ladder of municipal political office. The architects of the Elberfeld system hoped that the decentralization of poor relief, the restriction of the responsibility of the poor guardian to four individuals or households, and the requirement that he reside in the quarter for which he was responsible would simultaneously serve two distinct but related goals: first, that it would re-create through modern techniques the face-to-face relations believed to prevail in traditional societies and reestablish patterns of social deference among the mobile populace of the new urban centers, and, second, that it would facilitate what contemporaries came to call the *individualization* of poor relief, that is, a closer, more constant assessment of the needs of the poor, the causes of this need, and the possibilities of its melioration, especially through the poor guardian's firsthand knowledge of both the character and personal circumstances of these parties and the local job market. This concept of individualization played a pivotal role in the modernization and rationalization of poor relief and charity, and, at bottom, the Elberfeld system was simply an institutional framework for the realization of the goals of personal help and individualized assistance, which together formed the conceptual core of poor relief, charity, and welfare from the 1850s into the Weimar Republic.[22]

The Elberfeld system was created at a key transitional moment in German history when the problem of pauperism was just beginning to subside and the *Arbeiterfrage*—that is, social problems raised by the emergence of a factory proletariat—was just beginning to assume clear contours. Consequently, although this reformed system of public poor relief undoubtedly helped depauperize the poor and integrate them into the expanding market society, it also played a pivotal role in disciplining both the migrants from the rural east and the urban laboring poor and, thus, in creating the urban working classes. The most important effect of this mid-century poor relief system was to force the able-bodied poor into the labor market and compel the unpropertied to accept whatever work they could find under whatever conditions it was offered. As the success of the cooperative movement in the 1850s and 1860s demonstrates, for a brief moment the liberal and Christian ideology of labor as a vehicle for self-improvement coincided with the realities of a market society in the initial stages of industrialization, when it was still possible for wage earners to themselves become propertied employers of labor. However, with the progress of industrialization, the separation of working-class and bourgeois public spheres, and the emergence of a distinct, increasingly ghettoized working-class subculture,

---

[22] Both Steinmetz, *Regulating the Social* and Richard Münchmeier, *Zugänge zur Geschichte der sozialen Arbeit* (Juventa Verlag, 1981) emphasize the modernizing function of the principle of individualization. Although poor relief reformers never tired of insisting on the absolute originality of the Elberfeld system and its underlying principles of individualization and decentralization, the same ideas had underlain the influential reform of poor relief in Hamburg in the 1780s. What was unique about the Elberfeld system was that it shifted responsibility for poor relief from the patriciate and the church charities to the middle classes while devising organizational forms appropriate to the new urban environment. On the Hamburg reforms, see Mary Lindemann, *Patriots and Paupers: Hamburg, 1712–1830* (Oxford University Press, 1990).

the principles of the Elberfeld system became an element of bourgeois dogma and a vehicle for class domination.

During the middle of the nineteenth century, both Christian conservatives and liberal social reformers regarded that form of demoralized and demoralizing indigence which they alternately characterized as pauperization or proletarianization as the result of individual moral failings, that is, as a willful refusal to conform to the dictates of Christian morality and middle-class respectability. These beliefs justified the quasi-criminalization of work-shyness (*Arbeitsscheue*), begging, vagrancy, excessive drinking, and juvenile delinquency. They also explain the fundamentally disciplinary, deterrent character of the municipal poor relief system. District poor relief authorities were required only to provide what the 1870 Reich Relief Residence Law called an "absolute existence minimum" (*unentbehrlicher notdürftigster Lebensunterhalt*), which included only food, shelter, clothing, emergency medical treatment, and a pauper burial. Both Prussian and subsequent Reich legislation simply established this broad framework for the determination of need and left the determination of both the "poverty level" and the scope and nature of relief to the discretion of local government. Generally, local poor relief authorities, however, set poor relief rates at or below the wages of unskilled labor in the area, which they generally used as a proxy for the local existence minimum. Assistance was provided on a strictly subsidiary basis only after the individual had exhausted all available personal and familial resources and had fallen into complete destitution. In addition, this assistance was always provided in a manner consciously intended to stigmatize its recipients, and the receipt of such assistance was always accompanied by political disabilities, including the forfeiture of the right to vote. To reinforce the fiction that the obligation of local officials to provide this existence minimum was an obligation they owed to the state, rather than the poor, and that, therefore, the poor had no legally enforceable right to relief, poor relief was provided in the legal form of a loan, which the recipient was, in theory, obligated to repay. Underlying this entire edifice was the Malthusian belief that only absolute material deprivation could motivate the poor to earn their daily bread and that any relief which exceeded the existence minimum which society was morally obligated to provide undermined the work ethic of the poor and thus increased the total misery of humankind.

The Elberfeld system rode the crest of the wave of industrialization which swept across the country after 1860 and was generally adopted by the larger industrial cities as they were forced to reorganize their poor relief systems by the pressures of urbanization and industrialization. In addition to the belief that the able-bodied poor were not deserving of public assistance because they were responsible for their own misfortune, the more or less unstated presupposition underlying this deterrent, disciplinary approach to poor relief was the belief that voluntary organizations would step in and provide supplementary support—beyond this existence minimum—to the deserving poor.[23] This, in turn, pro-

---

[23] German poor relief and charity reformers never succumbed to the English illusion that outdoor relief could be eliminated through the rigorous application of the workhouse principle, and, as the

vided the stimulus for the expansion and rationalization of voluntary charity. As a result, the adoption of the spread of the Elberfeld system was accompanied in many cities by the establishment of societies for the prevention of poverty and begging, which represented the local German equivalent to the English Charity Organization Society.

During this period, charity reformers regarded indiscriminate charity provided without an adequate, individualized knowledge of the applicant as the most serious danger to the moral fiber of the poor and the integrity of the public poor relief system. However, the efforts of these German charity organization societies to modernize and coordinate the activity of voluntary charitable associations created a set of problems which were to beset social reformers through the Weimar Republic. Both charity workers and poor relief officials deeply believed that, since charity obeyed only the imperatives of love and could not tolerate the slightest compulsion, any attempt to regulate voluntary activity ran the serious risk of denaturing it instead of rendering it more rational. As Emil Münsterberg, the leading Progressive welfare reformer from the 1890s until his death in 1911, told the DV in 1891, "It is precisely . . . love, which accomplishes so much, but which tolerates nothing more poorly than force and regimentation. . . . It will act on behalf of one specific end, for one particular person, but fails completely when this specific end, when engagement for this particular person, is prohibited. Any serious constraints in this respect would in fact have no other effect than a substantial decrease in voluntary donations and the complete disappearance of personal engagement."[24] These concerns were heightened even further when these efforts to rationalize voluntary charity threatened to infringe upon the historic privileges of church charities—especially Catholic organizations—which insisted that dictates of faith took priority over the requirements of charity organization. These problems were complicated by the fact that public officials were required to take into account the support provided to the so-called deserving poor by voluntary associations—which was intended to supplement poor relief—in determining need and by the resulting conflict between the subsidiarity of poor relief and the aims of voluntary charity. Despite the continued reservations of Christian conservatives of both confessions to state-mandated poor relief, the commitment of public welfare to the provision of an existence minimum in a deterrent, disciplinary manner and the focus of voluntary welfare on the provision of supplemental support

---

English became increasingly aware of the limits of the 1834 poor law, they began to view the German system as a model to be emulated. See Michael Rose, "Die Krise der Armenfürsorge in England 1860–1890," in Wolfgang Mommsen and Wolfgang Mock, eds., *Die Entstehung des Wohlfahrtsstaates in Großbritannien und Deutschland 1850–1950* (Klett-Cotta, 1982), pp. 57–78. On American attempts to grapple with the dilemma of workhouses versus outdoor relief, see Michael Katz, *In the Shadow of the Poorhouse* (Basic Books, 1986).

[24] Münsterberg, "Die Verbindung der öffentlichen und der privaten Armenpflege," *SDV* 14 (1891), pp. 25–26. In addition, social reformers constantly reiterated their belief that voluntary charity was inherently superior to statutory poor relief because it was free to seek out the many needs of the poor and pioneer new ways of meeting these needs, while public poor relief could only lamely follow in its footsteps.

to the deserving poor provided the basis for a *modus vivendi* which lasted until World War I.

The social insurance legislation of the 1880s had originally been conceived by Bismarck and the state bureaucracy as much as a strategy for poor law reform as a social policy measure designed to win the loyalty of the working classes.[25] This legislation was ultimately passed by the Reichstag with such relative ease because it did not entail a significant redistribution of wealth between classes; taxes paid by the middle classes to cover poor relief costs were transformed in part into insurance contributions, while the working classes only acquired a legal entitlement to insurance benefits by assuming a substantial proportion of the costs of these programs. However, the net impact of the social insurance system on municipal poor relief was limited. Disability pensions were only adequate to support those skilled, better-paid workers who had long, unbroken work histories, but they were intrinsically inadequate for all other persons, who continued to depend on poor relief for at least part of their support in case of disability. While the sickness insurance program had a much more direct effect on municipal poor relief costs than did disability insurance, it also had a large direct impact on the poor relief system because it encouraged the working classes to seek out preventive medical treatment. However, from the point of view of poor relief officials, the sickness insurance program suffered from several important shortcomings. First, because the insurance programs were only obligated to pay for the hospital care of a sick person for a limited period of time, poor relief authorities were still frequently obligated to step in in the case of long-term illnesses. Second, since the family allowance provided to support the dependents of the insured worker in case of hospitalization seldom sufficed to meet the actual needs of the family, poor relief had to supplement this allowance whenever there was a large number of children or the mother was unable to work. Lastly, until after the turn of the century, only industrial workers were eligible for social insurance and large categories of workers—including domestic servants, agricultural workers, and independent artisans—were excluded. Into the 1920s, poor relief officials and social reformers continued to push for the further expansion of the social insurance system, including the creation of an unemployment insurance system.

In 1885, national poor relief statistics were gathered to provide a benchmark against which to measure the impact of the social insurance legislation. The results of the two surveys—one by the Imperial Statistical Office, the other undertaken by Viktor Böhmert, the most influential liberal poor relief and charity reformer from the 1860s through the 1880s, on behalf of the DV—are given in table 1. The most surprising and important result of both sets of statistics was the extent to which illness, old age, disability, and the death of the main breadwinner emerged as the leading causes of poverty among persons of

---

[25] Lujo Brentano, "Die beabsichtigte Alters- und Invaliden-Versicherung für Arbeiter und ihre Bedeutung," *Jahrbücher für Nationalökonomie und Statistik* N.F. 16 (1881), pp. 1–46.

TABLE 1
Poor Relief Survey Results

Imperial Statistical Office[26]		Böhmert/Deutscher Verein[27]	
Accident-related		Illness	44.89
Personal injury	2.1	Old age	15.75
Injury of breadwinner	0.2	Unemployment or low earnings	10.33
Death of breadwinner	.9	Orphanage	5.57
Non-accident-related		Too many children	4.94
Death of breadwinner	17.5	Insanity, mental retardation	3.37
Illness of relief recipient or fam-		Abandonment by breadwinner	2.53
ily member	28.4	Imprisonment of breadwinner	1.69
Physical or mental disability	12.3	Accident/Injury	1.09
Other		Blindness	1.08
Infirmity due to old age	14.9	Physical defect	1.01
Too many children	7.1	Drink	.96
Unemployment	5.4	Work-shy	.75
Drink	2.1	Juvenile Verwahrlosung	.64
Work-shy	1.2	Other	.59
Miscellaneous	7.8	Pauper burial	.22
Cause not given	.1	Physical or mental infirmity of breadwinner	.21
		Death of breadwinner caused by accident	.03

all age groups and, conversely, the relatively small proportion of reported poverty which could be attributable to moral failings, such as drink and work-shyness. Despite their obvious methodological shortcomings, these statistics helped point beyond both the moralistic conception of poverty which had dominated German discourse on the social question since the *Vormärz* and the fiscal perspective which governed the thinking of most poor relief administrators.

Beginning in the 1880s, the social landscape of the *Kaiserreich* was altered beyond recognition by the combined influence of industrialization, mass migration, and urbanization, and during these years a new generation of social reformers began to challenge mid-century views on poverty. Increasingly, they began to argue that living and working conditions in the new industrial metropolises were rendering the urban, working-class family—which was thenceforth to become the privileged object of their concern—structurally incapable of insuring the biological and social reproduction of the working classes. Social reformers were so obsessed with this development because they feared that it posed a mortal threat to both the domestic stability of the *Reich* and its position in the world. Without denying the reality of individual moral fail-

[26] Kaiserliches Statistisches Amt, ed., *Statistik des Deutschen Reiches*, N.F. Bd. 29: *Statistik der öffentlichen Armenpflege im Jahre 1885* (Berlin, 1887), p. 40. The figures cited apply only to the parts of the Reich covered by the relief residence system.

[27] Viktor Böhmert, *Das Armenwesen in 77 deutschen Städten* (Dresden, 1886), Allgemeiner Teil, p. 114.

ings, these reformers maintained that the widespread social problems of the highly industrialized and urbanized society being created during this period were primarily attributable to general social and economic forces and that distress could be prevented through a distinctly Progressive approach—known, in contrast to both poor relief and charity, as *soziale Fürsorge* or "social relief"— which aimed at eliminating poverty by returning behind the individual manifestations of distress to its general, social causes.[28]

The acceptance of this social perspective was clearly reflected in the new set of categories employed by welfare reformers to analyze the increasingly complex and differentiated problem of urban poverty in industrial society. The new concept of poverty replaced the older concept of "the poor" (*die Armen*), which implied that the existence of a class of materially destitute persons existing on society's margins was a natural phenomenon rooted in the frailty of the human condition. Poor relief and charity were increasingly viewed as forms of "social work," which emerged as a distinct discipline and occupation during this period; unemployment and housing were recognized as specific problems of urban, industrial society; illness was transformed from a matter of individual morality to a hygienic problem directly related to living and working conditions; and juvenile delinquency and criminality, which had long been viewed in religious terms, were increasingly reconceptualized in social scientific, criminological, and psychological terms.

However, these reformers were precisely that—reformers, not revolutionaries—and their goal was to compensate for the structural inadequacies of the reproductive sphere within the existing social order and, in this way, (re)integrate the needy into middle-class society and the national community. As the working-class family became the focus of social relief, the Progressive reformers who played the leading role in this reconceptualization of need slowly began to articulate a new vision of social citizenship which postulated that society had the obligation to secure the realization of those social rights that would enable the needy to discharge the obligations imposed upon them by society. These ideas, as well as the growth of middle-class apprehensions about the spread of Social Democracy, gave birth to a dense network of social relief programs, which were undertaken on a voluntary basis both by local associations and municipal government. These programs focused on such issues as unemployment, inadequate housing and sanitation, alcoholism and contagious diseases, infant mortality, the needs of pregnant women and working mothers, the needs of working-class children (especially out-of-wedlock children), and the problems of juvenile delinquency, and they were designed to secure as far as possible—within the framework of bourgeois society—the three major social rights: the rights to work, health, and education.

Unemployment was obviously the greatest existential risk of working-class life. As cyclical downturns during the *Kaiserreich* began to convince social reformers and politicians that unemployment was an unavoidable structural fea-

---

[28] The classic contemporary statement of this new approach was Münsterberg, "The Problem of Poverty," *American Journal of Sociology* 10 (1904), pp. 335–53.

ture of the capitalist economy which could not be reduced to individual moral failings, the desire to reduce the social insecurity of the labor market led to the creation of a number of social relief programs designed to make it a bit easier for the unemployed to secure work or, in the absence of such, to provide unemployment assistance which was more adequate than poor relief and which was not encumbered with social and political disabilities. These programs included in-kind relief stations and workshops for migrant workers (*Naturverpflegungsstationen* and *Wanderarbeitsstätten*), which were designed to facilitate migration in search of work while making it easier for local authorities to distinguish between the able-bodied unemployed legitimately seeking work, the disabled homeless, and the vagrants and beggars (*Landstreicher*) who populated the nation's roads. Increasingly, these programs were linked to local labor exchanges which, especially in the south, were operated by municipal government on the basis of the equal representation of workers and employers. After the turn of the century, the first attempts by local government to devise a viable unemployment insurance scheme were modeled on the so-called Gent system, according to which municipal government provided supplements to the benefits paid by unions to their unemployed members. Emergency public works played only a minor role in providing assistance to the unemployed. However, relief for the unemployed was the politically most sensitive field of social engagement, and, even as the limitations of the Gent system became increasingly clear, there was little political space for further initiatives in this area before the war.[29]

Although the right to health had been championed in 1848 by such radical democratic medical reformers as Rudolf Virchow and Salomon Neumann, it was not until the problems of health and hygiene were qualitatively transformed by urbanization and the emergence of social hygiene as a field of intellectual inquiry in the 1890s that this right became the focus of social relief programs.[30] The primary objects of social hygiene programs were, first, such chronic, contagious diseases as tuberculosis and, second, infant mortality and related maternal health problems, all of which were intimately related to the housing problem. The first programs in this area were rural holiday or convalescent camps (*Feri-*

---

[29] Anselm Faust, *Arbeitsmarktpolitik im Deutschen Kaiserreich. Arbeitsvermittlung, Arbeitsbeschaffung und Arbeitslosenversicherung, 1890–1918* (*VSWG*, Beiheft 79, 1986), Karl Christian Führer, *Arbeitslosigkeit und die Entstehung der Arbeitslosenversicherung in Deutschland, 1902–1927* (Berlin, 1990), and Steinmetz, *Regulating the Social*.

[30] On the development of social hygiene and social relief, see Max Mosse and Gustav Tugendreich, eds., *Krankheit und soziale Lage* (München, 1913), Gustav Tugendreich, *Die Mutter- und Säuglingsfürsorge* (Stuttgart, 1910), E. G. Dresel, *Soziale Fürsorge. Sozialhygienischer Teil*, 2d ed. (Berlin, 1922), George Rosen, "What is Social Medicine?" *Bulletin of the History of Medicine* 21 (1947), pp. 674–733, Daniel Nadav, *Julius Moses und die Politik der Sozialhygiene in Deutschland* (Gerlingen, 1985), Paul Weindling, *Health, Race and German Politics Between National Unification and Nazism, 1870–1945* (Cambridge University Press, 1989), Alfons Labisch, "'Hygiene ist Moral—Moral ist Hygiene'. Soziale Disziplinierung durch Ärtzte und Medizin," in Christoph Sachße and Florian Tennstedt, eds., *Soziale Sicherheit und soziale Disziplinierung* (Suhrkamp, 1986), pp. 265–85, and Richard Evans, *Death in Hamburg: Society and Politics in the Cholera Years 1830–1910* (Clarendon Press, 1987).

enkolonien, Walderholungsstätten, and, from 1914 onward, the *Landaufenthalt für Stadtkinder*) to send needy children to the countryside where they could enjoy the benefits of fresh air, healthy food, and exercise which they were all-too-frequently denied in the city. To combat tuberculosis, associations were established to sponsor sanitarium stays for needy persons in order to facilitate their recovery and block the transmission of the disease by removing this source of infection from the cramped working-class household. In many cities, municipal government joined with these voluntary associations to establish tuberculosis clinics (*Tuberkulosefürsorgestellen*) which disseminated medical advice and provided monetary incentives to encourage hygienic behavior by the sick. Poor relief authorities also began to expand their definition of the existence minimum to include sanitarium stays for the sick and additional support for the families of these persons to achieve these same goals.

Infant mortality also became the object of widespread public concern in the 1890s because, against the background of growing imperialistic rivalries, the combination of astronomical infant mortality rates among the lower classes and declining fertility appeared to pose an immediate threat to strength and productivity of the nation. From 1905 on, maternity care and infant welfare centers (*Mutterberatungs-* and *Säuglingsfürsorgestellen*) were established in many cities through joint public and private initiatives. They disseminated hygienic advice and sterilized milk. Moreover, since bottle-feeding was widely recognized as one of the major causes of infant mortality, these maternity care and infant welfare centers frequently provided financial incentives to encourage working-class women to breast-feed their infants, and in many cases visits to these centers were complemented by house visits by increasingly specialized social workers. While the organization of social relief programs around the working-class household, family, and reproduction provided a means of integrating conceptually and practically the increasingly diverse programs to treat the various aspects of the social question, this trend focused attention on the inseparability of infant and maternal welfare. While many women received some maternity benefits through the sickness insurance system, many more did not. Although women social reformers agitated unsuccessfully for a maternity insurance program before 1914, during World War I a program to cover delivery costs, midwife attendance, lost wages for eight weeks after delivery, and premiums to encourage breast-feeding was finally created, and this program was retained during the Weimar Republic. In addition, there were programs to teach urban working-class girls what one social reformer called "the grand art of living."[31]

Youth welfare was the last of the major fields of social relief. In the 1880s, the problem of rising juvenile delinquency and criminality assumed an unprece-

---

[31] Marie Baum, "Wohnung und Familie," in Badischer Landeswohnungsverein, ed., *Wohnung und Frau. 5 Vorträge* (Karlsruhe, 1912), p. 4. For the reform discourses dealing with the social effects of women's factory work, see Kathleen Canning, *Languages of Labor and Gender: Female Factory Work in Germany, 1850–1914* (Cornell University Press, 1997).

dented public importance. Both Christian conservatives and liberals were concerned because the relative availability of unskilled industrial labor and other forms of commercial employment allowed urban youth of both sexes to enjoy an unprecedented independence which middle-class reformers feared was undermining both parental discipline and the authority of other traditional socializing institutions, such as schools and the church. They believed that the characteristic expressions of this youthful emancipation represented a rebellion against the very principles of property and authority and a willful rejection of all of the virtues upon which bourgeois society was built. However, the youth welfare programs devised to secure the child's right to education and a degree of socialization which would enable the child to meet the demands of adult society aroused such violent emotions because the effective implementation of these reform programs appeared to require both the abandonment of fundamental categories of liberal-conservative jurisprudence and the definitive extension of public authority into the sphere of family and social reproduction.[32]

The most important means of combating the rising level of juvenile delinquency was compulsory correctional education (*Zwangserziehung* or *Fürsorgeerziehung*) in a foster home, house of salvation, or other institution, which had been permitted by the Criminal Code as an alternative to criminal punishment. While liberal-conservative jurisprudence could easily sanction such measures for juvenile offenders, the key issue for social reformers was whether such a law should be limited to those children who had already committed a crime or whether it should strive to prevent delinquency by allowing for the commitment of children who had not actually committed a crime, but who were manifestly endangered or neglected (*verwahrlost*). The proponents of this latter position initially invoked considerations of public order and national efficiency, and their arguments were reinforced by juvenile justice reformers, who argued that juvenile delinquents and offenders required education, not punishment, because they lacked the intellectual insight and moral maturity which was the precondition of the state's right to punish. However, after the turn of the century Progressive youth welfare reformers such as Wilhelm Polligkeit began to argue that the state had a duty to act, not to preserve public order, but rather to insure the realization of the right of endangered and neglected children to an adequate moral and civic education. The resulting conflict between the subsidiarity of public poor relief and the strategy of prevention dominated—and often paralyzed—youth welfare debates in the prewar years.[33]

In the prewar years, youth welfare reformers focused on two goals which they regarded as the key to realizing the child's right to education: 1) the establishment of juvenile court assistance programs (*Jugendgerichtshilfe*) to provide the rapidly expanding network of juvenile courts with detailed descriptions of the character and personal circumstances of juvenile offenders and exercise protective supervision over those children whose criminal sentences had been

---

[32] On the development of youth welfare in this period, see the literature cited in chapter 2.

[33] Polligkeit, "Das Recht des Kindes auf Erziehung," *Jahrbuch der Fürsorge* 2 (1907), pp. 1–86.

provisionally suspended in favor of pedagogical measures; and 2) the reform of guardianship, which was to be one of the main points of contention in subsequent youth welfare legislation. As reformers became aware of the crucial role of guardianship in reducing infant mortality, especially among out-of-wedlock children, there was a broad movement to have a public agency appointed as guardian of all such children. This automatic, legally mandated guardianship over specific categories of children was known as general guardianship (*Generalvormundschaft*). In the early years of the century, Christian Jasper Klumker and Othmar Spann, who were both employed by the Frankfurt *Centrale für private Fürsorge*, were the leading advocates of the employment of trained, salaried professional guardians (*Berufsvormundschaft*) to discharge these expanding public obligations, and they hoped that public guardianship would become the cornerstone of a comprehensive social relief organization to combat both infant mortality and the consequences resulting from the inability of the family—especially single, working-class mothers—to adequately socialize the young. The consolidation of juvenile court assistance and professional guardianship programs under the authority of municipal agencies or, as in Frankfurt, a voluntary association, provided the conceptual and administrative foundation for the subsequent development of youth welfare offices during and after the war. However, this Progressive project provoked the opposition of both liberal social reformers and Christian conservatives who challenged both the Progressive conception of poverty as a social, rather than an individual, moral problem and the belief that state action was in fact capable of positively influencing the personality of the poor. Instead, these groups insisted that this responsibility should remain with voluntary, societal organizations, a demand which was asserted even more firmly by the church charities, which hoped to forestall the further dechristianization of this important area of public life.[34]

Since the late 1890s, the concept of *Wohlfahrtspflege* had been used to describe all of those activities undertaken on a voluntary basis by charity organizations, municipal government, and employers to meliorate those social ills which were directly related to the social and economic system, but which had not yet become the object of social policy legislation or which were believed, by their very nature, not to be susceptible to such statutory remedies. As long as state welfare activity had remained limited to the provision of minimalist, disciplinary poor relief and had no broader aspirations, this definition of the essentially voluntary character and moral function of such activity had faithfully mirrored the liberal-conservative conception of the separation of state and society. However, between the turn of the century and World War I, the slow but steady expansion of voluntary social relief programs began to raise important issues regarding the reform of the poor laws themselves because the underlying discourse on social rights provided a positive rationale for expanded state activ-

---

[34] Georg Schmidt, *Die Organisation der Jugendfürsorge*, SDV 92 (1910), *Stenographischer Bericht über die Verhandlungen*, SDV 94 (1910), and Dickinson, *The Politics of German Child Welfare from the Empire to the Federal Republic*.

ity, which contradicted the deterrent, disciplinary function and the subsidiary nature of poor relief. In the prewar years, this logic of prevention began to undermine both the traditional distinction between statutory social policy programs and poor relief, on the one hand, and welfare or social work, on the other and the previous division of labor between poor relief and voluntary charity.

From the turn of the century onward, the conflict over social rights and the relation between subsidiarity and prevention led to a heated debate over the "social evolution" (*soziale Ausgestaltung*) of poor relief. Some Progressive welfare reformers argued that the scope of the deterrent, disciplinary poor relief system should be reduced by requiring public authorities to expand the network of preventive social relief programs in order to provide a greater degree of social security than that guaranteed by the key institutions of bourgeois society. These arguments pitted them against other reformers (above all Frankfurt municipal councilor Karl Flesch), who argued that the assumption of these preventive programs by municipal welfare would disrupt the functioning of those institutions—the labor contract, private property, and the family—which were the foundation of bourgeois society and the source of the general prosperity of the entire nation. In response to the proponents of the social evolution of poor relief, Flesch argued that the best strategy for increasing the social security of the working classes was through social policy legislation which would improve the position of the working classes in the labor market and thus place them in a position where they too could enjoy the benefits of these institutions.[35] In an effort to insure that those preventive social relief programs undertaken voluntarily by municipal government would have the greatest possible impact, in 1909 the Reichstag specified that certain programs were not to be considered poor relief in the sense of the 1869 electoral law and were, therefore, not to entail the loss of political rights. These programs included medical care, institutional care for relatives due to physical or mental infirmity, occupational training, and youth welfare programs. However, the political constitution of the *Kaiserreich* imposed strict limits upon the social evolution of poor relief before 1914, and, despite the important Progressive innovations implemented in many larger cities, the narrow scope of poor law reform debates in the immediate prewar years reflected the general paralysis of German domestic politics. It was ultimately the war and the revolution which fundamentally altered the parameters of poor relief and charity reform.

World War I precipitated a contradiction in the conditions of social reproduction in Germany because the social programs undertaken to mobilize the home

---

[35] Karl Flesch, "Die soziale Ausgestaltung der Armenpflege," *SDV* 54 (1901), pp. 1–30, Adolf Buehl, Rudolf Flemming, Rechtsrat Fleischmann, and Rudolf Schwander, *Die heutigen Anforderungen an die öffentliche Armenpflege im Verhältnis zur bestehenden Armengesetzgebung*, *SDV* 73 (1905), and *Stenographischer Bericht über die Verhandlungen*, *SDV* 75 (1905). These debates must be read in conjunction with Sidney and Beatrice Webb, *The Minority Report of the Poor Law Commission. Part I: The Break-up of the Poor Law*, Part II: *The Public Organisation of the Labor Market* (London, 1909).

front and the increasingly industrialized war effort tended to undermine those relations of political authority and social deference which the war was being fought to preserve.[36] With regard to poor relief, support for the families of enlisted soldiers, pensions for the wives and children of men who had been killed or disabled in the war, and voluntary charity, the effects of the war were complex and contradictory. While the Reich provided monetary allowances to the families of servicemen (*Kriegsfamilienunterstützung*), Reich and state governments repeatedly urged local authorities to voluntarily supplement these soldiers' family allowances with municipal wartime welfare programs (*Kriegswohlfahrtspflege*), which were to remain administratively separate from municipal poor relief, entail none of the traditional disabilities associated with public assistance, and suffice to enable these families to maintain their prewar standard of living. Wartime welfare, especially for disabled veterans, war widows, and their children, provided the impetus for the systematization of prewar social relief programs, and the broad "social" considerations upon which these innovative programs were based—often at the initiative of the War Ministry—threw an increasingly harsh light upon the presuppositions underlying nineteenth-century poor relief.[37]

The legitimacy of the poor relief system was also called into question from another direction as both Reich and Prussian government began to urge local authorities to expand these wartime welfare programs to all persons who had become needy as a result of the war, including those persons who would otherwise have been considered eligible only for municipal poor relief. Many local welfare officials resisted such an extension of wartime welfare—especially to previous poor relief recipients—because they feared that this would undermine the integrity of a poor relief system based on the principles of subsidiarity and deterrence. The existence of two qualitatively different systems of public assistance—poor relief and wartime welfare—generated widespread popular discontent with the perceived inequities in the treatment of the different categories of recipients, especially in view of the government's depiction of the war as a classless enterprise, while the introduction of a de facto means test for soldiers' family aid and the wide degree of discretion permitted local officials in the determination of need further highlighted the contradictory motives underlying these programs.

The destruction of human life during the war and the massive disruption of traditional family structures provided the impetus for the first attempts to put into practice the ideas of prewar youth welfare reformers through the national

---

[36] Elisabeth Domansky, "Militarization and Reproduction in World War I Germany," in Eley, ed., *Society, Culture, and the State in Germany 1870–1930*, pp. 427–63.

[37] On these new departures in wartime welfare, see *Schriften des Arbeitsausschusses für Kriegerwitwen und -waisenfürsorge*, especially vols. 1, 5, 9, *Soziale Fürsorge für Kriegerwitwen und Kriegerwaisen*, SDV 103 (1915), Hermann Luppe, ed., *Das Wesen und die Aufgaben der Kriegshinterbliebenenfürsorge im Deutschen Reich* (Leipzig, 1917), Edmund Friedberg and Siddy Wronsky, *Handbuch der Kriegsfürsorge* (Berlin, 1917), and *Theorie und Praxis der Kriegshinterbliebenenfürsorge* (Berlin 1916).

regulation of youth welfare and the establishment of a nationwide network of public youth welfare offices.[38] However, these first attempts to regulate youth welfare in Prussia and at the national level, as well as the efforts of the government to regulate the activity of the proliferating number of charitable organizations, intensified the prewar conflicts over the relation between public and voluntary welfare, as well as those among the many voluntary organizations active in every field of charitable endeavor.[39]

Many of these wartime initiatives were the product of an expanded notion of public responsibility for the welfare of the individual,[40] even though this new attitude was initially embodied in authoritarian policies in the areas of population policy, sexuality, and youth welfare.[41] However, conflicts over the future of the punitive, deterrent poor relief system and the role which wartime welfare and the other innovative social relief programs might play could not be resolved without a comprehensive reform of public assistance. During the last years of the war, Progressive reformers began agitating for such comprehensive reform on Progressive principles. At the 1917 DV conference, Kurt Blaum, one of the most active Progressive youth welfare reformers during and immediately after the war, called for the "socialization" of public assistance which, through the

[38] *Jugendämter als Träger der öffentlichen Jugendfürsorge im Reich. Bericht über die Verhandlungen des Deutschen Jugendfürsorgetages am 20. und 21. September 1918 in Berlin* (Berlin, 1919).

[39] Young-Sun Hong, "The contradictions of modernization in the German welfare state: gender and the politics of welfare reform in First World War Germany," *Social History* 17:2 (May 1992), pp. 251–70, and, among the extensive contemporary literature, Albert Levy "Ziele und Grenzen der staatlichen Aufsicht über Unternehmungen der Kriegswohlfahrtspflege," in *Gekürzter Bericht über die Tagung der "Freien Vereinigung für Kriegswohlfahrt"* (n.p., n.d. [December 1916]), Friedrich Zahn, *Staatliche Aufsicht über die freiwillige Wohlfahrtspflege? Kritische Betrachtungen (= Archiv der Hamburgischen Gesellschaft für Wohltätigkeit*, no. 8, 1916), *Stenographisher Bericht über die Verhandlungen, SDV* 107 (1918), pp. 114–99, 227–29, and *Schriften der Zentralstelle für Volkswohlfahrt*, N.F., no. 14, pp. 4–92. One important landmark in this process of polarization was the draft of a youth welfare law which was presented to the Prussian legislature in June 1918 (but which was not debated before the revolution) and the response by the Caritasverband to this Prussian draft. See *Drucksachen des Preußischen Abgeordnetenhauses*, 22. Legislaturperiode, Drucksache 1213 and *Denkschrift des Deutschen Caritasverbandes . . . zum preußischen Jugendfürsorgegesetz-Entwurf* (Freiburg, 1918).

[40] This new attitude comes through most clearly in the minutes of the three major welfare conferences held during the war: *Soziale Fürsorge für Kriegerwitwen und Kriegerwaisen, SDV* 103 (1915), *Die Erhaltung und Mehrung der deutschen Volkskraft. Verhandlungen der 8. Konferenz der Zentralstelle für Volkswohlfahrt in Berlin vom 26.-28. Oktober 1915, (= Schriften der Zentralstelle für Volkswohlfahrt*, N.F. 12, 1916), and Deutsche Zentrale für Jugendfürsorge, ed., *Gesamtbericht der Tagung in Frankfurt a.M. am 7.-9. Oktober 1915 (Gegenstand der Verhandlungen: Die Aufgaben der Jugendfürsorge nach dem Kriege, namentlich in der Kleinkinderfürsorge* (n.p., n.d.), as well as *Gekürzter Bericht über die Tagung der "Freien Vereinigung für Kriegswohlfahrt"*.

[41] Eve Rosenhaft, "Restoring Moral Order on the Home Front: Compulsory Savings Plans for Young Workers in Germany, 1916–19," in Marilyn Shevin Coetzee and Frans Coetzee, eds., *Authority, Identity and the Social History of the Great War* (Berghahn, 1995), pp. 81–109, and Cornelie Usborne, "Pregnancy Is the Woman's Active Service," in Richard Wall and Jay Winter, eds., *The Upheaval of War: Family, Work and Welfare in Europe, 1914–1918* (Cambridge University Press, 1988), pp. 389–416.

expansion of social relief programs would render poor relief, with its subsidiary character and deterrent approach, increasingly superfluous.[42]

Since 1914, the government had responded to wartime social dislocation in an ad hoc, piecemeal manner in the false but comforting belief that the war would be brief and, later, as the result of a conscious decision not to take any measures which would prejudice postwar developments in the field of poor relief and welfare. While all prewar attempts to justify comprehensive poor law reform in class terms had been rejected, after the total mobilization of society for the war had linked the political and social structure of the postwar nation to an unprecedented extent to the outcome of the war, the arguments in favor of innovative social welfare programs which had been advanced by the military during the war could—after 1918—be easily linked to Progressive arguments concerning population quality, national efficiency, and social citizenship.

In the immediate postwar period, welfare reform acquired an unprecedented importance because the revolution, the exigencies of reconstruction, and the opportunities afforded by the drafting of a new constitution linked social reproduction to state form far more directly than would have been possible before the war. As one contributor to the *Kölner Volkszeitung* explained in 1920, the war and revolution

> have not only politically placed our polity on a new foundation, but rather their effects have perhaps been of deeper significance for future development in the economic and social realms. Many signs appear to indicate that here a revaluation of all values is taking place. Concepts and standards such as we knew before the war have in many cases already become alien to us. Other economic principles and new forms of social life are preparing to emerge. The new relations, which the legacy of the lost war has brought with it, are struggling to achieve a new shape and are placing state and community before great new tasks with new purposes and new aims. One of the most important preconditions for the social and economic reconstruction of our sorely tested fatherland may well be found in the creation of a public poor relief and welfare system, which is permeated by a social spirit and a profound understanding of the need of the people. As a form of service to the people, public welfare has to fulfill one of the most important tasks with respect to the gradual recovery and rise of our German people.[43]

The constitution, which was approved on August 11, 1919, contained a lengthy list of fundamental social rights which established the framework for, but not the concrete significance of, subsequent welfare legislation. Article 7 gave the Reich government legislative competence in the areas of poor relief (which had previously been reserved to the states), population policy, maternity protection, youth welfare, public health, and labor law, while Article 9 extended

---

[42] Blaum, "Die öffentliche Armenpflege nach dem Kriege," *Die Armenpflege nach dem Kriege, SDV* 105 (1917), pp. 64ff. and *Die Uebergangsfürsorge vom Krieg zum Frieden, SDV* 106 (1917).

[43] Friedrich Meffert, "Die Neugestaltung der öffentlichen Armenpflege," *Kölnische Volkszeitung* (November 4, 1920).

Reich competence to include the new but undefined area of welfare (*Wohlfahrtspflege*). Article 161 gave the Reich the authority to create a comprehensive social insurance system to preserve the health and productivity of the people, protect motherhood, and insure against the economic consequences of age, disability, and the vicissitudes of life. While the first paragraph of article 163 imposed upon all citizens—without detriment to their personal freedom—the moral obligation to "employ their spiritual and physical forces in a manner conducive to the common welfare," the second paragraph stated that every German should have the opportunity to support him- or herself through productive labor, but that, insofar as appropriate work could not be found, the necessities of life were to be provided. The very important question of how these rights were to be satisfied was to be settled through subsequent legislation.

Despite the turmoil of the immediate postrevolutionary period, there quickly emerged a broad consensus across the entire political spectrum that the creative reconstruction of German society would require expanded and more aggressive state welfare policies. As Polligkeit, the chair of the DV and the single most influential welfare reformer during the Republic, argued in 1920, since labor power was the only resource left to the German people after the conclusion of the Versailles treaties, it was more necessary than ever before to create a welfare system to improve both the level of public health and the overall quality of the nation's human capital. He warned against being misled by fiscal considerations into cutting back on social programs and retreating from the social ideals championed by prewar reformers, and he argued instead that welfare reform could simultaneously serve both social-ethical ideals and economic reconstruction.[44]

Such considerations—which were widely shared—overrode historical objections to the expansion of state welfarist activity and made it more urgent than ever for the voluntary welfare organizations to insure that control over the public welfare system did not fall into the hands of their political opponents. Moreover, public concern for the quality and productivity of the population was not the exclusive domain of welfare reformers in the narrow sense, and frequently welfare reform discussions became the point of intersection for a multiplicity of related discourses on such issues as sexuality, population and family policy, social hygiene and eugenics, and household rationalization, as well as the campaign for morality legislation, which was often regarded as a necessary complement to, and sometimes as a substitute for, welfare reform.[45] Although the pro-

---

[44] Polligkeit, "Die Krise in der Wohlfahrtspflege," *Concordia* (November 1, 1920), pp. 201–5, citation p. 202. These ideas were reaffirmed at a major conference on population policy held the following year. See *Bericht der Verhandlungen des Bevölkerungspolitischen Kongresses der Stadt Köln* (n.p., 1921). On Polligkeit, see Carl Ludwig Krug von Nidda, *Wilhelm Polligkeit. Wegbereiter einer neuzeitigen Fürsorge* (Cologne, 1961) and Florian Tennstedt, "50 Jahre von 100. Wilhelm Polligkeit und der 'Deutscher Verein,' " Christoph Sachße/Florian Tennstedt, eds., *Jahrbuch der Sozialarbeit* 4 (1981), pp. 445–68.

[45] On Weimar morality legislation, see Atina Grossmann, *Reforming Sex: The German Movement for Birth Control and Abortion Reform, 1920–1950* (Oxford University Press, 1995), Cornelie

posed Reich welfare ministry was never created, the newly created Labor Ministry functioned as an effective surrogate until the end of the Republic.[46]

In the first months after the revolution, there was a spate of emergency government decrees and ad hoc legislation designed to prevent the further political radicalization of returning troops and gain a handle on the problem of demobilization and the transition to a peacetime economy. However, by 1920 welfare reformers and politicians had begun to settle down to the arduous work of crafting welfare legislation which would lay the basis for Germany's postwar reconstruction and put into practice the programmatic statements of the Weimar constitution. Between 1922 and 1924, three major pieces of welfare legislation were passed: the National Youth Welfare Law (*Reichsjugendwohlfahrtsgesetz*, RJWG [June 1922]); the National Social Welfare Law (*Reichsfürsorgepflichtverordnung*, RFV [February 1924]); and the National Guidelines for the Determination of Need, the Nature, and the Scope of Public Welfare (*Reichsgrundsätze über Voraussetzung, Art und Maß der öffentlichen Fürsorge*, RGr [December 1924]). This legislation, together with the 1927 Unemployment Insurance Law, represents the most important landmark in the history of the German welfare system between the Relief Residence Law of 1870 and the welfare legislation of the early 1960s, which simply reaffirmed the political principles and organizational innovations codified in the legislation of the 1920s.[47]

The numerous attempts in the postwar period to define "welfare" (*Fürsorge* or *Wohlfahrtspflege*)—as well as its relation to poor relief and social insurance—reflected a clear awareness that the extension of state activity far beyond the carefully circumscribed limits imposed by the rule of law in bourgeois society was blurring the traditional distinction between the public and the private spheres.[48] While the social evolution of poor relief had already begun to call

---

Usborne, *The Politics of the Body: Women's Reproductive Rights and Duties* (Macmillan, 1992), and Andreas Wollash, *Der Katholische Fürsorgeverein für Mädchen, Frauen und Kinder (1899– 1945). Ein Beitrag zur Geschichte der Jugend- und Gefährdetenfürsorge in Deutschland* (Freiburg, 1991).

[46] Although the Social Democrat Gustav Bauer served for a brief time as the first Reich Labor Minister, Heinrich Brauns, the former director of the *Volksverein für das katholische Deutschland*, held the post from 1920 until 1928, when he was replaced by the Social Democrat Rudolf Wissell. Adam Stegerwald, the general secretary of the Christian Trade Unions, became the first Prussian Minister for Public Welfare in 1919, though he ceded the post to Heinrich Hirtsiefer (Center) when he became Prussian Minister President in 1921. After the collapse of the grand coalition in 1930, Stegerwald served as Labor Minister under the Brüning administration from 1930 to 1932. On the Prussian ministry, see Stegerwald, *Wege der Volkswohlfahrt* (Berlin, 1920), and Hirtsiefer, *Die staatliche Wohlfahrtspflege in Preußen, 1919–1923* (Berlin, 1924). In Bavaria, Baden, and other states, welfare ministries were established immediately after the revolution, and in other states the authority of labor ministries was expanded to include welfare policy.

[47] The texts of the major Reich and state welfare laws, as well as the relevant implementation guidelines, can be found in Ernst Behrend/Helen Stranz-Hurwitz, eds., *Wohlfahrtsgesetze des Deutschen Reiches und Preußens*, 2 vols. (Berlin, 1923–25).

[48] The most important postwar contributions to this debate are Helene Simon, *Aufgaben und Ziele der neuzeitlichen Wohlfahrtspflege* (Stuttgart, 1922), Alice Salomon, *Leitfaden der Wohlfahrtspflege*, 3d ed. (Lepzig, 1923), Siddy Wronsky, "Wohlfahrtspflege," in Oskar Karstedt et al., eds.,

this definition into question, the distinctions upon which it was based were completely undermined after 1918, and the various definitions of welfare advanced in the postrevolutionary period reflected the growing awareness of the impossibility of identifying moral activity solely with voluntary charity or the rectification of structural causes of poverty with state social policy. As Johannes Steinweg of the Inner Mission clearly pointed out, "Today the state regards itself in principle as the bearer of primary responsibility for social welfare. . . . It does not aspire simply to be a state of order, police and law, but also wants to be a culture and welfare state (*Kultur- und Wohlfahrtsstaat*) as well."[49] Both the confessional charity organizations and, to a lesser extent, the Progressives objected to the colonization of voluntary charity by the emergent welfare state and feared the detrimental consequences of the bureaucratization, juridification, and professionalization of public assistance and social work for the moral and material well-being of the poor. As Friedrich Mahling, the historian of the Inner Mission, insisted, all attempts to codify this voluntary dimension of personal help simply denatured the idea of welfare, rather than enriching the idea of the state.[50] However, after the war it became increasingly difficult to defend such a position as the focus of debate shifted from the question of whether or not the state should intervene directly into the sphere of social reproduction to the question of the substantive values informing such intervention.

THE STRUCTURE OF THE BOOK

Chapter 1 examines the relationship between the worldviews espoused by Workers' Welfare, the Caritasverband, the Inner Mission, and Progressive welfare reformers; their respective visions of the individual, the family, and the state; and their understanding of how the social welfare should be reformed in order to facilitate the realization of these ideals. Chapter 2 shows how these differences shaped the National Youth Welfare Law (RJWG), which was the most important and controversial piece of welfare legislation passed during the Republic. The debate leading up to the passage of the RJWG pitted the Social Democrats against the confessional welfare organizations. While the former argued for the primacy of public welfare and the subordination of voluntary welfare groups to local democratic institutions, the latter insisted upon the pri-

---

Handwörterbuch der Wohlfahrtspflege (Berlin, 1924), pp. 442–49, Friedrich Mahling, *Die sittlichen Voraussetzungen der Wohlfahrtspflege* (Berlin, 1925), Hans Muthesius, *Die Wohlfahrtspflege* (Berlin, 1925), Hans Maier, *Die rechtlichen Grundlagen und die Organisation der Fürsorge einschließlich des Armenrechts und des Rechtes des Kindes* (Berlin, 1926), Else Wex, *Vom Wesen der sozialen Fürsorge* (Berlin, 1929), and Wex, *Die Entwicklung der sozialen Fürsorge* (Berlin, 1929).

[49] Steinweg, "Die Innere Mission der Evangelischen Kirche und die Wohlfahrtspflege," in *Verhandlungen des 40. Kongress für Innere Mission und der Ersten Kontinental Konferenz für Innere Mission und Diakonie*, ed. Central-Ausschuss für Innere Mission (Wichern Verlag, 1922), pp. 48–49. See also Maier, *Die rechtlichen Grundlagen*, p. 1.

[50] Mahling, *Die sittlichen Voraussetzungen*, pp. 9–10.

macy of voluntary welfare, the centrality of religious concerns, and the merely subsidiary role of public welfare. In this confrontation, the Progressives occupied an unstable middle position which sought to combine their advocacy of the extension of social rights and social obligations with a defense of the voluntarist tradition. The political compromises ultimately embedded in the National Youth Welfare Law clearly affirmed the subsidiarity of public welfare and guaranteed voluntary welfare a substantial role in the government of the public youth welfare offices established under the law. However, by failing to require these public agencies to delegate the direct provision of social services to voluntary welfare, the law created a permanent conflict between the principles of direct democratic control and the societal corporatism advocated by the church charities and the Progressives. This decision concerning the political structure of the governing committees of the municipal welfare offices further reinforced the tendency of the major welfare organizations to isolate themselves from one another and, by institutionalizing their mutual antagonism, accelerated the fragmentation and hollowing out of the sphere of public, parliamentary debate.[51]

The structure of the state envisioned by these welfare reform groups (corporatist, direct democracy, or some Progressive middle ground) also determined their understanding of the logic of social rationalization and the function of the welfare system. These debates illustrate with exemplary clarity the reciprocal relationship between the conceptions of the nature and scope of state activity advocated by these groups and their respective visions of family and civil society. In its simplest terms, a welfare system shaped by Catholic corporatist principles and designed to instill in children the love of God and respect for authority would have looked very different from both the Progressive vision of social hygiene and pedagogy programs administered by voluntary associations and the Social Democratic hope that extensive social programs, carried out by a strictly public welfare system, could help bring about the evolutionary transition from capitalism to socialism. As a result, the decision regarding state form also entailed a concrete decision about the substantive values informing public youth welfare work—as well as the methodology of social work. All of these issues had moved to the forefront of public debate since the revolution.

Chapters 3 and 4 trace the codification of preventive, therapeutic principles in the general welfare system (which were adopted in the youth welfare field with the RJWG) and the conflicts generated by the efforts of the Progressives to make their own need-based, work-centered—productivist—vision of social citizenship the basis for a comprehensive reform of poor relief and welfare legislation. Chapter 3 follows the conflicts which accompanied the development of special welfare programs for the "new poor" created by the war and the inflation: the unemployed, disabled veterans and the survivors of those men who had been killed in the war (i.e., widows, orphans, and dependent parents), recipients of pensions from the disability insurance funds (whose assets had been

---

[51] See Michael Geyer, "Nation, Klasse und Macht. Zur Organisation von Herrschaft in der Weimarer Republik," *AfS* 26 (1986), pp. 28ff.

annihilated by the inflation), and small rentiers (whose wealth had been destroyed in the same manner). The privileged treatment—including higher benefits, eligibility for therapeutic social services, representative rights in the welfare offices, and freedom from the disabilities historically entailed by the receipt of public assistance—granted to these new poor was based on the presumption that their need was somehow more directly related to misguided state policies than that of other groups of the needy, whose need was ostensibly due to individual moral failings. However, their insistence upon preserving these group-based privileges entangled them in a conflict of principle with the Progressives (and the Social Democrats) at the very moment when the distinction upon which these privileges were based was becoming increasingly difficult to maintain. The Progressives argued that the generalization of their need-based, work-centered approach was the best means of promoting the general welfare. However, there was an unavoidable conflict between this Progressive vision, which would have favored the needs of those persons who could be expected to (again) become productive members of the national community of labor, and the concrete interests of the elderly and disabled, who made up a large proportion of the new poor. The organizations representing the new poor feared that they would be the losers in a general reform such as that proposed by the Progressives, and they demanded the recognition of group entitlements to status-oriented welfare services, which, if achieved, would have amounted to public pensions to compensate these persons for the losses they suffered during the inflation.

Chapter 4 analyzes the forces which provided the impetus for a general reform of poor relief and welfare and the resulting three-way conflict between Progressive reformers, the new poor, and Labor Ministry officials over the National Social Welfare Law (RFV) and the National Guidelines for the Determination of Need, the Nature, and the Scope of Public Welfare (RGr). The outcome of this conflict was an unsatisfactory compromise between Progressive principles and group entitlements which resulted from the attempts by the Labor Ministry to employ means-tested, subsidiary forms of public assistance as a mechanism for reducing Reich social spending and equitably redistributing the costs of the war and the inflation. This compromise institutionalized the postwar conflicts among these three groups and overburdened municipal welfare with the financial costs of supporting the new poor and the political costs resulting from the use of a single public assistance system to serve two contradictory goals. Between 1924 and 1930, welfare reformers hoped that they could simultaneously solve both of these problems by promoting the expansion of social insurance and old age security programs in order to remove from municipal welfare rolls all of those persons who were not the proper object of individualized personal help. However, fiscal and political constraints limited progress in this direction, and these nagging conflicts continued to exercise welfare reformers and public officials until the end of the decade.

Chapter 5 analyzes the development of the social work profession during the Republic. The first section shows how the leaders of the social work profession attempted to legitimate their belief in the primacy of helping over politics and how such helping was reinterpreted with pedagogical—that is, preventive, therapeutic—intent in conjunction with the RJWG and the RGr. While the conflict between personal help and bureaucracy was inherent in the modernization of the welfare system, the division of labor between male bureaucrats and female field workers gave this conflict a strong gender dimension. The middle sections of chapter 5 examine, first, the highly idealized professional ethos shared by these women social workers and, second, the conflicts over wages, working conditions, and administrative authority through which this gendered conflict between bureaucracy and personal help found its most direct expression. By the end of the decade it was clear that the entry of women into the social work field had failed to transform the political culture of the welfare bureaucracy or that of the nation at large, and the disappointment at this failure gradually transformed the leading social work educators into disillusioned critics of the welfare system, which they had originally hoped would be a vehicle for both the reconciliation of class antagonisms and their own political emancipation. The chapter then examines the emergence of a distinctly Social Democratic theory of social work, which throws into sharp relief the presuppositions underlying the vision of social work as organized helping which was shared by both the Progressives and the confessional welfare organizations. It concludes with an analysis of both the ways in which these social workers attempted to subjectively work through the contradictions created by that repression of politics which underlay their own vision of the social work profession and the implications of these experiences for the political life of the Republic.

Chapter 6 attempts to assess the impact of the clash of worldviews examined in chapters 1 and 2 on the nature of the Weimar state and the structure of public life. One of the distinctive characteristics of the German welfare system as it emerged during the Weimar Republic was its corporate structure, in which responsibility for the primary provision of social services was delegated—in conjunction with public subsidies—to a number of semipublic welfare organizations divided along religious and political lines.[52] By 1925, there were seven welfare organizations which were officially recognized by the Labor Ministry as *Spitzenverbände* or "peak associations" endowed with quasi-public status and the right to distribute state subsidies—without being subject to direct control by either local or Reich government—to their member organizations. The most important included the Caritasverband; the Inner Mission; Workers' Welfare; the Red Cross; and the Fifth Welfare League (*Fünfter Wohlfahrtsverband*, which was formed in 1924 when an organization representing a number of male-dominated social hygiene

---

[52] The only other account of these institutional developments is Jochen-Christoph Kaiser, *Sozialer Protestantismus im 20. Jahrhundert. Beiträge zur Geschichte der Inneren Mission 1914–1945* (Oldenbourg, 1989). On the similarities between the corporatist system established during the Weimar period and that of the Federal Republic, see Dickinson, *The Politics of German Child Welfare*, pp. 244ff., Heinze and Olk, "Die Wohlfahrtsverbände im System sozialer Dienstleistungsproduktion," and Alfred Rinken, *Das Öffentliche als verfassungstheoretisches Problem, dargestellt am Rechtsstatus der Wohlfahrtsverbände* (Berlin, 1971).

associations absorbed the leading bourgeois women's welfare association). There were also two other peak associations which played only a minor role in politics of welfare reform: the Central Welfare Bureau for German Jewry (*Zentralwohlfahrtsstelle der deutschen Juden*) and the Central Welfare Committee for Christian Workers (*Zentralwohlfahrtsausschuß der christlichen Arbeiterschaft*, which had been formed by the Christian Trade Unions as a counterweight to Workers' Welfare). With the exception of Workers' Welfare, which remained committed to the primacy of public welfare, all of the *Spitzenverbände* were represented within a corporatist organ (the German League for Voluntary Welfare), through which these organizations represented their common interests against both Workers' Welfare and public welfare.[53]

In 1925/26, the DV sponsored a series of conferences, whose minutes are a singularly fascinating document which clearly shows how dissatisfaction with the compromises reached in the early 1920s and the persistent three-way conflict between public welfare, the church charities, and Workers' Welfare accelerated the search for alternatives to parliamentary democracy. This struggle against parliamentary democracy and cultural pluralism increased the attractiveness of a corporatist organization of the welfare sector which, the participants hoped, would guarantee the autonomy of voluntary welfare by removing it even further from the sphere of public control. However, this reprivatization and reconfessionalization of social work was impossible within the political framework of the Republic. The incompatibility of the ultimate ends advocated by the major welfare organizations led to a virtual *Weltanschauungskrieg* in the welfare sector, and the translation of these fundamental conflicts over the nature of the welfare system to the level of constitutional questions at the end of the 1920s played an important role in the crisis of the Weimar Republic.

All of the contradictions of the republican welfare system which had been generated by the attempt to employ an extensive public welfare system to secure the social rights of the needy and thus solve the problem of social insecurity in an acquisitive society had become evident to astute observers by 1928 or so: the destabilization of parliamentary democracy resulting from this *Weltanschauungskampf* and the resulting trend toward authoritarian corporatism, the resistance by the new poor to Progressive welfare reform, the ambiguous rela-

[53] The accurate description of the peculiar status of these organizations entails substantial terminological difficulties. Although these *Verbände* were formed through the national organization of local voluntary associations (*Vereine*), as poverty became a specifically public, political problem across the middle of the nineteenth century, it was increasingly recognized that these organizations performed a distinctly public function, though their activity continued to be distinguished from that of statutory public poor relief by its voluntary character. In light of the increasingly public character of the work of what would normally be called private associations, it is improper to speak of an opposition between public poor relief or welfare and private charity, and I have decided to contrast *public* and *voluntary* welfare, despite the fact that this terminology grates against anglophone lexicographical sensibilities, and to describe these organizations as "societal" organizations. Similar terminological difficulties beset contemporary attempts to distinguish between statutory social policy programs (*Sozialpolitik*), social work (*Fürsorge*), and welfare (*Wohlfahrtspflege*).

tion between the emancipatory and disciplinary dimension of preventive, therapeutic welfare practices, and the contradictions of social pedagogy as experienced by both social workers and their clientele. The depression merely accelerated the search for a solution. Chapters 7 and 8 explore the implications of these trends for both the republican welfare system and the republican welfare state.

Chapter 7 deals with the external crises and the internal contradictions of the republican welfare system and the increasingly antiliberal, antidemocratic reform strategies proposed by both the Progressive and confessional architects of the republican welfare system. This chapter shows, first, how the dismantling of the unemployment insurance system under Chancellor Heinrich Brüning led to a massive fiscal crisis which forced municipal welfare to suspend the ambitious preventive and therapeutic programs established during the 1920s and, second, how the fiscal crisis of municipal welfare and the political disarray of the Progressives provided an unexpected opportunity for voluntary welfare to again challenge the very legitimacy of public welfare and democratic control over the welfare sector.

In addition, between 1928 and 1933 there was a growing awareness in many quarters that those same forces which were driving the evolution of the social welfare system were also making it difficult, if not impossible, for these highly bureaucratized institutions to achieve their original goals. As a result, these Progressive reformers argued, the continued expansion of public welfare was leading to a fatal imbalance between social rights and social duties and transforming their positive ideal of a social, democratic *Volksstaat* into a welfare state, in the pejorative sense of the word. During this period, the Progressives articulated a complex genealogy of the contradictions of the republican welfare system. They traced the origins of all of these problems to the emergence of that sociological perspective on poverty in the 1880s and 1890s which had provided the conceptual foundation for their own most important achievements in the intervening decades and to the resulting bureaucratization of helping. These arguments simply brought to the surface the contradiction in Progressive thought between collective public responsibility and voluntary social engagement, between their belief in the importance of environmental reform and conviction of the necessity of personal help, which had been latent in the Progressive project from the very beginning. However, the Progressives were so deeply wedded to the idea of individualized help that their reform proposals increasingly tended toward a retreat from parliamentary government, the dismantling of the public welfare system, and the reprivatization of public welfare within the broad framework of an authoritarian, Christian state. All of these arguments were echoed by the confessional welfare organizations which, however, argued that Progressivism itself, rather than its bureaucratic distortion, was the root of the problem. Although both the Progressives and the confessional welfare organizations hoped that the Nazi seizure of power would make possible the creation of a viable corporatist system, the goal of the Nazis was not the reprivatization and confessionalization of welfare, but the total mobilization of society and the marginalization of confessional welfare organizations. As a result, the Nazi seizure of power set in motion a new round of cultural struggles which revealed the intrinsic contradictions of the corporatist solution advocated by so many welfare reformers during the 1920s.

Although growing authoritarianism of both the Progressives and the confessional welfare organizations enabled them to make common cause with the Nazis, it is misleading to view National Socialism as the apotheosis of pathologies latent in Progressive therapeutic practices. Peukert's version of the social discipline paradigm pivots on his account of the birth of German fascism out of the spirit of Progressive social engineering and the role of the proposed correctional custody law in this process. The program of prevention and therapy codified in the first years of the Republic was based on the presumption that the ostensible beneficiaries of these programs were willing to accept this help on the terms that it was offered, that is, that they were willing to let themselves be helped. However, this raised important questions about the nature of state welfarist intervention, especially regarding the treatment of that residual stratum of persons—prostitutes, the work-shy, migrant casual laborers, beggars, drunkards and endangered youth—who resisted the assistance proffered by social workers, but who persisted in forms of conduct which were generally regarded as harmful both to these persons and to society at large. Through the end of the decade, the debate over a proposed correctional custody law continued to reflect Progressive and Christian concern for the realization of the individual personality, which was reinforced by a broad optimism with respect to the possibility of reconciling individual interests and those of society through the proposed form of therapeutic correctional custody.

Peukert argues that Progressivism was transformed into its inhumane *Doppelgänger* by a growing reliance upon discipline and segregation to eliminate that resistance to therapeutic normalization which could not be overcome through social pedagogy and that this transformation was exemplified by the emergence of a new conception of correctional custody which stripped away all of the pedagogical connotations associated with the idea through the 1920s. However, despite their increasingly vociferous criticisms of the republican welfare system, the Progressives and the church charitites by and large remained faithful to the humanistic principles which they shared with the Social Democrats and which had informed their vision of welfare and social work since the founding of the Republic. Peukert notwithstanding, chapter 8 argues that the crisis of Progressivism did not provide the spiritual energies which underlay the Nazi vision of the racial reconstruction of civil society and determined the role of correctional custody in this program. Rather, these new impulses were supplied by the eugenic reformers who played a growing role in welfare reform debates between 1928 and 1933. These eugenic reformers regarded social pedagogy and social hygiene as wasteful, if not dysgenic, and demanded that preventive, therapeutic *Fürsorge* for needy individuals be replaced by a collective *Vorsorge*, which would subordinate the rights of the individual to those of the supraindividual, supragenerational entities of *Volk* and race. Consequently, in the welfare sector, the most direct continuities between the Weimar Republic and the Third Reich are to be found not in the apotheosis of the latent pathologies of Progressivism, but rather in the rejection of the spiritual foundations of the republican welfare system by both eugenic welfare reformers and their Nazi supporters.

The Politics of Welfare Reform, 1919–1923

Social Democracy, Progressivism, Christian Conservatism, and the Shaping of the Weimar State

The revolution fundamentally altered the position of Social Democracy within the German political system, and the effects of the revolution were no less profound in the welfare sector, where it created a complex antagonistic relationship between socialist welfare reformers and organized church charities, than in other spheres of German society. Although the SPD founded its own national welfare organization Workers' Welfare (*Arbeiterwohlfahrt*) in December 1919, the Protestant Inner Mission and the Catholic Caritasverband had a head start of three-quarters of a century, and Workers' Welfare never became as large as its confessional counterparts, which still had broad support both within the government and in the public at large.[1] Nevertheless, Workers' Welfare was extremely influential in the subsequent development of the Weimar welfare system because of both the reforms it advocated and the tremendous catalytic effect which its mere existence had on the Inner Mission and the Caritasverband.

In the immediate postwar period, the Inner Mission was extremely vocal in its opposition to Social Democracy, revolution, and the Republic, and it maintained close relations to the DNVP (*Deutschnationale Volkspartei*). On the other hand, thanks to the support of the Center Party, which played a pivotal role in the Weimar coalition, the Caritasverband was quite successful working within the system, and the efforts of the Catholic organization to preserve the rights of voluntary welfare redounded to the benefit of the Inner Mission as well as bourgeois charity organizations.[2] In the long run, this mutual provocation forced both Workers' Welfare and the organized church charities to articu-

---

[1] The archives of Workers' Welfare were destroyed in 1933. The most important studies of the organization are Christiane Eifert, *Frauenpolitik und Wohlfahrtspflege. Zur Geschichte der sozialdemokratischen 'Arbeiterwohlfahrt'* (Campus Verlag, 1993), Anneliese Monat, *Sozialdemokratie und Wohlfahrtspflege. Ein Beitrag zur Entstehungsgeschichte der Arbeiterwohlfahrt* (Stuttgart, 1961), Karen Hagemann, *Frauenalltag und Männerpolitik. Alltagsleben und gesellschaftliches Handeln von Arbeiterfrauen in der Weimarer Republik. Untersucht am Beispiel des sozialdemokratischen Milieus in Hamburg* (Bonn, 1990), and, from a Catholic perspective, Karl Bopp, *Die Wohlfahrtspflege des modernen deutschen Sozialismus* (Freiburg, 1930).

[2] On the position of the Caritasverband in the postwar period, see Lorenz Werthmann (the head of the Caritasverband), "Tagesströmungen auf dem Gebiete der deutschen Wohlfahrtspflege. Vertrauliche Denkschrift des Deutschen Caritasverbandes" (1920), ADCV CA XX 49, and Constantin Noppel, "Die Caritas im neuen Deutschland," *Stimmen der Zeit* 99 (1920), pp. 33–49.

late more fully their own visions of the role of welfare in the new Republic and become more strident and comprehensive in their criticisms of their opponents. While the Inner Mission and the Caritasverband maintained that Social Democratic demands for far-reaching social reforms were, in fact, symptoms of that moral decline which—as had been the case in 1848—had culminated in revolution, the Social Democrats argued that social reform was the precondition for moral renewal because a social order based on private property was the ultimate cause of mass poverty. The Social Democrats dismissed the attacks by the confessional charities upon their materialism and political sinfulness, as well as the insistence by the church charities upon the primacy of moral renewal, as thinly veiled attempts to retain class privileges so that they could continue to propagate notions of deference and subordination which had no place in a social, democratic republic. In turn, these Social Democratic attacks on the pernicious political effects of bourgeois and church charity and the implication of these groups in the authoritarian system of the *Kaiserreich* forced voluntary organizations to claim with increasing fervor that they had rights which preceded those of the state and that they could never be subordinated to the authority of democratic, parliamentary government or supplanted by the socialized welfare system envisioned by Workers' Welfare.

Although Progressive reformers were assured of a pivotal role in the shaping of the Weimar welfare system by virtue of their longtime engagement in the cause of welfare reform, they occupied an ambiguous position. Like the Social Democrats, the Progressives regarded labor as the essential characteristic of citizenship, and they sought to construct a new social contract by arguing that the state was obligated to guarantee—through preventive, therapeutic social services—those social rights to work, health, and education which would enable the individual to fulfill the more extensive social obligations imposed upon the citizen by the welfare state. Their goal was to create a social, democratic *Volksstaat* which would transcend both bourgeois individualism and the excessive collectivism of the Social Democratic and Communist parties. However, in contrast to the Social Democratic argument that the poor should have a legal entitlement to assistance under specified conditions, the Progressives insisted that the moral right to public assistance could never be legally codified. They argued instead that the democratic goal of equal opportunity could best be achieved through the individualized determination of need by trained social workers and by the continued provision of these social services on a subsidiary basis. The Progressives also maintained that state social policy programs could never completely obviate the need for voluntary welfare and that individualized personal help would always be necessary to supplement state social policy programs. While this emphasis on the necessity of voluntary welfare created substantial common ground between the Progressives and the confessional welfare groups, the focus of the Progressives on work and social rights and their understanding of need as primarily a social phenomenon, rather than the result of individual moral failings, had much more in common with the Social Democrats than with either the confessional organizations or the organizations representing the various groups of the new poor created by the war and the inflation.

Like the DDP itself, however, Progressive reformers were increasingly faced with the problem of bridging the gap between their claim to transcend differences of class and confession and the realities of Weimar politics. Although Progressive welfare reformers castigated what they perceived as the particularism of the organizations representing the new poor and argued with increasing vehemence that only the further professionalization of social work could provide an effective antidote to the undue politicization of personal help, they were themselves constantly tossed back and forth between Workers' Welfare, the major confessional welfare organizations, the interest groups representing the new poor, and the Labor Ministry. Although the Progressives ultimately played a major role in shaping the Weimar welfare system, they were only able to do so in alliance with the other major reform groups and, all too frequently, on the terms established by these groups.

"WE ARE THE SUBJECT, NOT THE OBJECT, OF SOCIAL WELFARE": SOCIAL DEMOCRACY AND WORKERS' WELFARE

Despite their growing influence in municipal politics, the Social Democrats had had little opportunity before World War I to participate in municipal poor relief and little inclination to theorize about poor law reform. Instead, they directed their reformist energies toward labor law and the social insurance system. During the war, the participation of some Social Democratic women in the National Women's Service had not fundamentally changed this situation, and only when they entered the government *en masse* after the revolution did the Social Democrats begin to reflect systematically on the problem of poor law and welfare reform.

The novelty of the Social Democratic strategy for welfare reform—and its permanent challenge to both confessional and bourgeois organizations—lay in its insistence that the social question could only be solved through political struggle and radical social change to eliminate poverty as a class phenomenon, rather than through personal help provided to indigent individuals.[3] The overriding aim of Social Democratic welfare reformers was the democratization of both charity and poor relief because they viewed this as the precondition for transforming public and private benevolence into a generalized system of social self-help. The Social Democrats detested the very idea of charity because the display of gratitude expected from the recipients of such largesse reinforced traditional patterns of political subordination and social deference which were incompatible with the idea of democratic equality. This antipathy extended to poor relief as well, and the Social Democrats made the democratization of

[3] Hedwig Wachenheim, "Soziale Fürsorge und Sozialdemokratie," *Die Gleichheit* 29:9–11 (1919), pp. 70–71, 79–80, 85–86.

charity and poor relief their top priority in order to demonstrate—to use one of their most popular slogans—that the working classes were "not only the object, but also the subject, of social work."[4]

However, private charitable activity had historically lain beyond the legislative competence of both Reich and local government, and the charities tenaciously resisted all attempts by the Social Democrats to "politicize" their work, especially the Caritasverband, which saw this challenge as yet another stage in its own *Kulturkampf* against the sovereign, secular state.[5] Nevertheless, the Social Democrats insisted that charity organizations had to be subjected to the sovereign authority of a democratically elected government because providing for the poor was one of the essential tasks of the state and could not, therefore, be left to the discretion of private individuals or associations. As Hedwig Wachenheim, the daughter of a wealthy banker who joined the SPD in early 1914 and became one of its leading welfare theorists, argued, democracy could only be perfected by subordinating the charities to democratic institutions and the authority of organized public opinion. Through the 1920s Wachenheim was the most vocal Social Democratic advocate of the "primacy of public welfare" and the most trenchant defender of the sovereignty of democratic self-government against the traditional privileges of church charities.[6] Ultimately, this democratization of voluntary welfare would have entailed its "communalization" and the transformation of welfare offices into the "executive organ of the public welfare will [*Fürsorgewillen*]."[7]

The goal of democratizing the welfare system and imbuing it with a socialist spirit was closely connected to the problem of social work training for working-class women because the Social Democrats insisted that only the participation of the working classes themselves could transform social work from a charitable undertaking into an expression of democratic solidarity.[8] However, the ma-

---

[4] Marie Juchacz and Johanna Heymann, *Die Arbeiterwohlfahrt* (Berlin, 1924), pp. 5, 26.

[5] While it could be argued that the Caritasverband was simply defending its traditional province against attacks by the Social Democrats and the Progressives, not itself attacking the state, the key point is to recognize that both the expansion of state activity and the Catholic response were simply contradictory dimensions of the same modernizing process.

[6] Wachenheim, "Soziale Fürsorge und Sozialdemokratie," p. 86, and Wachenheim, "Der Vorrang der öffentlichen Wohlfahrtspflege," *AW* 1:3 (November 1, 1926), pp. 65–72. Wachenheim served as *Regierungsrätin* in the Prussian Interior Ministry in 1923–33, and she edited the party's leading welfare reform journal *Arbeiterwohlfahrt* from 1926 until 1933. See her autobiography, *Vom Großbürgertum zur Sozialdemokratie* (Colloquium Verlag, 1973). On the Social Democratic understanding of the state and democracy during the Weimar Republic, see Heinrich Potthoff, "Das Weimarer Verfassungswerk und die deutsche Linke," *AfS* 12 (1972), pp. 433–83 and Walter Euchner, "Sozialdemokratie und Demokratie. Zum Demokratieverständnis der SPD in der Weimarer Republik," *AfS* 26 (1986), pp. 125–78.

[7] Sophie Schöfer, *Ausbau der Kinderfürsorge durch die Gemeinde* (Berlin, 1921).

[8] Wachenheim, "Ausbildung zur Wohlfahrtspflege," *Die Neue Zeit* 39:13 (June 24, 1921), pp. 302–7. However, bourgeois and confessional charity organizations feared that working-class women, who had imbibed the Marxist doctrine of class struggle and did not accept their own ethics of selfless service, would abuse their positions for party-political ends. Alice Salomon, "Zum Eintritt in den sozialen Beruf," *Die Gleichheit* 29:22 (July 19, 1919), pp. 171–73.

jor obstacle to social work training for these women was the fact that they could not afford the tuition demanded by the existing social work schools. Since the fall of 1919, Social Democratic women had been calling for the establishment of special courses to give working-class women a knowledge of the fundamentals of social work. In response to both this pressure and a request by the Interior Ministry, the Conference of German Social Women's Schools (*Konferenz Sozialer Frauenschulen*)—which had been founded in January 1917 by representatives of the existing social work schools (or social women's schools, as they had been known since the turn of the century) to represent the collective interests of these schools and the nascent profession—decided in early 1920 to sponsor six-month training courses at the social work schools in Berlin, Munich, and Hamburg.[9] Approximately 150 women took part in these courses, which were funded by the socialist trade unions, the Interior Ministry, and the Labor Ministry. Even though these courses were generally regarded as successful, the *Konferenz* feared that they would lower the level of social work training, and thus the status of the profession, and they were not repeated after their initial offering. Instead, the *Konferenz* proposed that those municipal governments which needed more social workers provide stipendia to permit working-class women to attend existing social work schools.[10] Workers' Welfare itself also offered a number of short-term courses to provide social workers with an overview of existing legislation. However, the hurdles faced by working-class women were raised even higher by the training regulations issued in October 1920 by the Prussian Interior Ministry.[11]

Beyond these programmatic statements and immediate goals, however, Social Democratic welfare experts did not initially have a concrete vision of what a modern democratic welfare system would look like. The decision to establish Workers' Welfare was taken primarily on pragmatic grounds which reveal more about the dynamic which propelled the organizational consolidation of voluntary charity in the early years of the Republic than about the Social Democratic vision of welfare reform. Social Democrats were often excluded from the official welfare policy committees because there was no organization to officially represent the interests of the working classes in these matters. These problems were further complicated by the fact that both the Reich Labor Ministry and the Prussian Ministry of Public Welfare, which were the most important sources of funding for charitable work, preferred to negotiate exclusively with the centralized welfare organizations. Both the Caritasverband and the Inner Mission already had nationwide networks and were consequently in a much more favorable position to obtain government sub-

---

[9] See the course description prepared by Salomon and the circular from the Interior Ministry to Bavarian government (November 28, 1919), both BayHStaA MK 42943.

[10] *Konferenz* minutes (October 24, 1921), ADCV DK 142/31.

[11] "Freie Bahn dem Tüchtigen," *Die Gleichheit* 29:15 (April 25, 1919), pp. 114–15, Salomon, "Schulung von Arbeiterinnen für Berufsarbeit in der Wohlfahrtspflege," *Concordia* 27:3 (February 1, 1920), pp. 31–32, and Salomon. "Die Ergebnisse der Sonderlehrgänge für Arbeiterinnen zur Ausbildung in der Wohlfahrtspflege," *SPr* 29 (1920), cols. 1216–20. On both the Conference and these Prussian regulations, see p. 149 below.

sidies and secure foreign relief than were socialist welfare activists. As Heinrich Schulz, State Secretary in the Interior Ministry, told the SPD central committee, although a great deal of money lay at the disposal of the Prussian Ministry of Public Welfare, he found himself in a difficult position when fifty church-affiliated organizations applied for funding, while there was no separate organization to represent the interests of the working classes. For this reason, he urged the SPD to create an organization "which corresponded to what the bourgeois parties called 'voluntary charity.'"[12]

Workers' Welfare was officially founded in December 1919 by the SPD as an affiliated organization. The head of the national organization was Marie Juchacz, a member of the Reichstag and chair of the SPD Women's Bureau, and its central committee was made up of representatives of the party and the socialist unions as well as experienced social workers. The women's movement had generally been marginalized within the SPD itself, and the women who played a leading role in Workers' Welfare—including Juchacz, Wachenheim, Dorothea Hirschfeld, Adele Schreiber-Krieger, Elisabeth Kirschmann-Röhl (Juchacz's sister), and Louise Schroeder—hoped that the organization would become a vehicle for advancing the goals of the women's movement within the party. As Juchacz later wrote, Workers' Welfare was "the ground on which the women's movement grows and thrives."[13] These women believed that it was necessary to establish an autonomous women's sphere within the socialist movement because, no matter how unresponsive or antagonistic their male comrades might be to their interests, the class differences between working-class and bourgeois women were still too great to allow them to join with bourgeois feminists to form an independent women's party.[14]

The preliminary guidelines which were published in June 1920 stated that the primary goals of Workers' Welfare were to promote the interests of the working classes by placing party comrades in key administrative positions in the growing network of municipal welfare offices; mobilize the working classes and provide them with the training necessary to enable them to occupy the many voluntary and honorary positions in these offices; and represent the working classes at all levels of government and in umbrella organizations of private charity organizations.[15] Although the leaders of the organization were either unaware of or not especially concerned by the ambiguous status of the organization as a voluntary, societal association devoted to the communalization of all such organizations, they nevertheless insisted that the activity of Workers' Welfare was qualitatively different from that of bourgeois and church charity orga-

---

[12] *Protokoll der Sitzung des Parteiausschusses der SPD vom 13. Dezember 1919* (Berlin, 1919), p. 44.

[13] Juchacz/Heymann, *Die Arbeiterwohlfahrt*, p. 45, and Fritzmichael Roehl, *Marie Juchacz und die Arbeiterwohlfahrt* (Hanover, 1961), p. 77.

[14] Antonie Pfülf, *Bericht über die Frauenkonferenz der Sozialdemokratischen Partei Deutschlands* (Berlin, 1920), p. 16. See also Christoph Sachße, *Mütterlichkeit als Beruf. Sozialarbeit, Sozialreform und Frauenbewegung 1871–1929* (Suhrkamp, 1986), pp. 173–86, and Margarete Jacobsohn, *Die Arbeiter in der öffentlichen Armenpflege* (Leipzig, 1911).

[15] Juchacz, "Arbeiterwohlfahrt," *Die Gleichheit* (June 19, 1920), p. 206.

nizations because it was not charity, but rather the organized self-help of free
and equal citizens, who recognized their solidaristic obligations to one another.
As Johann Caspari, the director of the Berlin-Neukölln youth welfare office and
later mayor of Brandenburg, argued, "Democracy does not exhaust itself at the
ballot box, but rather means the intensive collaboration of the individual in the
common welfare and interest."[16] This maxim was applied in a very concrete
manner in the fund-raising activity of the organization. Unlike the older and
better-established organizations, Workers' Welfare could not depend on either
government subsidies or the contributions of affluent benefactors, and its important source of funding came from union members who worked overtime and
donated their wages from these *Wohlfahrtsstunden* to the organization (and
from employers who were also expected to contribute part of the profits from
these extra hours).[17] As Minna Todenhagen, the director of the Berlin branch of
Workers' Welfare, explained, the democratization of the welfare system depended as much on the activity of the local Workers' Welfare associations as it
did on the democratization of the welfare bureaucracy. These local organizations, she argued, "must understand and undertake their work as social service
in the service of the state." No matter whether they worked in an official or a
voluntary capacity, she argued, the members of Workers' Welfare represented
an auxiliary service for public welfare, not a private, societal organization, and
they should "provide the points of contact from which a coordinated stream
flows through the entire welfare system."[18]

The first national Workers' Welfare conference was held in September 1921
in Görlitz in conjunction with the SPD party and women's conferences, and in
her keynote address to the conference Helene Simon—a prominent bourgeois
social reformer who had joined the SPD in 1919—undertook to provide a comprehensive theoretical foundation for a Social Democratic strategy for welfare
reform.[19] Since the turn of the century, Simon had played a key role in articulat-

---

[16] Caspari, "Zweck und Aufgaben der Arbeiterwohlfahrtspflege," *Essener Arbeiter-Zeitung* (November 3, 1921), as well as Caspari, "Fremde Wohltat—eigene Würde," *Vorwärts* (November 14,
1920) and "Der organisatorische Aufbau der Wohlfahrtspflege," cited in "Sozialdemokratischer
Wohlfahrtstag," *Vorwärts* (September 16, 1921).

[17] Through the entire existence of the Republic, public funding for voluntary organizations was
distributed by the Labor Ministry to these organizations based on the number of beds in the various
institutions—hospitals, workhouses, children's homes, and correctional education institutions—
they maintained. This gave a permanent advantage to the older and more well-established organizations, especially since Workers' Welfare initially opposed establishing its own institutions and never
received more than 9% of these monies. In *Arbeiterwohlfahrt*, Juchacz and Wachenheim carried on
a running battle with the Labor Ministry and the confessional organizations over these funding
arrangements.

[18] Minna Todenhagen, "Partei und Wohlfahrtsausschüsse," *Vorwärts* (September 16, 1921).

[19] Helene Simon, *Aufgaben und Ziele der neuzeitlichen Wohlfahrtspflege* (Stuttgart, 1922). See
also Simon, "Sozialismus und Wohlfahrtspflege," *AW* 1:1 (October 1, 1926), pp. 3–9 and "Voraussetzungen, Begriff und Entwicklung der Wohlfahrtspflege," in Hauptausschuß für Arbeiterwohlfahrt, ed., *Lehrbuch der Wohlfahrtspflege* (Berlin, 1927), pp. 91–108. On Simon's life and
work, see Sabine Klöhn, *Helene Simon* (Frankfurt & Bern, 1982), and Walter Friedländer, *Helene
Simon. Ein Leben für soziale Gerechtigkeit* (Bonn, 1962).

ing within the welfare reform community the idea of a social contract between the citizen and the state. Building upon these ideas, she argued that this social contract could only be secured through the creation of a modern welfare system which would eliminate the causes of class poverty. Simon inverted the nineteenth-century equation of poverty with immorality, sloth, and crime and argued instead that welfare was the precondition for increasing the productivity of the individual and the nation. Her definition of welfare was very broad and covered all measures intended to improve the health, education, working conditions, and more generally the quality of life of the unpropertied masses. She envisioned a comprehensive social security system which would not limit itself to meliorating the worst external manifestations of need, but rather would strive to eliminate poverty as a class phenomenon by combating its deeper-lying structural causes.

While existing social insurance and other pension programs were based on private-law contracts according to which individuals acquired the right to specific benefits in consideration for their insurance premiums, Simon insisted that the social insurance and pension system could be transformed into a general social security system by expanding this individualistic concept of labor into a broader concept of social labor. This concept would have to be adapted to both the stages of the productive life cycle and the requirements of social reproduction in order to include the entire range of other activities, such as motherhood, child-raising, and military service, which were necessary and beneficial to society, but which were not included in bourgeois notions of labor. While all persons were obligated to work to support themselves and thus contribute to the welfare of society as a whole, Simon argued that the state had the obligation to protect the health of all citizens, help the young acquire intellectual skills as well as the physical and moral strength necessary for them to fulfill their future civic obligations, provide the permanently disabled with a sufficient level of support, and help the partially disabled recover their labor power. In its most general terms, she concluded, this meant that "from the obligation to perform socially useful labor flow the legal entitlements necessary to prepare one for this labor." The goal of this need-based, work-centered approach was to restore the independence of the needy person while providing assistance to bridge the gap between what the individual could be expected to earn through his or her own labor—depending on the person's position in the productive life cycle— and the income required to maintain a social existence minimum. Simon regarded the new maternity welfare program as a perfect example of this new approach because it extended to needy women the legal entitlement to specific social services—regardless of whether they had contributed to the health insurance funds—based on a broader understanding of child-bearing and -raising as a form of socially necessary labor.[20]

---

[20] Simon, *Aufgaben und Ziele*, pp. 5–6, 18, 20, "Sozialismus und Wohlfahrtspflege," p. 3, and "Ueber Versorgung und Fürsorge. Ein Beitrag zur Begriffsbildung," *SPr* 31:33–35 (August 1922), cols. 857–60, 894–96, 939–40, citation col. 896. Many of Simon's ideas were echoed by Reichstag

Maternity, infant, and youth welfare programs were of special concern to Simon, and they clearly illustrate the ambiguities in her concept of social citizenship. Although pregnant women and mothers of young children should be entitled to welfare services, she insisted that, since social citizenship imposed upon these women the obligation to care for and educate their children to become productive citizens, the state must, therefore, bear "ultimate responsibility" for insuring that mothers properly discharged these communal obligations which had been entrusted to the parents by the state. Simon insisted that her proposals were intended to strengthen, rather than weaken, the family, and she was sanguine about the potential negative implications of this expansion of state intervention into the familial sphere.[21]

Simon came to Social Democracy from Progressivism and social reform, and her ideas were influenced more directly by Robert Owen's theories on the organization of labor, by the proposals of Sidney and Beatrice Webb (whose minority report of the English Poor Law Commission she translated) for the prevention of class poverty, and by Progressive attacks on nineteenth-century poor relief than by Marx's analysis of class struggle in capitalist society, and her reform goal might best be described as a synthesis of Fordism and Owenite socialism, that is, the rationalization of production and consumption. She rejected Marx's immiseration theory and instead argued that, by improving the quality of life and level of education of the working classes, the reform of the welfare system was itself the precondition for the development of class consciousness: "Immiseration and a *Lumpenproletariat* [the underclasses] might lead to Bolshevism, but never to socialism. Class consciousness arises and thrives as the condition of the working classes improves."[22] In her work, Marx's prediction that capitalism would collapse as a result of the immiseration of the proletariat and the intensification of class struggle receded behind a faith that welfare reform would transform capitalist society from within and thus bring about the evolutionary transition to socialism.[23]

Simon's arguments both reflected and facilitated the transformation of the SPD into a reformist party. Even though the tide of revolutionary enthusiasm for the communalization of charity and poor relief had already begun to ebb, Wachenheim still maintained that Workers' Welfare was not a private organization, but rather an auxiliary to public welfare. She continued to insist that Workers' Welfare still had to work toward the integration of all voluntary charity associations into municipal welfare offices because this was the only way to

---

delegate and welfare activist Sophie Schöfer in her address to the 1921 SPD women's conference on the topic of "human economy" (*Menschenökonomie*). Schöfer, "Soziale Frauenarbeit in der Gemeinde," in *Reichsfrauentag der Sozialdemokratischen Partei Deutschlands am 17. und 18. September 1921 in Görlitz* (n.p., n.d.), pp. 11–21.

[21] Simon, *Aufgaben und Ziele*, pp. 11–14.

[22] Ibid., p. 4.

[23] Simon, "Sozialismus und Wohlfahrtspflege," p. 9, and "Von Owen bis Ford," *SPr* 34:31–32, cols. 673–76, 697–701.

completely eliminate the odium otherwise associated with public assistance.[24] However, with the passage of the RJWG and the proclamation of the RFV, both of which sanctioned the participation of voluntary organizations within municipal welfare and youth welfare offices and thus institutionalized the privileged status which Wachenheim had argued had to be overcome through the democratization of the welfare system, it became increasingly difficult to maintain the fiction that the status of Workers' Welfare as a voluntary organization was only a provisional arrangement.

At the second Workers' Welfare conference in September 1924, Hermann Heimerich, Nuremberg city councilor and one of the leading Social Democratic municipal welfare politicians, assessed the implications of the new political situation for the organization. The goal of Social Democracy remained the elimination of class poverty through the transformation of the economic system, not simply the creation of the most extensive welfare system. However, Heimerich concluded that, until this goal was achieved, and even in a socialist society, a welfare system would be necessary to a limited extent to care for the disabled, and the asocial. Although he argued that the evolution of the many different welfare programs had the potential to transform capitalism from within, he also pointed out that public welfare could only be reformed in accordance with socialist ideas if the Social Democrats were in a position to influence public welfare policy and practice. As long as the Social Democrats did not dominate the government, this goal could only be achieved through a societal organization: "The state can not be set in motion in a specific direction overnight; rather, it is moved and influenced by the life of free societal forces. . . . We must first demonstrate our goals to the state through voluntary activity and thus compete with the other tendencies of voluntary welfare." While it would be wrong for the Social Democrats to categorically oppose the existence of private welfare simply because they themselves believed in the primacy of public responsibility for the needy, it would be just as wrong to sulk and wait for the socialist utopia to fall into their laps, and he called upon the members of Workers' Welfare to devote themselves with renewed energy to shaping public welfare through their paid and voluntary work within the municipal welfare offices.[25]

Heimerich's analysis of the changing role of Workers' Welfare and the legit-

---

[24] *Reichsfrauentag der Sozialdemokratischen Partei Deutschlands am 17. und 18. September 1921 in Görlitz*, pp. 21–26 and "Auftakt zum Görlitzer Parteitag," *Vorwärts* (September 18, 1921), as well as Caspari, "Wohlfahrtspflege. Ein Rückblick auf die Görlitzer Wohlfahrtstagung," *Vorwärts* (September 28, 1921).

[25] Hermann Heimerich, "Die Zusammenarbeit der öffentlichen Fürsorge mit der privaten Fürsorge und den Trägern der Sozialversicherung," *Allgemeine Fürsorge. Referate auf der Reichstagung der Arbeiterwohlfahrt am 12.–13. September 1924 (= Kommunale Praxis*, 1924, no. 2), pp. 78–80. On Heimerich's life and work, see Susanne Krauß, *Kommunale Wohlfahrtspolitik in der frühen Weimarer Republik am Beispiel der kommunalpolitischen Tätigkeit Dr. Hermann Heimerichs in Nürnberg vom ersten Weltkrieg bis 1925* (Magisterarbeit, Erlangen-Nürnberg, 1986) and Heimerich, *Lebenserinnerungen eines Mannheimer Oberbürgermeisters*, aus dem Nachlaß hrsg. Jörg Schadt (Stuttgart, 1981).

imacy of voluntary organizations reflected a more fluid understanding of the relation between state and society which differed from the Rousseauean vision of democracy espoused by Wachenheim and others immediately after the revolution, and this, in turn, foreshadowed a dual transformation in the political tactics of the organization. If Workers' Welfare were to successfully make this transformation, it would have to abandon its pretension to represent the general will and instead work to reshape the welfare system in accordance with its own worldview in order to rally public opinion behind its flag. At the same time, the organization began to turn inward and devote more energy to cultivating its traditional constituency—the skilled, organized working classes—in order to retain their loyalty and demonstrate the validity of its own ideas to both the confessional charities and the Communists. As Workers' Welfare became aware of this new status, it found itself compelled to adopt a less overtly political and more professional approach to its work. This change was reflected in the January 1925 reorganization of its advisory council, which was replaced by a set of specialized subcommittees devoted to specific areas of welfare reform and social work, and the realization of the long-standing goal of establishing its own social work training school in 1928.

CHRISTIAN CONSERVATISM, THE CHURCH CHARITIES, AND THE REPUBLIC

By the end of 1924, the Weimar political system had assumed a very different shape than it had possessed in early 1919, and the Social Democratic approach to welfare reform had evolved with it. However, the development of Workers' Welfare heightened, rather than meliorated, the opposition of the confessional organizations, which retained their traditional hostility to socialism and democracy, resisted the communalization of voluntary charity, opposed the idea of a legal entitlement to social services, and continued to condemn the entire Social Democratic strategy for welfare reform as a product of a flawed view of human nature. The confessional charity groups—or welfare organizations, as they were coming to style themselves—believed that the revolution was itself the result of a crisis of authority which was at once familial, religious, and political, and they argued that the primary aim of the welfare system should be to halt the de-Christianization of public life and reinforce traditional family values, which were the wellspring from which all other virtues flowed.[26]

At the first postwar congress of the Inner Mission, Inner Mission vice-president Reinhold Seeberg argued in terms which had changed remarkably little since Wichern's analysis of the 1848 revolution that the revolution of 1918 and the decline of public morality which followed in the wake of this political upheaval had been caused by the humanistic anthropology shared by the liberals and the socialists. Seeberg rejected both the belief in the intrinsic goodness of the natural will and the "pathological emphasis on the autonomous

---

[26] See Constantin Noppel, "Zurück zur Familie!" *Stimmen der Zeit* 100 (1921), pp. 161–70.

personality, its rights and claims," which grew out of this doctrine.[27] "All revolutions," he reiterated the following year, "begin with the optimistic belief that man is naturally good."[28] Reinhard Mumm, one of the leading DNVP welfare politicians, insisted that the only cure for this crisis of authority was to reintroduce into political life the concept of sin because "whoever does not know sin remains unshakable in the belief in the goodness of the human soul and will persevere in a politics of illusion."[29] Only a renewed respect for the normative authority of tradition—behind which lay a thinly veiled desire for the restoration of the monarchy and the reestablishment of the Lutheran church—could, they argued, halt the demoralization and spiritual impoverishment of the nation.[30]

In contrast to the reform plans laid out by the Social Democrats, the confessional welfare organizations insisted that poverty was primarily a spiritual problem, which manifested itself in materialism, the decline of public morality, the weakening of the family, the *Verwahrlosung* of those persons who had been deprived of the protection of those social institutions which had traditionally served as a bulwark against sin, and, ultimately, communism, atheism, and revolution. At the 1920 Inner Mission congress, one speaker argued that both the Progressive-Social Democratic strategy for welfare reform and the revolution itself were simply two manifestations of the same secular worldview. The revolution, he argued, was nothing other than the "most loathsome outburst of the basest instincts" and the product of the "fallacy as though the external milieu would have to be improved before an inner renewal was possible."[31] As one DNVP delegate argued in the Prussian Landtag, communism was born "from the misery which the individual had to bear when he focuses his life only on the here and now. . . . Christianity and Christianity alone can give mankind a moral anchor in its misery."[32] It was this preoccupation with the problem of authority which led the leadership of the Inner Mission to equate emancipation with sin, castigate the Social Democratic concern with social reform as mammonism and materialism, and repeatedly insist that revolutionary politics was the symptom

[27] Reinhold Seeberg, "Wo hinaus?" *Der 38. Kongress für Innere Mission*, ed. Central-Ausschuss für Innere Mission (Wichern Verlag, 1919), pp. 13–14. On the close connections between the DNVP and the women's organizations related to the Inner Mission, see Doris Kaufmann, *Frauen zwischen Aufbruch und Reaktion. Protestantische Frauenbewegung in der ersten Hälfte des 20. Jahrhunderts* (Munich, 1988), pp. 43ff. Those Protestants who seriously tried to build bridges between religion and the problems of industrial society gravitated toward the *Evangelisch-Sozialer Kongress*, which maintained close connections with the Progressives in the DV.

[28] Seeberg, "Die gegenwärtige geistige Lage und die Stellung der lutherischen Kirche zum Kulturproblem," *Der 39. Kongress für Innere Mission*, ed. Central-Ausschuss für Innere Mission (Wichern Verlag, 1920), p. 144.

[29] *Der 38. Kongress für Innere Mission*, p. 110.

[30] Seeberg, "Die gegenwärtige geistige Lage," pp. 145–47, and Gerhard Füllkrug, "Die Innere Mission und die Republik," *IM* 14:1 (January 1919), pp. 1–7.

[31] Wurster, "Der Zusammenbruch der Moral in unserm Volk und der Weg zu ihrem Wiederaufbau," *Der 39. Kongress für Innere Mission*, pp. 14, 26, 28.

[32] Dallmer, *Verhandlungen des preußischen Landtags*, 179. Sitzung (November 25, 1920), col. 13976.

of spiritual distress, not the solution to it. To the Social Democratic rhetoric of class struggle, the Inner Mission contrasted its own goal of saving lost souls through brotherly love, which would bind together the rich and the poor into a new, authentic national community and thus overcome those conflicts that had rent the fabric of bourgeois society.[33]

Since the nineteenth century, both the Inner Mission and the Caritasverband had concentrated their energies on the struggle against alcoholism and "sexual immorality," and in the postrevolutionary period these two areas of interest increasingly converged on the question of the family. For both confessional organizations, the family was as much the symbol of the conservative order as the object of real social-political concern, and they viewed the restoration of a healthy family life as the antithesis of, and the antidote to, the political sinfulness of the liberals and socialists. Of all the evils of postwar society, Christian conservatives of both confessions were most alarmed by the spread of birth control and the declining birth rate because, for them, the separation of sexual pleasure from the responsibilities of familial life symbolized the victory of rationalist individualism over revealed authority. They looked askance at the "new woman" and viewed changes in family and sexual mores as the cause of social decay, not as the product of social change. As one DNVP delegate argued in the Prussian Landtag, the most important task of the new Ministry of Public Welfare was to "discover and redeem the culture of the family" because all of the "ills from which our *Volk* is suffering, the corrosive, nearly incurable ills are predominately caused by the fact that our *Volk* no longer has a healthy family life."[34]

Although both the Inner Mission and the Caritasverband argued that their work was inspired solely by a spirit of Christian love and served no ulterior political or missionary aims, confessional charity was intrinsically conservative. However, while Thomist natural law permitted the Catholics to build bridges between charity and social reform, the charity reformers in the Inner Mission denied that any specific conclusions regarding political or economic life could be drawn from Lutheran theology and advanced no concrete social reform ideas. Instead, they continued to rail against the materialism, hedonism, and atheism into which the Protestant working classes had allegedly fallen.[35] During the revolution, the status of the Inner Mission had been threatened both by the disestablishment of the Evangelical Church and by the widespread hostility among the socialist parties to organized church charity. The Social Democrats had nothing but contempt for the incorrigible condescension of "bourgeois ladies," and the Communists accused the religious charity organizations of "cook[ing] their confessional soup on the fire of social work."[36] It was precisely

[33] Friedrich Mahling, *Die sittlichen Voraussetzungen der Wohlfahrtspflege* (Berlin, 1925), pp. 39, 72, 74.

[34] Bronisch, *Verhandlungen des preußischen Landtags*, 51. Sitzung (September 19, 1919), cols. 4098–4100.

[35] Seeberg, *Der 38. Kongreß für Innere Mission*, pp. 17, 69.

[36] *Stenographische Berichte über die Sitzungen des II Landtags von Thüringen*, 25. Sitzung (January 12, 1922), pp. 792–93, 797.

these charges that inspired the Inner Mission to return to its original principles and again become the "vanguard in the struggle for the souls of the endangered and those persons who are alienated [from God] and for the preservation and restoration of the Christian foundations of our entire national life."[37] Nevertheless, although the revolution did breathe new life into the Inner Mission, its preoccupation with authority and its inability to understand the forces which had made the revolution made it extremely difficult for the organization to communicate with the parties of the left or to strike deep roots among the Protestant working classes. In addition, the Inner Mission's prospects of rechristianizing the masses seemed further imperiled by the continued expansion of public welfare, especially in the larger cities, where personal help on a religious basis ran up against both Social Democratic hostility and a militantly expansive public welfare bureaucracy.

The history of the Inner Mission during the postrevolutionary period is of special interest because it shows clearly how the political and fiscal pressures of the period forced it and the other voluntary welfare organizations to rationalize their organizational structures.[38] While the Caritasverband had emerged from the war with a much stronger organizational structure and much greater public authority thanks to its recognition as the official representative of Catholic charities by the 1916 Fulda bishops' conference, the Central Committee for Inner Mission remained a loose association of notables active in church charities. Consequently, it was unable to serve as the forum for the formulation of common policy for Evangelical charities, coordinate their activity, or effectively represent their interests at the national, state, or local levels.

To overcome these organizational handicaps, the *Centralverband* of the Inner Mission, which united the forty-four state and local associations and the seventy specialized, functional organizations, was founded in 1920. At the same time, the Central Committee of the Inner Mission, which became the executive organ for the *Centralverband*, was reorganized to include both representatives chosen by the regional and specialized associations belonging to the *Centralverband* and a number of individuals who were co-opted for lifelong membership and who perpetuated the older tradition of the Central Committee as a notable association. Although the creation of the *Centralverband* represented an important step toward the modernization of the Protestant charities, it did not completely eliminate the dualism between the new, more hierarchical and professional *Centralverband* and the older associations of the notables, and relations between the two groups remained a source of friction through the decade. To prevail in the coming struggle and represent their common religious interests vis-à-vis both public welfare and charitable organizations inspired by other worldviews, Seeberg argued that organized Protestant charity needed a greater

[37] Schoell, "Die Innere Mission und die Öffentlichkeit," *Der 38. Kongreß für Innere Mission*, p. 173, and Füllkrug, "Die Innere Mission und die Republik."

[38] For accounts of the organization and activity of the Inner Mission in the 1920s, see Johannes Steinweg, *Die Innere Mission der evangelischen Kirche* (Heilbronn, 1928), and Mahling, *Die Innere Mission*, 2 vols. (Gütersloh, 1935).

degree of professional expertise among its charity workers and the stronger support of the institutional church. However, since the very idea of an "inner mission" was predicated on the commitment of pious individuals to charitable service to those in need, the organization could never obtain the recognition of the institutional church in the same way as the Caritasverband without deviating from its fundamental precepts. Seeberg hoped to resolve this ambiguity between personal piety and the authority of the institutional church by convincing the clergy of the importance of this charitable activity for the rechristianization of public life and the reestablishment of a Lutheran *Volkskirche*.[39]

At the same time that they were modernizing its organizational structure, reformers within the Inner Mission—including Gerhard Füllkrug (the director of the *Volksmission*), Otto Ohl (the director of the Inner Mission in the Rhineland), and Steinweg—were pushing forward with the creation of a network of local organizations, known as the Evangelical Welfare Service (*Evangelischer Wohlfahrtsdienst*). Its purpose was to mobilize Church members for charitable activity, provide them with the necessary schooling, and thus enable the organization to both bridge the gap between the Church and the people and effectively represent the interests of Lutheran charities in every locale and at every level of government. These reformers believed that such a counteroffensive was necessary if the Church were to maintain its influence in the face of the attacks by political Catholicism and Social Democracy. As Wilhelm Zoellner wrote, "The battle of the confessions will be fought on the battlefield of charity."[40] Increasingly, the Inner Mission recognized that its ability to influence welfare policy at the local level would depend not only on its ability to mobilize the Lutheran middle classes, but also upon its ability to provide these new recruits with enough professional training and knowledge of the specialized fields of welfare work to enable them to hold their own in public competition with other organizations.

THE PROGRESSIVE PATH TO THE WELFARE STATE: SOCIAL CITIZENSHIP, THE NATIONAL COMMUNITY OF LABOR, AND INDIVIDUALIZED PERSONAL HELP

In the early years of the Republic, the Progressives definitively abandoned the Malthusianism and the moralism which had characterized both public poor relief and voluntary charity in the nineteenth century and emerged as the leading advocates of a preventive, therapeutic approach to welfare reform and the professionalization of social work within the framework of a system of public

---

[39] Seeberg to *Evangelischer Oberkirchenrat* (May 24, 1922), ADWRh 24.1. In many respects, the expansion of the Caritasverband provided a model for—and a challenge to—the Inner Mission. See Jochen-Christoph Kaiser, *Sozialer Protestantismus im 20. Jahrhundert* (Oldenbourg, 1989), pp. 78–94, Mahling, *Die Innere Mission*, pp. 1015–26, 1352–58, Steinweg, "Die evangelische Liebestätigkeit und die neuesten Vorgänge auf dem Gebiet der allgemeinen Wohlfahrtspflege," *IM* (1920), pp. 178–83, and Füllkrug, "Evangelisch-kirchliche Wohlfahrtspflege," *SPr* 31:5 (February 1, 1922), cols. 132–36.

[40] Cited in Mahling, *Die Innere Mission*, p. 1022.

welfare offices. The groundwork for the development of Progressive thought since the war had been laid by Christian Jasper Klumker, whose *System of Social Welfare* was the first systematic, theoretical attack on that equation of material need with crime and immorality which had dominated discourse on the social question since the time of Malthus.[41] In this work, Klumker inverted the fundamental categories of bourgeois-Christian thought and argued that the essential characteristic of poverty was not immorality but "uneconomicalness" (*Unwirtschaftlichkeit*). By uneconomicalness, Klumker meant the absence of the habits of frugality, thrift, and providence which could affect either the work ethic or consumption patterns in such a way that, under given economic circumstances, the person was unable to maintain his or her economic independence and was thus forced to depend on support from others. All of those character traits which had historically been adduced to demonstrate that material need was caused by personal immorality—frivolity, dissipation, sloth, deceptiveness—were, he argued, secondary psychological effects of the loss of economic independence; the resulting material impoverishment so narrowed the economic horizon of these persons and subjected them to such existential uncertainty that they were unable to maintain a rational, disciplined lifestyle. Klumker insisted that, since uneconomicalness was essentially a social or economic phenomenon, it was impermissible to render a moral judgment upon someone simply because they were dependent on the support of others. Therefore, the task of social work was to educate the uneconomical, help them learn how to make the best use of their capabilities in order to support themselves, and assist those who were unable to support themselves. No matter how much religion might help achieve these goals, he insisted, social work was primarily directed toward social ends and should not be conflated with pastoral activity.

Up to the revolution and beyond, the "poor" had been constructed in negative terms as persons who depended upon the support of others. However, as the sociologist Georg Simmel had argued shortly before the war, this negative definition had blinded observers to the actual process of impoverishment. According to Simmel, the status of the poor as a liminal group had prevented society from viewing the poor as ends in themselves, and, instead, society had approached the problem of poor relief from the perspective of the effect of the poor on society itself. This move limited the potentially unlimited claims of the poor upon society—which grew out of the right to existence—and permitted society to treat poor relief as a means for either protecting society against the potential criminality of the poor or fulfilling the moral obligation of the propertied to help the poor. This instrumental approach had given rise, Simmel argued, to an arrangement in which public poor relief had provided an absolute existence minimum to all persons bereft of economic resources, while leaving

---

[41] Klumker, *Fürsorgewesen. Einführung in das Verständnis der Armut und der Armenpflege* (Leipzig, 1918). While Malthus had condemned charity and the poor laws for fostering sloth and excess population growth among the poor, Klumker criticized Malthus for rejecting the individual's right to existence and, thus, for questioning the purpose of welfare.

voluntary charity the freedom to provide additional support based on its assessment of the moral worthiness of the individual poor.[42] Klumker's attack on the moralistic underpinnings of poor relief and charity made it possible to view the indigent as integral and potentially productive members of society, and it shifted attention from the security needs of society to the existential needs of the poor themselves.

In the postwar period, Progressive welfare reformers conceived of the national community as a "community of labor" and argued that social services should be graduated according to the degree and nature of individual need, rather than the presumptive origins of this need, a position which permitted them to make labor power the focus of a comprehensive system of social services whose benefits would be extended to all citizens. They envisioned a comprehensive system of public health, juvenile education, and occupational training and rehabilitation programs which would attack the causes of need by promoting labor power, preventing disability, meliorating that disability which could not be prevented, and providing long-term support for those persons who were unable to work.[43] Moreover, as Polligkeit argued, since it was impossible to compensate for the churning of class structures since the war through public assistance, it was senseless to set relief rates at a higher level simply because the recipient at one time belonged to a higher social stratum. Even when providing a social existence minimum, he insisted, the productive value of the recipient for the economic and social life of the nation must be the primary consideration.[44]

While the Social Democrats argued that an expanded public welfare system should primarily function as a redistributive mechanism in order to compensate for the inequalities in capitalist society, the Progressives argued that the primary goal of their need-based, work-centered approach to welfare reform was to foster a sense of rational self-discipline among the needy, promote a spirit of self-help, and thus assist these persons in regaining their economic and moral autonomy. The Progressives believed that productive labor was both the key to individual self-development and the bridge which spanned the interests of the individual and of society. As Harold Poelchau wrote, the individual performing productive labor "produces for others, for society, and through his labor integrates himself into the larger whole; he becomes social."[45] However, this shifting of the boundaries between state and citizen within the republican welfare

---

[42] Georg Simmel, "The Poor" (1908), in *On Individuality and Social Forms*, ed. Donald Levine (University of Chicago Press, 1971), pp. 150–78.

[43] Gerda Simons, "Entwicklungstendenzen der Wohlfahrtspflege," *SPr* 30:4 (January 26, 1921), cols. 81–84.

[44] Polligkeit, "Über grundsätzliche Gesichtspunkte für die Aufstellung von Unterstützungssätzen des Wohlfahrtsamtes Frankfurt a.M.," cited in Willi Cuno, "Voraussetzung, Art und Maß der Fürsorge," *SPr* 33:10 (1924), col. 210. One of the most systematic statements of Progressive welfare policy was provided by Otto Wölz, *Aufgaben deutscher Wohlfahrtspolitik* (Berlin, 1925).

[45] Harold Poelchau, *Das Menschenbild des Fürsorgerechts. Eine ethisch-soziologische Untersuchung* (Potsdam, 1932), p. 56.

state cut in both directions, and the Progressives constantly reiterated their belief that the extension of social rights had to be accompanied by the expansion of the obligations of the individual toward the community. "The guarantee of a right to assistance," wrote Polligkeit, "is unthinkable without the explicit emphasis that every person is obligated to the extent of his ability to support himself through his own labor, to safeguard his health, and to educate his children."[46]

Like the Social Democrats, the Progressives depicted welfare as an expression of social solidarity and a form of mutual assistance free from all connotations of deference and dependence.[47] However, while the Progressives hoped that their new vision of social solidarity would transcend the material conflicts which increasingly dominated Weimar political life, they were obsessed with the possibility that the expansion of social services would further aggravate these tendencies. There was a distinct tendency among Progressive welfare reformers—which became much stronger later in the decade—to emphasize the national, social dimension of their concept of productive social citizenship while downplaying the importance of individual rights. As Marie Baum, one of the leading bourgeois feminists active in the social reform field and *Oberregierungsrätin* in the Baden Interior Ministry from 1920–26, warned,

> The concept of the *Rechtsstaat* is often understood to imply that the state is there to distribute rights and that every citizen has the right to insist upon his rights. However, in our national community life would become a hell if the emphasis on rights and services were brought to the fore and the community of beliefs (*Gesinnungsgemeinschaft*) were not regarded as primary. . . . We must, however, be completely clear about the limits of state activity.[48]

The influential Progressive labor law expert Heinz Potthoff warned that the most pressing task was to educate the people to democracy and a sense of civic responsibility because, "above all, the German Republic lacks republicans. The broad masses in every social class . . . do not regard civic rights as a means of devoting themselves to the state, for assuming their share of the labor, burdens and responsibility for the whole, but rather as a means for securing privileges from society at the cost of the whole, that is, at the cost of others."[49] Potthoff was worried about the potential contradictions of what he called "welfare democracy," and he hoped that a form of non-Marxist social democracy, which would combine the best features of liberalism and socialism, would succeed in

---

[46] Polligkeit, "Die künftigen Ziele der sozialen Fürsorge," in *Künftige Ziele der sozialen Fürsorge* (Frankfurt, 1919), citation pp. 16–17.

[47] Aloys Fischer, "Ueber das Verhältnis des Staates zu den Aufgaben der Wohlfahrtspflege . . . ," *Bayerische Fürsorgeblätter* 3:3 (March 10, 1928), cols. 89–102.

[48] "Niederschrift über die Mitgliederversammlung des 'Deutschen Vereins' am 16 Oktober 1919," *ZfA* 20:10–12 (October/December 1919), p. 287.

[49] Potthoff, "Wandlungen der Sozialpolitik," *SPr* 31:50–52 (1922), cols. 1375–76, 1401–4, 1435–37, citation cols. 1401–2. See also Potthoff, *Der Volksstaat. Wesen und Aufgaben sozialer Demokratie* (Munich, 1919).

bridging the chasm which yawned between "the obligation to work and the joy of living" in bourgeois society.[50]

Although the Progressive emphasis on labor as the foundation of citizenship and their view of welfare as the precondition for social citizenship bore many similarities to those of the Social Democrats, the Progressives were far less optimistic about the possibility of eliminating poverty through state social policy than were the Social Democrats. They insisted that no alteration of economic relations could ever completely eliminate the individual causes of need, that is, that distress which was caused by what Polligkeit called "personal economic crises," even if such reforms could remove the general causes of class poverty, because, as Hans Maier—a prominent welfare reformer in Frankfurt and Saxony who moved from the Progressives to the Social Democrats in the mid-1920s—argued, sloth, drink, and uneconomicalness would still exist in a socialist society. Precisely because this residual distress was rooted in the character of the individual, it could only be treated in an individual, personal manner.[51]

The Progressives were just as opposed to the communalization of voluntary charity as were the confessional organizations themselves. At an October 1919 DV conference devoted to the question of the role of voluntary welfare in the new polity, the representatives of both humanitarian and confessional welfare declared the privilege of discharging their holy obligation of charity toward others to be a fundamental, inalienable right.[52] In addition, the Progressives and confessional organizations never tired of praising the role of voluntary welfare as a "pathbreaker," which ferreted out new social ills and staked out new fields of action into which public welfare could later follow. Ultimately, they concluded that any attempt to bring voluntary welfare under public control would mean its sterility, not its communalization.[53]

The response by both the Progressives and the confessional welfare organizations to the socialist challenge was colored by a deeply felt conviction that state bureaucratic activity could exert no positive moral influence. There was, Baum argued, a complete antithesis between social work and charity: "The life to which [social work] devotes itself is personal and individual, and everything personal and individual resists force and power and seeks to follow its own laws." Its schematic and generalizing mode of work imposed intrinsic limita-

[50] Potthoff, "Wandlungen der Sozialpolitik," col. 1403, and *Der Volksstaat*, pp. 5–6, 33–34.

[51] Polligkeit, "Die künftigen Ziele der sozialen Fürsorge," p. 14, Hans Maier, "Die Stellung der sozialen Fürsorge in der neuen Zeit," *SPr* 29:37–38 (June 15, 1920), cols. 865–69, 894–98, and Eduard von Hollander, "Die Zukunft der Wohlfahrtspflege im neuen deutschen Reich," *ZfA* 21:7 (July 1920), pp. 192–204.

[52] "Kundgebung: Die Stellung der privaten Fürsorge im neuen Staat," in Deutscher Verein, ed., *Gekürzter Bericht über die Tagung 'Die künftige Stellung der privaten Fürsorge im neuen Staat' 17. und 18. Oktober 1919 zu Berlin* (Frankfurt, n.d.), pp. 27ff., 79, and *ZfA* 21:1–2 (January/February 1920), pp. 23–24.

[53] Heinrich Ruhland, "Die 'Kommunalisierung' der privaten Fürsorge vom Standpunkte des Steuerzahlers," *ZfA* 21:5 (May 1920), pp. 96–102.

tions upon public welfare and would always have to be supplemented by voluntary engagement because public welfare "reaches its limit where it is a question of the individual dimension of social work . . . Caritas is more than justice, it is infinite goodness."[54] As Polligkeit put the matter, the enthusiasts for communalization forgot that the effectiveness of rationalized social work was limited by "the irrational dimension of human nature" and that the creation of a bureaucratic framework often obscured the fact that social work was ultimately the "cultivation of the personality."[55]

Polligkeit felt that the problem of the relationship between public and voluntary welfare could be solved through the proper organizational form, and he reiterated his wartime call for a kind of "mixed operation" in which public welfare would coordinate and lead, but not dominate, societal welfare organizations. Those problems which were peculiarly suited to bureaucratic, administrative treatment—primarily public health—were to be assigned to public welfare, while all of those areas which touched on questions of education and culture—especially youth welfare—were to be reserved for voluntary welfare. The result would be a symbiotic relationship between state and society in which the strengths of each partner would compensate for the intrinsic weaknesses of the other.[56]

In the heated political climate of the immediate postwar period, both the Progressives and confessional welfare reformers were occupied with the problem of convincing public opinion of the legitimate role of voluntary charity in public life without at the same time opening the door to the politicization of their ostensibly nonpartisan, purely professional work.[57] However, the Progressives also felt that the future of social work was threatened just as much by the postrevolutionary disaffection of the middle-class women who were giving up their voluntary work either because they were bitter at the course of the revolution, because they themselves now needed to pursue gainful employment, or because they were being pushed out of public welfare offices by determined Social Democrats. Despite these trends, Alice Salomon, a prominent bourgeois feminist and leading social work educator, tried to rally the middle-classes behind the flag of social work and social reform by encouraging those social workers who remained distant toward the new Republic to recognize the equality of the working classes and to embrace those aspects of the revolution which were consonant with their own vision of social work. The question, she asked herself and others, was whether, "in such a deeply divided society, there is still room for a type of social work which wants to provide more than mere material help, which strives to bring about understanding between classes and is in its

---

[54] Baum, "Warum ist auch künftig der Staat auf die Mitwirkung der privaten Fürsorge angewiesen?" *Die künftige Stellung*, pp. 7–13.

[55] Polligkeit in "Die künftigen Ziele," p. 20.

[56] Polligkeit, "Das Zusammenarbeiten der Wohlfahrtsvereine," in *Schriften der Zentralstelle für Volkswohlfahrt*, N.F. no. 14 (1918), pp. 50–52, and Polligkeit, "Die Frage der Kommunalisierung der privaten Fürsorge, in *Die künftige Stellung*, pp. 14–22.

[57] *Die künftige Stellung*, pp. 15, 29.

most basic aims a labor of reconciliation." She insisted that social work as a labor of reconciliation and a vehicle for expiating class antagonisms and "social guilt" implied a positive attitude toward socialism and revolution because both social reform and social revolution shared a belief in what she called a "social worldview" (*soziale Weltanschauung*), "without which no true social work is possible."[58]

This social worldview, she wrote in words which sum up all of the pathos of the prewar bourgeois women's movement, meant "being filled with the desire for a social order in which the individual does not enjoy privileges at the cost of the whole." It entailed a "decisive rejection of economic individualism, of unrestrained profit-seeking, of the right of the strong to exploit the weak." No upright person could, she wrote, look at the wretched housing of the poor, the exploitation of the working classes, or the dreary existence of working women without experiencing a sense of "genuine brotherliness, true human community." It was the historical mission of the social work profession, Salomon maintained, "to fill the middle classes with a spirit which would enable them to comprehend the spirit of the revolution and accept it voluntarily" because neither economic class struggle nor the vicious circle of revolution and reaction could be broken unless the previously privileged classes were also emancipated from within by a new sense of social idealism. Salomon believed that this social worldview could transcend the conflicts among the parties vying for influence in the social welfare sector because Judeo-Christian religion, Enlightenment humanism, nationalism, and socialist class solidarity were all inspired by the same quasi-religious belief in the sanctity of human community and a common conviction "that mutual aid is the law of life, that the essence of life does not rest with ourselves, but that it can be realized only in our relations with other human beings. We can never make our life something real, something complete, unless we can make it overflow with sympathy, friendship, love, and action, unless we pass over the threshold which separates the 'I' from the 'thou.' "[59]

In the immediate postrevolutionary period, the attempt by the Progressives to defend voluntary welfare—as the sole possible remedy for that poverty which could never be eliminated through statutory social policy programs and bureaucratic help—entangled them in an extended conflict with Workers' Welfare over the relative priority and ultimate goal of poor law and welfare reform. At the same time, their hope that Salomon's social worldview would provide a firm foundation for both cooperation within and the rationalization of a deeply fragmented voluntary welfare sector involved them in an equally intractable conflict with the confessional welfare organizations, who were nearly as fearful

---

[58] Salomon, "Wie stellt sich der einzelne Sozialarbeiter oder die einzelne Organisation der privaten Fürsorge auf die neuen Verhältnisse ein?" *Die künftige Stellung*, pp. 43–52.

[59] Salomon, "Die sittlichen Ziele und Grundlagen der Wohlfahrtspflege," in *Verhandlungen des Deutschen Vereins*, SDV N.F. 2 (1921), pp. 1–12. Salomon presented a revised version of this talk in the United States in 1923. See *Proceedings of the National Conference of Social Work* (Chicago, 1923), pp. 228–31, from which the above translation is taken.

of the interconfessionalism of the Progressives as they were of the outright antireligious views of the Social Democrats. However, these efforts by the Progressives to distinguish their own position from that of both Social Democracy and Christian conservativism backed them into an uncomfortable, ambiguous position in which they could establish their own distinct identity only at the cost of alienating themselves from their potential allies. This process of mutual repulsion will be analyzed in the remaining two sections of this chapter.

PROGRESSIVISM, SOCIAL DEMOCRACY, AND WELFARE REFORM, 1919–1922

From 1919 onward, Progressive welfare reformers struggled to rethink their understanding of welfare and adapt their ideas to the political and economic realities of the postwar period, while at the same time continuing those innovative social welfare programs for disabled veterans and war survivors which had been pioneered during the war. Although their long-term goal was the passage of a comprehensive national welfare law, the most immediate concern of the middle-class reformers in the DV was the reform of the 1870 Relief Residence Law.[60]

Poor law reform was so urgent in this period because, with the expected dismantling of wartime welfare, responsibility for these persons would then devolve upon municipal poor relief.[61] The decision to give poor law reform priority over the drafting of a national welfare law aroused some opposition within the DV, especially from bourgeois feminists, who argued that poor law reform was a hopeless and reactionary undertaking which would only perpetuate existing inequities. As Marie Kröhne, a leading family welfare activist in Düsseldorf, argued, instead of reforming the poor laws, the concept of the "poor" should itself be abandoned: "In a welfare law, we have to take precautions that we do not create any long-term poor, any second-class persons; the will to self-help is to be strengthened through nursing and pedagogical measures. Our purpose is not to care for the poor, but for human beings."[62]

These plans for poor law reform provoked a more systematic response by the Social Democrats, who for the first time were actively involved in the DV.

---

[60] In February 1919 the DV changed its name from the German Association for "Poor Relief and Charity" to the German Association for "Public and Private Welfare" in order to reflect the new political realities of the postwar world. Georg Schlosser (the vice-chair of the DV), "Die Aufgaben unseres Vereins" (December 18, 1918), IfG 227.

[61] The DV central committee had charged Colmar Justizrat Friedrich Diefenbach with drafting new proposals for poor law reform, which were discussed at the association's 1919 and 1920 conferences. Diefenbach, *Ein Reichsarmengesetz* (Karlsruhe, 1920), Diefenbach, "Die Reform der öffentlichen Armenpflege," in Deutscher Verein, ed., *Gekürzter Bericht über die Tagung der Fachausschüsse für städtisches und ländliches Fürsorgewesen am 13. u. 14 Februar 1920* (n.p., n.d.), pp. 5–29, and *Verhandlungen des Deutschen Vereins*, SDV N.F. 1 (1920).

[62] *Verhandlungen des Deutschen Vereins*, SDV N.F. 1 (1920), p. 38.

These criticisms soon involved Helene Simon in a wide-ranging debate with Polligkeit which focused on the relationship between poor relief, welfare, and social insurance and the potential impact of poor law reform on the structure of the bourgeois state. While Progressives wanted to improve the level of both municipal and voluntary welfare through the extension of preventive, therapeutic programs, they nevertheless insisted that the needy could never have an entitlement to such services, which had to be provided on a subsidiary, individualized basis. Simon, on the other hand, insisted that their bourgeois prejudices prevented Progressive reformers from realizing that the rigorous pursuit of their own preventive, therapeutic approach would ultimately require the "break-up" (*Abbau*) of the poor laws—to borrow a phrase from the Webbs—and their transformation into a comprehensive system of social legislation designed to prevent poverty as a class phenomenon.[63]

Simon argued that this ambitious goal could be achieved through broad reforms in three key areas: public health legislation, a comprehensive youth law, and labor legislation. Simon believed that the increasing acceptance of a preventive approach had largely supplanted the older, deterrent function of poor relief and transformed it into a program to prevent or cure the worst *effects* of poverty, without, however, fully comprehending the necessity of more systematic social policy measures to attack the deeper-lying structural *causes* of poverty. She proposed replacing the existing poor relief, social welfare, and social insurance systems with a single tax-based social security system in which the legal entitlement to pensions and therapeutic social services would be based upon an expanded notion of social citizenship. Although this focus upon the rights and obligations growing out of the concept of productive citizenship provided Simon with a rationale for maintaining some sort of disciplinary mechanism to deal with those asocial or work-shy persons who failed to fulfill these obligations, she nevertheless insisted that only "the principle of a social labor obligation and corresponding legal entitlements [would make it] possible to free the welfare system from its superannuated disciplinary forms and uphold the dignity of the person even in its most extreme degradation."[64]

[63] Simon developed her ideas in a series of articles: "Sozialreform und Reichsarmengesetz," *SPr* 29:22 (1920), cols. 488–89, "Abbau oder Reform der Armenpflege?" *SPr* 29:51–52 (September 22 & 29, 1920), cols. 1199–1203, 1223–27, "Wohlfahrtsamt und Armenamt," *SPr* 30:16 (1921), cols. 420–22, "Wohlfahrtspflege," *SPr* 30:30 (July 27, 1921), cols. 761–66, and "Ueber Versorgung und Fürsorge."

[64] Simon, "Ueber Versorgung und Fürsorge," cols. 859, 896. Simon herself did not use the term social security, but she never found a single term which captured all of the different dimensions of her vision of a "welfare system reformed with social-political intent" (*sozialreformerisch ausgebaute Wohlfahrtspflege*). She rejected the concept of social policy because it was historically identified with the evolution of labor law and had no intrinsic connection to preventive, therapeutic social services. Although the term *Versorgung* implied an entitlement to benefits, it also had no connection to therapeutic social services. On the other hand, neither of the German words for welfare (*Wohlfahrtspflege* and *Fürsorge*) could be lexically connected to the idea of a legal entitlement to either pensions or therapeutic social services. Simon was the leading Social Democratic advocate of a correctional custody law. See Simon, *Aufgaben und Ziele*, pp. 10, 17, and chapter 8 below.

Initially, the nonsocialist members of the DV responded to Simon's proposals by reiterating their belief that, in one form or another, poor relief would always be necessary. Since it was impossible, they insisted, to eliminate those human foibles and failings which lay at the root of most poverty, no matter how much the social insurance system might be improved, the existence of such persons represented the intrinsic limit of Simon's call for the break-up of the poor laws.[65] For this reason, Polligkeit argued that, even though it was necessary to draw a sharp distinction between poor relief and social policy, it was wrong to say that the struggle against class poverty and the individualizing, subsidiary treatment of residual poverty were mutually exclusive. Consequently, while Simon had warned that the mere reform of poor relief posed a threat to its ultimate break-up, Polligkeit called for the simultaneous break-up reform *and* of poor relief through its further social evolution.[66]

These responses failed to address directly Simon's most important claim: that poverty could only be prevented through social policy legislation which attacked its causes and that the subsidiary provision of therapeutic services by a reformed poor relief system would always remain half-hearted and ineffective measures. However, in the ensuing discussion, the broader theoretical issues were overshadowed by practical concerns, and opinion was sharply divided over how to respond to the rising tide of need because any welfare program which sought to provide for all of the new poor would either be prohibitively expensive or its benefits would have to be set at such a uniformly low level that it would be inadequate to meet the needs of these people. As Maier pointed out, state economic policies "create wounds which we can heal in any individual case. However, we can not compensate for economic policies through social welfare programs." Although everyone agreed that further across-the-board increases for social insurance were unacceptable, the absence of any general definition of need which could be applied to all applicants for public assistance appeared to leave social reformers with little choice but to continue the two-tier strategy of creating separate programs—each with their own eligibility criteria and benefits—to meet the needs of each privileged group of the new poor while at the same time seeking to shore up a poor relief system which was creaking under the weight of its own administrative apparatus. As one member of the DV concluded, "The only thing we can do is to prevent as much as we can. We have to put poor relief in a position to insure that we in fact achieve that which still lies within our power."[67]

The fiscal crisis of the public assistance system continued to deepen as the scope of poverty expanded through 1921 and 1922, while the proliferation of specialized welfare programs for the new poor and the open insolvency of the

[65] Hollander, "Abbau oder Reform der Armenpflege?" *SPr* 30:21 (May 25, 1921), cols. 545–50, Polligkeit, "Zur Reform des öffentlichen Unterstützungswesens," *ZfA* 21:10–11 (October/November 1920), pp. 237–43, and Blaum in minutes of the HADV (February 28, 1921), IfG 229.

[66] *Verhandlungen des Deutschen Vereins*, SDV N.F. 1 (1920), p. 16, and minutes of HADV (February 28, 1921).

[67] Maier and Karl Sperling in munutes of HADV (February 28, 1921).

disability insurance system made a more thorough examination of the relationship between welfare and social insurance both increasingly urgent and increasingly difficult. At the March 1922 DV meeting, Simon and Polligkeit squared
off over the issue. While Simon restated the arguments which she had advanced
at the September 1921 SPD convention in Görlitz, Polligkeit presented a revised version of the reform plan which he had presented the previous spring.[68]
Although the sphere of welfare described in the constitution encompassed both
social insurance and public assistance, Polligkeit argued that it was wrong to
consolidate the two in "a general social security system for all possible causes
of distress" and that, instead, each system should be separately reformed on the
basis of preventive, therapeutic principles. In an insurance system reformed in
this manner, the schematic provision of monetary payments on the basis of
paid-in premiums would have to be scaled back, and the benefits actually provided would have to correspond to the degree of disability and be designed to
eliminate, or at least reduce, the degree of disability: "The mere fact of illness,
accident, disability, or inability to work in one's profession are not the cause of
need and must not determine the level of insurance benefits, but rather [the
question of] whether and to what extent one of these causes has limited or
destroyed the ability to work." On the other hand, the reform of the welfare
system would have to begin by breaking with the postwar policy of creating
new specialized programs, with their different eligibility requirements and separate administrative apparatus, for each group of the new poor. Instead, the goal
must be the consolidation of all of these specialized programs into a general
welfare program based on a unitary definition of need. Although Polligkeit
shared Simon's belief that individualist categories of bourgeois political economy had to be abandoned in favor of a more "social" view of citizenship and
individual rights, he drew opposite conclusions from this principle. While Simon wanted to break up the poor laws and anchor preventive, therapeutic programs in legislation which would establish an entitlement to specific social
services, Polligkeit's proposal to graduate insurance benefits according to individual need and supplant the right to monetary payments with therapeutic services would have broken up the social insurance system by undermining its
basic contractualist principles. Polligkeit's implicit call for the "break-up of the
social insurance system" through the introduction of an individualizing, need-
based approach represented a distinctly Progressive, but no less radical, social
reform strategy than Simon's call for the break-up of the poor laws, and, by
gradually eliminating the most salient differences between welfare and insurance, it would have opened the way to their consolidation, though on a very
different principle than that envisioned by Simon.

While most leading Progressive welfare experts supported the thrust of Polligkeit's proposals, Hermann Luppe, the vice-chair of the DV and a leading

---

[68] Polligkeit, "Vorschläge für eine einheitliche reichsgesetzliche Neureglung der öffentlichen
Wohlfahrtspflege," *SPr* 31:26 (1922), cols. 705–10, and "Bericht über eine Tagung des Hauptausschusses des Deutschen Vereins," *SPr* 31:27 (1922), cols. 729–32.

DDP politician, attacked his ideas and defended the liberal, individualist premises of the social insurance system against both Polligkeit and Simon. Luppe argued that the principle of a legal entitlement to insurance benefits—apart from all questions of individual need—was a sign of economic and social progress which had to be upheld in principle. On the other hand, he attacked the idea of a noncontributory social security system (*allgemeine Volksfürsorge*) because he felt that this would undermine both the work ethic and the incentive to provide for one's own future and thus lead to an undesirable leveling of social distinctions. He urged that the welfare system place an even greater emphasis on individual self-help because an impoverished nation could not afford to schematically supplement inadequate social insurance pensions from tax revenues without insuring that the applicants for support had first exhausted all of their own resources.[69]

This three-way debate between Simon, Polligkeit, and Luppe revolved around the question of how best to guarantee those social rights championed by both the Progressives and the Social Democrats without undermining the work ethic and the social obligations which both groups agreed were the necessary correlate to these rights. While Simon argued that these rights could only be secured by anchoring them in law, Polligkeit and Luppe argued that a legal entitlement to social services would undermine personal responsibility. However, while Simon and Polligkeit both envisioned a comprehensive system of preventive and therapeutic social services, Polligkeit insisted that this goal could only be achieved without undermining individual responsibility by providing these services on the basis of individual need as determined by social service experts, rather than as legal entitlements. This, in turn, reintroduced that moment of external authority—and the potential for its abuse—which Workers' Welfare had hoped to eliminate through the democratization of the welfare system and which Luppe believed could only be forestalled by the principle of social insurance.

Between 1920 and 1922, it had become increasingly evident that the reform of poor relief, welfare, and social insurance had important implications for the structure of the Weimar state. In fact, the confrontation between Simon and the Progressives in the DV antedated and foreshadowed the later and better-known "crisis of social policy."[70] As the fiscal crisis narrowed the horizons of these welfare reformers, the DV continued to pursue the two-tier reform strategy

---

[69] Minutes of the HADV (March 22, 1922), IfG 229, and Luppe, "Versicherung und Fürsorge," *SPr* 31:48 (November 30, 1922), cols. 1305–8. Luppe had begun his career in Frankfurt working under Karl Flesh. He was elected deputy mayor of Frankfurt in 1912 and played a key role in the creation of the city's welfare office during and after the war. He was elected to the National Assembly in 1919 and became Nuremberg mayor in January 1920. Luppe was recognized as one of the leading authorities on municipal welfare and social policy, and in the 1920s he played a leading role in the Städtetag and its welfare subcommittee. See Hermann Hanschel, *Oberbürgermeister Hermann Luppe. Nürnberger Kommunalpolitik in der Weimarer Republik* (Verein für Geschichte der Stadt Nürnberg, 1977), and Luppe, *Mein Leben* (Nürnberg: Selbstverlag des Stadtrats, 1977).

[70] Ludwig Preller, *Sozialpolitik in der Weimarer Republik* (Athenäum, 1978), pp. 204ff.

which Simon had attacked so bitterly. On the one hand, the DV created a special committee to draft an emergency law for the reform of the Relief Residence Law; this was submitted to the Interior Ministry, which was responsible for poor relief, in October 1922.[71] On the other hand, the DV also began preliminary work on a national welfare law along the lines of Polligkeit's proposals, which Labor Ministry officials—who were responsible for all of the postwar welfare programs—had already praised as a promising basis for a future Reich welfare law.[72] In practice, the confrontation between the Progressives and the Social Democrats, which remained unresolved at the theoretical level, was increasingly resolved in favor of the Progressives by the deepening fiscal crisis, which precluded ambitious welfare reforms for the foreseeable future; by the renewed influence of the bourgeois and religious parties; and by the proliferation of specialized postwar welfare programs, which forced Progressive reformers to shift their attention to the call for entitlements by the various groups of the new poor. This will be the theme of chapters 3 and 4.

PROGRESSIVISM AND THE CHURCH CHARITIES BETWEEN COOPERATION AND CORPORATISM

The expansion of state involvement in (and regulation of) the sphere of voluntary welfare during the war and the specter of communalization in the immediate postwar period provided a greater incentive than ever before for the creation of an umbrella organization to insure the most efficient use of available resources and more effectively represent the collective interests of voluntary welfare in the legislative process. Between 1919 and 1921, the DV—under Polligkeit's leadership—attempted to take the initiative in the formation of such an organization. These efforts were guided by the belief that the many conflicts of religion and worldview which were the cause of the excessive fragmentation and inefficiency of voluntary welfare could be transcended through the rational, functional division of labor among voluntary welfare and the further professionalization of social work on the basis of an individualizing, casework methodology and the commitment of trained social workers to a nonpolitical ethics of selfless service. Unfortunately, the Progressives failed to realize the extent to which the confessional organizations regarded these proposals as a direct threat to their own religious-political identity, to which they had been forced to cling more firmly than ever before by the revolution, or the extent to which their humanism and utilitarianism clashed with the views of the confessional charities. Consequently, and paradoxically, the efforts by the Progressives to promote more systematic cooperation among the major voluntary welfare organizations set off a countermodernization on the part of the confessional organizations and intensified that very politicization of social work which the Progressives hoped

[71] "Entwurf eines Notgesetzes zum U.W.G.," *Nachrichtendienst* 30 (October 1922), p. 265.
[72] Minutes of HADV (March 22–23, 1922), IfG 229, p. 24a.

such cooperation would eliminate. By sharpening their mutual understanding of the cultural and political differences dividing them and forcing these organizations to turn inward to seek a homogeneous religious-cultural milieu within which they could pursue their own visions of social reform through social work, the failure of cooperation in the early 1920s became the precondition for the development of a corporatist system in the middle of the decade.

Since the 1890s, the Progressives had been searching—with only a minimal degree of success—for a viable means of coordinating both voluntary charity and its collective relations with public welfare, and these efforts had been intensified in response to the proliferation of charitable organizations during the war. Part of the problem was that in 1919 there were more than one hundred central, nationwide organizations divided along functional and political lines. Although Polligkeit recognized that the creation of a giant umbrella organization embracing all of these organizations was entirely unrealistic, he did believe that some organizations had to represent "the idea of unity" and focus on those general problems which transcended political and functional boundaries. To achieve this goal, Polligkeit hoped to bring about a sort of personal union among the three most important existing umbrella organizations: the venerable, semi-official, and hopelessly patriarchal *Zentralstelle für Volkswohlfahrt*; the DV; and the German Central Association for Youth Welfare (*Deutsche Zentrale für Jugendfürsorge*), the leading national organization in the field.[73] While many organizations feared that any attempt to direct their work toward specific ends or limit their freedom would inevitably cripple the voluntaristic impulse which was so crucial to the achievement of their goals, Polligkeit argued that this goal could be achieved through the creation of a self-governing body based on collegial rather than parliamentary principles. He hoped that this organization would serve as a kind of "intellectual general staff" to formulate plans and priorities for the collective work of voluntary welfare and function as a national welfare council which the government would have to consult on all fundamental questions of social and economic policy.[74]

These ambitious plans were quickly overtaken by events. Although the need to create a central organization to represent all German charities in negotiations with international philanthropic organizations led in 1920 to an abortive attempt to transform the German Red Cross (which had been reorganized into a peacetime social hygiene organization) into such an umbrella organization, most of the other charity organizations regarded the Red Cross as a hostile interloper, not as their legitimate representative, and the idea was quickly dropped.[75] How-

[73] Polligkeit, "Formen der Arbeitsgemeinschaft zwischen den Zentralbehörden der staatlichen Wohlfahrtspflege und Zentralvereinigungen der freien Wohlfahrtspflege," *Concordia* 26:23 (December 1, 1919), pp. 213–21, and Polligkeit(?), "Neue Ziele der Zentralstelle für Volkswohlfahrt" (July 19, 1919), BAP RAM 9039.

[74] Polligkeit, "Die Krise in der Wohlfahrtspflege," *Concordia* 27:20–21 (November 1, 1920), p. 203, "Planmäßige Wohlfahrtspflege auf arbeitsgemeinschaftlicher Grundlage," *Concordia* 27:24 (December 15, 1920), pp. 257–59, and "Formen der Arbeitsgemeinschaft . . ."

[75] "Denkschrift des Reichsarbeitsministeriums über die Bildung einer deutschen Roten Kreuz-

ever, the episode did suffice to convince these organizations to form such an association on their own. In his suggestion that the DV was the natural candidate to serve this representational function, Polligkeit gave the matter a revealing sense of urgency: "We face a crisis similar to that which has led to a planned economy in the economic sphere. We face the same danger in the social welfare sector." He conceded, however, that no single organization was capable of representing the interests of all because, "as little as we are politically ripe enough for a unitary state . . . we are equally so in the welfare sector." Effective cooperation could, therefore, only be achieved on the basis of a "working community [*Arbeitsgemeinschaft*], which ultimately rests on mutual trust," not on democratic, parliamentary principles.[76]

In March 1921, the *Reichsgemeinschaft von Hauptverbänden der Deutschen Wohlfahrtspflege* (Reich Association of German Social Welfare Peak Associations), the first nationwide societal welfare umbrella organization, was officially founded.[77] Financial considerations were of foremost concern in the decision to establish the *Reichsgemeinschaft*, and it worked hard to obtain larger subsidies from all levels of government.[78] The *Reichsgemeinschaft* limited its membership to those major national welfare central organizations whose activity covered the entire range of social welfare services, including the DV, the Inner Mission, the Caritasverband, the Central Welfare Bureau for German Jewry, and the German Association for Rural Welfare (*Deutscher Verein für ländliche Wohlfahrts- und Heimatpflege*).[79] From the beginning, however, relations between the *Reichsgemeinschaft* and both Workers' Welfare and the German Red Cross—both of which were invited to join—were strained. Polligkeit hoped that the invitation to Workers' Welfare would demonstrate that the traditional bourgeois and confessional organizations were in step with the changing times and willing to welcome the working class as an equal partner in the field of social work and that the affiliation of Workers' Welfare would commit it to cooperating with the other groups and thus prevent the further "politicization" of the welfare sector. However, the leadership of Workers' Welfare was divided over its own goals

---

Gemeinschaft" (1920), BAP RAM 9234. Werthmann regarded the Labor Ministry proposal as "one of the most significant documents of the last decades" regarding the organization of the welfare sector. Werthmann, "Tagesströmungen."

[76] Minutes of the HADV (September 23, 1920), IfG 229.

[77] Circular from Polligkeit announcing the creation of the *Reichsgemeinschaft* (February 17, 1921), ADCV 460 and *SPr* 30:12 (1921), cols. 307–9.

[78] "Niederschrift der Verhandlungen über die Gründung einer Reichsgemeinschaft der Hauptverbände der freien Wohlfahrtspflege" (March 2, 1921), ADCV 460.

[79] Minutes of the *Reichsgemeinschaft* meeting (March 12 and May 10, 1921), ADCV 460.040. Smaller private welfare organizations in specialized fields of welfare activity were encouraged to form their own associations, which would then meet the organizational requirements of the *Reichsgemeinschaft*. Those organizations working in the social hygiene area considered forming their own national organization in order to qualify for membership in the *Reichsgemeinschaft*. However, rather than affiliating with the *Reichsgemeinschaft*, the social hygiene organizations combined to form an independent organization, the *Arbeitsgemeinschaft sozialhygienischer Reichsfachverbände*.

and ultimately declined the offer.[80] Relations with the German Red Cross also remained unclear, though it did join the *Reichsgemeinschaft* later that year.

However, beyond sponsoring a public campaign against luxury, a charity drive for impoverished pensioners, and an important conference on social work training, the *Reichsgemeinschaft* accomplished relatively little, and it never became the dynamic organization envisioned by Polligkeit. Polligkeit's plan to create a politically neutral intellectual general staff to coordinate the activity of voluntary welfare failed because the scope of the organization simply displaced into the *Reichsgemeinschaft* all of the persistent cleavages of the Weimar polity itself. In addition to their unconcealed hatred for the Social Democrats—which was intensified by the traditional anti-Semitism of the Caritasverband and the Inner Mission—and their barely concealed mistrust of the Red Cross, there was also a sharp antagonism between these confessional organizations and the DV itself. This antagonism continued to intensify because, despite Polligkeit's protestations, the DV was itself becoming an eminently political association representing the interests of municipal welfare officials and a distinct group of Progressive and, increasingly, Social Democratic reform ideas.

Cooperation with and within the DV would have required the confessional organizations to give up what they were coming to value most—their distinct confessional identity—and dampen their traditional hostility to liberalism and Social Democracy. Although Salomon had hoped that her social worldview would transcend the cultural and political differences dividing the major voluntary welfare organizations, the church charities had little sympathy for either Salomon's ecumenical suggestion that the Christian religion simply represented one among many manifestations of a natural feeling of human solidarity or for Klumker's definition of indigence.

In the early 1920s, the Caritasverband was especially concerned with distinguishing Christian charity from the secular, humanitarian idea of "welfare" advocated by the Progressives and the Social Democrats. Caritas, argued the Breslau theologian Joseph Löhr, was something unique and different from all other similar forms of activity. It was "something supernatural, a religious habitus; it is the love—which immediately and necessarily flows forth from the theological virtue of the love of God—of the likenesses and the children of the one heavenly Father."[81] In addition to this supernatural dimension of charity, which the Caritasverband naturally shared with the Inner Mission, Löhr insisted that caritas was also something specifically Catholic which could only be perfected within the institutional Church. The Catholics insisted that this distinctly confessional conception of charity could in no way be confused with the syncretism of Salomon's social worldview. They constantly and invidiously contrasted these supernatural motives with the merely sentimental humanitarianism

---

[80] Minutes of the *Reichsgemeinschaft* meeting (May 10, 1921), ADCV 460.040.

[81] Löhr, "Grundsätzliches über Caritas und Caritaswissenschaft," *Caritas* N.F. 1:5–6 (1922), pp. 168–83, citation p. 170.

which underlay all nonreligious forms of social work and with distributive justice, which was the aim of state social policy.[82] While caritas was inspired by
religious motives, secular welfare, argued Löhr, was concerned exclusively with
the earthly well-being of men and women, not their salvation.[83] Although caritas
was distinguished from the directly pastoral activity of the Church by the fact
that it aimed at the alleviation of distress and that its scope was not limited, as
was pastoral activity, to the members of the Church, Löhr insisted that caritas
nevertheless ultimately served religious, not economic or social, ends. The
struggle against spiritual distress—sexual immorality, *Verwahrlosung*, venereal
disease, alcoholism, and the declining birthrate—was the highest and most no-
ble task of caritas as well as its privileged sphere. Only religion and charitable
activity undertaken with pastoral intent could cure these forms of spiritual distress: "If those fail, then all other methods will be pointless in any case and the
monies spent will be wasted state expenditures."[84] These arguments were part of
a conscious countermodernization of Inner Mission and Catholic caritas in response to the Progressive and Social Democratic provocation, and this modernization led to the founding in 1925 of a Catholic institute for "charitable science" (*Caritaswissenschaft*) at the University of Freiburg and to the founding of
a comparable Protestant institute in Berlin later in the decade.

While the Progressives originally hoped to forestall conflicts over religion
and politics by introducing supposedly value-neutral scientific social work and
the functional division of labor as the universally valid norms and methods
governing the welfare sector, the Progressive vision of a depoliticized, func-
tionally organized welfare sector failed as religious and cultural forces inevitably entered in through the back door as soon as attention was focused on either
the specific values which inspired the personal engagement of the social worker
or on the goals of such activity. The cleavages dividing these organizations
mirrored the divisions of the German polity itself, and conflicts over politics and religion overshadowed those conflicts arising out of the functional
division of labor. During this period, the confessional welfare organizations
became increasingly aware that they would have to create stronger organizations, with a broader political base and a much clearer consciousness of
the specificity of those religious beliefs which distinguished their understanding of social work from that of the Progressives, before it would be
possible to seriously consider cooperating with humanitarian organizations
and public welfare. In view of these trends, it is hardly surprising that the
representatives of the major voluntary welfare organizations decided—with
the apparent consent of the Labor Ministry, but behind Polligkeit's back—
to let the *Reichsgemeinschaft* slowly die and to form a new organization of

[82] Franz Rappenecker, "25. Deutscher Caritastag," *Caritas* N.F. 3:7 (1924), pp. 125–39.
[83] Löhr, "Geist und Wesen der Caritas," *Caritas* N.F. 1:1–2 (1922), pp. 18–27, 55–72, citation p. 68.
[84] Löhr, "Geist und Wesen der Caritas," citation p. 27.

their own. All of these developments were part and parcel of the mutual repulsion of Progressive, Social Democratic, and Catholic organizations, and, as these trends were played out in the 1922 debate on the National Youth Welfare Law, these antagonisms would have important implications for the character of political discourse in the Republic.

Weltanschauung and *Staatsauffassung* in the Making of the National Youth Welfare Law

CHURCH, STATE, AND THE NATURE OF PUBLIC AUTHORITY

The path leading to the passage of the RJWG was long and arduous, and the bill which emerged from the complicated negotiations among the coalition parties and the many interested ministries and welfare reform groups differed in important respects from the initial draft prepared by the government. The Caritasverband had opposed the national regulation of youth welfare because it feared the waning influence of religion on social reproduction in an increasingly pluralistic and irreligious society. The Social Democrats, however, insisted on the primacy of public welfare as the precondition for its democratization and for the emancipation of the young from the authoritarianism of traditional youth welfare practice. From a Catholic perspective, the interconnection between state form and civil society was reflected in the modern, yet antiliberal efforts to remove social work as much as possible from public control in order to perpetuate an approach to juvenile socialization which viewed the family as the primary site for inculcating in the young that love of God and respect for authority which Christian conservatives regarded as the ultimate foundation of the social and political order.

The terms of the debate had been framed by the Progressive advocacy since the turn of the century of a right to education, and the door to further politicization of these issues had been opened by those portions of the Weimar constitution dealing with marriage, children, and the family. For welfare reformers, the key issue was the extent to which public authorities should have the right and obligation to intervene into family life to insure the satisfaction of this right. The views of the various organizations concerning the scope of public authority, on the one hand, and the nature of family and civil society, on the other, pivoted around the divergent answers which they gave to this question. Although the Progressives were the most active proponents of national youth welfare legislation, the final version of the law was a great disappointment for both the Progressives and the Social Democrats because the Center Party and the Caritasverband were able to give the law a very different effect from that envisioned by its sponsors. Ultimately, these Catholic organizations succeeded in transforming a law which would have curtailed the autonomy of humanitarian and confessional welfare into one which guaranteed their influence within the newly established municipal youth welfare offices and codified instead the subsidiarity of public youth welfare.[1]

---

[1] The most important contemporary commentaries on the RJWG are Edmund Friedberg and Wilhelm Polligkeit, *Das Reichsgesetz für Jugendwohlfahrt*, 2d ed. (Berlin, 1930), and Bäumer/

In the first months after the revolution, Progressive youth welfare activists in the DV and the *Archiv Deutscher Berufsvormunder* called upon both the government and the National Assembly to remove the two most important legislative barriers to the further development of preventive youth welfare: the subsidiarity of public assistance as spelled out in Relief Residence Law and the sections of the Civil Code dealing with parental rights. Although the Prussian Landtag had already begun debate on a state youth welfare law in the summer of 1918, the new Prussian government agreed to postpone further consideration of this law in favor of national regulation because comprehensive reform at the state level was impossible without prior Reich legislation regulating such matters as support for indigent children and the family law provisions of the Civil Code. However, in October 1919 Württemberg did pass its own Youth Office Law, which was regarded by Progressive youth welfare reformers as a model for future legislation.[2]

At the Reich level, the Interior Ministry had already begun drafting a youth welfare law in the summer of 1918, and in May 1919 discussions began among the various Reich ministries concerned with youth welfare. The task of drafting the law was delegated to an Interior Ministry committee chaired by Privy Admiralty Councilor Otto Köbner. The initial draft was a lineal descendant of Progressive youth welfare reform proposals stretching back to the prewar years. Köbner argued that the law should be a broad youth education law encompassing both youth cultivation and youth welfare (*Jugendpflege* and *Jugendfürsorge*) because the success of their work depended on avoiding the appearance that the youth welfare offices were concerned only with mentally or physically defective, fallen, or endangered youth. The law must, Köbner maintained, establish the right of all German children to an intellectual and moral education which would make them capable of fulfilling their civic obligations and affirm

---

Hartmann/Becker, *Das Reichsgesetz für Jugendwohlfahrt auf Grund des amtlichen Materials herausgegeben* (Berlin, 1923). On youth welfare during the Weimar Republic, see Gary Finder, *"Education not Punishment": Juvenile Justice in Late Imperial and Weimar Germany* (dissertation, University of Chicago, 1997), Edward Ross Dickinson, *The Politics of German Child Welfare from the Empire to the Federal Republic* (Harvard University Press, 1996), Marcus Gräser, *Der blockierte Wohlfahrtsstaat. Unterschichtsjugend und Jugendfürsorge in der Weimarer Republik* (Vandenhoeck & Ruprecht, 1995), Elizabeth Harvey, *Youth and the Welfare State in Weimar Germany* (Oxford University Press, 1993), Andreas Wollash, *Der Katholische Fürsorgeverein für Mädchen, Frauen und Kinder* (Lambertus, 1991), pp. 122ff., Carola Kuhlmann, *Erbkrank oder Erziehbar? Jugendhilfe als Vorsorge und Aussonderung in der Fürsorgeerziehung in Westfalen von 1933–1945* (Juventa, 1989), pp. 26–50, Detlev Peukert, *Grenzen der Sozialdisziplinierung* (Bund-Verlag, 1986), Rüdiger Baron, "'Ballastexistenzen': Sparmaßnahmen in der Krise: Fürsorgeerziehung im Übergang zum Dritten Reich," in Georg Vobruba, ed., *"Wir sitzen alle in einem Boot." Gemeinschaftsrhetorik in der Krise* (Campus Verlag, 1983), pp. 138–59, and Christa Hasenclever, *Jugendhilfe und Jugendgesetzgebung seit 1900* (Göttingen, 1978), pp. 48–87.

[2] The Württemberg law provided for the establishment of a network of local youth welfare offices whose activity was in principle limited to statutory, bureaucratic tasks; they were only permitted to directly provide social services if voluntary organizations were unwilling to assume these tasks. Kurt Blaum, "Die württembergische Jugendfürsorgereform," *Zentralblatt* 11 (1919/20), pp. 169ff.

the obligation of public welfare authorities to secure this right when and to the extent that the family was unable to do so.[3]

Ministerial discussions were completed by the end of 1919, and the first draft was sent to the Reichsrat in February 1920. However, despite the great public interest in the law, the draft immediately ran aground in the Reichsrat, where the Bavarian government objected to virtually every major provision of the law. The Bavarian government maintained that the Reich did not have the authority to require local welfare offices to provide specific services because this infringed on the authority of the federal states, and it insisted that the Reich law should only provide a national framework, while leaving the specific provisions to the discretion of state and local government. Moreover, although the Bavarian government supported the aims of the law in principle, it insisted that the declaration of a right to education could not be a binding legal norm and did not, therefore, belong in the law itself.[4] Consideration of the law was also delayed by disagreements over the financing of the new programs required by the law. Finance Minister Matthias Erzberger (Center) maintained that state and local government, not the Reich, should be responsible for funding the youth welfare programs regulated by the law and that the Reich should only be responsible for monitoring compliance with the provisions of the law. Despite these reservations, Erzberger grudgingly agreed to provide 50 million marks annually for the first three years to help fund the youth welfare offices.[5] However, this tentative compromise aroused deep concern on the part of the states. In particular, Prussian Finance Minister Albert Südekum protested that the proposed Reich subsidy would come nowhere near providing state and local government with resources necessary to carry out the tasks imposed upon them by the law, while local government, whose finances had already been stretched to the limit, was incapable of bearing the additional costs.[6]

In view of these objections, by early summer 1920 it appeared that the legislative initiatives of the previous decade might flounder, and further Reichsrat discussion was suspended. However, in November, thirty-three women Reichstag delegates from all political parties sponsored an interpellation demanding that the government present a draft of the law to the current session of the Reichstag.[7] In response, the Interior Ministry finally presented the draft to the Reichstag on March 15, 1921. The preamble restated the basic Progressive position that the problems of the youth welfare system were due more to the absence of legislation specifying the scope and authority of public youth wel-

---

[3] "Aufzeichnung über das Ergebnis der . . . kommissarischen Beratung über die reichsgesetzliche Reglung der Jugendwohlfahrt" (May 5, 1919), and "Vorentwurf des Reichs-Jugendwohlfahrtsgesetzes nach der Fassung der kommissarischen Beratungen . . ." (July 9, 1919), BAP RJM 1514.

[4] "Bemerkungen und Anträge Bayerns zum Entwurf eines Reichsjugendwohlfahrtsgesetzes . . ." (March 17, 1920), BAP RJM 1514.

[5] Erzberger to Justice Ministry (February 10, 1920), BAP RJM 1514.

[6] Südekum to Koch (March 8, 1920), BAP RJM 1514.

[7] I. Wahlperiode (1920/24), Drucksache Nr. 921, and *Verhandlungen des Reichstags* 58. Sitzung (January 27, 1921), pp. 2172–86.

fare than to the shortcomings of either youth welfare theory or the administration of youth welfare in those cities with innovative programs. The most pressing need was to create a central point—the youth welfare office—"around which the various organizations working together can gather, coordinate, and distribute" the tasks to be done.[8] The first article proclaimed the right of every German child to "physical, spiritual and moral education" and required local government to establish youth welfare offices which were to intervene if the family failed to satisfy this right. Contemporary opinion was unanimous in the belief that the significance of the RJWG lay in the codification of a pedagogical approach to youth welfare, which made the child's right to education as important as the right of society to protect itself from the consequences of juvenile delinquency, and the reorganization of youth welfare on the basis of this principle.[9]

The second section of the law described the competence and organizational structure of the new public youth offices. In many respects, these provisions simply systematized and codified Progressive ideas on professional guardianship and municipal youth welfare offices which had been advanced before the war, while mandating their implementation by local authorities. The competence of the youth welfare offices was expanded to include the supervision of foster children, monetary support for indigent children, guardianship for orphans and out-of-wedlock children, correctional education, and juvenile court assistance. More important, the draft also permitted both Reich and local government to assign additional responsibilities to the youth welfare offices. This provision, as well as those parts of the law which described the composition of the governing bodies of the public welfare offices and their relation to voluntary welfare, all generated substantial conflict.

The third section defined the obligations of youth welfare offices with regard to the supervision of foster care, while the fourth section established uniform national regulations concerning statutory guardianship, which was extended to include all out-of-wedlock children. The draft included clauses intended to insure that the religion or worldview of the parent(s) was taken into account to "as great an extent as possible" in the appointment of public guardians. The fifth section regulated responsibility for the relief of indigent children, which was henceforth to include the cost of their education and occupational training. The sixth section established uniform national regulations for protective supervision and correctional education. Protective supervision was permitted if it appeared necessary and adequate to prevent physical or moral *Verwahrlosung*, even if the child had not been convicted of a criminal offense, and, in contrast to earlier Prussian legislation, the law eased the conditions under which children could be committed to correctional education. Lastly, the law obligated the Reich to contribute 100 million marks annually for at least the first three years

---

[8] I. Wahlperiode (1920/24), Drucksache Nr. 1666, pp. 1237–76, citations pp. 1237–38. This breakthrough was made possible by the willingness of the Prussian government to compromise on its demand that the Reich pay for all of the additional costs entailed by the law.

[9] Hasenclever, *Jugendhilfe und Jugendgesetzgebung*, pp. 73–74.

to help state and local government defray the costs entailed by the law. The law was to take force in April 1924.

After its first reading, the bill was referred to committee for further consideration. From the very beginning, the women members of the Reichstag were especially active in securing the passage of this law, and thirteen of the twenty-eight members of the Reichstag committee were women. At the same time, the bill was being carefully studied by a commission established by the Caritasverband and by a so-called experts' commission—chaired by Polligkeit—established jointly by the DV, the *Archiv deutscher Berufsvormunder*, and the *Deutsche Zentrale für Jugendfürsorge*.[10] Agnes Neuhaus, the head of the *Katholischer Fürsorgeverein für Mädchen, Frauen und Kinder*, was the only person who belonged to all three committees, and the ultimate passage of the law owed much to her ability to forge a coalition among the bourgeois and confessional parties while maintaining good relations with the Social Democrats.[11]

In all of these committees, the debate over the extent of state intervention into the familial sphere to guarantee the right to education illustrate the reciprocal relationship between state form and the role to be played by public welfare in shaping the sphere of social reproduction. The Progressives emphasized the social purpose of this right to education.[12] As Gertrud Bäumer, the chair of the national Federation of German Women's Associations (*Bund Deutscher Frauenvereine*, BDF) and a leading social work educator, wrote, "The child is to be educated for society, and the goal of education is determined by the usefulness of the child for society."[13] Summarizing the conclusions of the experts' committee, Polligkeit pointed out that the assertion in §1.2 that the law did not affect the historic rights and duties of parents was patently false.[14] In a later essay, he argued that the right of parents to educate their children was based on the presumption that the family was in fact capable of providing the necessary education and that the community, therefore, need only watch over the parents and insure that they fulfill this duty. However, this fiction was becoming increasingly untenable due to social change, and he concluded that in the future the actual pedagogical achievements of the family would increasingly

---

[10] This commission provides a perfect example of both the growing influence of experts in the formulation of public policy and the corporatist inclusion of organized interest groups in the legislative process. *Protokoll der Beratungen der Caritaskommission zum Reichsjugendwohlfahrtsgesetzentwurf* (December 9–10, 1921, and March 5–7, 1922, of which there are two transcripts), ADCV 319.4 E.II.6 (in the following, this will be cited as *Caritaskommission* I, II, and III), Deutscher Caritasverband, ed., *Denkschrift zum Entwurf eines Reichs-Jugendwohlfahrtsgesetzes* (Freiburg, 1920), and Deutscher Verein, ed., *Materialien zum RJWG vom 9.7.1922* (Frankfurt, 1961). The report of the experts' committee was published separately as Polligkeit/Hilde Eiserhardt, eds., *Denkschrift zu dem Entwurf eines Reichsjugendwohlfahrtsgesetzes* (Frankfurt, 1921).

[11] On Neuhaus's role, see Wollash, *Der Katholische Fürsorgeverein*, and *Caritaskommission* II, p. 2.

[12] See Polligkeit's comments in *Materialien zum Reichsjugendwohlfahrtsgesetz*, pp. 154ff.

[13] Bäumer/Hartmann/Becker, *Das Reichsgesetz für Jugendwohlfahrt*, p. 36.

[14] Polligkeit/Eiserhardt, *Denkschrift*, pp. 5–6.

lag behind this historical norm. Although Polligkeit protested that he respected the traditional rights of parents, he also argued that this right was accompanied by an obligation to raise children who were physically, mentally, and morally capable of fulfilling their civic and social obligations, and he insisted that the state had both the right to supervise parental education and the obligation to render the parents capable of fulfilling their duty. The programmatic significance of §1 lay in the codification of this new conception of social rights and obligations which permitted the collective responsibility of state and society to supplement the individual responsibility of the parents. This was, he concluded, constitutive of the transition from the *Rechtsstaat* to the welfare state.[15]

However, everyone involved in the drafting of the law was conscious of the gaping chasm between the programmatic intentions announced in §1, which envisioned a broad public youth *education* law, and the remaining provisions, which in fact amounted only to a youth *office* law. Klumker complained that the law simply cobbled together legislative proposals dealing with various aspects of youth welfare without subordinating them to a clear, overarching vision or providing for a unitary source of funding. In addition, Progressive ideas were still riven by an apparent contradiction between, on the one hand, their desire to establish a public education authority responsible for the spiritual welfare of children of all classes and, on the other hand, their belief that this educational mission could best be realized through voluntary organizations, whose rights had to be guaranteed by the youth welfare law. Klumker hoped to resolve this contradiction by assigning a broad public importance to the work of voluntary welfare and insuring it the right to work within the youth welfare offices.[16]

During the revolution, the leftist parties had hoped to reduce the influence of organized religion on public life, especially by eliminating religious instruction from public schools, and they remained extraordinarily mistrustful of confessional charity organizations, particularly of correctional education institutions run by these organizations. All too often, these organizations, argued the leftist parties, proffered help "only in order to shear a sheep for their ecclesiastical and confessional goals," and they accused correctional institutions of abusing their charges, exploiting them as a source of cheap labor, and devoting more energy to proselytizing and punishing their charges than educating them.[17] In contrast

---

[15] Polligkeit, "Die programmatische Bedeutung von §1 RJWG," in Wilhelm Polligkeit, Hans Scherpner, and Heinrich Webler, eds., *Fürsorge als persönliche Hilfe. Festgabe für Prof. Dr. Christian Jasper Klumker* (Berlin, 1929), pp. 151–58, reprinted in Friedeberg/Polligkeit, *Das Reichsgesetz für Jugendwohlfahrt*, pp. 58ff.

[16] *Materialien zum Reichsjugendwohlfahrtsgesetz*, pp. 28ff., "Bericht über die Mitgliederversammlung und Konferenz der Deutschen Zentrale für Jugendfürsorge," *Die Jugendfürsorge* 15:3 (July/September 1920), pp. 55–59, Klumker, "Jugendamt und Berufsvormundschaft," *ZfA* 20:1–3 (January–March 1919), pp. 9ff., and Klumker, "Reichsjugendwohlfahrtsgesetz. Ein Wort in letzter Stunde," *Kommunale Praxis* 22 (1922), pp. 377–80.

[17] Gründler, *Stenographische Berichte über die Sitzungen des II. Landtags von Thüringen*, 25. Sitzung (January 12, 1922), p. 802. See also Wachenheim, "Die Demokratisierung der Wohlfahrtspflege," *AW* 4:13–14 (1929), pp. 438–39, and Adolph Hoffmann, *Verhandlungen des preußischen Landtages*, 22. Sitzung (May 22, 1919), col. 1676. The socialist attempt to secularize public school-

to the Progressives, the Social Democrats argued that the state, rather than societal organizations, bore primary responsibility for the welfare of every member of society, and, while the Progressives hoped to anchor the role of voluntary welfare firmly in the youth welfare law, Kurt Löwenstein, the leading USPD educational reformer, called for the establishment of a genuinely public national youth authority (*ein wirklich öffentlich-rechtliches, behördlich gesichertes Reichsjugendamt*) which would represent the general will and thus transcend the particular, frequently antidemocratic views represented by voluntary welfare.[18]

At the other end of the political spectrum, the draft of the RJWG did little to ease the Catholic insistence upon the primacy of familial and religious concerns in youth welfare. The efforts by the Caritasverband to defend its position helped crystallize a new Catholic notion of subsidiarity which was to greatly influence the shape of the German welfare system in both the Weimar Republic and, after 1945, the Federal Republic. While the traditional notion of subsidiarity had simply meant that the individual had to exhaust all of his or her resources before becoming eligible for public assistance, the new doctrine maintained that the priority of voluntary, confessional welfare was rooted in the order of creation itself because the family represented a complete society which preceded the existence of all other forms of society and whose rights and obligations were prior to those of the state. Children must, therefore, remain subject to the authority of their fathers until they learn to discipline and control their free will.[19] These arguments were further developed in the 1929 encyclical "The Christian Education of Youth," which stated that "the family holds directly from the creator the mission and hence the right to educate the offspring, a right inalienable because inseparably joined to the strict obligation, a right anterior to any right whatever of civil society and of the state, and therefore inviolable on the part of any power on earth." Civil society had the duty to protect and to foster, "but by no means to absorb the family and the individual, or to substitute itself for them."[20] Building on these doctrinal pronouncements, Catholic charity reformers argued that Catholic charitable associations represented a new form of sociation which had emerged as industrialization had undermined the function of the family and that, therefore, in those cases of seriously impaired families, these associations represented an extension of the family and, as such, also enjoyed rights which were prior to the existence of the state and which could not be infringed upon or abridged by public authority. Should parents prove unable to fulfill their obligations toward their children, it was the right and the duty of the Church and its charitable organizations to step in and fill this gap

---

ing was one of the major points of conflict within the Weimar coalition, and the controversy hardened the battle lines over control over juvenile socialization even before debate began on the RJWG.

[18] *Verhandlungen des Reichstags*, 226. Sitzung (June 14, 1922), pp. 7801–6.

[19] "The Condition of Labor," *Five Great Encyclicals* (New York, 1939), pp. 6–7.

[20] "The Christian Education of Youth," *Five Great Encyclicals*, pp. 37–68, citations pp. 45, 48.

because the primary community within which the family existed was the religious community, not the sovereign nation-state.[21]

The Caritasverband was especially worried about the proposed Reich regulation of statutory guardianship, which one member of the organization characterized as a socialist idea and the first step toward the "communalization of the child."[22] Cardinal Adolph Bertram (the head of the Fulda bishop's conference) insisted that the very idea was unacceptable because it automatically granted the youth welfare office—which, by its nature as a state institution, was incapable of insuring the religious education of its charges—guardianship over all out-of-wedlock children. However, Neuhaus argued that the best way to secure the religious education of these children was not to oppose statutory guardianship, but rather to increase the number of Catholic social workers working within the youth welfare offices.[23]

Although the Caritasverband insisted that the rights of family and church could only be protected if the law placed strict limits upon the scope of state welfare activity, Karl Neundörfer, the director of the Caritasverband in Mainz and one of the most influential Catholic welfare experts, pointed out that the programmatic declaration of a child's right to education could be interpreted as supporting the radical socialist desire to communalize public life and destroy the family. There was nothing in the text of the law which could prevent public welfare offices from interpreting this right in such a way that most families would be incapable of fulfilling their obligation to their children. The failure of the law to place strict limitations on state intervention into family life raised the specter of educational communism, and Neundörfer lamented that the only effective barrier to such an overextension of state activity "appears to be our financial distress."[24] Initially, Catholic welfare activists were bitterly divided over whether they should participate in the drafting of the law or, as Neuhaus phrased the problem, "abandon everything to those who have made the revolution?"[25] The attitude of the Commission members toward the law was largely determined by a pragmatic assessment of whether Catholic interests would best be served through national or state youth welfare legislation. Commission members from more conservative states, such as Bavaria, continued to favor state legislation. Constantin Noppel, the Caritasverband director in Munich, pointed to Bavarian legislation which he hoped would "destroy the red domination of communal government."[26] Gradually, however, most of the commission members came to favor cooperation with the socialists, providing that they were able

[21] Constantin Noppel, "Zurück zur Familie!" *Stimmen der Zeit* 100 (1921), pp. 161–70.

[22] Wolff in *Caritaskommission* I, p. 63.

[23] Neuhaus, "Im Auftrag des Herrn Präsidenten Marx. . . . [to Bertram]" (June 4–5, 1922), ADCV 319.4 E.II.6.

[24] Neundörfer, "Widerstreitende Mächte im Reichsgesetz für Jugendwohlfahrt," in Joseph Beeking, ed., *Das Reichsgesetz für Jugendwohlfahrt und die Caritas* (Freiburg, 1925), pp. 51–54, and Caritasverband, *Denkschrift*, p. 5.

[25] *Caritaskommission* II, p. 42.

[26] Ibid., p. 20.

to win those concessions which they considered necessary to protect their own vital interests.

Within the Reichstag committee, the bourgeois and confessional parties were united in their opposition to the radical left, and they agreed that the autonomy of voluntary welfare could best be secured by specifying that, if the parents were unable to fulfill their duties toward the child, public welfare would act *only if* voluntary welfare failed to meet the educational needs of the child and would intervene "without detriment to the collaborative work of voluntary charity."[27] However, the hope that potential abuses of state power could be forestalled in this manner was severely undermined by the ambiguity of those passages of the text regulating the relations between public and voluntary welfare, and the Caritasverband demanded changes in several key provisions of the draft. The Caritasverband insisted that §5, which permitted Reich or local government to assign additional responsibilities to the youth welfare offices, be eliminated because it feared that this article could provide a carte blanche for the limitless expansion of public welfare. These fears were shared by other voluntary welfare organizations, and this paragraph was eventually deleted by the Reichstag committee. These organizations were also concerned about §7, which required the youth welfare offices to promote, support as far as possible, and collaborate with voluntary welfare organizations while respecting their autonomy. They were worried because it was unclear as to whether public welfare officials could themselves establish and administer social programs or whether they could only do so if societal welfare was unable or unwilling to act. In plenary debate, the Reichstag ultimately eliminated the qualifier "as far as possible" and added a new clause requiring the youth welfare office to draw upon voluntary welfare and involve these organizations in the office's work. These two changes substantially strengthened the position of voluntary welfare, though they did not definitively resolve the problem. Lastly, §11 permitted the youth welfare offices to delegate specific tasks to voluntary welfare, but did not require them to do so. This article remained unchanged during the drafting of the law, and it generated substantial controversy through the end of the decade.

However, all of the conflicts raised by the RJWG were condensed in §10, which regulated the composition and authority of the governing body of the youth welfare offices, and the willingness of the Center Party to support the law depended on its success in winning substantial revisions of the draft version of this article. The initial draft simply stated that the youth welfare offices were to have a board of directors and an advisory council, but left it up to the states to determine their composition and authority. The Caritasverband suspected that the creation of two separate bodies was a socialist trick to force the Catholics

---

[27] This formulation was chosen because it appeared to reserve a role for voluntary welfare without going so far as to state categorically that the involvement of voluntary welfare was itself adequate to satisfy the right to education and thus preclude the necessity of intervention by public welfare. Such a position would have been unacceptable to the Social Democrats.

out of the policy-making board of directors and relegate them to a powerless advisory council.[28]

The Caritasverband was not the only voluntary organization which felt that its autonomy—even its existence—was threatened by the original wording of §10. The experts' committee also insisted that voluntary welfare could only avoid being squeezed out by public welfare if it were guaranteed representation in the policy-making body of the youth welfare office. It recommended that the advisory council be eliminated and that at least 2/5 of the seats on the board of directors be reserved for the representatives of voluntary welfare; the remaining seats were to be filled at the discretion of local government, with the proviso that doctors, clergy, and representatives of religious organizations who might be appointed by local authorities occupy only the remaining seats so that these official appointments could not be used to reduce the influence of voluntary welfare representatives in these bodies.[29] The experts' committee also wanted to insure that municipal government did not appoint people without adequate practical youth welfare experience, because the members regarded this as the best means of forestalling the politicization of youth welfare by the Social Democrats. Also, a number of amendments were proposed in the Reichstag committee to insure that the voluntary charity organizations active in a district could not be arbitrarily excluded from the youth welfare office.[30] Although some members wanted to reserve as many as 2/3 of the seats on the board of directors for voluntary charity, such proposals were patently unacceptable to local government, which could hardly be expected to fund the youth welfare office without having any control over the way in which these monies were spent, and the Reichstag eventually settled on a formula, according to which 2/5 of the non-official members of the board of directors would be reserved for voluntary welfare.[31]

The municipal officials who were appointed to the board, which was to be chaired by the mayor, generally included the director of the youth welfare office, the district physician, a judge from the local juvenile court, and the district school supervisor. Catholic, Protestant, and, if necessary, Jewish clergy were guaranteed seats on the board, though they were not to be considered as representatives of voluntary welfare. Those seats which were to be filled by official appointment were generally distributed in proportion to the relative strength of the different parties represented in the local government. Although the confessional welfare organizations were concerned about this provision, it was simply impossible to eliminate the influence of local parties in the youth welfare office.

The greatest fear of the Caritasverband was that public officials would simply not assign it any cases and that it would thus be marginalized and left to

---

[28] *Caritaskommission* II, p. 24.
[29] Polligkeit/Eiserhardt, *Denkschrift*, pp. 13–14.
[30] Aktenstück Nr. 3959, Anträge 18, 63, 166.
[31] *Caritaskommission* I, p. 76.

'ay slowly."[32] In Mainz, Neundörfer complained, the public youth office had not assigned the Caritasverband any preventive supervision ᴗes in the preceding six months, and he insisted that "we have to participate in communal government. We have to have a voice. We achieve this through the law."[33] In view of these concerns, voluntary welfare came to regard the law as an important achievement precisely because it legitimated the public role of voluntary welfare and guaranteed its representation in the youth welfare offices.[34] As one member of the Caritasverband pointed out, in the long run, it was impossible to govern against both the Catholics and the Protestants, and, as long as the individual confessional organizations were well organized and willing to cooperate with one another, the law would serve to protect vital Catholic interests.[35]

These revisions made the final version of the law far more palatable to the Catholics than the original draft. The cumulative effect of these changes was to transform the original text, whose purpose was to create a public youth education and socialization system, into a law which protected voluntary welfare against the expansive ambitions of public youth welfare officials and which institutionalized the public status and function of voluntary welfare, whose activity was, henceforth, to be actively supported and subsidized by local government. With some justice, Neuhaus could report that events had shown that active participation in the drafting of the law had been the right decision: "If we had rejected collaboration because in principle we could not work together with the Social Democrats on a law which touched upon cultural questions, things would have become very grim for us."[36]

But these same revisions had so deeply alienated so many of the original liberal and socialist supporters of the bill, and the coalition supporting the final version had become so fragile that any additional demands or delays would upset the entire deal. Progressive reformers in Hamburg, Frankfurt, and Nuremberg opposed the final version of the law for several reasons. It weakened many of the key provisions regarding public guardianship and maintained the principle of individual guardianship—which the church charities argued could alone insure that guardians were of the same confession as their wards—and the position of the more conservative guardianship judges who were responsible for enforcing these guarantees.[37]

Already in May, one prominent Catholic charity reformer reported that he had been sounded out by someone whom he presumed to be acting on behalf of Luppe and his "radical wing" in the Städtetag about whether the Caritasverband would be willing to drop the law.[38] The enthusiasm of the Social Democrats was

---

[32] Ibid., p. 18.
[33] *Caritaskommission* III, p. 32.
[34] *Caritaskommission* II, p. 17, and Neundörfer, "Widerstreitende Mächte," p. 71.
[35] *Caritaskommission* II, pp. 52, 46.
[36] Ibid., p. 61.
[37] Neuhaus, "Im Auftrag des Herrn Präsidenten Marx. . . . [to Bertram]."
[38] Albert Lenné to Zillken (May 12, 1922), ADCV 319.4 E.II.6.

so markedly dampened by the revisions of the original draft that Juchacz confidentially asked Neuhaus whether she would have believed it possible to achieve all of the concessions contained in the final version.[39] Even Johannes Straubinger, the Caritasverband director in Stuttgart, admitted that, if he were a Social Democrat, he would not vote for the law.[40] Neuhaus wrote to Bertram that it was especially important to pass the law as soon as possible because any further demands on their part would upset the agreement over statutory guardianship, which had only been reached by the slimmest of margins within the Reichstag committee.[41]

The strains between and within the parties of the Weimar coalition were evident at the final reading of the bill on June 13–14, 1922. The speeches by Juchacz, Neuhaus, and Marie-Elisabeth Lüders (a prominent bourgeois feminist who was the DDP spokeswoman in these negotiations) were colorless. They all feared that any programmatic statement would alienate the doubters within their own parties and further antagonize the opposition in the ranks of their coalition partners. Instead, they emphasized the spirit of goodwill and reconciliation which had supposedly prevailed within the Reichstag committee. Neuhaus simply reaffirmed her belief that the RJWG in no way represented the first step toward educational communism or the nationalization of voluntary welfare. Juchacz, on the other hand, pointed out that politics was the art of the possible and expressed her hope that the framework provided by the RJWG would soon be fleshed out by further legislation. Lüders, too, maintained that the law could be improved, but urged the Reichstag to pass the law and not to let the better be the enemy of the good.[42] On the other hand, KPD delegate Max Heydemann went even further than the Social Democrats, arguing that the education of the next generation and the protection of all youth was exclusively the duty of society and the state, not the family, and he complained that the proclamations of concern for the welfare of the young could be nothing more than pure hypocrisy in the mouths of the defenders of the capitalist system.[43]

Despite the intensity of Heydemann's sense of moral indignation, it was Löwenstein who provided the most insightful analysis of the final version of the law. Löwenstein's comments gave expression to the traditional resentment of the Social Democrats toward voluntary welfare, whose mere existence reflected the contradictions of bourgeois society. Since, by its very nature, voluntary welfare obscured and reinforced those relations of domination which made its own existence possible, youth welfare could only be genuinely fruitful if it bore a public character and was based on a recognized public right. While the Catho-

---

[39] *Caritaskommission* II, p. 3, and Neuhaus, "Im Auftrag des Herrn Präsidenten Marx. . . . [to Cardinal Bertram]."

[40] *Caritaskommission* II, pp. 46–47.

[41] Neuhaus, "Im Auftrag des Herrn Präsidenten Marx. . . . [to Bertram]."

[42] *Verhandlungen des Reichstags* 225. Sitzung (June 13, 1922), pp. 7786–89, and 226. Sitzung (June 14, 1922), pp. 7806–10.

[43] *Verhandlungen des Reichstags* 226. Sitzung (June 14, 1922), pp. 7812–15.

lics hoped to use their political influence to protect their vision of authoritarian, familial education and insure the reproduction of their antidemocratic culture, Löwenstein argued that the creation of a public welfare system, which was built upon democratic values, promoted the spirit of cooperative self-help, and bore primary responsibility for juvenile socialization, was the precondition for the promotion of democratic values *by* the welfare system. "What we want," Löwenstein demanded, "is that public institutions remain under public, political control." The state was itself, he continued, nothing other than the sum of the political parties, and the political principles which animated the class struggle for control of the state were also at stake in the debate over youth welfare reform. Unfortunately, the crossfire between the confessional parties and secular conservatives had completely altered the original intent of the law and transformed the RJWG from a substantive to a mere framework law. All that remained of the original idea of a national, public youth welfare system was, Löwenstein lamented, "an agglomeration of a series of voluntary associations and confessional organizations held together by public officials." He bemoaned the fact that in the final version of §10 "the role of the youth welfare office has been taken over by a cartel of voluntary organizations under the protectorate of the government and the Reich," and he feared that this cartel "would only serve to give the confessional and other conservative organizations a firmer foundation and the financial subsidies which they also need in these times."[44]

In the end, the coalition parties managed to push their carefully stacked apple cart through the Reichstag, despite rapidly growing reservations on the part of both the Social Democrats and the Progressives.[45] Although the many revisions made in the original draft insured that voluntary welfare would have a large voice in the affairs of the local youth welfare offices, precisely which organizations would be represented on the board of directors was more a matter of political power than of law. As Neundörfer rightly suggested, the RJWG satisfied the wishes of the Social Democrats as much as it did those of the Catholics, and the compromises regarding the composition of the board of directors and the delegation of the direct provision of services displaced these bitter cultural struggles over juvenile socialization from the national level into the local welfare offices, which were to be established in the following years. Since municipal officials would be free to make policy as they saw fit, if there was any dissension among the representatives of voluntary welfare on the board of directors, Neundörfer pointed out that it was all the more important to expand and coordinate the local Caritas organizations in order to influence welfare policy at the local level and to create a mechanism for resolving the conflicts among voluntary welfare.[46]

---

[44] Ibid., pp. 7802–6. These sentiments were echoed by Mathilde Wurm (USPD) in her own speech, ibid., pp. 7816–17. Neundörfer, "Widerstreitende Mächte," p. 70, cited the evident unhappiness of the USPD with the law as evidence of the Caritasverband's success.

[45] The Reichsrat raised no objections to the version approved by the Reichstag and the law was published on July 9, *RGBl.*, I, 1922, pp. 633ff.

[46] Neundörfer, "Widerstreitende Mächte," pp. 72–75.

However, the political issues raised in the Reichstag debates did not go away. In drafting the state implementation law for the RJWG, the Prussian government proposed reserving seats in the youth welfare office for Catholic and Protestant clergy by virtue of their church office, and in the Landtag these proposals set off a bitter debate which further highlighted the growing conflict between the corporatist arrangement envisioned by organized church charity and the democratic self-government championed by the Social Democrats. While the parties on the left decried the increasing confessionalization of youth welfare and objected to the prerogatives granted to the churches, all of the other parties insisted that the active participation of the clergy was necessary for the youth welfare office to perform its pedagogical mission.[47] In contrast, the Social Democrats argued that, since youth welfare programs were funded almost exclusively by local taxes, the composition of the boards of directors of the youth welfare offices should, within the limitations imposed by the RJWG, be determined in accordance with the relative strength of the parties represented in local government. They complained that the reservation of seats for the clergy beyond that to which the confessional parties were entitled by their representation in local government violated the principle of democratic self-government and illegitimately privileged the members of the two Christian confessions in comparison with the adherents of other religions or worldviews.[48]

This conflict could not easily be resolved through parliamentary debate, and, in one form or another, it continued to dominate welfare reform debates through the end of the decade. However, in the near term, the hyperinflation and the fiscal crisis of both Reich and local government added a new dimension to this conflict, and the resistance of municipal government to the youth welfare offices as a "foreign body" in their own self-governing body politic was compounded by their increasingly evident inability to pay for the additional programs mandated by the law. While the Städtetag called for the indefinite postponement of the effective date of the RJWG, the DV demanded that the original April 1924 effective date be adhered to. However, both organizations called upon the Reich to release local government from the requirement that separate youth welfare offices be established and scale back the programs mandated by the law.[49] Not without reason, voluntary welfare regarded these proposals as a surreptitious attempt to amend the key provisions of the RJWG guaranteeing their representation in the youth welfare offices, and many members of the Caritasverband would have preferred no national youth welfare law to one in which these guarantees were weakened.[50]

On February 14, 1924, the government issued—in conjunction with several other stabilization measures which also decisively influenced the development

---

[47] See the comments by Dallmer (DNVP) in *Verhandlungen des preußischen Landtags* 305. Sitzung (March 19, 1924), cols. 21610–11.

[48] *Verhandlungen des preußischen Landtags* 306. Sitzung (March 20, 1924), cols. 21647ff.

[49] Dickinson, *The Politics of Child Welfare*, pp. 162–68.

[50] Kreutz and Beeking to Interior Ministry (December 19, 1923), and Beeking to Neuhaus (December 27, 1923), as well as Neuhaus to Beeking (January 5, 1924), ADCV 319.4 E.II.6.

of the republican welfare system—an emergency decree modifying the RJWG. The decree freed Reich, state, and local officials for the indefinite future from the obligation to implement those provisions of the law which mandated either new programs or the substantial expansion of existing programs. The decree permitted local government to assign the responsibilities of the youth welfare office to existing government agencies (such as welfare or health offices), instead of establishing them as independent bodies, and it left the establishment of state youth welfare offices to the discretion of the states. It nevertheless stipulated that the 2/5 representation of voluntary welfare had to be guaranteed within these other agencies.[51] Although youth welfare reformers had long recognized that the success of their plans depended on unifying financial support for indigent children and preventive welfare programs in a single office, the RFV— which had been issued the previous day—reversed this unification and again placed responsibility for financial support for these children in the hands of the general welfare office. These provisions virtually eliminated all hope that the youth welfare offices might become an independent, public juvenile socialization agency, as the Progressive advocates of the law had originally hoped. At the 1924 DV conference, Klumker bemoaned the fact that statutory guardianship, which provided the conceptual and organizational foundation for the educational work of the youth welfare offices, had been further weakened by the decree: "Either the youth welfare office is statutory guardianship or it is not statutory guardianship, in which case it is nothing at all."[52] Although numerous attempts were made in the second half of the decade to restore the original version of the RJWG, none of these proposals was approved.

Nevertheless, welfare reformers continued to be preoccupied by the issues raised by the RJWG: the scope and nature of state authority, the clash between, on the one hand, corporatist self-government within voluntary welfare organizations virtually free from public oversight and, on the other hand, the Social Democratic vision of direct democratic control over such activity, and the dispute over the substantive values which were to guide state intervention in the social sphere.[53] These unresolved conflicts also cast a long shadow over the youth welfare offices which were being established in 1924–25, and in the welfare system, as in the political system itself, the deep and often unbridgeable cleavages within the German polity fueled that search—which will be examined in chapter 6—for alternatives to parliamentary democracy.

---

[51] *RGBl.* 1924, I, pp. 110–11.

[52] *Die Neureglung der öffentlichen Fürsorge unter dem Druck der Finanznot, SDV* N.F. 3 (1924), p. 109. See also Klumker, "Der Erziehungsgedanke im Jugendwohlfahrtsgesetz," in Ludwig Clostermann, ed., *Der Erziehungsgedanke im modernen Jugendrecht* (Bonn, 1927), pp. 29–38.

[53] See the confrontation between the Social Democrat Gottlieb Binder, Albert Lenné, and Noppel in *Die Neureglung der öffentlichen Fürsorge unter dem Druck der Finanznot, SDV* N.F. 3, (1924), pp. 112–13, 118, 128.

The New Poor and the Politics of Group Entitlements, 1919–1923

IN the postwar period, the different components of the "new poor" began to emerge as distinct social and political groups: disabled veterans and war survivors (i.e., widows, orphans, and dependent parents of soldiers killed or disabled in the war), the unemployed, and both social insurance pensioners (*Sozialrentner*) and rentiers whose financial assets had been devastated by the inflation (*Kleinrentner*).[1] During the war, eligibility for wartime welfare had been predicated on the assumption that need was directly related to the war, and this principle continued to shape welfare policy after the war. However, although the constantly accelerating inflation and the general decline in the standard of living made it increasingly difficult to credibly maintain that the need of any single individual was more directly related to the war and ill-guided state policies than that of other persons, whose need was ostensibly due to their own moral failings, the government was extremely reluctant to force these new poor to turn to municipal poor relief. Consequently, as more and more social groups were drawn into the inflationary whirlpool, local and, later, national government initially responded in an ad hoc manner by establishing special social welfare programs (*Sonderfürsorge*) which were means-tested, but which built upon the preventive, therapeutic principles of prewar social relief and wartime welfare programs.

The benefits granted to the new poor were never sufficient to enable these groups to maintain their prewar social status and standard of living, much less to meet their demands for compensation, and the increases in the level of public assistance granted to these persons constantly lagged behind the spiraling cost of living. Nevertheless, between the revolution and the hyperinflation, the political mobilization of the new poor and the formation of organized groups to represent their interests played an important catalytic role in the development of the German welfare system. The competition among the different groups of the new poor to secure benefits comparable to those provided to disabled veterans and war survivors—the most privileged groups of public assistance recipients—was part of the ongoing struggle to redistribute the costs of the war, and it led to a constant escalation of political rhetoric which helped give public life in the early years of the Republic its characteristic shrillness.

---

[1] The question of unemployment relief and the creation of an unemployment insurance in the Weimar Republic has recently been treated in three studies and will only be dealt with in the present work in passing. See Peter Lewek, *Arbeitslosigkeit und Arbeitslosenversicherung in der Weimarer Republik 1918–1927* (= *VSWG* Beiheft 104, 1992), Karl Christian Führer, *Arbeitslosigkeit und die Entstehung der Arbeitslosenversicherung in Deutschland, 1902–1927* (Berlin, 1990).

The political mobilization of the new poor in these years contributed to the collapse of the system which had been created to meet their needs, but which was hopelessly overburdened—fiscally, politically, administratively—by the hyperinflation. In turn, though, this collapse provided further support to Progressive and Social Democratic calls for the consolidation of these specialized social welfare programs into a general, unitary welfare system based on preventive, therapeutic principles and their own need-based, work-centered vision of social citizenship. Progressive and Social Democratic welfare reformers argued that such a reform would enable them to extend the benefits of innovative social welfare programs to the hundreds of thousands of persons whose economic existence had been destroyed by the war and the inflation, but who, for various reasons, were not eligible for these programs. On the other hand, the beneficiaries of these specialized welfare programs feared that such a general welfare system would simply be municipal poor relief by another name, and they demanded the retention of these programs, whose higher level of benefits and freedom from the political disabilities and social stigma which accompanied the receipt of general municipal welfare were predicated on the ostensible connection between their need and the economic consequences of the war. However, despite the opposition to these Progressive and Social Democratic reform plans, the efforts by the various parties to extend the benefits of these specialized welfare programs to more and more of the newly impoverished groups ultimately obscured the very distinctions upon which these programs were based.

DISABLED VETERANS AND WAR SURVIVORS

The first major social welfare program established after the revolution was the one for disabled veterans and war survivors, the politically most sensitive group of the new poor.[2] Although the Reich had insisted throughout the war that social services for disabled veterans and war survivors was the responsibility of local government and voluntary welfare, in a decree issued on February 8, 1919, the Reich government finally assumed responsibility for these programs and extended into peacetime the nationwide network of state and district welfare bureaus (*Fürsorgestellen*), which had been established during the war to coordinate social services for war widows and orphans. These *Fürsorgestellen* were to remain distinct from local poor relief offices.[3] The *Fürsorgestellen* were re-

---

[2] These laws and the subsequent implementation guidelines and amendments are reprinted in Ernst Behrend/Helene Stranz-Hurwitz, eds., *Wohlfahrtsgesetze des Deutschen Reichs und Preußens*, 2 vols. (Berlin, 1923–25), I:5ff. and I:102ff. On welfare for disabled veterans and survivors, see Robert Whalen, *Bitter Wounds: German Victims of the Great War, 1914–1939* (Cornell University Press, 1984), and Christoph Sachße/Florian Tennstedt, *Geschichte der Armenfürsorge in Deutschland* 3 vols. (Kohlhammer, 1980–92), II:89ff.

[3] *RGBl.*, 1919, I, pp. 187–90, and Direktor Kießling, "Die Reichsverordnung vom 8. Februar 1919 über die soziale Kriegsbeschädigten- und Kriegshinterbliebenenfürsorge," in *Künftige Ziele der sozialen Fürsorge* (Frankfurt, 1919), pp. 38–46. However, the Reich government did not as-

quired to set up advisory councils composed of representatives of employers, workers, voluntary welfare, and organizations of disabled veterans and war survivors. Disabled veterans and war survivors were given the right to participate in the formulation of welfare policy, and their representatives were to make up at least half of the membership of the advisory council. At the national level, the wartime Reich Committee for Welfare for Wounded and Disabled Veterans (*Reichsausschuß der Kriegsbeschädigten- und Kriegsbehindertenfürsorge*) was integrated into the Labor Ministry, which assumed responsibility for military pensions when the War Ministry was dismantled in accordance with the Versailles treaties. The Reich Committee had the right to approve guidelines governing the administration of these new welfare programs and advise the Labor Ministry on issues relating to the welfare of disabled veterans and war survivors.[4]

There were seven major organizations representing disabled veterans and war survivors, and their representation in the Reich Committee was proportional to their membership.[5] In addition to their mutual antipathies, these organizations also accused the Labor Ministry of failing to involve the Reich Committee in a timely manner in the formulation of these policies. While these organizations suggested that the Reich Committee be given a status comparable to that of the Reich Economic Council, the Labor Ministry insisted that both the Committee and the advisory councils of the welfare bureaus were nonpartisan working groups, not political bodies, and that they should not be used as forums for promoting the interests of either their organizations or of any political party.[6]

The material provisions of the social welfare programs for war victims were spelled out by the Military Pensions Law (*Reichsversorgungsgesetz*, RVG), which was passed on May 12, 1920.[7] In Germany pensions for disabled veterans were determined by economic and fiscal considerations to a greater extent

---

sume legal responsibility for the cost of these welfare programs until May 1920, when the Reichstag passed a law eliminating Reich subsidies for local wartime welfare programs, which were to be dismantled and shifted to the *Fürsorgestellen*. *RGBl.*, 1920, I, pp. 1066–67. The Reich paid all of the program costs and 80% of the administrative costs.

[4] The *Reichsausschuß* was composed of representatives of the major, nationwide organizations of disabled veterans and war survivors, the heads of the state *Fürsorgestellen*, the *Ludendorff-Spende*, and the National Foundation for War Survivors, as well as representatives of the major welfare organizations.

[5] These organizations included the *Reichsbund der Kriegsbeschädigten und Kriegshinterbliebenen* (SPD, 13 seats), the *Zentralverband Deutscher Kriegsbeschädigten und Kriegshinterbliebenen* (Hirsch-Duncker, 5 seats), the *Kyffhäuser Bund* (conservative, 4 seats), the *Einheitsverband der Kriegsbeschädigten und Kriegshinterbliebenen Deutschlands* (liberal, 4 seats), *Internationaler Bund der Opfer des Krieges und der Arbeit* (KPD, 4 seats), the *Deutscher Offiziersbund* (conservative, 2 seats), and the *Bund erblindeter Krieger* (neutral, 1 seat). *Reichsbund* to Labor Ministry (November 8, 1921), BAP RAM 8905. On the politicization of veterans, see James Diehl, "The Organization of German Veterans, 1917–1919," *AfS* 11 (1971), pp. 141–84, and Whalen, *Bitter Wounds*, pp. 95ff.

[6] Minutes of the *Reichsausschuß* meetings (July 9, 1920), BAP RAM 8906 and (March 2–3, 1921), BAP RAM 8907, pp. 5ff.

[7] *RGBl.*, 1920, I, pp. 989–1019.

than in other countries through the graduation of pensions according to the degree of disability and the partial replacement of schematic monetary payments by individualized medical treatment and social services, including occupational rehabilitation and training, which had been provided for by the February 1919 decree.[8] Although the disruption of the economy and the massive costs of reconstruction provided the impetus for this linkage, the integration of therapeutic welfare programs into the military pension system was nevertheless regarded as an indispensable means for helping disabled veterans regain their economic independence, maintain that social position which they could have been expected to occupy had they not been injured, and again become productive members of society. It was this innovation—which was praised by welfare reformers—which integrated pension programs for disabled veterans and war survivors into the broad network of therapeutic social service programs which had been created since the war.[9]

At the beginning of 1920, there were an estimated 1,537,000 disabled veterans and 1,945,000 war survivors in Germany.[10] During the course of 1920, the number of disabled veterans eligible for military pensions was reduced by some 262,000 by giving a lump-sum settlement to all veterans with a disability of less than 10%. The government repeated this process in 1923 for all those veterans who were less than 25% disabled in the hope that this step would decrease the total costs of the pension system. This reduced the number of veterans receiving pensions by an additional 553,000. However, in 1924 there were still more than 720,000 veterans entitled to military pensions and related social services.[11]

While the graduation of pensions according to the degree of disability was designed to compensate for the reduced ability to work, this scheme did not take account of individual differences in earnings, and special provisions were made for persons who had suffered severe injuries—such as the loss of a leg— but whose ability to work had not been impaired. Although there was broad support for a unitary pension scale, the RVG provided for a 25% supplement to

---

[8] Michael Geyer, "Ein Vorbote des Wohlfahrtsstaates. Die Kriegsopferversorgung in Frankreich, Deutschland und Großbritannien nach dem Weltkrieg," *GuG* 9:2 (1983), pp. 230–77. One of the greatest sources of discontent among veterans was the official determination of the disability assigned to specific wounds. This "*Knochentax*" specified that the loss of an arm or leg entailed a 50% disability, the loss of a lower leg or arm 40%, facial mutilation 20–50%, etc.

[9] Polligkeit, "Renten- und Fürsorgeprinzip als Grundlagen der Reform der Militär-Versorgungsgesetzgebung," in Deutscher Verein, ed., *Gekürzter Bericht über die Tagung des Fachausschusses für städtisches Fürsorgewesen am 13. Oktober 1919* (n.p., n.d.), pp. 4–11.

[10] *Drucksachen des Reichstags, Denkschrift über das Versorgungswesen* (April 5, 1923), I. Wahlperiode, Aktenstück Nr. 5725, p. 6613, and "Die Zahl der Kriegsbeschädigten und Kriegshinterbliebenen in Deutschland," *WuS* 5 (1925), pp. 28–30.

[11] "Die Zahl der versorgungsberechtigten Kriegsbeschädigten und Kriegshinterbliebenen Deutschlands im Mai 1932," *Reichsarbeitsblatt* II (Nichtamtlicher) Teil 12:21 (July 1932), pp. 287–91. There were also approximately 1,150 disabled women war veterans, primarily nurses who had contracted serious diseases treating the wounded.

the basic pension for persons who before the war had worked in an occupation requiring substantial knowledge or skills, and this supplement was increased to 50% for those persons who had occupied positions of special responsibility and authority. The guidelines permitted the *Fürsorgestellen* to provide long-term support in those cases where pensions and additional earnings did not enable disabled veterans to satisfy their basic needs, and they also stipulated that, as far as possible, war victims should not have to depend on municipal poor relief, except in those cases of long-term dependence which was not directly related to the war. Although these guidelines for the administration of the RVG stated that the prewar social status of the pensioners was to be taken into account, they also emphasized that the interests of these veterans would have to be balanced against those of the rest of society and that benefits would also have to reflect the general decline in the standard of living since the war.[12] This decision to base pensions on civilian social status and income, as well as the degree of disability, rather than military rank, which had been the case before the war, was one of the clearest indicators of the extent to which the industrialization of warfare and the massive mobilization of society had undermined the autonomy of the professional military caste in Germany. The RVG emphasized that even disabled veterans were obligated to work, and their pensions were not so generous that they could escape this obligation if they did not have private resources. This work obligation was complemented by the April 6, 1920, law on the employment of severely disabled veterans, which took steps to insure that positions were available for both these persons and—against the opposition of some veterans groups—workers who had been disabled by industrial accidents.[13]

The RVG also granted pensions to the widows, orphans, and dependent parents of men who had been disabled or killed in the war.[14] In October 1924, approximately 365,000 war widows, 962,000 half orphans, 65,000 full orphans, and a total of 194,000 dependent parents were receiving public support through the military pension system.[15] Widows were only entitled to 30% of the pension to which the deceased would have been entitled if he had been completely disabled. This was raised to 50% if the woman was unable to work, if child raising prevented her from working, or if she was over fifty.[16] These pensions were set at such a low level to encourage these women to remarry, and thus reduce the Reich pension costs, and to provide themselves and their children with a source of paternal authority. Approximately 40% of these war widows

---

[12] Behrend/Stranz-Hurwitz, eds., *Wohlfahrtsgesetze*, I:136.

[13] *RGBl.*, 1920, I, pp. 458–64, and the minutes of the *Reichausschuß* meeting (January 24, 1922), BAP RAM 8907.

[14] Minutes of the *Reichausschuß* meeting (February 18, 1920), BAP RAM 8906.

[15] "Die Zahl der versorgungsberechtigten Kriegsbeschädigten und Kriegshinterbliebenen Deutschlands im Mai 1932," p. 289.

[16] In 1928, 10.5% of these widows were considered capable of supporting themselves, 72.1% had young children to care for, and 17.1% were over 50. Franz Rappenecker, *Das Problem der Fürsorge für die Kriegsopfer* (dissertation, Münster, 1928), p. 33.

remarried between 1919 and 1924; thereafter, the number remained constant at about 360,000.[17] If these widows married a German man, they were entitled to a lump sum settlement equal to three times their annual pension. Half orphans were entitled to a pension amounting to 15% of the pension to which their fathers would have been entitled, and this was raised to 25% for children who had lost both parents. The pension granted to out-of-wedlock children whose fathers had died in the war was only half of that granted to legitimate children. Parents of those men who had been killed during the war were also entitled to small pensions if they were needy and unable to support themselves. However, war survivors did not have a right to therapeutic welfare programs, especially medical care. This created widespread problems because few of these women were covered by the health insurance funds, and they generally could not afford to pay for medical care for themselves and their children. The Labor Ministry was reluctant to extend such benefits because of the difficulty in establishing a causal connection between the war and many of the diseases and ailments from which these persons suffered and suggested, instead, that the needs of war widows could be met through supplementary welfare benefits provided by local authorities or voluntary welfare.[18]

The RVG required the immediate creation of a massive bureaucracy to determine—for every occupation and profession—the degree of disability resulting from the myriad of possible injuries and the appropriate forms of medical treatment and vocational rehabilitation. This placed a great deal of power in the hands of doctors and welfare experts and created abundant cause for discontent among the beneficiaries. In addition, not even the pensions granted to disabled veterans and war survivors, which had originally been set at a low level, were immune to the ravages of the inflation. By January 1922 their real value had already been so eroded that pensions for completely disabled veterans were less than two-thirds of the officially established poverty line, while pensions for other beneficiaries were wholly inadequate even as a supplement to other income.[19] The declining value of these pensions, as well as the fact that even the most poorly paid public officials were better supported by the state than disabled veterans and war widows, inevitably generated a great deal of hostility toward the government. On June 23, 1923, the RVG was finally amended. Although the revision adjusted pensions to the rising cost of living, it also contained several provisions whose effect was to reduce both the level of benefits for disabled veterans and war survivors and the total costs of the pension sys-

[17] Whalen, *Bitter Wounds*, pp. 109–10.

[18] Minutes of the *Reichausschuß* meeting (August 6, 1919), BAP RAM 8906. The systematic provision of medical care for war survivors did not begin until 1921 and was paid for out of special funds allocated for youth welfare for war orphans. A 1922 survey confirmed that a substantial portion of the cost of social welfare programs for survivors was attributable to medical treatment, hospital care, and convalescence. See Dorothea Hirschfeld in minutes of the *Reichsausschuß* (January 24, 1922), BAP RAM 8907.

[19] See the figures cited in Whalen, *Bitter Wounds*, p. 148.

tem. Consequently, in many instances municipal welfare still had to pay part of the cost of supporting these persons.

From early 1921 onward, the question of the relation between the social welfare programs for disabled veterans and war survivors and those general welfare programs sponsored by municipal government moved into the center of public debate. While veterans groups frequently complained that their privileged status was not adequately guaranteed and feared that their right to representation and participation would be eliminated if their programs were consolidated with other social welfare programs,[20] Progressive and Social Democratic welfare reformers called for the merging of these programs into the general welfare system in order to insure that all of the indigent population would benefit from the innovations contained in these laws. They called on veterans groups to abandon their exclusivism and recognize that persons who had been rendered indigent due to accident, disease, or death of a family member were just as deserving of public assistance as those whose indigence was the direct result of the war.[21] However, before the end of 1922 neither financial pressures on the city nor the arguments of Progressive reformers had generated enough momentum to overcome the staunch resistance of these war victims.

SOZIALRENTNER

Before the war, assets such as stocks, bonds, mortgages, savings accounts, and insurance policies and annuities, had made up approximately one-half of Germany's total wealth, and income from these assets accounted for approximately one-sixth of the nation's total income. By 1924, approximately 90% of the real value of these assets had been destroyed by the hyperinflation. The social effects of this inflationary redistribution and expropriation of wealth were complex and traumatic. This wealth had been distributed among all strata of German society from working-class social insurance pensioners, via middle-class homeowners and mortgage holders, to the plutocratic elite, and much of the

[20] The *Reichsbund* did not reject the idea outright, but believed that such a step was impossible until the level of municipal services had itself been improved substantially. Hirschfeld, "Die Ueberleitung der sozialen Kriegsbeschädigten- und Kriegshinterbliebenenfürsorge auf die gemeindliche Wohfahrtspflege," *SPr* 32:11 (1923), cols. 231–34, Lorenz, "Die Kriegsbeschädigten- und Kriegshinterbliebenenfürsorge an einem Wendepunkt," *SPr* 32:32 (1923), cols. 748–51, Ernst Barth, "Kriegsbeschädigten- und Kriegshinterbliebenenfürsorge oder Armenpflege?" *SPr* 32:37 (1923), cols. 834–37, and Lade, "Zur Verschmelzung der Kriegsopferfürsorge mit der allgemeinen Wohlfahrtspflege," *SPr* 32:48 (1923), cols. 942–44.

[21] Simon, "Wohlfahrtsamt und Armenamt," *SPr* 30:16 (1921), cols. 420–22 and her comments in Minutes of the *Reichausschuß* meeting (March 1–3, 1921), BAP RAM 8905, Gerda Simons, "Entwicklungstendenzen der Wohlfahrtspflege," *SPr* 30:4 (January 26, 1921), cols. 81–84, Wölz, "Lehren der Kriegsbeschädigten- und Kriegshinterbliebenenfürsorge für die Gestaltung der allgemeinen Wohlfahrtspflege," *SPr* 30:43–44 (1921), cols. 1105–11, 1140–43, and Heimerich in *Verhandlungen des Deutschen Vereins*, SDV N.F. 2 (1921), pp. 24–25.

wealth which was lost by creditors was acquired by debtors belonging to the same social classes.[22]

The process of the inflation and the churning of prewar class structures created two new, distinct sociological groups who were increasingly dependent upon public assistance because the inflation was rapidly eroding the real value of the assets from which they drew their income and who were increasingly well mobilized to insure that the state took action to meet their needs. On the one hand, there were the *Sozialrentner*, who lived on pensions from the disability insurance funds, their widows and dependents, as well as the much smaller number of beneficiaries of the old-age and accident insurance funds. The substantial assets of the disability insurance funds were simply annihilated, and the previously acquired pension rights supported by these assets were largely devalued and could only be upheld by drawing upon the public purse, either in the form of Reich subsidies to the insurance funds or by shifting the burden of supporting the beneficiaries onto municipal public assistance. On the other hand, there were the *Kleinrentner*, who before the war had lived on interest from their savings, income from mortgages and other investments, and annuities. Unlike the owners of real property, the holders of financial assets were the real losers during the inflation, and, to the extent to which they lived on the income from these assets, they were economically impoverished and socially declassed. They either had to reenter the workforce or, if they were unable to work and could not depend upon their families for support, became dependent on public assistance. Although the indigence of both groups was attributable primarily to the indirect effects of the war upon public finances, the two groups had different social origins and they justified their demands for public support in different terms and with different degrees of success. The bitter debate over the precise nature of public support to be provided to these groups was an important element of the ongoing, multifaceted struggle to allocate the costs of the war, and its outcome defined one important dimension of the Weimar welfare state.

Although the *Sozialrentner* were originally eligible for unemployment relief, in May 1920 those who were more than 67 percent disabled were declared to be incapable of work, and thus ineligible for such benefits.[23] Moreover, even before the war only those persons who were completely disabled could afford to live on their pensions alone. As a result, a substantial portion of them, especially those partly disabled, had been forced to either take part-time work or low-

[22] Franz Eulenberg, "Die sozialen Wirkungen der Währungsverhältnisse," *Jahrbücher für Nationalökonomie und Statistik* 12 (1924), pp. 748–94.

[23] On the *Sozialrentner*, see Karl Christian Führer, "Für das Wirtschaftsleben 'mehr oder weniger wertlose Personen'. Zur Lage von Invaliden- und Kleinrentnern in den Inflationsjahren 1918–1924," *AfS* 30 (1990), pp. 145–80, Sachße/Tennstedt, *Geschichte der Armenfürsorge*, II:92–93, Greg Eghigian, "The Politics of Victimization: Social Pensioners and the German Social State in the Inflation of 1914–1924," *Central European History* 26:4 (1993), pp. 375–403, and David Crew, "'Wohlfahrtsbrot ist bitteres Brot': The Elderly, the Disabled and the Local Welfare Authorities in the Weimar Republic 1924–1933," *AfS* 30 (1990), pp. 217–45.

paying jobs or depend on poor relief to supplement their inadequate pensions. Moreover, by the end of the war the real value of disability pensions had already been seriously eroded by the inflation. In April 1919 Augsburg *Sozialrentner* were receiving only 78 pfennig per day, while unemployment relief benefits provided 4 marks per day, and the flooding of discharged veterans into the labor market was making it more difficult for pensioners to supplement their pensions through work, as they had done during the war.[24] While the municipalities were unable or unwilling to create special welfare programs for these pensioners, these *Sozialrentner* did everything in their power to avoid having to turn to poor relief. Local officials in many cities instituted ad hoc programs to help these pensioners, including supplements to their pensions from discretionary public funds or charitable institutions administered by the city and in-kind support. For example, Nuremberg established a special *"Mittelstandshilfe"* for the *Sozial-* and *Kleinrentner*, and many cities provided one-time allowances to help them pay off past-due rent or gas bills.[25]

The political import of the impoverishment of these pensioners became clearer with the creation of a nationwide league of local pensioner associations, the Central Association of German Invalids and Widows (*Zentralverband der Invaliden und Witwen Deutschlands*), in July 1920.[26] The Central Association, which in 1922 claimed to represent some 120,000 pensioners and their survivors, insisted that the Reich government had an obligation to support these "civil pensioners," and it demanded that the Reich establish both a special social welfare program for pensioners, comparable to that already provided for military pensioners, and an advisory council through which the *Sozialrentner* could represent their interests.[27]

In 1918, 1919, and 1920, the Reich government had ordered the disability insurance funds to provide across-the-board supplements to their pension payments in a half-hearted attempt to keep pace with the inflation, but had funded these subsidies in a way which permitted the Reich to avoid accepting direct responsibility for the welfare of the estimated 4 million disability pension recipients.[28] However, government officials were reluctant to set a precedent by establishing a special welfare program for these pensioners, and they generally argued that these persons would have to rely on municipal poor relief. The consensus among welfare reformers and municipal officials was that the needs

---

[24] Führer, "Für das Wirtschaftsleben 'mehr oder weniger wertlose Personen,'" p. 151.

[25] *Nachrichtendienst* 2 (March 1920), pp. 1–4.

[26] Prussian authorities opposed the foundation of the Central Association because they believed both that it would only increase the inefficiency within the already overfragmented welfare sector and that the interests of these pensioners were already adequately represented through the unions. Staatskommissar für Kriegswohlfahrtspflege to Zentralverband (April 11, 1921) and Hans Maier to Reichsamt für Arbeitsvermittlung, (June 29, 1921), BAP RAM 9132. In 1932, the organization claimed a membership of 300,000. Zentralverband to Labor Ministry (October 17, 1932), BAP RAM 9132. Although the Zentralverband was the largest organization representing the *Sozialrentner*, its representative monopoly was challenged by two other organizations.

[27] Zentralverband to Reich Labor Ministry (June 22 and November 26, 1921).

[28] Ernst Behrend, "Unterstützung der Kapitalkleinrentner" (August 1921), BAP RAM 9195.

of the *Sozialrentner* could best be met by improving the level of municipal welfare, and they opposed further across-the-board increases to pensions. However, they also opposed either establishing a separate welfare administrative apparatus for the *Sozialrentner* or transferring them to the *Fürsorgestellen* for war survivors because they feared that this would grate against the sensibilities of disabled veterans and their families.[29] Both local and state officials protested to Reich authorities that, under existing poor laws, they could not afford to provide these people with benefits more generous than those provided by poor relief, and in 1920 the Prussian, Saxon, and Bavarian governments all asked the Reich to take some action in order to improve the situation of the *Sozialrentner*. However, Reich officials rejected these requests, insisting that the state did not have any special obligation toward these pensioners beyond that owed to any other indigent citizens, and they continued to maintain that state and local government, and not the Reich, bore primary responsibility for assisting them, either through poor relief or supplementary municipal welfare programs.

As the mark lost an additional two-thirds of its value in the second half of 1921, the Reich was finally compelled to step in. On December 7, 1921, the Reichstag passed an emergency law which required the reluctant municipal governments to establish special assistance programs for the *Sozialrentner* which would make up the difference between the actual income of these pensioners and a minimum annual income set by the law.[30] The Reich paid 80% of the program costs, and it was expected that the 20% share to be paid by local government would be offset by a corresponding decrease in poor relief costs. However, these supplements were limited to those actually in need, thus effectively depriving those who had other sources of income of the rights established by their previous premium payments. The first 2,000 marks of outside income earned annually by these pensioners were to be excluded in determining need, as were the first 600 marks in pensions received from former employers; all benefits received from the different insurance funds were to be included. Moreover, income was calculated on a household or family—rather than individual—basis, and support which other family members were legally obligated to provide was taken into account in determining eligibility. Although this law established a direct Reich responsibility for supporting the *Sozialrentner*, the inclusion of a means test and the characterization of the law as an emergency measure were designed to limit the scope of this obligation to the subsidiary provision of supplemental public assistance (beyond that provided by municipal poor relief) while at the same time rejecting as a matter of state policy the obligation of the Reich to fully compensate these pensioners for the losses they suffered during the inflation. Municipal officials were also dissatisfied with this emergency law because the guaranteed minimum income reduced their discre-

[29] *Nachrichtendienst* 7 (October 1920), pp. 6–10, and minutes of the HADV (October 27, 1920), pp. 4–8.

[30] *RGBl.*, 1921, pp. 1533–35, and "Notstandsmaßnahmen für Sozialrentner und Kleinrentner," *Nachrichtendienst* 21 Sonderausgabe (January 1922).

tion in determining need, and they feared that the very fact of establishing a legal right would encourage pensioners who had previously avoided seeking public assistance to apply for support.

The stipulation that all family support obligations were to be considered in the determination of need also led to friction between the *Sozialrentner* and local officials, who often included such support regardless of whether these family members were actually capable of meeting this obligation, and authorities threatened to take family members to court should they refuse to provide this support.[31] Moreover, the law was also only of dubious benefit to its ostensible beneficiaries. Because it granted the right to a minimum income to qualified persons and did not take into account the cost of living in different areas, this minimum was set at a uniformly low level which lay substantially below the benefits already provided by poor relief authorities in many cities.[32] The manifest inadequacy of the promised welfare payments prompted the Saxon branch of the Central Association to attack the Reichstag for its ignorance of economic affairs or for consciously adopting "a system which is intentionally designed to destroy those persons who are permanently incapable of working." They demanded that the program be modified in a number of ways to restore their "human rights": that pensions be brought into relation with the actual cost of living and set at a level equal to one-third of the average earnings of skilled workers; that the program be financed exclusively by the Reich and the pensions distributed through the postal savings system rather than municipal welfare offices; that the obligation of children to support their parents be eliminated; that they also receive free medical treatment; and that they have consultative representation in the Reich Economic Council.[33]

However, whatever material benefits might have been provided by the December law were more than offset by the accelerating inflation, the elimination of price controls on grain in February 1922, and the discontent caused by the law itself, and in July 1922 the *Sozialrentner* relief program was completely overhauled. The primary goal of this reform was to reduce government expenditures, not to improve the position of these relief recipients, and it further eroded the rights of pension recipients. The minimum income was transformed into a maximum in the belief that many pensioners could largely support themselves through work or that they would be supported by their families. As a result, at the end of 1922, only one-third of the *Sozialrentner*—one-half in some of the larger cities—were actually receiving benefits under this program.[34]

---

[31] Richter, "Vermerk" (May 8, 1922), BAP RAM 9185, and "Niederschrift über die Besprechung der Dezernenten . . ." (February 18, 1922), BAP RAM 9184. The *Sozialrentner* argued that these provisions should be eliminated because their need was the result of government policies, not the lack of filial piety.

[32] Zentralverband to Labor Ministry (February 28, 1922), BAP RAM 9188 and Führer, "Für das Wirtschaftsleben 'mehr oder weniger wertlose Personen,'" pp. 160–61.

[33] Sächsische Invaliden-Vereinigung to Reichstag (February 2, 1922), BAP RAM 9188, and petition by Sozialinvaliden-Renter in Löwenberg (February 5, 1922), BAP RAM 9184.

[34] Führer, "Für das Wirtschaftsleben 'mehr oder weniger wertlose Personen,'" p. 161, and Sachße/Tennstedt, *Geschichte der Armenfürsorge*, II:93.

These changes drove the *Sozialrentner* to new depths of despair and their political rhetoric to new heights. The Central Association objected sharply to the Reichstag's "interminable, immiserating improvisation" and characterized the July law as "a sprawling patchwork which mocks the misery which it does not understand." They presented themselves as "victims of labor" and demanded "a genuinely social piece of legislation which, in accordance with their recognized rights, has no loopholes and guarantees that they can continue to live as human beings." They characterized the means test as a "brutal exceptional law" against their economically weaker and defenseless comrades and were deeply offended by the presumption "that in their old age they should go begging for alms from all those who owe them nothing, while the Reich barely, if at all, fulfills its contractual obligations."[35] Although the disproportion between pension benefits and the cost of living assumed grotesque dimensions as the year progressed, these exhortations to the state to insure justice to its citizens were not easily translated into concrete policies, especially in view of the fact that Labor Minister Brauns was himself convinced that the economic crisis was even making it necessary to extend the welfare principles of means testing, in-kind support, and work obligations to the social insurance system to a much greater degree than in the past.[36]

The cumulative effect of the inflation, and of the hyperinflation which began in the fall of 1922, was to expropriate the pension rights which these disabled workers had acquired through their insurance premiums. As they frantically cast about for anchors in the constantly rising oceans of currency, they focused increasingly on two firm measures of value through which to convert their moral outrage into better benefits: the gold standard and the social welfare benefits provided to war victims.[37] However, the provision of social services equal in real value to the paid premiums was out of the question, and, no matter how great or how real their need, these civil pensioners could never establish a greater claim upon public sympathies and the public purse than that of disabled veterans and war survivors. The recognition of a loosely defined right to subsidiary welfare benefits was the compromise imposed upon the *Sozialrentner* by the political and economic constraints of the period. Although tax-based welfare benefits represented an increasingly large proportion of the total assistance provided to these *Sozialrentner*, their economic situation continued to be determined primarily by their success in finding work.

---

[35] Zentralverband, "Protest an die Reichs-Regierung" (June 20, 1922), BAP RAM 9189.

[36] Brauns in Rabeling, "Uebergang des Armenwesens vom Reichsministerium des Innern auf das Reichsarbeitsministerium" (September 4, 1922), BAP RAM 9258.

[37] Zentralverband to Labor Ministry (October 26, 1922), BAP RAM 9190, and petition from an unidentified branch of the Zentralverband to the Labor Ministry (September 18, 1922), BAP RAM 9189. For the impact of the inflation on the social insurance system and the relationship between the finances of the social insurance system and those of local and Reich government, see Gerald Feldman, "The Fate of the Social Insurance System in the German Inflation, 1914–1923," in Feldman, et al., eds., *Die Anpassung an die Inflation* (Berlin, 1986), pp. 433–47.

KLEINRENTNER

While the social identity of the *Sozialrentner* derived from their previous status as wage earners, the *Kleinrentner* were a much more diffuse group. It included segments of the middle and lower middle classes who were not eligible for social insurance or the welfare programs established for the *Sozialrentner*. As a result, they found themselves in an increasingly desperate situation as the inflation destroyed the real value of the financial assets upon which they depended to support themselves. As the extent of this damage to their income and social status became clear, their demands focused on compensation and revaluation, and they never ceased to regard public assistance in any form as a temporary and unsatisfactory expedient.[38] Although the very diffuseness of the *Kleinrentner* meant that they were slower to emerge as a distinct social group and more difficult to mobilize politically, the category itself was much more flexible than that of *Sozialrentner*, and legislative attempts to define the *Kleinrentner* increasingly focused public attention on the problematic assumptions underlying the concept of war-related need and the ambiguous status of all of the special welfare programs. As the effects of the inflation penetrated deeper into the middle classes, the category was expanded *ad absurdum* until it became a general "war consequences assistance program" (*Kriegsfolgenhilfe*) for those—generally older—members of the middle classes who no longer, or who never had, worked, whose income could not keep pace with the inflation, but whose need was deemed to be qualitatively different from that of the traditional recipients of municipal poor relief.

In 1920, there were an estimated 200,000 *Kleinrentner*, 50,000 of whom belonged to the most important *Kleinrentner* organization, the German Rentiers' League (*Deutscher Rentnerbund*).[39] Despite their heterogeneity, the *Kleinrentner* perceived themselves as forming a distinct segment of the middle classes, the *Rentnerstand*. They depicted themselves as the very embodiment of the bourgeois virtues of self-reliance, saving, and self-denial, and they quickly came to stylize themselves as the quintessential victims of the inflation. In their

---

[38] All of these resentments and demands are bundled up in their "Offener Brief an den Herrn Reichsarbeitsminister," *Der Rentner* (March 1924) and "Entschädigung, Fürsorge oder Almosen? Zur gegenwärtigen sozialen Lage der deutschen Kleinrentner," *Der Rentner* (September 1924). For the legal basis of their claims, see Michael Hughes, *Paying for the German Inflation* (University of North Carolina Press, 1988).

[39] On the *Kleinrentner*, see Wilhelm Schickenberg, *Die Reichsversorgung der Kleinrentner* (Berlin, 1927), *Denkschrift zur Kleinrentnerfürsorge* (April 27, 1923), I. Wahlperiode, Reichstag Drucksache Nr. 5770, Oskar Karstedt and Heinrich Rabeling, *Die öffentliche Kleinrentnerfürsorge unter besonderer Berücksichtigung der Reichsmaßnahmen* (Berlin, 1923), Führer, "Für das Wirtschaftsleben 'mehr oder weniger wertlose Personen,'" and Robert Scholz, "'Heraus aus der unwürdigen Fürsorge'. Zur sozialen Lage und politischen Orientierung der Kleinrentner in der Weimarer Republik," in Christoph Conrad and Hans-Joachim von Kondratowitz, eds., *Gerontologie und Sozialgeschichte. Wege zu einer historischen Betrachtung des Alters* (Berlin: Deutsches Zentrum für Altersfragen, 1983), pp. 319–50.

own eyes, they were "members of the productive estates," that is, former merchants, artisans, farmers, professionals, and, especially, their widows and daughters, who had saved enough to support themselves in their old age and insure their children an appropriate education. However, the onset of the inflation entangled them in a vicious circle as the declining real value of their income forced them to dip into their capital and thus take the fatal first step down the slippery slope to irreversible poverty. They were the inevitable losers in the inflationary compromise between labor and business which helped buoy the German economy in the postwar years.[40]

The *Kleinrentner* characterized themselves as the victim of their bourgeois and patriotic virtues. During the war, they argued, they had "sacrificed everything for the Reich, their gold, their valuables, their jewelry, even their clothing and linen, on the altar of the fatherland, and thus given everything . . . which they had earned in a long, laborious life and scraped together in such a miserly manner."[41] They argued that they in turn had been sacrificed and that the products of this life of labor and self-denial destroyed by the unscrupulous politicians and agitators who had made the revolution and caused the inflation. Although there was a natural affinity between this self-image of the *Kleinrentner* and the scurrilous attacks on the republic by the DNVP, the Center Party, the SPD, and the DDP all vied for their loyalty and votes.

However, neither aspect of this "victim theory"[42] adequately captures the more ambiguous reality of the *Kleinrentner*. Contemporaries understood under *Kleinrentner* persons who before the war had enjoyed an income of 600 to 3,000 marks annually, which they derived from capital worth between 15,000 and 60,000 marks, and the large majority of *Kleinrentner* fell within these parameters.[43] The security of their income and the fact that they did not have to work secured their status as rentiers, even though their modest standard of living—often a life of genteel poverty—frequently did not surpass that of skilled workers. Most of the *Kleinrentner* were over sixty, and a large majority—75–85% by most estimates—were women who had inherited this capital. According to one survey, nearly half of the *Kleinrentner* were women without a previous occupation, either spinsters or "*Haustöchter*," who had never been engaged in paid wage labor and who survived on their modest inheritances; another quarter were either retired merchants or former female white-collar workers.[44] However, despite contemporary rhetoric, the *Kleinrentner* had generally placed most of their money in secure investments, and had sacrificed only a small proportion of their wealth for the war effort.[45] In fact, it was the size of

---

[40] See the February 1921 petition from the Rentnerbund reprinted in Karstedt and Rabeling, *Die öffentliche Kleinrentnerfürsorge*, pp. 1–2.

[41] Karstedt and Rabeling, *Die öffentliche Kleinrentnerfürsorge*, p. 11.

[42] See Schickenberg, *Die Reichsversorgung der Kleinrentner*, p. 8, for statistics which confirm this definition.

[43] Ibid.

[44] Schickenberg, "Hannover," in *Die örtliche und soziale Herkunft öffentlicher unterstützten Personen* (Leipzig, 1927), p. 101.

[45] Paul Peters, "Die Vermögens- und Wohnverhältnisse der Kleinrentner in der Stadt Hanover,"

their investments and their inability to participate in the speculative profits to be made during the period, and not their sacrifices on behalf of the war effort, which explains why the *Kleinrentner* were hit so hard by the inflation. Nevertheless, this gap between the self-image and the social reality of the *Kleinrentner* did not mean that their need was any less real, and their self-perception as upright members of the middle classes did make it unusually difficult for them to "apply for a form of public assistance which is intentionally made to resemble poor relief."[46]

While the *Kleinrentner* had been able to live a modest but independent life before the war, by early 1920 they were no longer able to keep their heads above water, and, although most older men could find some type of employment, the women who made up the majority of the *Kleinrentner* had little success in finding remunerative employment. Despite their sympathy with the plight of these older rentiers, it was legally impossible for municipal officials to regard people who still owned homes, expensive furnishings, and *objets d'art* as indigent in the sense of the poor laws, even though their actual income did not suffice to afford them even a modest standard of living. When the DV considered the problem, most members firmly rejected the idea that the wealth of these rentiers could be protected by providing them with public assistance without—as the Rentiers' League had demanded—applying a means test and encumbering this assistance with the usual obligations "since it can not be the duty of the state to permit laughing heirs to benefit at public expense." Heimerich proposed instead that these rentiers could turn over a substantial portion of their remaining capital to local government in exchange for a lifetime annuity or that local government assume responsibility for administering their property in return for a guaranteed minimum monthly income which would be composed of income from this property, payments from principal, and a municipal supplement.[47] Although these proposals were endorsed by the Städtetag, they aroused the ire of the *Kleinrentner* because they feared that to give in to these demands would mean the end of their economic autonomy and, with this, a substantial portion of their social identity.[48]

From late 1920 onward, a number of state governments began to provide subsidies to local governments to support relief programs for *Kleinrentner*.[49] However, by the fall of 1921, the needs of this group, whose number had by then increased to an estimated 400–500,000, continued to exceed the resources of state and local governments. In December of that year, the Reich government

---

Wohlfahrtswoche [Hanover] 2:26 (June 26, 1927), pp. 217–21. Of the 2,375 *Kleinrentner* in the city, most had prewar assets valued between 5,000 and 40,000 marks, and their average wealth was 32,600 marks.

[46] *Denkschrift zur Kleinrentnerfürsorge*, p. 6711.

[47] Heimerich, "Zur Frage der Gewährung von Ausgleichsunterstützungen und Sozialversicherungsrentner und Kleinkapitalrentner," *SPr* 30:4 (January 26, 1921), cols. 95–100, *Verhandlungen des Deutschen Vereins*, *SDV* N.F. 2 (1921), citation p. 24, and Gerald Feldman, *The Great Disorder* (Oxford, 1993), pp. 555–56.

[48] *Denkschrift zur Kleinrentnerfürsorge*, p. 6712.

[49] Ibid., pp. 6704ff.

finally agreed to provide 100 million marks to local government to subsidize relief programs for the *Kleinrentner* for the second half of the 1921 fiscal year. While the guidelines for the distribution of these funds basically codified existing local programs, the need to define more precisely who the *Kleinrentner* were and the nature of their rights and obligations raised some important issues. According to the final guidelines for the distribution of these monies, *Kleinrentner* were persons who before January 1920 had secured for their old age an annual income of at least 600 marks from real estate or other assets. These funds were limited to those *Kleinrentner* in need—which was defined in accordance with the unemployment and *Sozialrentner* relief laws as an annual income of less than 3,000 marks—who, because of age or the inability to find work, depended on this income. Moreover, in the original draft guidelines, the Labor Ministry had insisted that eligibility be restricted in principle to those persons who had acquired or preserved their property through their own labor, or, in the case of widows, the work of their husbands.[50] However, under pressure, the Labor Ministry agreed to expand these guidelines to include other groups: *Haustöchter* who had maintained their parents' households, persons who had devoted their lives to philanthropic activity, and persons who lived on their inheritances because mental or physical infirmities prevented them from working. This significantly broadened the scope of the law.

The Labor Ministry insisted on financing support for the *Kleinrentner* through subsidies to local government, rather than direct relief to needy *Kleinrentner*, in order to reinforce the principle that local government bore primary responsibility for supporting these persons and that it was the duty of the states and the Reich to fill the gap only if the demands of the moment exceeded the resources of local government. The guidelines also insisted that these subsidies represented loans advanced against the remaining property of these *Kleinrentner*, and they required that municipal officials obtain a lien against this property to insure that local government would be reimbursed for these expenditures when these rentiers died. However, the extent to which municipal authorities could draw on the property of these *Kleinrentner* was limited by the stipulation that they had to take into account the age, wealth, and other circumstances of these elderly persons.[51]

In May 1922, the Reich government proposed that an additional 200 million marks be appropriated for the 1922 fiscal year. The Reichstag itself increased

---

[50] Karstedt and Rabeling, both Labor Ministry officials, defended this position (*Die öffentliche Kleinrentnerfürsorge*, p. 8), arguing that the public could hardly be obligated to provide a privileged level of support to people who had never worked.

[51] Behrend, "Denkschrift über die Unterstützung notleidender Kleinrentner" (November 14, 1921), Prussian Ministry for Public Welfare to Reich Labor Ministry (December 5, 1921), and "Niederschrift über die Sitzung des Sozialausschusses . . . betr. Kleinrentner" (December 15, 1921), BAP RAM 9195. The January guidelines are reprinted in *Denkschrift zur Kleinrentnerfürsorge*, p. 6713 and "Notstandsmaßnahmen für Sozialrentner und Kleinrentner." The Rentiers' League dismissed the 100 million mark subsidy as "perfectly laughable," and insisted that only long-term support which was indexed to the inflation rate could substantially reduce the misery of the *Kleinrentner*. Rentnerbund to Labor Ministry (January 2, 1922), BAP RAM 9195.

this amount to 500 million marks. The guidelines issued in August for the distribution of these funds lowered to 500 marks the minimum income from capital required to qualify as a *Kleinrentner*, prohibited local officials from forcing these persons to alienate their property if their net worth was less than 50,000 marks, or demanding reimbursement from their estates if these rentiers were married or if they had other descendants or relatives entitled to inherit this property. Even though it fell far short of the demand for compensation, the limitation of these reimbursement requirements and the guarantee of a minimum income for eligible *Kleinrentner* went a long way toward establishing a legal entitlement to a state pension, though the accompanying obligation lay as much with local government as with the Reich.[52]

With the onset of the hyperinflation, even 500 million marks proved to be entirely inadequate, and, by the spring of 1923, the number of *Kleinrentner* had increased substantially above the estimate from the fall of 1921.[53] The subsidies provided to *Kleinrentner* were almost always lower than those provided to the *Sozialrentner*, and in many big cities they were even lower than the assistance provided by poor relief.[54] In response to proposals by both the DDP and the Center, in January 1923 the Labor Ministry submitted to the Reichstag a draft of a national law requiring local government to establish a special social welfare program for the *Kleinrentner*.[55]

The law was intended as a war consequences assistance program for those members of the middle classes who had been impoverished by the economic impact of the war. The government draft took the audacious step of expanding eligibility to include not only those persons who had actually provided for their old age before the inflation, but also those persons who had not yet managed to make such provision, but who could have been expected to provide for their own old age if they had not been prevented from doing so by the war and the inflation. The Social Democrats proposed a twofold modification of this draft. They wanted to further extend the benefits of this new program to include all those whose need was a consequence of the general economic situation. While this would have broken with the principle that certain groups were entitled to privileged treatment because their need was in some way more directly related to the war than that of the other poor, their second proposal to base benefits on need, rather than the prior possession of capital or the ostensible cause of need, reintroduced into the debate the demand for a general reform of all existing special welfare programs in accordance with the principles laid out by the Progressive and the Social Democrats.[56]

[52] These August guidelines are reprinted in *Denkschrift zur Kleinrentnerfürsorge*, pp. 6714–15.

[53] Ibid., p. 6704.

[54] *Verhandlungen des Reichstags*, 294. Sitzung (January 31, 1923), p. 9565.

[55] The following discussion is drawn from ibid., pp. 9561–76. The government draft is contained in *Denkschrift zur Kleinrentnerfürsorge*, pp. 6718–20 and the final version of the law and the accompanying guidelines are reprinted in Behrend/Stranz-Hurwitz, ed., *Wohlfahrtsgesetze*, I:199ff.

[56] Behrend, "Das Gesetz über Kleinrentnerfürsorge und seine Bedeutung für die allgemeine Reichswohlfahrtsgesetzgebung," *SPr* 32:11 (March 15, 1923), cols. 250–54.

In the Reichstag social affairs committee, the bourgeois and confessional parties opposed these Social Democratic proposals, as well as the Communist call for the creation of a social security system (*allgemeine Volksfürsorge*). However, with surprising ease, all of the parties—except the Communists— reached a compromise based on the principle that social welfare benefits should be extended to all those persons who could have been expected to provide for their own old age if they had not been prevented from doing so by forces beyond their control. The only people who were explicitly excluded from this compromise—were it to be generously interpreted in practice—were those who were eligible for other government social welfare programs and those whose indigence was due to their own "gross negligence," that is, those persons who, *even without* inflation and other consequences of the war *would not* have been able to provide for their own old age or disability and who would have depended on poor relief.

Although the Reich assumed 80% of the program costs and local government the remaining 20%, the law also stipulated that the Reich's obligation to reimburse local government was limited by the funds made available by the Reichstag. This proviso created a huge gap between the assistance obligations placed upon local government and the obligation of the Reich to reimburse local authorities and undermined to a certain degree the rights granted to this group of needy citizens by the Reichstag. In the plenary session, State Secretary in the Labor Ministry Hermann Geib insisted that the broader question of poor law and welfare reform had to be separated from emergency measures to alleviate the mass distress caused by the economic consequences of the war, and he portrayed the *Kleinrentner* law as the last link in a long chain of similar war consequences assistance programs, whose principles and benefits were gradually being brought into line with one another. While SPD delegate Louise Schroeder pleaded with her fellow delegates not to cause more discontent by creating additional artificial distinctions among the millions of indigent citizens, DNVP delegate Ernst Oberfohren argued that, in view of the abominably low level of support currently being provided to the *Kleinrentner*, it was necessary to spell out the minimum level of assistance to be provided by local officials.[57]

The law was approved by the Reichstag without any major revisions on January 31, 1923. The implementation guidelines issued in May reaffirmed the obligation of the *Kleinrentner* to support themselves through their own labor as much as possible and consume their capital to pay for the necessities of life, as well as the right of municipal officials to secure reimbursement from their estate for the support they provided. They also stated that the criteria for the determination of need should be interpreted in generous terms. Although these were the only salient differences between the welfare program for *Kleinrentner* and *Sozialrentner*, who by definition did not have an estate to consume, these regulations nevertheless aroused the opposition of both the Städtetag and the *Kleinrentner*. While the Städtetag complained about the schematic provision—

---

[57] *Verhandlungen des Reichstags*, 294. Sitzung (January 31, 1923), pp. 9567–68.

in accordance with the *Sozialrentner* law—of a minimum income to the *Klein-rentner*,[58] the *Kleinrentner* themselves were frightened by the work obligation, even though most of them were exempted because they were unable to work or at least, in the words of one official, "not used to work." In any case, the requirement was seldom invoked for elderly women, while elderly men sometimes took on office jobs. Even though the guidelines also made more generous exceptions to the reimbursement requirement than those already contained in the earlier guidelines, these requirements offended the *Kleinrentner* because they still smacked too much of poor relief and reminded them that they had failed to achieve their goal of public pensions to compensate for their losses during the inflation.

This *Kleinrentner* welfare law took to its logical extreme the idea of a war consequences assistance program for all of those persons whose indigence in this time of economic and social upheaval was believed to be in some way more directly attributable to the economic consequences of the war than that of the traditional recipients of municipal poor relief. However, in so doing the *Kleinrentner* welfare law helped crystallize the distinction between such a program, whose purpose was to meliorate the consequences of the war and uphold traditional social distinctions, and a general reform of the welfare system in accordance with Progressive and Social Democratic ideas. This further undermined the political and social functions of poor relief and thus removed many of the remaining barriers to the passage of a comprehensive welfare law. Although the specialized welfare programs for war victims, the unemployed, and *Sozialrentner* and *Kleinrentner* vastly expanded the scope of direct Reich responsibility for supporting the needy, the concrete significance of these measures nevertheless remained limited by the crisis of local and Reich finances and the insistence that they were merely subsidiary measures which were intended only to compensate for the direct effects of the war, rather than attack the more general problem of social inequality.

INFLATION, THE SHIFTING BALANCE OF PUBLIC AND VOLUNTARY WELFARE, AND THE PROBLEM OF REFORM

The war, its economic and social consequences, and the creation of the different specialized welfare programs to combat the resulting mass distress all had a deep impact on municipal finances, and in the summer of 1921 the DV and the Städtetag jointly sponsored a survey to determine how these events had affected municipal social spending in thirty-four larger cities.[59] The survey documented the quantitative expansion of municipal social services since 1913, the qualitative transformation of these services under the combined influence of wartime welfare and Progressive reform ideas, and the shifting balance between public

---

[58] Städtetag to Labor Ministry (June 25, 1923), BAP RAM 9234.

[59] *Verhandlungen des Deutschen Vereins*, SDV N.F. 2 (1921), pp. 79–99. See also Polligkeit, "Finanznot und Wohlfahrtspflege," *SPr* 31:3 (January 18, 1922), cols. 73–77.

and voluntary welfare. In every major city welfare expenditures increased at a far greater rate than both total municipal expenditures and municipal tax revenue and were consuming a progressively larger portion of the municipal budget. While total municipal expenditures increased by an average of 700% in nominal terms between 1913 and 1921, total welfare costs rose by an average of 1,066%. From 1913 to 1919, however, the percentage of municipal social spending devoted to poor relief declined substantially in almost every city because many people who had been supported by the poor relief before the war had become eligible for wartime welfare; the relatively small increases in poor relief costs during the war simply reflected the rising cost of living, not higher levels of support or greater numbers of recipients.

On the other hand, not only was total municipal social spending increasing dramatically; the proportion of these expenditures which were devoted to social welfare programs—that is, preventive, therapeutic social services and public health programs—increased substantially in every major city. Total social welfare expenditures, which had not exceeded poor relief expenditures in any city before the war, had far surpassed poor relief costs in every city by 1919. However, between 1919 and 1921, the relative percentage of the population supported by poor relief again began to rise as the inflation created a growing number of new poor who were not eligible for existing specialized social welfare programs. A substantial portion of the increase in total social expenditures between 1919 and 1921 was in many cases attributable to increased costs for unemployment relief and higher administrative costs associated with the establishment of public welfare offices and the employment of professional social workers. The survey also showed that the growth of public social spending evident in all of the cities surveyed took the form of a massive expansion of direct municipal social services (frequently at the expense of voluntary welfare), substantial increases in municipal subsidies to voluntary welfare, and the takeover by local government of many voluntary programs and institutions—especially maternity, infant, and youth welfare programs—which had been rendered insolvent by the inflation. The financial difficulties of many voluntary organizations working in the youth welfare field provided an opportunity for municipal government to extend its authority into what had heretofore been regarded as the privileged domain of voluntary welfare. Some welfare reformers welcomed these developments because they gave municipal welfare the chance to bring under its control those social programs which were necessary to create a comprehensive public welfare program, but which had previously been run by voluntary organizations. As Heimerich argued, the assumption of public responsibility for these programs represented the "culmination of the entire edifice of public youth welfare . . . and such an important institution must not be left outside the [authority of the] youth welfare offices."[60]

---

[60] Heimerich, "Neuordnung der öffentlichen Jugendfürsorge in Nürnberg" (February 11, 1920), cited in Susanne Krauß, *Kommunale Wohlfahrtspolitik in der frühen Weimarer Republik* (Magisterarbeit, Erlangen-Nürnberg, 1986), pp. 160–61.

The establishment of the various specialized social welfare programs in the early 1920s created special problems for local government, which was burdened with both its share of the program costs and substantial additional administrative costs which were attributable to the method of financing made necessary by the tax reforms pushed through by Erzberger in 1919–20. Before the war, municipal government had financed poor relief and other programs primarily by imposing supplements to income and property taxes, which were levied by the states, not the Reich, whose finances depended on indirect taxes and the so-called matricular contribution by the individual states. However, Erzberger's tax reforms fundamentally altered the relation between the Reich, state, and local government by reserving to the Reich the authority to levy taxes on income and real estate. While Erzberger was convinced that the costs of the war could only be repaid if the fiscal resources of the nation were centralized in the hands of the Reich, he also viewed tax reform as a vehicle for creating a sovereign nation-state out of an alliance of monarchical states, whose fiscal autonomy had been the most tangible symbol of their former status, and redistributing a greater share of the nation's wealth toward the working classes. Because these reforms deprived local government of its most important sources of income, the Reich agreed to return a specified portion of the revenue from the income and property taxes to state and local government.

Because these tax reforms left local government bereft of financial resources, it was incapable of bearing the costs of welfare for war victims, unemployment relief, and the programs later established to support the *Sozial-* and *Kleinrentner.* Instead, the Reich required the municipalities to administer these programs and then reimbursed local government for a specified percentage of the program costs. However, this so-called dotation system itself entailed substantial administrative costs, because local government had to maintain a small standing army of clerical workers and officials to calculate how much the city was due from the Reich according to the different eligibility requirements and funding arrangements for each of these programs. Municipal politicians constantly complained that, by requiring local government to administer programs over which it had no control, these arrangements hollowed out the substance of local self-government and transformed it into a mere agent of the Reich. Moreover, both the Reich and municipal officials complained that the separation between the granting and distribution of welfare benefits, on the one hand, and the raising of the funds to pay for these programs, on the other, deprived local government of the incentive to administer these programs as economically as possible and tempted local officials to include marginal or unqualified cases under the Reich-funded specialized welfare programs in order to reduce the burden upon locally financed poor relief. While municipal officials argued that the dotation system should either be eliminated entirely or the detailed calculation of reimbursement for individual recipients replaced by lump-sum payments, it was impossible to restore the degree of fiscal autonomy commensurate with the administrative responsibility demanded by local government without completely overhauling the tax system which had just been so laboriously created by Erzberger. At the same time, the fiscal crisis of municipal government constantly narrowed horizons of welfare reformers. In early 1922, the DV was still divided over the relative merits of expanding the different specialized social welfare programs or transforming municipal welfare into a unitary war consequences assistance program, and public discussion focused more on increasing the effectiveness and efficiency of municipal welfare than on the more abstract and controversial issues raised by Simon and Polligkeit.[61]

However, the collapse of the welfare system was the result of a complex concatenation of forces.[62] By the winter of 1922, the coexistence of so many separate welfare and public assistance programs, each based on their own principles with their own system of benefits and their own administrative apparatus, had led to the hypertrophy of the welfare bureaucracy, which was costly, inefficient, ineffective, and so complicated that few persons understood the entire complex set of regulations. The effect of these problems was complicated by Erzberger's tax reforms, which made it impossible for local authorities, who were directly responsible for administering all of these programs, to raise the necessary funds on their own authority. Moreover, while the new poor feared being abandoned to the discretion of local officials and saw direct Reich responsibility and funding as the only way of protecting their rights, the extension of direct Reich responsibility and the issuance of detailed regulations specifying the level of benefits entailed a greater degree of Reich supervision and control which threatened to render local political autonomy entirely illusory. All of these problems were further intensified by the hyperinflation, which substantially reduced the real value of the funds transferred from the Reich to local government, thus forcing the Reich itself to assume a constantly increasing share of the direct costs of these programs and, eventually, to pay for the enormous local bureaucracy required to administer them and calculate the reimbursements due from the Reich under each program.[63]

All of these problems were inextricably entangled with one another. Although the November 1923 Public Finance Law (*Finanzausgleichsgesetz*), which specified what percentage of the different sources of public revenue was to be distributed to each level of government and prohibited the Reich from imposing any additional spending requirements upon state and local government without at the same time providing them with the revenue necessary to cover these additional expenses, represented an initial attempt to return a degree of fiscal and administrative sovereignty to local authorities, its complex system of subsidies and advances created as many problems as it solved.[64] Ultimately,

---

[61] "Das örtliche Zusammenwirken der Träger der fürsorgerischen Arbeit und die Vereinheitlichung der Gesetzgebung als seine Voraussetzung," *SPr* 30:52 (1921), cols. 1350–53, and "Tagung des Hauptausschusses des Deutschen Vereins," *SPr* 30:47–48 (1922), cols. 1300–1302, 1331–34.

[62] See "Wichtige Äußerungen zur Frage einer Reform der Wohlfahrtspflege" (January 1923), BAP RAM 9234.

[63] Wölz, "Die Notverordnung über die Wohlfahrtspflege," *SPr* 33:6 (1924), cols. 102–9.

[64] Luppe, "Landessteuergesetz und Wohlfahrtspflege," *SPr* 32:6 (February 8, 1923), cols. 119–21 and "Zu §61 des Finanzausgleichsgesetzes," *SPr* 32:46 (November 15, 1923), cols. 979–81.

welfare reform could only be undertaken in conjunction with a thorough refc of Reich finances, and the political will to attempt such a gigantic undertaking had to await the collapse of the economy and the decision to stabilize the currency. In chapter 4 we will examine the origins of these reforms and the conflicts which they generated.

Between Public Assistance and Social Security

THE RFV, THE NEW POOR, AND THE
CONTRADICTIONS OF PROGRESSIVE WELFARE
REFORM, 1922–1930

The National Social Welfare Law (RFV) and the National Guidelines for the Determination of Need, the Nature, and the Scope of Public Welfare (RGr), which provided uniform regulations for the implementation of key provisions of the RFV, brought about the most far-reaching reform of the German poor relief system since the 1842 Prussian poor relief law. Contemporary observers all agreed that the RFV and the RGr represented the triumph of a modern, Progressive conception of public assistance, which, through the provision of individualized personal help by trained, professional social workers, aspired to prevent or overcome social distress. This new sensibility was reflected in the terminology of this legislation, which no longer spoke of the "poor" and "poor relief" (*Armen* and *Armenpflege*), but rather of "necessitous persons" and "welfare" (*Hilfsbedürftigen* and *Fürsorge*).[1] Although this praise accurately captured the broad intentions of the framers of the law, here, as with RJWG, this Progressive project was refracted through the conflicts arising out of the contradiction between the abstract Progressive-Social Democratic vision of social citizenship and the concrete interests of those persons whom this reform plan was ostensibly designed to benefit, and the final versions of both the RFV and the RGr bear the scars of the ensuing conflicts.

While the depreciation of the currency had helped reduce unemployment and maintain social stability from 1919 to 1921, the perceptible acceleration of inflation from August 1922, the virtual bankruptcy of the social insurance system, and the complete collapse of the currency and the economy in the fall of 1923 vastly expanded the scope of poverty. One informed observer estimated that, between 1913 and the end of the hyperinflation, per capita income had fallen by 50% in real terms and that the war and the inflation had together rolled back all of the economic progress made by the nation since the 1890s.[2] In the spring of 1923, 6.6 million persons, or more than 10% of the population, were receiving

---

[1] Alice Salomon, "Betrachtungen zur Entwicklung der sozialen Fürsorge," *DZW* 1:1 (April 1925), pp. 3–6, Hans Muthesius, "Wie weit haben die Reformideen der letzten Zeit ihren Niederschlag in den Reichsrichtlinien zur FV. gefunden," *DZW* 1:1 (April 1925), pp. 10–13, and Johannes Horion, "Definition and Progress of Social Work," *First International Conference of Social Work,* 3 vols. (Paris, 1929), I:607–31, especially 622ff.

[2] Franz Eulenberg, "Die sozialen Wirkungen der Währungsverhältnisse," *Jahrbücher für Nationalökonomie und Statistik* 122 (1924), pp. 748–94, citation p. 752.

welfare benefits from the Labor Ministry; this figure excludes the recipients of municipal poor relief.[3] In September 1924, some 4.5 million persons, or 7.2% of the population, were still receiving some form of public assistance. This figure included an estimated 768,000 disabled veterans, 420,000 war widows with 1,020,000 children, 54,000 full orphans, 1,400,000 recipients of disability and old-age pensions, 160,000 recipients of widows'/widowers' pensions, 190,000 dependent parents of soldiers killed in battle (*Kriegseltern*), and an estimated 500,000 poor relief recipients.[4] The undernourishment of the populace, the precipitous decline in public health, the deterioration of living conditions, and a host of other social ills were widely documented.

The debates leading up to the promulgation of the RFV involved a three-way conflict between Progressive and Social Democratic reformers in the DV, the organizations representing the new poor, and the Labor Ministry in which the debate over the principles of welfare reform was inextricably connected with the problem of redistributing the costs of the war and the inflation. The Progressives hoped that the comprehensive reform of existing welfare legislation on the basis of their need-based, work-centered approach would increase the level and quality of municipal welfare programs, while at the same time promoting a greater degree of equality among the needy. They also called for the reform of the organizational structure of the welfare system and the devolution of both administrative autonomy and fiscal authority from the Reich back to local government. While the new poor insisted that they were entitled to welfare benefits which exceeded those to which they would have been entitled solely by virtue of their status as needy citizens because this assistance represented a form of state compensation for either irresponsible state policies, their own service to the nation during the war, or that of their family members, both the Progressives and the Social Democrats charged that the mere existence of these programs was helping to preserve and harden illegitimate social distinctions. Consequently, the claims by these privileged groups involved them in a conflict of principle with the Progressives and the Social Democrats at the very moment when the general impoverishment of the nation was rendering the distinction between the traditional poor and those whose need was directly related to the war entirely untenable. This was why the distinction between a broad war consequences assistance program and a comprehensive reform of the welfare system on the basis of Progressive principles had all but disappeared in the debate over a *Kleinrentner* welfare law.

However, despite Progressive protestations, it was difficult to say with certainty whether such a reform would lead to the leveling upward of municipal general assistance or the leveling downward of the existing special welfare programs, and the new poor were legitimately concerned that a unitary program such as that advocated by the DV would erase all substantive distinctions be-

---

[3] Brauns, "Übergang des Armenwesens vom Reichsministerium des Innern auf das RAM" (March 21, 1923), BAP RAM 9258.

[4] Beisiegel and Richter, "Begründung" to RGr (September 16, 1924), BAP RAM 9260. These figures were estimates and they do not exactly match the statistics given in chapter 3.

tween them and those work-shy, asocial, and criminal elements who had always been the responsibility of local poor relief. The new poor were able to mobilize political support to pressure the Labor Ministry into building into the RFV and RGr assurances that their benefits and political rights would be protected. The problem was so intractable because, although the Labor Ministry was sympathetic to both Progressive reform plans and the political demands of the new poor, its freedom of action was limited by the deplorable state of both the economy and Reich finances. The outcome of this three-way struggle was an unsatisfactory compromise between Progressive principles and group entitlements, and the intrinsic contradictions of this policy could be traced back to the desire by the Labor Ministry to guarantee a certain minimum level of support for the new poor (as well as their privileges with respect to the recipients of municipal general assistance) while at the same time employing means-tested, subsidiary forms of public assistance as a mechanism for reducing total public assistance costs and equitably redistributing the costs of the war and the inflation.

FROM POOR LAW REFORM TO WELFARE LEGISLATION

While the DV had been slowly preparing the groundwork for the reform of the poor laws in the spring of 1922, public pressure for comprehensive welfare reform was mounting, and on May 17, 1922, the Reichstag passed a resolution asking that all existing public assistance programs, including poor relief, be transferred from the Interior Ministry to the Labor Ministry.[5] The Reichstag resolution unleashed a flood of memoranda and countermemoranda between the Labor and Interior Ministries. Labor Ministry officials argued that responsibility for poor relief should be transferred to the new ministry because the disciplinary apparatus of the Interior Ministry in the field of poor relief remained hopelessly bound to outdated prewar views, which were incompatible with the basic values of the new state, whose goal was to promote the welfare and autonomy of all citizens through a modern social welfare system. This preoccupation with the preservation of public order, they argued, rendered the Interior Ministry incapable of modernizing the poor relief system. In addition, Labor Ministry officials maintained that the centralization of all welfare programs under *its* authority would substantially reduce administrative costs; since the Labor Ministry was already responsible for welfare programs for some 6.5 million people, it was wasteful to maintain a separate department in the Interior Ministry to administer a program for the mere 300,000 people who were still supported by poor relief when these duties could be performed within the Labor Ministry at no additional cost.[6]

[5] *Verhandlungen des Reichstags* 212. Sitzung (May 17, 1922), pp. 7283ff., especially p. 7305 and Drucksache Nr. 4181 IIa 1.

[6] Wölz to Brauns, "Übergabe des Armenwesens auf das Reichsarbeitsministerium" (February 16, 1923), and "Denkschrift zur Frage des Übergangs des Armenwesens vom Reichsministerium des

Interior Minister Rudolf Oeser (DDP) marshaled a variety of counterarguments in hopes of retaining the ministry's control over poor relief. Oeser insisted that poor relief and social welfare programs had to retain their separate identities because they served different functions; while the special welfare programs created since the war were based on the presumption that the indigence of the recipients was directly related to the war or the inflation, poor relief, he argued, must continue to adhere to its minimalist, deterrent principles in order to avoid weakening the self-responsibility of the poor. The transfer of poor relief to the Labor Ministry would bring it under the influence of ideas that were foreign to its nature, and the resulting "overextension" (*Überspannung*) of the concept of welfare would obliterate the important distinction between these two forms of public assistance.[7] Oeser also feared that the transfer of poor relief would further accelerate the questionable development of the Labor Ministry into a national welfare ministry and that the resulting centralization of power would undermine the autonomy of the federal states while overburdening the Reich government with financial costs which had previously been borne by local government.[8]

The failure of the government to quickly resolve this conflict prompted the Reichstag to pass a second resolution on July 15, 1922, requesting that poor relief be transferred to the Labor Ministry without further delay. The Reichstag also asked that the Labor Ministry submit a memorandum outlining its plans for a comprehensive national welfare reform.[9] However, the Labor Ministry had already begun to work on a national welfare law in 1921, and in May 1922—a month before the original Reichstag resolution—Erwin Ritter, Ministerial Director responsible for the welfare department within the Labor Ministry and the person directly responsible for drafting the RFV, submitted a memorandum spelling out his plans for the reform of existing welfare programs.[10] Ritter's primary goal was to unify all public assistance programs at the local level within new district welfare authorities, which were to replace the existing poor relief authorities, because the latter were regarded as too small to effectively administer a modern welfare system.[11] In the memorandum which he submitted

---

Innern auf das Reichsarbeitsministerium" (unsigned, undated [probably fall 1922]), BAP RAM 9258.

[7] Oeser, "Denkschrift über die Belassung des Armenwesens beim Reichsministerium des Innern" (February 27, 1923), BAK R43 I/842, and Oeser to Brauns (October 13, 1922), BAP RAM 9258.

[8] Oeser, "Denkschrift über die Belassung des Armenwesens," and Brauns, "Übergang des Armenwesens vom Reichsministerium des Innern auf das RAM" (March 21, 1923), BAP RAM 9258. Both the Städtetag and the *Verband der Deutschen Landkreise* supported the transfer of poor relief to the Labor Ministry. See the letters (June 21 and July 14, 1923), respectively, in BAP RAM 9258.

[9] *Verhandlungen des Reichstags*, 252. Sitzung (July 15, 1922), pp. 8578–81, Drucksache Nr. 4764, and minutes of the meeting of the Reichstag social affairs committee (July 12, 1922), in BAP RAM 9258.

[10] See Ritter's untitled memorandum (May 12, 1922), and the draft of the RFV prepared by Rabeling on the basis of Ritter's memorandum (June 15, 1922), BAP RAM 9234.

[11] Although the initial drafts of the RFV required these districts to have a minimum population of 10,000, the final draft left the size of the districts to the discretion of the states.

to the Reichstag in February 1923, Ritter argued that the impoverished nation could no longer bear the social and financial burdens imposed by a fragmented and inefficient welfare system. However, the attainment of his goal of "clear and simple rules, more help, less administration" depended on the reform of the underlying principles of public welfare. Although the scope of welfare programs would necessarily be limited in the immediate future by the general economic situation, the proposed national welfare law should, he argued, build upon the important innovations of wartime welfare and the postwar welfare programs in order to establish a firm framework for the future evolution of the public welfare system. The goal of public welfare must be to strengthen the will of the indigent individuals so that they could, through their own labor and initiative, support themselves without, at the same time, destroying their self-reliance, family loyalty, or self-respect. Although thoroughgoing preventive public assistance was more effective and efficient than the post-facto treatment of social ills, Ritter warned that such assistance must also be withdrawn in a timely manner in order to prevent the recipients from becoming dependent on this assistance. To this end, the reformed welfare system would have to rely upon individualized personal help (*Hilfe von Mensch zu Mensch*) and, wherever necessary, therapeutic services, rather than the schematic provision of monetary support; the level and nature of these services would have to be determined on the basis of an individualized examination of character and circumstance. He hoped that the unification of the various special welfare reform programs on the basis of this principle would lead to the simplification of the complex, inefficient welfare bureaucracy. If implemented, this far-reaching plan would have effectively transformed the Labor Ministry into a Labor *and* Welfare Ministry.

While the DV had advocated a unitary welfare system which would graduate relief in relation to the anticipated future productivity of the recipient, Ritter, despite his general agreement with Progressive ideas, sought to preserve some of the distinctions among recipients. He justified this position by warning that the level of social services would be much lower if they were provided to all citizens simply by virtue of their status as needy members of the community (*lediglich kraft seines Daseins*) than if the recipients had acquired a specific right through either service to the nation or the prior provision for old age and time of need.[12]

The responses to the Labor Ministry's draft were as varied as the German political landscape, as fragmented as the welfare system, and as contradictory as the period itself. Although everyone agreed with the assessment by the Städtetag and the DV that the current state of legislation and administration was "completely and totally untenable," they all hoped for and feared different things from the proposed reforms.[13] While some groups believed that the accel-

---

[12] "Denkschrift des Reichsarbeitsministeriums über die Vorarbeiten zu einem Reichswohlfahrtsgesetz," BAK R86 2318. The salient portions of this memorandum are reprinted in Julia Dünner, ed., *Reichsfürsorgerecht* (Munich, 1924), pp. 74–81.

[13] DV (Polligkeit and Luppe) to Labor Minister (April 23, 1923), ADCV 319.4 E II 6.

erating deterioration of public finances made comprehensive welfare reform all the more necessary, others argued that such reform was impossible for precisely the same reason. Most of the states wanted some kind of reform, but they insisted that the proposed welfare law be only a framework law which left most authority in their own hands. The Württemberg Interior Ministry objected in no uncertain terms: "Welfare is primarily the responsibility of the states *and must remain so*."[14] However, the cities expected far more from the proposed reforms, especially the elimination of both the dotation system and the minimum income guaranteed by the *Sozial-* and *Kleinrentner* welfare programs, and they hoped that this would be achieved in conjunction with the devolution of fiscal authority and administrative autonomy from the Reich to local government.[15]

On October 13, 1923, the Reichstag passed an Enabling Act giving the government the power to implement the measures necessary to reform the welfare system, and on December 8 the Reichstag approved a revised Enabling Act which gave the conservative coalition headed by Wilhelm Marx (Center) the powers necessary to stabilize the currency and end the hyperinflation. This revised Enabling Act provided the legal foundation for the proclamation of the RFV on February 13, 1924, and it was issued in conjunction with several other closely related decrees: the Third Emergency Tax Decree, the decree altering the National Youth Welfare Law, and the reform of unemployment relief. The RFV, which represented an attempt to simultaneously lay the foundations for future welfare reform and reduce government expenditures for public assistance in a time of rapidly increasing need, was scheduled to take effect April 1, 1924.[16]

The RFV was primarily an organizational law. In conjunction with the Third Emergency Tax Decree and the Public Finance Law, which made possible the effective decentralization of public welfare by restoring to local government much of the fiscal autonomy which had been taken away by Erzberger's tax reforms, it consolidated poor relief and all of the existing welfare programs for war veterans and survivors, *Sozial-* and *Kleinrentner*, maternity programs, sup-

---

[14] Württemberg Interior Ministry to Labor Ministry (April 19, 1923), BAP RAM 9234.

[15] Städtetag to Labor Ministry (June 25, 1923), "Wichtige Äußerungen zur Frage einer Reform der Wohlfahrtspflege," pp. 10, 13–24, and Städtetag to Labor Ministry (June 25, 1923), BAP RAM 9234.

[16] *RGBl.*, 1924, I, pp. 100ff., reprinted in Dünner, ed., *Reichsfürsorgerecht*, pp. 1ff. The extraparliamentary origins of the RFV may at least partly explain why the decree does not figure in any of the major accounts of the political economy of the Republic. The most important contemporary commentaries on the RFV are Otto Wölz, Fritz Ruppert, and Lothar Richter, *Die Fürsorgepflicht* (Berlin, 1925), Dünner, ed., *Reichsfürsorgerecht*, Siddy Wronsky, ed., *Die Fürsorgepflicht* (Berlin, 1924), and Hans Muthesius, *Die Wohlfahrtspflege. Systematische Einführung auf Grund der Fürsorgepflichtverordnung und der Reichsgrundsätze* (Berlin, 1925). The provisions of this decree also corresponded to a large degree with the recommendations made by the DV in September 1923 at the peak of the hyperinflation. See "Dringlichkeitsantrag des Deutschen Vereins betr. Notgesetz über allgemeine Fürsorge," *Nachrichtendienst* 42 (October 1923), pp. 417–20, the minutes of the meeting of the DV's executive committee (September 26, 1923), IfG 228, Polligkeit, "Notstandsmaßnahmen zur Sicherstellung der öffentlichen Fürsorge," *SPr* 32:42 (October 18, 1923), cols. 915–20, and "Reform der Kriegsfolgenhilfe" (August 16 and October 16, 1923), BAP RAM 9234.

port for indigent children and the severely handicapped; it delegated the administration of these programs to state and district welfare authorities which were to be established by the individual states. The RFV definitively abandoned the relief residence system and made the district where a person maintained his or her customary residence ultimately responsible for supporting the person in case of indigence. In contrast to the controversial vagueness of the RJWG, it specified that district authorities were not to establish new programs or institutions as long as these needs were adequately met by societal welfare, although district welfare authorities did retain ultimate legal and financial responsibility for these public programs.

The RFV left the regulation of the participatory rights of welfare recipients to the states, though it did specify that these rights were to be at least as extensive as those guaranteed by existing welfare programs. In broad terms, the RFV reaffirmed the obligation to work and the familial obligations defined by earlier legislation. It also stated that, in appropriate cases, public assistance could be made dependent upon a work test, and it permitted authorities to confine to a workhouse persons whose indigence was the result of their "moral faults" (*sittliches Verschulden*) and who persistently refused to work or fulfill their familial support obligations.[17] Lastly, the RFV delegated to the states the authority to determine—within broad national guidelines to be established by the Labor Ministry—when need existed and the type and level of services to be provided. This question was certain to attract the attention of the beneficiaries of the specialized welfare programs, and the drafting of these National Guidelines generated far more controversy than the RFV itself.[18]

On February 23, 1924, the Labor Ministry distributed a first draft of the proposed guidelines (RGr) to state governments, representatives of the welfare recipients, and leading private welfare organizations.[19] In principle, these guidelines codified the need-based, work-centered approach long advocated by the Progressives, and they reflected the Progressive belief in the importance of prevention and therapy. The concept of need contained in the draft guidelines was defined primarily in economic terms. An individual was to be considered needy if and insofar as 1) complete or partial disability prevented the person from securing the "indispensable necessities of life" through the fruits of his or her own labor; 2) the person was unable to work because he or she was too young, too old, or otherwise occupied with child-raising or household duties; and 3) the person was not legally entitled to support from third parties, such as family members or social insurance funds. Partially disabled persons were expected to employ their remaining labor power, and they were only to be considered needy

---

[17] However, this morality provision was seldom applied to single persons because—when threatened with internment in a workhouse—most of them chose to forego further public assistance.

[18] "Besprechung mit den Verbänden der Kriegsbeschädigten und Kriegshinterbliebenen am 29. Februar 1924," and Zentralverband der Invaliden und Witwen Deutschlands to Labor Ministry (February 22, 1924), both BAP RAM 9259.

[19] Labor and Interior Ministry, "Referententwurf" (February 23, 1924), BAP RAM 9259 and ADCV R307 I.

if and insofar as work could not be found which they could reasonably—i.e., in view of their age, health, and domestic obligations—be expected to perform.

The draft guidelines emphasized the importance of education, occupational training, and job placement services, especially for children and persons who were only partially disabled. It also provided for extensive maternity benefits and specified that the family, rather than the individual, was to be considered the basic unit of support, though they did not extend the legal support obligations among family members as the DV had recommended. Within these broad guidelines, the precise determination of the level and nature of support was left to the discretion of state and local government. However, the draft guidelines did enumerate specific groups of welfare recipients who, "due to social considerations," were entitled to a "somewhat higher standard of living." These privileged recipients included all of the previous beneficiaries of the various specialized welfare programs. Benefits for poor relief recipients who were unable to work and, especially, those persons whose need was self-incurred were to be limited to an absolute existence minimum (*das zum Fristen des Lebens Unerlässliche*).

As Hans Maier noted, the RFV had a Janus face: "It can thrust all forms of welfare back to the level of prewar poor relief, but it can also lead to great social progress,"[20] and the provision for enhanced welfare benefits for groups enumerated in the draft guidelines was intended to reassure these groups that the Reich did not wish the administrative reform to become a pretext for reducing the level of their benefits. However, the very act of enumerating these groups meant that other groups were by definition excluded, even if they did not belong to the traditional groups of poor relief recipients. Although the desire to extend the benefits of social welfare programs to these excluded persons had been one of the main motives behind welfare reform proposals since 1922, the clarification of this intrinsic ambiguity in the draft guidelines was rendered more difficult by the beneficiaries of the specialized welfare programs, who feared that their social status would be degraded, their benefits lowered, and their rights abridged if the administration of these programs was placed in the hands of district welfare authorities.

By the end of February, the Labor Ministry was already inundated with petitions from disabled veterans, war survivors, *Sozial-* and *Kleinrentner*, as well as various state governments (including Bavaria, Württemberg, Hesse, and Mecklenburg, but not Prussia) protesting the ostensible plan to lump these groups together with traditional poor relief recipients in a general social welfare system. The issue was so politically explosive that Ritter considered simply not issuing any guidelines at all.[21] The organizations representing disabled veterans and war survivors protested that "no rationally thinking person will disapprove

---

[20] *Verhandlungen des Deutschen Vereins, SDV* N.F. 3 (1924), p. 19.

[21] Wölz, "Durchführung der Verordnung über die Fürsorgepflicht nach §6, 32 II, und 34" (February 21, 1924), BAP RAM 9259, and his article by the same title in *SPr* 33:16–18, 20–22 (1924), cols. 318–20, 342–44, 364–66, 397–98, 429–31, 436–38.

of our justified anger over such a step when you consider that the government has nothing in mind but to conflate the sacred rights of those persons who have shed their blood for the existence of the Reich, who have lost their breadwinner, with public poor relief."[22] They also feared that the devolution of Reich responsibility onto local government would have a negative impact upon their welfare. As the *Kyffhäuserbund* put it, "Despite the restoration of the fiscal sovereignty of the states, the obligation of the Reich to provide welfare can not be watered down, much less given up."[23] Organizations representing *Sozial-* and *Kleinrentner* also objected to the government's plan to foist responsibility for their benefits onto the cities, whom they regarded as their worst enemies. They protested against the government's cost-cutting measures, "which have heretofore been carried out only at the cost of the lower strata of the population, who are intentionally used to impress the stamp of poor relief upon social welfare in order to deter those persons who have a right to social help from availing themselves of their rights and in this way to reduce these costs." They demanded that *Sozial-* and *Kleinrentner* receive the same benefits as disabled veterans and survivors and that these programs be kept separate from poor relief.[24]

The *Kleinrentner* were utterly exasperated because they felt that their economic existence was being ground to dust between the Third Emergency Tax Decree, which substantially increased their tax burden, and the RFV, which appeared to deny them the right to a decent and honorable existence. They feared that the transfer of responsibility for their welfare benefits from the Reich to the district welfare authorities would amount to abandoning them to the unlimited arbitrary authority of municipal poor relief officials. They objected to the "disgraceful" plan "to place us together on the same level with charity recipients and work-shy idlers" and resented the fact that, at the end of a rich yet laborious life, the RFV held out to them the prospect of compulsory labor and life in a workhouse. They detested both the obligation to work and the fact that public welfare was only subsidiary to familial support, "since it was not our children who plunged us into misery, but rather the Reich through the abandonment of the gold standard and its monstrous tax legislation."[25] Ultimately, the *Kleinrentner* wanted the state to compensate them for the losses by providing them with a pension equal to their prewar income without regard to their present need and income, and they demanded that the work and family support obligations, as well as the reimbursement requirements, be eliminated because this pension was to be considered state compensation, not welfare.[26] All

---

[22] Letters from the branches of the Reichsbund (February 9 and 16, 1924), BAP RAM 9238.

[23] *Verhandlungen des Deutschen Vereins, SDV* N.F. 3 (1924), p. 50.

[24] Letter from mid-April 1924, BAP RAM 9238.

[25] See the letters from local pensioner organizations from March 1924 in BAP RAM 9239, the letter from the Neustettin branch of the *Rentnerbund* to the Labor Minister (February 27, 1924), BAP RAM 9238, and the spring and summer issues of *Der Rentner*. One local group demanded that pensioners be treated in the same way as retired civil servants (*Beamten*), whom they regarded as their social peers.

[26] "Forderungen des Deutschen Rentnerbundes an den hohen Reichstag," *Der Rentner* (July 1924), pp. 1–2.

of the recipients' organizations felt that it was increasingly important to secure their representation in welfare offices to insure that they had a voice in the formulation of welfare policy.

This apprehension about the transfer of social welfare programs from the Labor Ministry to district authorities was not entirely unjustified. Municipal politicians were uncertain regarding both the general economic situation of the nation and the effects of the Third Emergency Tax Decree. At a time when it was impossible to foresee the extent to which it would be possible to maintain even a minimal level of public services, they warned the Reich against making promises which local government could not keep. Instead, they argued that the proposed guidelines should contain as few requirements as possible and be limited to specifying which groups were eligible for enhanced welfare. However, although many municipal politicians doubted the ability of the new welfare authorities to undertake any preventive programs, Otto Wölz (DDP)—ministerial councilor in the Labor Ministry and head of the policy division of the welfare department—argued that such programs could produce substantial savings and were, in any case, politically unavoidable.[27]

At a meeting between the Labor Ministry, representatives of the state social ministries, voluntary welfare, and the DV, Polligkeit presented a comprehensive counterproposal which attacked the very principle of group distinctions which had been perpetuated in the Labor Ministry's draft guidelines. He argued for a unitary system which differentiated on the basis of the particular needs of the individual, rather than membership in an externally defined group.[28] At the 1924 DV conference, which began the next day, Polligkeit's criticisms were echoed by many Progressive and Social Democratic municipal politicians. Former DV chair Otto Lohse argued that the distinction between self-incurred and war-related need was completely artificial because almost all need was in some way related to the war and its consequences. He insisted that the decisive criterion in determining the nature and level of welfare benefits in any particular case had to be whether welfare programs could prevent need or cure existing need or whether they would simply provide for the basic needs of persons who could not be expected to contribute to the common good.[29] Moreover, as Heimerich argued, considerations of equity mitigated against the distinctions which the Labor Ministry was attempting to draw; there was simply no reason why a woman with dependent children had to depend on municipal general assistance because her husband had abandoned her, while another woman qualified for better support because her husband had been killed in the war.[30] The principle of individualization meant, Polligkeit concluded, that the same state of need required the same type and level of treatment regardless of whether or not the

---

[27] Polligkeit, "Vorschläge für endgültige reichsrechtliche Grundsätze gemäß §6 der F.V.," *Nachrichtendienst* 47 (March 1924), pp. 37–38, and "Besprechung mit den Kommunalspitzenverbänden am 28.2.1924," BAP RAM 9259.

[28] Wölz, "Vermerk: Grundsätze auf Grund des §6 der Fürsorgepflichtverordnung" (March 15, 1924), BAP RAM 9259.

[29] *Verhandlungen des Deutschen Vereins*, SDV N.F. 3 (1924), pp. 8–9.

[30] Ibid., p. 26.

needy person belonged to a certain legally defined category of persons, and he believed that the supposedly nonpolitical determination of need on an individualizing basis would put an end to the postwar "orgies of group egoism" among the new poor.[31]

Although the Labor Ministry had originally hoped to issue the final guidelines by April 1, these criticisms forced the ministry to issue temporary guidelines, which were to be effective from April 1 to July 1, and to form a commission to attempt to resolve these differences.[32] While these meetings and the ensuing political maneuvering reveal the strength of the political forces favoring enhanced welfare benefits for privileged groups of the needy, this resistance also helped crystallize the Progressive conception of welfare and social work, which had been evolving since the war.

In his alternative draft of the guidelines, which formed the basis for the commission's work, Polligkeit called in stronger terms than ever before for the universal application of the principle of individualization to all categories of welfare recipients and argued that differentiation of welfare benefits according to the peculiar nature of the individual's need (*eine der Eigenart ihres Notstandes entsprechende, im übrigen aber einheitliche Fürsorge*) would provide an objective standard which was consistent with the demands of both democracy and economy. In addition, he expanded the accepted definition of the basic necessities of life to include, beyond physical needs (food, shelter, clothing, and basic medical care), those social services necessary to render indigent individuals capable of fulfilling their social obligations (i.e., the obligation to work, maintain their health, and provide their children with a proper moral education and adequate occupational training).[33]

Polligkeit criticized the RFV and the original draft guidelines for using the term "moral failings" to distinguish between these privileged groups and those persons whose indigence was considered to be the result of personal immorality, vice, and crime. He did not believe that such a category was useful in practice, and he felt that it contradicted the Progressive principle of a graduated, individualized determination of need and assistance.[34] Polligkeit agreed that assistance to these persons should be limited to an absolute minimum, but suggested that this moralizing terminology be replaced by a more objective, productivist formulation. He proposed instead that benefits be reduced in such a manner for "work-shy and manifestly uneconomical persons" who persistently refused appropriate work or failed to fulfill their family support obligations. These ideas drew the logical consequences of the idea of individualization and

---

[31] Ibid., pp. 40, 67.

[32] The minutes of these meetings and other relevant material can be found in BAP RAM 9259. These temporary guidelines were ultimately extended through the end of the year.

[33] "Reichsrechtliche Grundsätze gemäß §6 der Verordnung über die Fürsorgepflicht," *SDV* N.F. 3 (1924), pp. 147–67.

[34] Wölz, "Vermerk: Grundsätze auf Grund des §6 der Fürsorgepflichtverordnung," and Polligkeit, "Vorschläge für reichsrechtliche Grundsätze," *SDV* N.F. 3 (1924), pp. 136–46, citation p. 144. See the discussion of correctional custody legislation in chapter 8 below.

the underlying vision of democratic equality of opportunity for the needy. His arguments were the most coherent, systematic statement of the Progressive vision of welfare reform advanced in the 1920s, and they marked the culmination of a process of intellectual development whose roots reached back into the 1890s.

Ritter, on the other hand, defended these distinctions. In view of the ambiguous implications of Progressive welfare reform proposals for the new poor, Ritter claimed that his goal was not so much to discriminate against those upright members of the community who had fallen between the cracks of the specialized welfare programs, as to insure that the enumerated groups did in fact receive preferential treatment by local authorities. However, he insisted that the extension of enhanced welfare beyond these enumerated groups was politically intolerable, theoretically indefensible, and economically unbearable.[35] But Ritter's argument failed to convince his opponents. Since, as Polligkeit and others noted, the enumerated groups made up between two-thirds and three-quarters of the total number of welfare recipients, the level of enhanced benefits would inevitably become the norm, thus further depressing the benefit levels of the other two groups.[36] Although the commission report clearly reflected Polligkeit's ideas, at the end of May Ritter told the commission that political factors—especially consideration for the *Kleinrentner*—compelled the Ministry to reject the commission's recommendations in favor of the retention of group distinctions.[37]

Although the Prussian government asked the Labor Ministry to refrain from publishing the guidelines until after the election scheduled for December 7, Brauns feared that such a delay would only reinforce the worst suspicions of the *Sozial-* and *Kleinrentner* about the Ministry's intentions, and on December 4 the Labor Ministry finally issued the RGr.[38] These guidelines, which were to

[35] "Niederschrift der Sitzung der Sachverständigenkommission zur Ausarbeitung von Grundsätzen . . . am 9. April 1924," p. 2, and Beisiegel, "Vermerk über die Sitzung des Sachverständigenausschusses vom 9. April, 1924," pp. 3–4, BAP RAM 9259. Ritter's position was supported by some members of the DV, such as Willi Cuno, who insisted that it was impossible to do without the concept of self-incurred need. Cuno to Labor Ministry (April 29, 1924), BAP RAM 9259.

[36] Luppe, "Vereinheitlichung des materiellen Fürsorgerechts?" *SPr* 33:37 (September 11, 1924), cols. 761–64.

[37] "Sitzung der Zehnerkommission zur Beratung von Sondergrundsätzen gemäss §34 RFV" (May 30, 1924), BAP RAM 9259. This led to howls of protest from Polligkeit, who insisted that such political considerations were entirely out of place in the work of this nonpolitical experts' committee.

[38] *RGBl* 1924, I, pp. 765ff., reprinted in Dünner, ed., *Reichsfürsorgerecht*, pp. 15ff. Prussian Minister President to Chancellor Wilhelm Marx (November 6, 1924), Brauns to Marx (November 8, 1924), and State Secretary in the Reich Chancellery to Prussian Minister President (November 11, 1924), all BAK R43 I/837. These letters report that the Reichstag social affairs committee unanimously supported the Labor Ministry's plan to guarantee enhanced welfare to disabled veterans, war survivors, *Sozial-* and *Kleinrentner*. Although there was yet another round of discussions between the DV, the Städtetag, and the Labor Ministry in July and August, it did not result in any fundamental changes in the positions of the parties involved. See "Gutachtliche Aeußerung des Vorstandes des Deutschen Vereins zu dem . . . vorläufigen Entwurf von Grundsätzen . . . ,"

take effect January 1, 1925, did not diverge in any significant respects from the draft which the Labor Ministry had prepared in July on the basis of Ritter's arguments.[39]

The RGr played an important role in helping crystallize Progressive ideas on welfare reform and, as such, must be regarded as one of the milestones in the development of the Weimar welfare system. However, as a mechanism for meliorating the mass poverty of the postwar period and definitively redistributing the cost of the war, they were a failure. The Weimar state was unable to bear the political costs entailed in the consequent pursuit of the Progressive vision of a need-based, work-centered approach or the economic costs involved in guaranteeing a minimum income for the many persons included in the privileged groups of welfare recipients. The result was a combination of, on the one hand, a welfare system based on individualization and means-testing and, on the other, a state pension system. While this compromise undoubtedly did help reduce state expenditures for public assistance, it could only achieve this goal at the cost of forcing municipal welfare to bear the political burden of distributing the costs of the war and the inflation—but to do so with hopelessly inadequate resources and in a way which threatened the integrity of a subsidiary, individualizing system of public assistance.

THE NEW POOR IN THE PERIOD OF RELATIVE PROSPERITY

With the devolution from the Reich to local government of fiscal responsibility and administrative authority for assistance to the new poor, the pre-1924 conflicts between the Labor Ministry, Progressive welfare reformers, and the new poor began again and continued until the end of the decade.

Even after the currency stabilization, social spending at the local level remained substantially higher than it had been before the war. Already in 1925/26, local officials were speaking of a crisis of public welfare resulting from the emergence of the new poor, persistently high levels of poststabilization unemployment, increases in welfare benefits to compensate for rising housing costs, and the reduction in the local share of tax revenue under the Public Finance Law.[40] It was estimated that 8–10% of the entire population received some form of public assistance.[41] According to a Frankfurt survey, the number

---

Nachrichtendienst 52 Sonderbeilage (August 1924), pp. 1–13, and Städtetag (Heymann) to Labor Ministry (August 15, 1924), BAP RAM 9260.

[39] For a concise statement of the motives behind the specific provisions, see Wölz, "Reichsgrundsätze über Voraussetzung, Art und Maß der öffentlichen Fürsorge," *SPr* 33:51–52 (December 18, 1924), cols. 1073–78, 1097–1100.

[40] Karl Sperling, "Die Krise der öffentlichen Wohlfahrtspflege," *DZW* 2:1 (April 1926), pp. 1–7.

[41] Oskar Mulert, "Wohlfahrtspflege und Gemeindefinanzen," *SPr* 36:4 (1927), cols. 73–77, "Zahlen zur Finanzlage der Städte," *Mitteilungen des deutschen Städtetages* (March 1, 1925), pp. 66–70, and the Städtetag memorandum in *SPr* 35:48 (1926), cols. 1227–38.

of households supported by municipal welfare had risen from an average of 5,142 in 1913 to 23,040 in 1924 and 26,510 in 1925 before skyrocketing to 40,760 in April 1926 during the poststabilization economic downturn, as can be seen in table 4.1. Including dependents, 15% of the population was dependent on public assistance, and another 5%, including unemployed persons not eligible for unemployment relief and *Kleinrentner* who refused to accept public assistance, had to be considered as indigent, even though these invisible poor did not appear on welfare rolls. As a result, municipal social spending also increased substantially, as can be seen in table 4.2. In 1913, Frankfurt welfare expenditures in the narrow sense had accounted for only 6.25% of the city budget, and all social spending had only accounted for 15%. By 1926, the figures had risen to 17.6% and 37%, respectively, and the city had to use 49% of its tax revenues to cover those social costs for which it was not reimbursed by Reich and state transfer payments.[42]

The first major changes to the settlement embodied in the RGr came from the revaluation of preinflation debt (*Aufwertungsgesetz*) and the commutation of public debt (*Gesetz über die Ablösung der öffentlichen Anleihen*), which were debated in the Reichstag in July 1925. They contained clauses specifying that the first 270 marks received annually on the basis of these laws—a sizable exemption—was to be excluded by local officials in the determination of need for *Kleinrentner*, and, as part of the political compromise reached to insure the passage of this legislation, a separate law was passed which established a comparable exemption for income received by the *Sozialrentner* from the social insurance funds. Municipal welfare officials objected to both of these provisions because they further undermined the principle of individualization and threatened to impose substantial additional financial burdens on local government. However, the Labor Ministry suspected that the intent of the RGr (which these provisions of the revaluation legislation were designed to reinforce) was being subverted by local officials. To resolve these problems, in early September the Ministry issued a decree which required local authorities to establish local welfare rates (*Richtsätze*) which had to provide for preferential treatment for *Sozial-* and *Kleinrentner* in addition to the exemptions contained in the revaluation laws.[43]

---

[42] Max Michel, *Städtischer Gemeindehaushalt und soziale Lasten vor und nach dem Kriege (Aufbau und Ausbau der Fürsorge*, no. 7, 1926). Although actual expenses are given in nominal terms, the percentage changes are adjusted by Michel for changes in the real value of the mark. On the social origins of the new poor, see Sächsische Landeswohlfahrtsstiftung, ed., *Die örtliche und soziale Herkunft der öffentlich unterstützten Personen* (Leipzig, 1927).

[43] *RGBl.*, 1926, I, p. 332 and the extensive materials on this whole affair in BAP RAM 9240. For the principles employed by welfare officials in establishing these rates, see Willi Cuno, *Grundsätzliches bei der Aufstellung und Handhabung von Richtsätzen für die Unterstützung Hilfsbedürftiger (Aufbau und Ausbau der Fürsorge*, no. 12, 1927), and Cuno, *Die Richtsätze der öffentlichen Fürsorge. Grundsätze für ihre Aufstellung und Handhabung (Aufbau und Ausbau der Fürsorge*, no. 19, 1933). The hasty passage of this law at the very end of the legislative session precipitated a minor constitutional crisis because the Reichstag failed to properly consult the Reichsrat, whose role in the legislative process was carefully defined by the constitution. Because of

TABLE 4.1
Persons Receiving Public Support in Frankfurt before and after the War

	1913		1924 (Average)		1925 (Average)		April 1926	
	Cases	Persons	Cases	Persons	Cases	Persons	Cases	Persons
1. Welfare office Total Welfare Recipients	3,344	8,111	11,593	20,787	10,773	19,248	13,800	24,959
a. General Welfare (prewar poor relief)	3,344	8,111	5,549	10,543	5,801	11,022	7,797	14,814
b. *Sozialrentner*	—	—	3,130	5,008	3,026	4,842	3,086	4,938
c. *Kleinrentner*	—	—	1,000	1,600	1,044	1,670	1,117	1,787
d. Unemployed persons without claim to unemployment relief								
1. *Ausgesteuerte*[a]	—	—	1,914	3,636	902	1,714	550	1,045
2. Other							1,250	2,375
2. Welfare Office for War Victims								
a. War Wounded	—	—	291	774	809	1,618	822	1,648
b. War Survivors	—	—	4,118	7,338	4,081	6,992	4,117	7,078
3. Youth Welfare Office	1,798	1,798	2,078	2,078	2,924	2,924	2,603	2,603
4. Labor Office								
a. Unemployed Persons Receiving Relief	—	—	4,960	8,899	7,925	4,215	18,868	32,216
b. Supplements for Short-Time Workers							550	1,027
Total	5,142	9,909	23,040	39,876	26,510	44,997	40,760	69,531

Source: Max Michel, *Städtischer Gemeindehaushalt und soziale Lasten vor und nach dem Kriege. Eine Untersuchung auf Grund der Haushaltspläne der Stadt Frankfurt a.M. (Aufbau und Ausbau der Fürsorge,* no. 7, 1926), p. 63.
[a]Persons whose eligibility for unemployment relief had expired.

In contrast to the RGr, which simply expounded general principles and left the establishment of assistance levels to the discretion of local authorities, the local welfare rates required by the Labor Ministry decree functioned in an entirely different manner. By requiring that municipal welfare officials make public these rates (which had long been used internally by many cities), this decree opened up support levels to public scrutiny and thus set in motion a gradual

their substantive and procedural objections, Reich officials refused to present the law to president Hindenburg for his signature. See the material in BAP RAM 9240. By the spring of 1926, the Reichstag and the Reich government were looking for a way to reconcile their differences, and on June 8, 1926, the Reichstag passed a law which affirmed the substance of the Labor Ministry's September decree. *RGBl.,* 1926, I, pp. 255–56.

TABLE 4.2
Social Expenditures in Frankfurt am Main before and after the War (all figures in millions)

	1913			1924			1926		
	Gross Outlay	Net Transfers	Net City Cost	Gross Outlay	Net Transfers	Net City Cost	Gross Outlay	Net Transfers	Net City Cost
1. Welfare Office	3.737	.738	2.999	10.787	1.095	9.692	12.493	1.133	11.360
2. Welfare for War Wounded and Survivors	—	—	—	1.827	1.642	.185	2.698	2.336	.362
3. Youth Welfare	Contained in 1			2.321	.514	1.807	3.452	.688	2.764
4. School Health programs[a]	.177	—	.177	1.314	.479	.835	1.889	.776	1.113
5. Labor Exchange and Unemployment Relief	.066	.014	.052	.583	—	.583	.878	—	.878
6. Public Health	4.450	2.707	1.743	10.268	6.877	3.391	11.573	8.468	3.105
7. Sports and Swimming	Contained in 4			.121	.010	.111	.153	.019	.134
8. Insurance Office	.089	.004	.085	.094	.005	.089	.105	.006	.099
9. Trade and Commercial Court	.026	.002	.024	.045	.013	.032	.066	.004	.062
10. Subsidy for Legal Advice Station	.012	—	.012	.052	.003	.049	.067	.001	.066
11. Housing Office (Wohnungsfürsorge and Rent Subsidies)	.026	—	.026	.438	.028	.410	.604	—	.604

TABLE 4.2 (Continued)

	1913			1924			1926		
	Gross Outlay	Net Transfers	Net City Cost	Gross Outlay	Net Transfers	Net City Cost	Gross Outlay	Net Transfers	Net City Cost
12. Rent Mediation Office	Contained in 11			.129	.127	.002	.131	.101	.030
13. Municipal Housing Construction	—	—	—	—	—	—	3.500	—	3.500
14. Taxes of District Welfare Authority	.594		.594	.662	—	.662	1.040	—	1.040
Total Ordinary Expenditures for Social Purposes	9.177	3.465	5.712	28.641	10.793	17.848	39.207	13.544	25.663
Total City Expenditures	59,952	30,345	29,607	98,172	48,554	49,618	105,923	53,197	52,776
Extraordinary Expenditures									
Housing						15.750			
Construction						+ 3.500 (from ordinary budget)			
Emergency Job Creation						2.276			

Source: Max Michel, Städtischer Gemeindehaushalt und soziale Lasten vor und nach dem Kriege. Eine Untersuchung auf Grund der Haushaltspläne der Stadt Frankfurt a.M. (Aufbau und Ausbau der Fürsorge, Heft 7, 1926), pp. 64–66.
[a]Includes 86,000 marks for kindergartens and school breakfasts.

leveling-up of rates in those areas whose rates were below those in comparable cities. Inevitably, this publicity tended to transform these rates into norms which were provided to all welfare recipients within a given category unless specific circumstances justified deviation in one direction or the other. Both the Labor Ministry and the recipients hoped that the publication of these rates would make it easier to influence local welfare officials, who were not directly subject to the authority of the Labor Ministry, and judge the validity of complaints by recipients.[44]

In response to continued complaints by the *Kleinrentner*, in the fall of 1926 the Labor Ministry conducted the first nationwide survey of local rates in order to monitor compliance with the September decree.[45] In many instances, welfare rates had already been increased during 1925 from their artificially low post-stabilization levels, and, to the extent that the rates published on the basis of the June 1926 law were adhered to in practice, between 1926 and the next survey in 1928, the increasing publicity of local welfare rates and the general prosperity led to an average increase in local rates of 17–18% in major metropolitan areas in Prussia. In comparison with a 5.2% increase in the cost of food, this meant that the real value of welfare benefits had increased 12–13%. Driven by competition between the various parties to curry the favor of the electorate in anticipation of the 1929 municipal elections, between 1928 and 1930 welfare benefits continued to increase in step with increases in wages, civil servant salaries, housing prices, and social insurance benefits, peaking in 1930 at a level which in major metropolitan areas was 30–33% higher in real terms in comparison with 1926 levels and 21–26% higher in smaller cities.[46]

However, although the publication of local rates in accordance with the Labor Ministry decree did increase the leverage of both Reich officials and recipient groups over local welfare officials, this alone was not capable of resolving the two fundamental problems of the post-1924 welfare system: the overburdening of municipal welfare and the problems resulting from the unhappy combination of a state pension system and an individualizing, means-tested public assistance program. Polligkeit argued that the only real solution to these problems was to remove from the welfare rolls those persons who were not the proper objects of individualizing assistance through a series of related legislative measures: transforming the unemployment relief program (which had been established in 1918 and thoroughly reformed in 1923/24 as part of the currency stabilization) into an unemployment insurance system; further revaluing the as-

---

[44] Richter, "Vermerk über einen Vortrag bei dem Herrn Minister am 22. Dezember 1925 . . . ," BAP RAM 9240.

[45] Labor and Interior Ministers to the social ministries of the federal states (July 31, 1926), BAP RAM 9240.

[46] These figures are calculated from *Statistik des Deutschen Reiches*, Bd. 512/I: *Die öffentliche Fürsorge im Deutschen Reich in den Rechnungsjahren 1932 bis 1936*, p. 58. The cost of food provides a more accurate measure of the cost of living of welfare recipients because public assistance for rent was generally determined on a case by case basis and was not calculated into municipal welfare rates.

sets of elderly and disabled persons; providing more ample pensions for disabled veterans and survivors; and, ultimately, establishing a comprehensive old-age security system.[47] But despite measurable improvements in the level of public assistance during this period, fiscal constraints continued to place strict limits on the efforts of welfare reformers to definitively resolve these problems in the manner recommended by Polligkeit.

The one area in which these reforms achieved notable success was the reform of unemployment assistance. Although welfare officials and social reformers greeted enthusiastically, though not uncritically, the passage of the Labor Exchange and Unemployment Insurance Law in July 1927, municipal welfare remained responsible for a large number of long-term unemployed. There was widespread agreement among welfare reformers that municipal welfare should not limit itself to simply providing monetary assistance, but should go beyond this in order to help maintain the work ethic and prevent the decline from unemployment to criminality and dependence.[48] As Johannes Horion, Landeshauptmann for the Rhineland and an influential figure in the Caritasverband, argued at the 1927 DV conference, although the unemployed had a right to work, this did not include the right to remunerative work at the prevailing wage, "but rather the right to the development of natural physical and mental capabilities, the right to be protected against the decay of their labor power, the right to happiness and health, as only work can guarantee." The conference participants hoped to link this belief in the salutary moral effects of work with existing emergency works programs through the idea of "welfare through productive work" or "workfare" (*Arbeitsfürsorge*), which gave a Progressive twist to traditional public works programs.[49] While these proposals reflected the centrality of work for therapeutic welfare, the optimistic assumption that municipal welfare would only be responsible for a small residuum of unemployed was quickly belied by unemployment levels which remained consistently above those anticipated by the law. Although the unemployment insurance system was originally supposed to bear primary responsibility for supporting the able-bodied

[47] Polligkeit, "Gegenwartsaufgaben der öffentlichen und der privaten Fürsorge . . . zugleich ein Versuch zu einem Arbeits-Program des Deutschen Vereins," IfG 290b, and Polligkeit, *Forderungen für den systematischen Ausbau der Altersfürsorge (Aufbau und Ausbau der Fürsorge*, no. 14, 1928). On the changing attitudes toward old age and the development of old-age support, see Christoph Conrad, *Vom Greis zum Rentner. Der Strukturwandel des Alters in Deutschland zwischen 1830 und 1930* (Vandenhoeck & Ruprecht, 1994).

[48] Welfare reformers were particularly concerned about the effects of unemployment on two overlapping groups: young workers and homeless, migrant, and casual laborers. On the problem of juvenile unemployment, see Elizabeth Harvey, *Youth and the Welfare State in Weimar Germany* (Oxford University Press, 1993), and Peter Stachura, *The Weimar Republic and the Younger Proletariat* (St. Martin's Press, 1989). On "migrant relief" (*Wandererfürsorge*), see Ewald Frie, *Wohlfahrtsstaat und Provinz. Fürsorgepolitik des Provinzialverbandes Westfalen und des Landes Sachsen 1880–1930* (Schöningh, 1993), pp. 211–24, and, in addition to the DV publications cited by Frie, the running commentary in the *Nachrichtendienst* and the extensive minutes of the DV commission on migrant relief in BAP RAM 9242.

[49] "Verlauf und Ergebnisse des 40. Deutschen Fürsorgetages," *Nachrichtendienst* 8:6 (June 1927), pp. 145–55, citation p. 146, *Die Verwertung der Arbeitskraft als Problem der Fürsorge*, SDV N.F. 9/10 (1927), and *Verhandlungen des Deutschen Vereins*, SDV N.F. 11 (1927).

unemployed, municipal welfare was soon overwhelmed by the rising number of long-term unemployed who depended on public assistance (known as the welfare unemployed), and municipal welfare officials quickly shifted their attention from individualizing help for the unemployed to the complex relationship between municipal welfare and the unemployment insurance system, whose dismantling under the Brüning administration shifted back to municipal welfare responsibility for supporting the rapidly increasing number of unemployed.

Disabled veterans and war survivors were faced with special problems because they had to deal with a bureaucracy of heretofore unimaginable proportions, complex regulations which were manipulated to reduce Reich pension costs, the distortion beyond all recognition of their subjective needs as they were refracted through the technical language of doctors and welfare experts, and a frighteningly complex and unfeeling appeals process. In the second half of the decade, the RVG was amended several times. The major reform approved in December 1927 doubled the pension benefits which disabled veterans had been receiving before a previous 1925 revision, and this increase, together with several other changes, also resulted in a substantial increase in the pensions granted to war widows and the parents of soldiers killed in the war. However, despite the increases in survivors' pensions in 1925 and 1927, the standard of living of war widows and their children declined substantially in comparison with that which they would have enjoyed were it not for the war and the inflation. The relative decline in the standard of living of women belonging to higher social status was far greater than that of working-class women, who, through the combination of military pensions, remunerative labor, and survivors' benefits from the social insurance funds, were often able to maintain their previous standard of living.[50] Of equal import was the decision by the Labor Ministry to reconsider claims by those veterans who were less than 30% disabled and had received settlements in previous years. The number of applicants under this program substantially exceeded the expectations of the Labor Ministry, and new pensions were granted to more than 100,000 veterans, thus quickly pushing actual pension costs above budgeted amounts. Although the Labor Ministry was already coming under pressure to reduce pension costs by early 1929, further pension reform plans were overtaken by events, and military pensions and survivors' benefits were also severely affected by the dismantling of welfare programs under the Brüning administration.[51]

The development of assistance for *Sozial-* and *Kleinrentner* generated more controversy, at least in welfare reform circles, than that of war victims and survivors. The position of the *Sozialrentner* was directly determined by the poststabilization reform of the disability insurance system.[52] Because of its

[50] Karl Nau, *Die wirtschaftliche und soziale Lage von Kriegshinterbliebenen* (*Aufbau und Ausbau der Fürsorge*, no. 16, 1930).

[51] See the running account of E. Claessens in *SPr* 34 (1925), cols. 797–99, 35 (1926), cols. 581–82, 36 (1927), cols. 585–88, 608–12, 1135–39, 1161–63, 1314–16.

[52] Martin Geyer, "Soziale Rechte im Sozialstaat. Wiederaufbau, Krise und konservative Stabilisierung der deutschen Rentenversicherung 1924–1937," in Klaus Tenfelde, ed., *Arbeiter im 20. Jahrhundert* (Klett-Cotta, 1991), pp. 406–34.

method of financing and the requirement that they hold a large portion of their assets in supposedly gilt-edged government bonds, rather than real assets, the disability insurance program had been hit especially hard by the inflation, which had destroyed the accumulated assets from which pension payments were funded. The system could only be upheld by switching from an accumulated entitlement system to a pay-as-you-go method of financing. Although the disability insurance funds paid only nominal benefits in 1924, disability pensions were increased every year between 1925 and 1929, and these higher pension benefits were funded through large increases in both contributions and Reich subsidies.[53]

Municipal welfare officials argued that these schematic increases in disability pensions, together with the exclusion of various amounts in the determination of need, had led to an unfair, wasteful situation in which slightly more than one-fourth of the 2 million disability pensioners and 400,000 widows' pensioners continued to depend on public assistance for at least part of their income, while at the same time benefits continued to be increased for those pensioners who already enjoyed an adequate income.[54] The root of the problem lay in the fact that, with the exception of men with long, unbroken work histories, disability pensions did not as a rule suffice to cover the necessities of life. According to a DV survey, what distinguished those social pensioners who did not depend on municipal welfare from those who did was the existence of supplemental sources of income because disability pensions were intrinsically inadequate for widows and for men who were not eligible for the maximum pension benefits. The DV concluded that, in principle, disability pensioners were not the proper objects of individualized personal help and that their needs should be satisfied by their pensions. Since the fiscal situation of the Reich precluded pensions generous enough to achieve this goal, the DV argued that schematic increases should be abandoned in favor of a system of means-tested supplementary pensions, which it hoped would 1) stem the corruption of the principle of subsidiarity and insure that available funds would be directed toward those social pensioners who needed them most, and, at the same time, 2) forestall the rush of new applicants for any future funds which might be made available by the government. However, by the time these proposals were advanced, the first signs of the depression had become visible, and there was no further need to devise an alternative to previous policies.[55]

Of all of the groups of the new poor, the *Kleinrentner* were least successful in the second half of the decade in achieving a substantial revision of the compromises embodied in the RGr. However, this failure did lead to the sharpest

---

[53] Alois Egger, *Die Belastung der deutschen Wirtschaft durch die Sozialversicherung* (Jena, 1929), pp. 149, 157.

[54] For one skirmish, see "Berücksichtigung der Sozialrentenerhöhungen bei Bemessung der Fürsorgeleistungen," *Nachrichtendienst* 10:9 (September 1929), p. 396.

[55] *Sozialversicherung und öffentliche Fürsorge als Grundlagen der Alters- und Invalidenversorgung*, SDV N.F. 14 (1930); the preliminary results of the DV's survey were published in *Nachrichtendienst* 10:10 (October 1929), pp. 464–72.

conflict between municipal welfare and the Labor Ministry. Because the re-valuation legislation of 1925 brought only minor relief, the *Kleinrentner* contin-ued to call for a special pension law to keep step with what they regarded as the privileged treatment of the *Sozialrentner* (to whom their fortunes had been linked since the inflation) resulting from the de facto revaluation of the assets of the disability insurance funds through increased Reich subsidies. In September 1925, the Rentiers' League circulated the draft of a *Kleinrentner* pension law which would have graduated pension payments according to preinflation assets.[56] Reich officials gave this proposal a cold reception because it would have ren-dered all of the settlements contained in the revaluation laws subject to renego-tiation and because they feared that the difficulties in delimiting the sphere of eligible persons would make the proposed program prohibitively expensive, especially because it was anticipated that the establishment of such a pension program would lead to a substantial influx of new applicants.[57]

Instead, between 1927 and 1929, the Labor Ministry attempted to gain greater control over local welfare policy by issuing increasingly restrictive guidelines for the determination of need and more precise reimbursement regu-lations.[58] Municipal welfare officials feared that the Reichstag would take the next, fateful step of establishing a legal entitlement to a minimum level of benefits, a step which would have contravened the principles of individualiza-tion and subsidiarity and substantially undermined the authority of local self-government.[59] The DV commission established to study the problem came to the same conclusion regarding the *Kleinrentner* that it had reached regarding the *Sozialrentner*: that they were not the proper objects for municipal public assistance and that their needs should be met through an old-age pension sys-tem.[60] However, Labor Minister Rudolf Wissell (SPD) insisted that the equitable treatment of *Kleinrentner* could, in fact, be achieved through the closer regula-tion of local assistance, and the Reichstag social policy committee cut the ground out from under the DV's strategy by rejecting the proposed pension

[56] Wilhelm Schickenberg, *Die Reichsversorgung der Kleinrentner* (Berlin, 1927), pp. 36ff., *Mate-rial zur Kleinrentnerfürsorge*, IV. Wahlperiode, Reichstag Drucksache Nr. 52 (November 1928), Drucksache Nr. 805 (1929), pp. 1157–1207, *Material zur Frage eines Rentnerversorgungsgesetzes (Aufbau und Ausbau der Fürsorge*, no. 11, 1927), *Das Rentnerversorgungs-Gesetz. Material zusam-mengestellt von der Pressestelle des Deutschen Rentnerbundes* (Kassel, 1929), and the running commentary in the *Nachrichtendienst*.

[57] Erwin Rawicz, "Die Ergebnisse einer Erhebung über unterstützte Kleinrentner," *Reichsar-beitsblatt* II, Nr. 18 (1927), pp. 16–20.

[58] "Verordnung zur Änderung der Reichsgrundsätze . . ." (March 29, 1928) in Drucksache Nr. 52, p. 32, and "Verhältnis von Unterhaltspflicht und öffentliche Fürsorge," *Nachrichtendienst* 9:5 (May 1928), pp. 160–61.

[59] Minutes of the HADV (June 4, 1928), IfG 228.

[60] "Die Gefährdung der Grundsätze der Individualisierung und Subsidiarität durch die wied-erholten Abänderungen des Fürsorgerechts," *Nachrichtendienst* 9:6 (June 1928), pp. 186–88, "Gut-achten der Geschäftsstelle zur Frage der Überprüfung des materiellen Fürsorgerechts gemäß RFV und RGr," *Nachrichtendienst* 9:8 (August 1928), pp. 262–68, and "Gekürzte Niederschrift über die Verhandlungen der Kommissison zur Ueberprüfung des materiellen Fürsorgerechts" (September 28–29, 1928), ADCV B I 3.

system and calling instead for the reform of existing *Kleinrentner welfare* legislation.[61] The distribution of draft guidelines in October 1929 provoked a sharp response by both the DV and the Städtetag.[62] However, this conflict between local and national democracy in the welfare sector remained unresolved, and it was the fiscal constraints imposed by the deepening depression which limited what the Labor Ministry could do to aid the *Kleinrentner*. By the end of 1930, Labor Ministry officials admitted that "it is indeed politically uncomfortable, but absolutely necessary, to declare that the *Kleinrentner* pension law must finally be buried."[63]

As can be seen in tables 4.3 and 4.4, both the social consequences of the inflation and the impact of welfare legislation on municipal finances are evident in the national welfare statistics, which were gathered in 1927 for the first time since the 1880s. The most striking fact revealed by these statistics is that the new poor made up 55–60% of the total heads of household supported by municipal welfare; the traditional poor and, increasingly, the unemployed, constituted the remainder. Between 1924 and the end of the Republic, the number of persons in each of the different groups of the new poor who were supported by public assistance and the level of support provided to each group varied in accordance with both changes in welfare legislation and economic and demographic trends.

As can be seen in table 4.5, the sheer number of persons dependent on public assistance placed an immense burden on municipal finances and consumed an ever larger proportion of those municipal expenses (known as the *Zuschußbedarf*) which were not funded through borrowing or specific taxes and had to be funded through general tax revenues and profits from municipal enterprises.

Above and beyond the leap in social spending between 1913 and 1924, social spending for both social insurance and public assistance continued to rise through the end of the decade.[64] Once the currency stabilization had limited their ability to pass on rising social costs to consumers, employers began to feel the impact of these costs on their profit margins, and from 1925 onward they conducted an increasingly violent polemic against rising social spending. While business groups claimed that social spending represented an unproductive, po-

[61] Drucksache Nr. 805, p. 15, and *Verhandlungen des Reichstages*, 46. Sitzung (February 18, 1929), p. 1160.

[62] *Nachrichtendienst* 10:10 (October 1929), pp. 438–64, and, for the response by the Städtetag, "Niederschrift über die Besprechung mit den Vertretern der kommunalen Spitzenverbände und der Kleinrentnerverbände . . ." (November 13, 1929), BAP RAM 9246.

[63] "Niederschrift über die Besprechung über Änderung des Fürsorgerechts" (December 11, 1930), BAP RAM 9247. During the depression, the RFV and the RGr were modified, but the basic system established in 1923/24 was preserved. See Reinhold Schleicher, *Die Wandlung der Wohlfahrtspflege durch den Nationalsozialismus* (dissertation, Heidelberg, 1939), and Christeph Sachße/Florian Tennstedt, *Geschichte der Armenfürsorge in Deutschland*, 3 vols. (Kohlhammer, 1980–92), vol. 3.

[64] "Der Zuschußbedarf der öffentlichen Verwaltung im Deutschen Reich in den Rechnungsjahren 1913/14 und 1925/26," *WuS* 7:21 (1927), pp. 886–91 estimated that 80% of the increase in total public spending (Reich, state, and local levels) was a direct or indirect consequence of the war. For a comparison of the structure and trends in social spending in Cologne, Frankfurt, Essen, Düsseldorf, Aachen, and Bonn for fiscal 1928, see "Die Wohlfahrtsausgaben der Stadt Köln," HAStK, Abt. 902, Nr. 198, Fasz. 3.

TABLE 4.3

Heads of Household Receiving Long-Term Support from District and Regional Welfare Authorities, 1927–1936

Date	War Disabled and Survivors	%	Sozialrentner	%	Kleinrentner[d]	%	Welfare Unemployed	%	Unemployed Receiving Suppl. Relief	%	Other Needy[a]	%	Total	Total Persons Including Dependents
	Heads of Household (in thousands)													
July 31, 1927	73.5	4.7	576.5	36.7	332.3	21.1			589.4[e]	37.5			1,571.7	
March 31, 1928	84.4	5.0	601.4	35.7	332.9	19.8			664.7[e]	39.5			1,683.3	
July 31, 1928	62.7	3.8	609.6	37.3	340.8	20.9	145.0	8.9	16.9	1.0	459.1	28.1	1,634.1	
March 31, 1929	71.1	4.0	627.3	35.2	339.2	19.1	209.3	11.8	36.5	2.0	497.5	27.9	1,780.9	2,833.0[b]
July 31, 1929	50.5	3.0	614.0	36.6	331.9	19.8	182.6	10.9	32.8	1.9	467.2	27.8	1,679.0	
March 31, 1930	57.9	2.9	629.3	31.7	330.2	16.6	387.6	19.5	66.5	3.4	514.2	25.9	1,985.8	3,227.0[c]
June 30, 1930	39.9	2.0	624.9	31.5	317.6	16.0	475.6	24.0	51.4	2.6	474.2	23.9	1,983.4	
Dec. 30, 1930	44.7	1.8	644.3	26.0	311.6	12.6	829.2	33.5	98.0	4.0	548.2	22.1	2,476.0	4,163.0[c]
Sept. 30, 1931	37.9	1.3	609.0	20.8	292.2	10.0	1,317.8	45.1	149.5	5.1	516.7	17.7	2,923.1	
March 31, 1932	40.6	1.0	574.2	14.9	283.7	7.4	2,139.4	55.5	216.2	5.6	600.4	15.6	3,854.5	
Sept. 30, 1932	33.2	.8	570.6	13.2	273.5	6.3	2,290.2	53.1	252.8	5.9	895.7	20.7	4,316.1	8,728.1[b]
Dec. 31, 1932	33.5	.7	585.1	12.7	269.6	5.8	2,473.3	53.7	228.8	5.0	1,018.0	22.1	4,608.2	
March 31, 1933	32.6	.7	529.5	11.3	266.4	5.7	2,344.1	50.2	252.4	5.4	1,183.4	25.3	4,671.3	
March 31, 1934	29.9	.9	595.7	17.9	253.7	7.6	1,038.0	31.2	222.2	6.7	1,188.2	35.7	3,327.9	
March 31, 1935	26.4	1.0	578.2	21.0	265.0	9.6	605.7	22.0	231.1	8.4	1,052.6	38.1	2,759.2	
March 31, 1936	25.4	1.0	569.7	23.0	258.0	10.4	338.3	13.8	225.6	9.1	1,058.4	42.8	2,475.0	

Source: Statistik des Deutschen Reiches, Bd. 421: Die öffentliche Fürsorge im Deutschen Reich 1927 bis 1931, p. 12 and "Die öffentliche Fürsorge im Deutschen Reich," WaS 17 (1937), pp. 206-12.

[a]Figures for Other Needy also included the following number of persons who were unemployed but were not recognized as Welfare Unemployed: 1933–439.4, 1934–424.2, 1935–332.9, 1936–255.6.

[b]Census data gathered only on these dates.

[c]Estimate.

[d]Including persons granted equal benefits by the Kleinrentner welfare law.

[e]This figure also includes Welfare Unemployed and Other Needy.

TABLE 4.4

Total Public Welfare Costs 1927–1936

(all figures in millions, except per capita)

	1927/28	1928/29	1929/30	1930/31	1931/32	1932/33	1933/34	1934/35	1935/36
Expenditures									
Direct Program									
Cost	936.3	106.5	1,217.7	1,544.3	1,955.6	2,409.3	2,221.4	1,703.8	1,408.9
Other[a]	297.7	356.5	405.5	400.1	353.2		155.4	169.9	358.1
Gross Spending by District Welfare	1,234.0	1,463.0	1,623.2	1,344.4	2,308.8	NA	2,564.7	2,051.5	1,767.0
Net Cost of District Welfare (*Zuschußbedarf*)[b]	1,101.5	1,309.1	1,383.5	1,680.1	1,860.6	NA	1,625.5	1,591.7	1,456.8
Gross Spending by Regional Welfare	NA	NA	246.1	260.2	242.9	NA	195.5	185.9	178.2
Net Cost of Regional Welfare	133.2	151.3	150.9	156.7	133.3	NA	113.0	103.0	96.2
Total Net Cost	NA	NA	1,534.4	1,836.8	1,993.8	1,887.8	1,738.5	1,694.7	1,553.0
Subsidies									
Reich					188.3[c]	711.8	712.0	244.9	92.5
	(80.3[d])	(75.9[d])	73.09	5.2					
State					81.4	138.1	53.6	32.4	25.2
Total Public Welfare Costs	1,234.7	1,460.4	1,607.4	1,923.0	2,263.5	2,737.7	2,504.1	1,972.0	1,670.7
Per capita	19.8	23.4	25.8	31.0	36.3	42.0	38.4	30.3	25.3

Source: Statistik des Deutschen Reiches, Bd. 421: *Die öffentliche Fürsorge im Deutschen Reich 1927 bis 1931*, pp. 32–35 and "Die öffentliche Fürsorge im Deutschen Reich," *WuS* 17 (1937), pp. 206–12, citations pp. 211–12.

[a]Includes: Administrative costs, subsidies to public institutions, reimbursements to other district welfare authorities, and subsidies to voluntary welfare and social insurance programs.

[b]Net Cost represented gross spending less income (primarily payments from social insurance and income from charitable foundations), transfer payments from other welfare authorities, and public subsidies. The method for calculating net cost was changed between the first publication of the first overview of Reich welfare statistics for the period 1927–32 and the later overview published in 1937. The revised 1937 figures, which are shown in the table for fiscal years 1929ff., are slightly higher than the figures originally published in 1933. In addition, the Net Cost of regional welfare for 1927/28 and 1928/29 is not entirely comparable with that of later years.

[c]Includes subsidies provided on the basis of the emergency decrees and smaller subsidies for *Kleinrentner*.

[d]Reich and state subsidies to district welfare. These amounts, which are used as proxies for total Reich and state subsidies, are already included in net cost for these years.

litical burden upon the economy which was reducing profits, investment, employment, and ultimately the prosperity of the entire nation, the issue was substantially more complex because it was impossible to quantify the extent to which social spending was necessary to insure either working-class social reproduction or economic productivity itself, much less the net redistributive effect of these programs.[65]

[65] See Egger, *Die Belastung der deutschen Wirtschaft durch die Sozialversicherung*, pp. 1–39, Jürgen von Kruedener, "Die Überforderung der Weimarer Republik als Sozialstaat," *GuG* 11

TABLE 4.5
Welfare Spending and the Development of Municipal Finances, 1913–1933
(millions, except per capita)

Year	Net Municipal Spending	Zuschußbedarf	Per Capita Zuschußbedarf	Welfare Costs	Per Capita Welfare Costs	Total Welfare[b] as % of Zuschußbedarf/ Support for Unemployed as % of Zuschußbedarf
1913/14	2,766.0	1,804.0	32.00	289.9	NA	16.1/8.8
1925/26	5,288.0	3,875.0	63.75	1,089.7	NA	28.1/20.6
1926/27	NA	4,345.0	70.70	NA	NA	NA
1927/28	NA	4,670.0	75.62	1,301.0	NA	27.9/19.3
1928/29	7,645.0	5,182.1	85.24	1,472.6	24.22	28.4/19.6
1929/30	8,030.4	5,397.4	88.79	1,593.6	26.21	29.5/20.9
1930/31	7,660.0	5,552.0	91.33	1,922.2	31.62	34.6/26.8
1931/32	6,720.0[a]	5,120.0[a]	84.22	2,475.0[a]	36.47	48.3/40.5
1931/32	6,500.0	4,900.0	80.60	2,255.0	32.82	46.0/37.8
1932/33	6,070.0[a]	4,670.0[a]	76.82	2,460.0[a]	40.46	52.7/47.0
1932/33	5,400.0	4,000.0	65.80	1,790.0	29.44	44.8/38.1

Source: These figures are taken from *Die Finanzlage der Gemeinden und Gemeindeverbände, WuS* Sonderheft 9 (1932), p. 7 and are supplemented and/or adjusted on the basis of "Die Ausgaben der Gemeinden und Gemeindeverbände für das Rechnungsjahr 1931/32," *WuS* 13 (1933), pp. 547–49, with data for years before 1928/29 taken from Siegmund Forell, "Die Finanzlage der deutschen Gemeinden," *Die Wirtschaftskurve* 12 (1933), pp. 245–58. Similar, though not identical, figures for part of this period can be found in *Die Finanzen des Reichs, der Länder und der Gemeinden (Gemeindeverbände),* Sonderbeilage zu *WuS* 13 (1933), Nr. 20, from which the figure for net municipal spending for 1932/33 has been taken. The data given in these various sources correspond only imperfectly with one another, and the data presented here have been selected to provide the greatest degree of internal consistency. One measure of the severity of municipal spending cuts in other areas is the fact that, despite huge increases in welfare costs, total municipal spending for 1932/33 fell below the level of 1926/27. See also Dieter Rebentisch, "Kommunalpolitik, Konjunktur und Arbeitsmarkt in der Endphase der Weimarer Republik," in Rudolf Morsey, ed., *Verwaltungsgeschichte* (Berlin, 1977), pp. 107–63.

[a] The 220 million mark Reich subsidy for municipal welfare unemployed for 1931/32 and the 672 million mark Reich subsidy for 1932/33 have been added back to these figures to give a more accurate measure of municipal welfare spending.

[b] Including youth welfare, public health, general assistance (*Wirtschaftsfürsorge*), and the 20% municipal share of crisis relief.

(1985), pp. 358–76, and two articles by Peter-Christian Witt: "Finanz- und wirtschaftspolitische Folgen der Inflation. Die Auswirkungen der Inflation auf die Finanzpolitik des Deutschen Reiches 1924–1935," in Gerald Feldman, ed., *Die Nachwirkungen der Inflation auf die deutsche Geschichte* (Oldenbourg, 1985), pp. 43–95, and "Finanzpolitik als Verfassungs- und Gesellschaftspolitik. Überlegungen zur Finanzpolitik des Deutschen Reiches in den Jahren 1930 bis 1932," *GuG* 8 (1982), pp. 386–414.

While much of the contemporary debate over the impact of social spending focused on social insurance, the question of welfare costs was generally neglected, even though total welfare spending was nearly half as large as aggregate social insurance contributions. Welfare reformers argued that the root of the problem lay in the efforts of private enterprise to socialize the costs of social reproduction by dismissing surplus workers, especially older workers who had been rendered redundant by rationalization, thus making municipal welfare bear the costs of industrial rationalization, while private enterprise reaped the benefits. Hans Muthesius, a Progressive Berlin municipal councilor and chair of the DV after World War II, argued that these costs should be borne directly by business because they represented a de facto cost of doing business. Both he and other welfare reformers constantly reiterated their belief that carefully designed and well-administered welfare programs were the foundation of a healthy economy, not an unproductive, parasitic burden upon it. However, as Frieda Wunderlich, the coeditor of the leading Progressive publication *Soziale Praxis*, explained, the debate over social spending and welfare reform was caught in a vicious circle because welfare costs could only be reduced and the system again placed in a position where it could devote its energies to the provision of individualized personal help if the social insurance system were expanded and the mesh of the network of insurance programs made even finer so that municipal welfare would only be responsible for the subsidiary support of those persons who were the proper object of such assistance. Welfare reform measures by themselves were incapable of breaking out of this circle. However, all of these reform proposals immediately ran up against the opposition of business groups. In this way, welfare reform was immediately entangled in the bitter debates over the relative primacy of wages vs. profits, consumption vs. investment, *Sozialpolitik* vs. *Wirtschaftspolitik*, and economic democracy (*Wirtschaftsdemokratie*) vs. free enterprise—all of which precipitated the eventual crisis of the Republic.[66]

---

[66] Muthesius, "Planwirtschaft in der Wohlfahrtspflege," *SBA* 8:9–10 (September/October 1928), pp. 1–6, Wunderlich, "Wirtschaft, Sozialpolitik, und Wohlfahrtspflege," *SBA* 9:1–2 (January/February 1929), pp. 3–7, Wunderlich, "Vom Sinn der Wohlfahrtspflege," *SPr* 39:49 (1930), cols. 1104–6, and Luppe, "Die gegenseitigen Beziehungen von Wirtschaft und Wohlfahrtspflege," *Die Stellung der Wohlfahrtspflege zur Wirtschaft, zum Staat und zum Menschen, SDV*, N.F. 15 (1930), pp. 30–43.

Gender, Social Discipline, and the Social Work Profession

IMAGINARY COMMUNITY: THE REPRESSION OF POLITICS AND THE CONSTITUTION OF THE SOCIAL WORK PROFESSION

Since the 1880s, the bourgeois women's movement had maintained that social work represented an exclusively women's sphere of social activity formed through the extension of their specifically feminine qualities of nurturing and caring from the domestic sphere to the sphere of public affairs. Up to World War I and beyond, this depiction of social work as a corrective to the socially corrosive effects of capitalism helped legitimate both this gender-specific conception of social work as a *bürgerlicher Frauenberuf* and the emancipatory aspirations of the women's movement.[1]

After the revolution, German women from all political parties—with the exception of the extreme right—believed that female suffrage had finally given them the opportunity to transform the political culture of the nation and reshape it in accordance with their own maternalistic values. Alice Salomon, the most influential figure in the development of the profession between the turn of the century and the end of the 1920s, summed up the new situation of women in the postrevolutionary period when she wrote that "German women are now

---

[1] An earlier version of parts of this chapter has appeared as "Gender, Citizenship, and the Welfare State: Social Work and the Politics of Femininity in the Weimar Republic," *Central European History* 30:1 (1997). The literature on the social work profession and the women's movement has mushroomed in the past decade. See Christoph Sachße, *Mütterlichkeit als Beruf. Sozialarbeit, Sozialreform und Frauenbewegung 1871–1929* (Suhrkamp, 1986), Sachße, "Social Mothers: The Bourgeois Women's Movement and German Welfare-State Formation, 1890–1929," in Seth Koven and Sonya Michel, eds., *Mothers of a New World: Maternalist Politics and the Origins of Welfare States* (Routledge, 1993), pp. 136–58, Dietlinde Peters, *Mütterlichkeit im Kaiserreich. Die bürgerliche Frauenbewegung und der soziale Beruf der Frau* (Bielefeld, 1984), Elisabeth Meyer-Renschhausen, *Weibliche Kultur und soziale Arbeit. Eine Geschichte der Frauenbewegung am Beispiel Bremens* (Köln, 1989), Irene Stoehr, "Organisierte Mütterlichkeit. Zur Politik der deuschen Frauenbewegung um 1900," in Karin Hausen, ed., *Frauen suchen ihre Geschichte* (Munich, 1983), pp. 221–49, Iris Schröder, "Wohlfahrt, Frauenfrage und Geschlechterpolitik. Konzeptionen der Frauenbewegung zur kommunalen Sozialpolitik im Deutschen Kaiserreich, 1871–1914," *GuG* 21 (1995), pp. 368–90, Rüdiger Baron and Rolf Landwehr, "Von der Berufung zum Beruf—Zur Entwicklung der Ausbildung für die sozialen Arbeit," in Baron, ed., *Sozialarbeit und Soziale Reform* (Beltz Verlag, 1983), pp. 1ff., and Young-Sun Hong, "Motherhood as Calling: Class and Gender in the Making of the German Social Work Profession," Konrad Jarausch and Geoffrey Cocks, eds., *German Professions* (Oxford University Press, 1990), pp. 232–51.

fully responsible citizens. They have not only the right, but also the duty, to work to shape the future fate of the nation, and they must do this as women."[2] Bourgeois women argued that, since women's lives and experiences were rooted in the family and differed in essential ways from those of men, women should participate in those areas of public life which permitted them to express most fully their own maternalistic qualities. It was no coincidence that two major bourgeois women's organizations—the *Allgemeiner Deutscher Frauenbund* and the BDF—devoted their first postwar conferences to the question of how women could expand their previous activity in "municipal housekeeping."[3] These ideas on gender difference were initially shared by many Social Democratic women. They too concentrated on issues which they regarded as distinctly women's issues and regarded social work as their most important field of public activity.[4]

Although the realization of these political and cultural goals depended on the ability of women social workers to reshape the rapidly expanding social service bureaucracy in their own image, the integration of social work into the welfare bureaucracy on a paid basis entangled these women in those very forces against which they defined their cultural mission, and their struggle for better pay and more responsible positions quickly became a struggle to determine whether the social work profession would be able to reshape from within this bureaucracy—and the public life of the nation more generally—or whether it would itself be deformed by those forces it opposed. While leading social work educators generally succeeded in shaping the social work schools in the image of the women's movement, they were never able to translate their own emancipatory rhetoric into the political power necessary to achieve their broader goals. By the end of the 1920s, most leading social work educators were deeply disillusioned with the state of the new profession, and their analysis of the causes of these developments led them toward a form of gendered *Kulturkritik* which alienated them from the Republic which they had originally expected would make possible the realization of the historical goals of the women's movement.

In addition to these challenges, the status of the profession was further undermined by the unfolding of the intrinsic contradictions of social work as a pedagogical undertaking. The constitution of a distinct sphere of social pedagogical action depended on the plausibility of the belief that all forms of need—poverty, *Verwahrlosung*, delinquency, and the like—were simply the external manifestation of internal, spiritual distress resulting from the breakdown of commu-

[2] Salomon, "Der Völkerbundsgedanke und die Frauen," *Frauenfrage* 21:5 (May 1, 1919), p. 35, as well as Gertrud Bäumer, "Die alte und die neue Macht der Frauen," *Die Frau* 28:5 (February 1921), pp. 137–39, and Rosa Kempf, "Frauenbefreiung und Mannesmut," *Die Frau* 29:4 (January 1922), pp. 115–18. See also Salomon, *Die Ausbildung zum sozialen Beruf* (Berlin, 1927), p. 2.

[3] Adele Beerensson, "Ein kommunalpolitisches Frauenprogramm," *Concordia* 26:20 (October 15, 1919), pp. 179–81, and Gertrud Israel, "Frauenaufgaben im neuen Deutschland," ibid., pp. 181–82.

[4] On Workers' Welfare and its relation to the subculture of working-class women, see Christiane Eifert, *Frauenpolitik und Wohlfahrtspflege* (Campus Verlag, 1993), and Karen Hagemann, *Frauenalltag und Männerpolitik* (Bonn, 1990).

nity and that the alleviation of this internal distress was the proper object of social work; although the social worker might provide material support, this was neither the distinguishing characteristic nor the most important aspect of her work.[5] Since the turn of the century, social workers of all political persuasions—with the exception of the Social Democrats—had attributed this distress to the alienation resulting from the colonization of all spheres of social life by a capitalist economy which regarded production and profits as ends in themselves and by the resulting hollowing out of community by organizations which were held together solely by material interests. "Social distress is a part, a dimension of this," wrote Maria Laarmann, *Regierungsrätin* in the Prussian government and director of the Catholic social work school in Münster, "and social work is the response."[6]

The *raison d'être* of professional social work was the (re)creation of community. As the Lutheran theologian and pedagogue Helmuth Schreiner maintained in an influential 1929 essay, "All distress is in some way a sign of shattered community, and it makes no difference if the origin of this distress lies in the guilt of the individual, in social guilt, or other causes. Therefore, the inner meaning, the substance of all help which one person gives to another consists of the will to create new community."[7] However, if community was the goal of social helping, it was also its precondition, and the entire theory of social work as organized helping pivoted on the faith—or fiction—that the social distance between social workers and their clients could only be bridged through the commitment by the social worker to the ethics of selfless service because, it was argued, such a commitment was alone capable of recreating those social bonds which had been broken by industrialization, urbanization, and the spread of an increasingly pluralistic culture. Else Wex, an influential commentator on the development of the profession, summed up all of these ideas when she wrote that the "pure type" of social helping could only be found "where the individual person desires nothing other than to help."[8]

---

[5] Alice Salomon, *Leitfaden der Wohlfahrtspflege*, 3d ed. (Leipzig, 1923), p. 21, Hans Achinger, "Zur Theorie der Fürsorge," in Wilhelm Polligkeit, Hans Scherpner, and Heinrich Webler, eds., *Fürsorge als persönliche Hilfe* (Berlin, 1929), pp. 1–24, and Antonie Morgenstern, "Grenzen der Wohlfahrtsarbeit," *FW* 2:12 (March 1928), pp. 529–34.

[6] Laarmann, "Die Wohlfahrtsschule als Ziel, Aufgabe und Methode," in Preußisches Ministerium für Volkswohlfahrt, ed., *Beiträge zur Methodenfrage der Wohlfahrtsschulen* (Berlin, 1931), pp. 1–16, citation pp. 10–11. Hermann Nohl, one of the leading advocates of the new pedagogy, expressed virtually identical sentiments in his *Jugendwohlfahrt* (Leipzig, 1927), pp. 23–24.

[7] Schreiner, "Zur Psychologie des Hilfsbedürftigen," *FW* 3:10 (January 1929), pp. 401–7, reprinted in Schreiner, *Pädagogik aus Glauben*, 2d ed. (Schwerin, 1931), pp. 137–47, citation p. 138. See also Else Wex, *Vom Wesen der Sozialen Fürsorge* (Berlin, 1929), pp. 14–15. Salomon herself once defined social work as "the science and art of creating community," cited in Dora Peyser, *Hilfe als soziologisches Phänomen* (dissertation, Berlin, 1934), p. 85. These ideas were shared, within limits, by some Social Democrats. See Karl Mennicke, "Der sozialpädagogische Sinn der öffentlichen Wohlfahrtspflege," *SPr* 33:29 (1924), cols. 581–82, and Mennicke, "Die persönlichen Voraussetzungen der sozialen Arbeit. Grundsätzliches und Methodisches zur Ausbildungsfrage," *DZW* 1:2 (May 1925), pp. 49–53.

[8] Wex, *Vom Wesen der Sozialen Fürsorge*, p. 15.

There was a broad consensus regarding this ideal of selfless service. Friedrich Ulrich, the director of the Berlin branch of the Evangelical Welfare Service, insisted that only love, not reason, was capable of bringing forth that act of self-sacrificing devotion, that erotic—in the Platonic sense—movement toward the other through which a genuine I-thou relationship was established. This act of self-overcoming enabled the social worker to recognize the infinite value of the personality of the client, resist the temptation to instrumentalize help for ulterior ends, avoid the danger of reducing all other individuals to a mere object, and thus make the transition to a general economy of love. Ulrich maintained that such love was not possible on a purely humanitarian basis, because, without God, the individual, not the absolute, would become the measure of all things; under such a false humanism, the existential encounter between the social worker and the client would lead to the subordination of the latter to the former, rather than a recognition by the social worker for the infinite value of the unique personality of the client.[9] While such ideas may have been self-evident propositions for the confessional organizations, they were also shared by large segments of the Protestant middle classes. Even Salomon argued that the ability to transcend one's own egoism, which inevitably led to the instrumentalization of others, depended on a transcendent worldview: "Without this faith in a common Father there is no faith in the brotherhood of mankind."[10] Even if spiritual motherhood provided the initial impetus for women's social work, this feminine vocation ultimately had to be perfected through religious faith.

However, if community was both the precondition and the goal of social work, these two moments were mediated by pedagogy, that is, by that advice and guidance which was given on a friendly, personal basis and whose purpose was to help the client rediscover that moral center which was necessary to overcome first inner then outer distress. As one social worker wrote, social work was essentially

> education . . . to transform the person who is enslaved—and thereby needy—into a free, valued member of the community. Through work in personal contact *von Mensch zu Mensch*, through advice and help . . . , social work aspires to free the person from enslavement, illness, danger of infection, economic or moral distress. . . . *The endangered person breaks through the bounds of community; the healthy person sustains and contributes to them.*[11]

---

[9] Ulrich, *Die weltanschaulichen Grundlagen der Wohlfahrtspflege* (Berlin, 1932), pp. 117–37. See also E. Nitzsche, "Die erzieherische Aufgabe der Wohlfahrtsschule," Preußisches Ministerium für Volkswohlfahrt, ed., *Richtlinien für die Lehrpläne der Wohlfahrtsschulen* (Berlin, 1930), pp. 96–103.

[10] Salomon, "Religiös-sittliche Kräfte in der sozialen Arbeit," in *Ratgeber für Jugendvereinigungen* (1920), pp. 157–62, cited in Friedrich Mahling, *Die sittlichen Voraussetzungen der Wohlfahrtspflege* (Berlin, 1925), p. 77. Although Salomon's school was nominally interconfessional, in *Leitfaden der Wohlfahrtspflege*, pp. 10–13, she did not identify any independent foundation for interconfessional social work.

[11] Anneliese Fröhlich, "Der Beruf der Wohlfahrtsbeamten," *SBA* 5:1–2 (January/February 1926),

For Salomon, the mission of public youth welfare was not the material provision for indigent children, but rather "education . . . education in the broadest possible sense." She believed that the therapeutic, pedagogical turn codified in the RJWG represented a decisive turn away from materialism, which worshipped at the altar of the natural sciences and idolized both the beneficial omnipotence of instrumental reason and the manipulation of the external environment in the struggle against need. It signified the breakthrough to a new pedagogical idealism: "Education does not only mean the creation of a favorable milieu, but also the strengthening of the character of the young person, through which he can overcome the influences of the milieu."[12]

The problem with this model of social pedagogical action was that it defined the process of social integration exclusively from the perspective of the social worker, and help had to proceed unidirectionally from the helper to the client. Since this model remained imprisoned within the subjective perspective of the social worker, it was structurally incapable of providing a compelling account of how the purity of the social worker's intentions could help her transcend the limitations of her own subjectivity and thus create a sense of community if such community were not present from the very beginning. Consequently, although this ethos of selfless service did provide a normatively binding orientation for the social work profession, it failed to address, much less transcend, the contradictions between therapeutic helping and social discipline.

CLASS, GENDER, AND SOCIAL WORK

During the demobilization, women of all political parties hoped to preserve the wartime women's employment bureaus (*Frauenreferate*) which they wanted to see transformed into women's social service offices—at the Reich, state, and municipal levels—with primary responsibility for matters affecting women and children. However, these ideas received virtually no support in the Reichstag, and these women had to content themselves with the token gesture of preserving the *Frauenreferate* for the duration of demobilization.[13]

---

pp. 1–2, citation p. 1, emphasis added. On the concept of social pedagogy as it was employed in the 1920s, see Bäumer, "Die historischen und sozialen Voraussetzungen der Sozialpädagogik und die Entwicklung ihrer Theorie," Hermann Nohl and Ludwig Pallat, eds., *Handbuch der Pädagogik*, 5 vols. (Langensalza, 1929), V:3–26, Aloys Fischer, "Das Verhältnis der Jugend zu den sozialen Bewegungen und der Begriff der Sozialpädagogik," in Fischer, *Leben und Werk*, intro. Karl Kreitmair (Munich, n.d.), Bd. 3/4, pp. 167–262, Karl Mennicke, "Das sozial-pädagogische Problem in der gegenwärtigen Gesellschaft," in Paul Tillich, ed., *Kairos. Zur Geisteslage und Geisteswendung* (Darmstadt, 1926), pp. 311–44, and Schreiner, *Pädagogik aus Glauben*, especially pp. 103–18.

[12] Salomon, "Die inneren Grundlagen der Jugendwohlfahrtspflege," *SBA* 2:5–6 (October/November 1922), pp. 17–21, citations pp. 17–18. Nohl, *Jugendwohlfahrt*, pp. 21–22 also criticized this "*Umweltfürsorge*," which neglected the personality of the needy.

[13] Petitions to Reichsarbeitsamt (November 18 and December 26, 1918), Ernst Francke and Helene Simon to Labor Minister Bauer (November 10, 1918), BAP RAM 8873, Josephine Levy-Rathenau, "Frauengedanken zur sozialen Übergangsfürsorge," *ZfA* 19:1–3 (January/March 1918),

In the immediate postwar period, the obstacles faced by women social workers in their efforts to secure better employment and working conditions posed a serious threat to the highly idealized vision of social work as a feminine calling and a labor of social reconciliation which they had articulated before and during the war. During the demobilization, many women were dismissed from positions which they had first occupied during the war. Social workers were not exempt from the threat of dismissal, and many of these women joined trade unions or professional associations in the first months and years after the war.[14] The membership of the German Association of Women Social Work Professionals (*Deutscher Verband der Sozialbeamtinnen*, DVS), which had been founded in 1917, grew from 603 in 1918 to 1,366 at the end of 1919, and then to 2,029 in 1920.[15] However, the leaders of the profession regarded this rush to join social worker unions and professional associations as a mixed blessing. Adele Beerensson, the chair of the DVS, warned the members of the association not to become intoxicated by the wave of unionization and strikes because the belief in the reality of class antagonisms which was implicit in the very idea of unionization was incompatible with their own ideal of class reconciliation through social work.[16] Some members of the DVS criticized this attempt to distinguish between an ostensibly value-neutral social work profession and other female white-collar work, and even the leadership of the social work associations had doubts about the ultimate success of their antiunion efforts. As Helene Weber, the chair of the Association of Catholic Social Workers, confessed in 1919, "Right now I just don't know how we will deal with all of the difficult local situations, because the times are bent on economic struggles and our members often have very little idealism."[17]

Although this ethos helped consolidate the identity of the new profession, its leaders soon became prisoners of their own antisocialism. The fear of losing both existing and potential members to other trade unions led these women to emphasize the unsoundness of both trade unionism and class conflict even more strongly than before. At the same time, even though the creation of professional associations during the war signified a certain break with the self-understanding of the first generation of bourgeois social workers, after the war both social work organizations *and* the welfare agencies again began to emphasize the dis-

pp. 19–28, *Verhandlungen der Verfassungsgebenden Preußischen Landesversammlung* (May 22, 1919), cols. 1609–10, 1641–44, (September 18, 1919), cols. 4022–23, (September 23, 1919), cols. 4173–76, 4210–14, the comments by Labor Minister Schlicke in *Verhandlungen der Nationalversammlung*, 84. Sitzung (August 20, 1919), pp. 2712–13, Marie-Elisabeth Lüders, "Die Auflösung der Frauenreferate," *SPr* 28:50 (1919), col. 898, Lüders to the Demobilization Office (January 31, 1919) and the Interior Ministry (February 1, 1919), BAP RAM 7000, and BDF to Prussian Finance Ministry (May 14, 1919), GStAM Rep. 151 I/C Nr. 11736.

[14] The DVS soon convinced the Interior Ministry to exempt social workers from the provision of the demobilization decrees which permitted employers to dismiss women from jobs they had first taken during the war, *Die Sozialbeamtin* 1:2 (December 1919), pp. 11–12.

[15] Deutscher Verband der Sozialbeamtinnen, ed., *10 Jahre soziale Berufsarbeit* (Berlin, 1926), p. 15.

[16] Beerensson, "Weg und Ziel," *Die Sozialbeamtin* 1:1 (October 1919), pp. 1–4.

[17] Letter to Elizabeth Zillken (December 29, 1919), ADCV 319.4 F I 1a.

tinctiveness of their professional ethos. They repeatedly argued that professional social work had to be clearly distinguished from manual labor and that the social obligations of the profession should take priority of the material welfare of social workers themselves.[18]

This idea of class harmony was first institutionalized in the General Association of Professional Social Work Organizations (the *Gesamtverband der Berufsorganisationen der Wohlfahrtspflege*) which was founded in December 1919 at the urging of the Caritasverband and the Inner Mission. The purpose of the General Association was to unite all social workers—voluntary and paid, male and female, religious and lay—in a single umbrella organization.[19] Both the Caritasverband and the Inner Mission hoped that the organization would protect their employees from the temptations of unionism and prevent the socialist unions from making further inroads into the social work profession, and the founders of the General Association emphasized both the peculiar nature of its ethics of selfless service and the commitment of its members to value-neutral professionalism.[20] However, although the General Association claimed some twelve thousand social service and charity workers, it was not able to effectively work to improve the wages and working conditions of women social workers. Even though the Labor Ministry recognized it as the collective bargaining agent for its members, its effectiveness depended to a large extent on the attitude of municipal authorities, who for the most part did not regard the General Association as a serious bargaining partner because it was not affiliated with any of the national unions.[21]

The weakness of the national leadership forced the local and regional branches of the individual social work associations to negotiate directly with local municipal authorities regarding pay, working conditions, and benefits.[22] In 1920 the social worker associations considered joining the larger and more

---

[18] Turnau, "Die Schwierigkeiten in der Organisation der Sozialbeamtinnen," *Die Sozialbeamtin* 1:2 (December 1919), and anonymous, "Berufsarbeit und öffentliches Leben," *Die Sozialbeamtin* 1:3 (February 1920), pp. 22–23. On the wages and working conditions of social workers in the 1920s, see Susanne Zeller, *Volksmütter—mit staatlicher Anerkennung. Frauen im Wohlfahrtswesen der zwanziger Jahre* (Düsseldorf, 1987).

[19] "Leitsätze für die Aussprache über die Frage der Organisation der Berufsarbeiter der Inneren Mission und verwandter Arbeitsgebiete," ADW CA 868.

[20] "Entwurf: Satzungen des Gesamtverbandes . . . ," the undated minutes (probably November 21, 1919), and "Richtlinien für die Arbeiten des Gesamtverbandes (Arbeitsprogram)," all in ADW CA 868.

[21] *Die Sozialbeamtin* 1:4 (April 1920), p. 29, and DVS, ed., *10 Jahre soziale Berufsarbeit*, p. 19.

[22] As part of a joint effort to improve the employment conditions of professional social workers, in April 1921 the three major social worker associations formed the *Arbeitsgemeinschaft der Berufsverbände der Wohlfahrtspflegerinnen Deutschlands* to represent—while respecting the autonomy of the member organizations—their common interests and operate a common job placement service. See Helene Weber, "Der Gemeinschaftsgedanke in der Sozialbeamtinnenbewegung," *SBA* 1:1 (April 1921), p. 1, Weber to Zillken (September 5, 1920), ADCV 319.4 F I 1a, and "Satzung der Arbeitsgemeinschaft der Berufsverbände der Wohlfahrtspflegerinnen Deutschlands," *SBA* 3:3–5 (March/May 1923), pp. 15–16. The official publication of the *Arbeitsgemeinschaft* was *Soziale Berufsarbeit*. The 1926 and 1927 issues of *SBA* carry the incorrect volume number. All further references to these volumes give the actual volume number and correct date.

influential Association of Prussian Municipal Civil Servants and Employees (*Komba*). However, negotiations with the civil servants' union ultimately collapsed because the social worker associations regarded it as essential to maintain their own women's organizations and because they were unwilling to recognize the use of strikes as a legitimate bargaining tool, as *Komba* demanded.[23] Many rank-and-file social workers criticized this decision because they felt that their isolation in women's organizations deprived them of all influence over their own working conditions and thoughtlessly sacrificed their own material interests to an abstract and distant principle. However, Antonie Hoppmann, the head of the Cologne branch of the Association of Catholic Social Workers, insisted that an autonomous, separate organization had to be preserved at all costs because affiliation with *Komba* on the terms demanded by that organization would be tantamount to abandoning their vocation and mission: "For us it is not a question here of women's rights, but of the right to be women (*Frauensein*)."[24]

Already in the early 1920s, many leading women politicians were beginning to express a sense of alienation resulting from their political marginalization. As Bäumer noted, "The entire structure of social and political life is so thoroughly and in every aspect masculine that women initially are repelled and oppressed by it and only with great difficulty learn to be themselves within this apparatus."[25] These women tended to demonize the characteristic features of modern political life as masculine phenomena which were alien and even antithetical to women's nature. Bäumer insisted that women should protect themselves from "frightful, slavish servitude" of party politics and that women's political engagement must also point toward an alternative, distinctly feminine conception of politics and society.[26] Rosa Kempf, a prominent bourgeois feminist and director of the Frankfurt social work school early in the decade, argued that contemporary politics consisted only of party squabbling which psychologically lamed the people and left them with a sense of helplessness, and she suggested that only charismatic leaders could "awaken a general, so to speak religious enthusiasm of the entire people through which divided hearts could be formed into a single will."[27] Not surprisingly, though, beyond such evocations of community, these women found it exceedingly difficult to specify the positive, concrete content of the new political culture and institutions they envisioned, and this search by Kempf and her colleagues for an authentically feminine form of politics increasingly relegated these women further to the margins of political life, where their sterile opposition could only undermine the Republic and prevent them from working to reform the system they so despised.

---

[23] Weber to Zillken (November 9, 1920), ADCV 319.4 F III 1a.

[24] Hopmann, "Unser Ringen um Selbständigkeit," *SBA* 2:1–2 (May/June, 1922), pp. 1–3.

[25] Bäumer, "Die alte und die neue Macht der Frauen," p. 138, and Mathilde Drechsler-Hohlt, "Mann und Frau in der Politik," *Die Frau* 28:1 (October 1920), p. 16.

[26] Bäumer, "Die alte und die neue Macht der Frauen," p. 139.

[27] Rosa Kempf, "Die politische Begabung der deutschen Frauen," *Die Frau* 28:6 (March 1921), pp. 181–82.

GENDER CONFLICT AND THE THEORETICAL FOUNDATIONS OF SOCIAL WORK
TRAINING IN THE 1920s

In the first months after the revolution, the most pressing task for social workers was to convince the Prussian government to revise the training and licensing
regulations which had been issued in September 1918. These regulations reflected the position of the male medical officials in the Prussian Interior Ministry, who held a much narrower view of the actual needs of female social workers than did bourgeois feminists and who opposed what they perceived as an
excessively liberal and theoretically oriented education in social scientific fields
provided by most of the existing social work schools. In February 1919, students at the leading professional social-work schools submitted to the Prussian
government a petition which criticized the excessive influence of male doctors
and school inspectors on the examination committees, and in April of that year
the Conference of German Social Women's Schools (*Konferenz der sozialen
Frauenschulen Deutschlands*) submitted its own ideas for the revision of the
licensing regulations.[28] Although Prussian health officials continued to insist
that, in view of the importance of public health in the postwar period, it was
essential for social workers to receive a thorough training in social hygiene,
official resistance to the views of social work educators was weakened by the
appointment of Helene Weber to oversee social work regulation in the Prussian
Ministry for Public Welfare. After much debate among Prussian state officials
and social work educators, the Prussian government issued revised licensing
requirements in October 1920.

The revised regulations, which provided the model for the subsequent regulation of social work training in many other states, reestablished the broad focus
of the curricula of the social women's schools and maintained the previous
tripartite division of the curriculum into social hygiene, youth welfare, and general assistance. Applicants for the social work schools had to have graduated
from a lyceum or a middle school for girls, but they permitted women who had
only an elementary school education to attend these schools if they passed an
admissions test. The regulations retained the traditional two-year training period. To obtain state certification, these women were required to pass a state
licensing exam after finishing their studies and complete a one-year probation-
ary period.[29]

---

[28] Petition (February 1919), the DV memorandum, "Gutachtliche Aeusserung über den Verlauf
der staatlichen Prüfung von Fürsorgerinnen . . ." (June 12, 1919) both in StAF, Magistratsakten:
Vereine 6/3, and Salomon, "Begründung zu einem Entwurf, Vorschriften über die staatliche Prüfung
von Sozialbeamtinnen und Wohlfahrtspflegerinnen" (April 1919), StAF Magistratsakten: Vereine
6/4.

[29] These Prussian regulations, the supplementary guidelines, and regulations issued by other states
are reprinted in Herbert Studders, ed., *Konferenz zur Beratung über die Fragen der Ausbildung zur
sozialen Arbeit veranstaltet von der Reichsgemeinschaft von Hauptverbänden der freien Wohlfahrtspflege* (n.p., n.d., [1921]). See also Salomon, "Die staatliche Prüfung von Wohlfahrtspflegerinnen,"
Volkswohlfahrt (1921), pp. 64–66.

Although the revised guidelines went a long way toward satisfying the demands of female social work educators, they were only a way station in the ongoing debate over the theoretical foundations of the profession and the organization of social work training. Part of the problem was that municipal administrators often regarded training in nursing and social hygiene as the best foundation for social work. This trend was strengthened by the medical establishment, which had long argued that hygiene rather than pedagogy should be the foundation for social work training. By the mid-1920s the demand for social hygiene workers to fill the new positions for family social workers (*Familienfürsorgerinnen*) had led to such an acute shortage of trained applicants that the Prussian Ministry for Public Welfare urged the social work schools to increase the number of students in this field.[30] Those schools operated by bourgeois feminists were so susceptible to these pressures because the inflation had so deeply undermined their finances that a number of them—including those run by Salomon (Berlin), Lüders (Düsseldorf), and Bäumer and Baum (Hamburg)—had become financially dependent on local government.[31] Moreover, at the same time that this renewed emphasis on the role of hygiene in social work training was threatening the influence of the women's movement on social work training, the Caritasverband was making a major push to gain control over the social work schools run by Catholic women's associations, which it charged were subordinating Christian charity to the aims of the women's movement. The Caritasverband even attempted to annex the Association of Catholic Social Workers, but decided to move slowly because the "feminist attitudes" of the organization were certain to provoke strong resistance.[32]

One aspect of this gendered struggle over the relative importance of hygiene and pedagogy was the ultimately unsuccessful attempt by middle-class women to establish their own *Spitzenverband* to promote their own vision of social reform, especially in the youth welfare field. At Bäumer's suggestion, in the early 1920s Anna von Gierke (DNVP), the chair of an influential Berlin youth welfare association, began to organize humanitarian organizations active in the youth welfare field into a regional association in Berlin, and similar umbrella associations were formed in Munich and the Rhineland. However, the leaders of these organizations soon recognized that they would have to form a nationwide central organization if they were to have an effective voice in the shaping of the welfare system and succeed in obtaining all-important state subsidies for their work. In June 1924 these organizations of humanitarian youth and maternal welfare associations merged with an organization—led by Siddy Wronsky, a leading Progressive welfare reformer who moved to the SPD in the late

---

[30] *Volkswohlfahrt* 4 (1923), p. 411.

[31] "Bericht über die Konferenz der sozialen Frauenschulen" (June 1–3, 1923), StAM Schulamt 3518.

[32] See the extensive correspondence in ADCV 142 and Kreutz to Freiburg Caritas director Eckert (December 6, 1924), ADCV 219.3.

1920s—active in the field of general assistance to form a new organization, Humanitas.[33]

Although Humanitas presented itself as neutral with respect to the political and religious views of its members, Gierke conceded that the establishment of a separate humanitarian *Verband* was a practical necessity because of the growing influence of other welfare *Verbände*: "It is a symptom of our times that movements everywhere seek to close off their adherents to a greater or lesser degree with respect to all other tendencies, to accentuate the differences dividing them, and to close off all possibility of purely human understanding with other movements."[34] In addition, the BDF feared that the failure to establish such a *Spitzenverband* would weaken the traditions of the women's movement and thus diminish its influence.[35] In the fall of 1924, the numerous member organizations of the BDF—including professional associations of women physicians, teachers, social workers, and nurses, as well as charitable organizations—combined into a "Special Division for Social Work," which then collectively joined Humanitas. The BDF hoped that this move would strengthen Humanitas's claim to recognition as a humanitarian *Spitzenverband*, and it both cemented the connections between Humanitas and the bourgeois women's movement and gave the humanitarian ideals of the organization a distinctly feminist orientation. As the draft statutes of Humanitas stated, "Welfare is . . . to be regarded as a special area for women's abilities; women must be accorded a leading role in this area."[36]

Gierke and Wronsky initially hoped to strike a deal with the German Association of Private, Philanthropic Health Care and Convalescent Institutions (*Vereinigung der freien privaten gemeinnützigen Kranken- und Pflegeanstalten Deutschlands*). The Association, which was headed by Leo Langstein, the director of the Kaiserin-Auguste-Krankenhaus and a leading figure in social hygiene circles, had been founded in 1920. However, the influence of the Langstein Association was limited because it only included organizations active in the social hygiene field. Since the Reich Labor Ministry dealt directly only with those organizations which were also active in youth welfare and work-related fields, the needs of Langstein's Association complemented those of Humanitas. Despite these common concerns, the unification of these two organizations proved to be extremely contentious. The Langstein organization had already been recognized by the Labor Ministry as a *Spitzenverband* in the spring of 1924, and the physicians who dominated the Association defined social hygiene in very broad terms and hoped to use this broad definition as a

---

[33] "Die Gründung eines allgemeinen Wohlfahrtspflegeverbandes 'Humanitas,'" *SPr* 33:46 (1924), col. 979.

[34] Gierke (n.d.) StADf XX 388.

[35] Gierke, "Der Fünfte Verband und seine Bedeutung im Rahmen der Wohlfahrtspflege" (n.d.), HLA 1–4/1, circular to BDF members (September 2, 1924), HLA 6–29/3, and Bäumer to Fifth Welfare League (January 22, 1925), BAP RAM 9149.

[36] Langstein to Labor Ministry (n.d.), BAP RAM 9149.

wedge to expand into the welfare organizations run by these women.[37] These men demanded that many of the programs and institutions belonging to Humanitas—including maternal advice stations and rural summer camps for urban children—be placed under their control, and they invoked this same rationale to support their claim that Humanitas itself should be subordinated to the Association.[38]

In response, Gierke and Wronsky asked the Labor Ministry to recognize Humanitas as an independent *Spitzenverband*.[39] This idea was supported by the Interior Ministry, as well as by a number of states, which regarded the organization as the legitimate democratic counterpart to those welfare organizations representing Catholic and Evangelical worldviews.[40] However, the leading officials in the Labor Ministry insisted that there could only be one humanitarian *Spitzenverband*. They supported instead the Langstein organization because they were determined to resist the attempt to "establish special privileges for women" in the welfare system. Otto Wölz insisted that he "could not accord an absolute predominance to women in these areas under any conditions. I believe that, especially in the area of social work, rational cooperation of men and women is absolutely necessary. It is especially appropriate that the economic aspects are as a rule directed by men."[41]

Langstein contrasted the expressly feminist orientation of Humanitas with the ostensible gender neutrality of his own organization.[42] With the support of the Labor Ministry, Langstein energetically worked to annex Humanitas and insisted that, as a condition for merging the two organizations, only those member organizations of Humanitas that were directly involved in social work would be permitted to join the new organization. This would have excluded the bulk of the associations belonging to the BDF. Erwin Ritter also criticized "the expressly feminist orientation of the Humanitas association," and he called for the outright absorption of Humanitas into the Langstein organization, rather than the perpetuation of their loose relationship. In the end, the support of the

---

[37] Minutes of the conference of the Fünfter Wohlfahrtsverband (April 27, 1924), and "Niederschrift der Landes- und Provinzialvertreter des Fünften Wohlfahrtverbandes" (April 27, 1924), both StADf XX 469.

[38] On the tentative agreement between the two organizations, see Langstein to Gierke and Wronsky (July 16, 1924), cited in Langstein to Labor Ministry (n.d.), BAP RAM 9149, and "Niederschrift der Landes- und Provinzialvertreter des Fünften Wohlfahrtverbandes" (April 27, 1924), StADf XX 469. The official publication of Humanitas was *Die Frau in der Sozialen Arbeit*.

[39] Humanitas to Labor Ministry (July 4, 1924), ADW CA 1184, and Gierke to Labor Ministry (October 25, 1924), BAP RAM 9149.

[40] Ernst Ranft to Langstein (February 24, 1925), BAP RAM 9149.

[41] Wölz to Hannes Kaufmann (August 2 & 11, 1924), BAP RAM 9149, and Humanitas to Langstein (July 8, 1924), cited in undated letter from Langstein to Labor Ministry, BAP RAM 9149. Langstein's opposition to Humanitas was reinforced by the confessional welfare organizations, which were concerned about the anticonfessional orientation of Humanitas, while Langstein himself repeatedly emphasized his willingness to work closely with these religious organizations. See Berlin Caritas director Johannes van Acken to Kreutz (November 29, 1924), ADCV 460.1.

[42] Langstein to Labor Ministry (n.d.), BAP RAM 9149.

Labor Ministry enabled Langstein to prevail in this struggle with Humanitas.[43] The new expanded organization was officially founded in December 1924, and in 1932 the name of the organization was changed from the colorless but descriptive Fifth Welfare League to its present *Deutscher Paritätischer Wohlfahrtsverband.*[44]

This conflict over the relative importance of pedagogy and hygiene in social work training was also the main issue at a major conference sponsored by the Prussian Ministry for Public Welfare in October 1924. At this conference, Polligkeit argued that the nature of social work training had to be determined by the practical needs of their future employers, not the ideals of the women's movement. Polligkeit insisted that hygiene should play a greater role in social work training because preliminary training in nursing provided the best way of judging whether social work students had that selfless devotion which was indispensable for their future vocation, and he reinforced this point by recommending that the regulations governing social work training should be altered to require two years of preliminary training in nursing and one year experience in pedagogy as the prerequisite for admission to the social work schools.[45]

Polligkeit's suggestions provoked the lively opposition of many of the women social work educators attending the conference. Among these women, there was a broad consensus that, the claims of the medical establishment notwithstanding, social hygiene—especially within the larger framework of family social work—was itself a pedagogical undertaking. As Idamarie Solltmann, a former member of the USPD who became a prominent Catholic social work educator, argued, it was not possible to cure dependent persons simply by giving them money to pay the rent or helping them find employment. Rather, "his will must be awakened, and he must be brought to the point where he raises himself up and again feels a sense of duty and responsibility to care for others, above all for his family. This means strengthening his sense of responsibility and duty."[46] This conviction that such personal help required an immediate,

---

[43] Circular from Langstein to the state and provincial directors of the Fünfter Wohlfahrsverband (March 24, 1925), StADf XX 471. Langstein boasted of his success in excluding "women's organizations and occupational organizations and thus spar(ing) the organization the odium associated with the idea that it represented an organization for the struggle of women against men in the welfare field."

[44] The organization adopted this name because it was generally named fifth—after the three confessional oranizations and the Red Cross—in any listing of the welfare *Spitzenverbände*. The statutes of the *Fünfter Wohlfahrtsverband* were crafted in such a way as to limit the influence of these women's groups, and Wronsky herself was denied a seat on the board of the new organization.

[45] Polligkeit, "Das Lehrziel der staatlich anerkannten Wohlfahrtsschulen unter besonderer Berücksichtigung der praktischen Anforderungen an den Beruf," in Preußisches Ministerium für Volkswohlfahrt, ed., *Grundsätzliche Fragen zur Ausgestaltung der staatlich anerkannten Wohlfahrtsschulen* (Berlin, 1926), pp. 5–16.

[46] Solltmann, "Wissen und Bildung im Beruf der Wohlfahrtspflegerin," *FW* 2:6 (September 1927), pp. 312–18, and Solltmann, "Sollen und können weltanschauliche Kräfte und Überzeugungen in der Familienfürsorge wirksam werden?" in *Ungelöste Fragen der Wohlfahrtspflege*

intuitive insight into the character and mental state of the client lay at the root of the argument that psychology and pedagogy had to form the core of the social work curriculum.[47]

Salomon's own arguments in support of the integration of pedagogy and psychology into the social work curriculum were part of her ongoing efforts to formulate a theory of social work and social work training. In her influential 1927 book *Education for a Social Vocation* (*Die Ausbildung zum sozialen Beruf*) Salomon systematized the experience of the first generation of social work educators whose vision of the profession had been shaped by the women's movement. Here, Salomon argued that social work schools occupied a position *sui generis* in the German educational system because social work schools pursued knowledge for the sake of practice, while universities pursued knowledge for its own sake.[48] On the one hand, the goal of social work training was not to master a specific body of facts, but rather to acquire "an understanding of people, of the peculiarity, uniqueness and indivisibility of every particular task which is related to individuals." On the other hand, social work schooling was a form of moral education toward a social worldview which gave the social worker an understanding of the mutual obligations and responsibilities of communal life and, at the same time, moved her to act upon this knowledge: "All social education remains sterile and without consequence, when it does not lead to a social attitude, when it does not make the person . . . into someone which she was not before."[49] Since the cultivation of this ethos of selfless service could only be achieved on the basis of a comprehensive worldview, social work schools, she argued, had to form a community in which a common set of beliefs grew out of shared experiences.[50] Social work schools, Salomon maintained, should neither content themselves with training nurses or social investigators, who would be subordinated to doctors and subaltern welfare officials, nor aspire to provide a comprehensive education in social science and philosophy, which would permit their students to comprehend the general social causes of need and thus take up the cause of social reform. Instead, this intermediate character of the social work schools as "higher" vocational schools corresponded to the

---

(= *Veröffentlichungen des Vereins katholischer deutscher Sozialbeamtinnen*, Nr. 1, 1929), pp. 14–38, citation p. 15. Along these same lines, Rosa Kempf argued—against those persons who insisted that social workers should have a more extensive knowledge of home economics—that social workers should only be responsible for "*soziale Schäden*" and should not be viewed as "*Mädchen für Alles*." Kempf, "Hauswirtschaftliche Ausbildung der Wohlfahrtspflegerin," *FW* 4:1 (April 1929), pp. 39–40.

[47] Louise Besser, "Das Lehrziel der staatlich anerkannten Wohlfahrtsschulen," and Eduard Spranger, "Psychologie und Pädagogik in der Wohlfahrtsschule," both in *Grundsätzliche Fragen*, pp. 17–23, 67–83, respectively.

[48] Salomon, "Die deutsche Akademie für soziale und pädagogische Frauenarbeit im Gesamtaufbau des deutschen Bildungswesens," *DZW* 5:3 (June 1929), pp. 137–44. Klumker was simply expressing a widely held opinion when he pointed out that social work training could not be integrated into the university system, "Hochschule und Ausbildung zu sozialen Berufen," *ASS* 62 (1929), pp. 589–601, and Salomon, *Die Ausbildung zum sozialen Beruf*, pp. 172ff.

[49] Salomon, *Die Ausbildung zum sozialen Beruf*, pp. 53, 204.

[50] Ibid., p. 204.

task of the social worker, whose concern for helping and influencing the needy demanded a greater degree of freedom and responsibility than that granted to nurses and secretaries, but whose concern for the suffering individual precluded a direct engagement in social reform.[51]

This vision of social work education was plagued by a dualism between the superficial, syncretic education of students in a number of ancillary disciplines and the development of a social worldview which would inspire students and sustain their devotion through the inevitable disappointments of their daily activity. The problem, Salomon lamented, was that there existed no science of social work (*Fürsorgewissenschaft*) which would integrate specialized scientific knowledge and the ethos of selfless service into a coherent practical discipline without subordinating practical experience—which was always concretely individual and oriented toward the unique personality of the client—to abstract theoretical schemata, which could not but denature this personal contact.[52] This search for a science of social work yielded so few concrete results because Salomon and her contemporaries failed to understand that social work training— as they envisioned and practiced it—was primarily a hermeneutic process through which the student internalized those norms which permitted her to apply in any individual case those empirical rules of thumb established by the experience of previous generations of social workers without having to reflect explicitly on the foundations of this knowledge. This method of training functioned adequately because the language of helping always contained at a preconscious, tacit level those empirical generalizations which constituted the distilled experience of the previous generation of women social workers. This self-enclosed language of helping made it possible for the social work student to internalize the norms and experiences of her teachers and, in so doing, led her to perceive the applicant for public assistance in a specific manner: as a person suffering from distress which could only be relieved through personal help. It was this unquestioned, preconscious conception of indigence as a spiritual problem—what one writer called a "therapeutic-pedagogical prejudgment"—and the resulting belief in the indispensability of personal help which transformed the presence of the social worker in the household of the client into an authentic house visit. However, the same antipathy toward abstract, general concepts which drove social work educators toward a "theory of practical experience" also blocked the path to critical reflection on the foundations of the discipline and reinforced the essentialism inherent in the definition of social work as organized helping.[53]

---

[51] Ibid., pp. 77, 90.

[52] Ibid., pp. 55, 109ff. Bäumer advanced similar arguments in "The Contribution of the Various Sciences to Social Work Training," in *First International Conference of Social Work*, 3 vols. (Paris, 1929), II:100–107. See the critical comments by Hans Scherpner, "Die Ausbildung zum sozialen Beruf. Zur Kritik der Schrift von Dr. Alice Salomon," *Zentralblatt* 20:2 (May 1928), pp. 39–42.

[53] For a critique of the conflation of fact and value underlying this essentialism, see Hans Achinger (the director of the *Centrale für private Fürsorge* in the late 1920s), "Vom Wesen der Fürsorge," *Zentralblatt* 21:5 (August 1929), pp. 174–77, Joachim Matthes, *Gesellschaftspolitische Konzeptionen im Sozialhilferecht* (Stuttgart, 1964), pp. 67–84, 109–25, and, for an analysis of this model of practical knowledge grounded in the self-interpreting structure of everyday language,

The debate over social work training and curriculum reform continued at two different levels through the end of the decade. While on the surface it was a question of whether the traditional three-track curriculum should be retained or abandoned in favor of a unitary curriculum which in theory corresponded more closely to the needs of family welfare work, the underlying issue continued to be the relative primacy of nursing or pedagogy and the respective positions of men and women in the welfare system. The 1930 guidelines issued by the Prussian Ministry for Public Welfare struck a compromise between the spirit of pedagogy and the letter of hygiene while continuing to rely upon the commitment to helping to overcome the syncretism of the new curriculum and thus establish the unity and autonomy of social work as a distinct profession. "The purpose of social work," the guidelines claimed, "is to overcome or meliorate the distress of the individual or society. Its realm is as broad as the realm of human distress and need. The collective term 'social work' thus encompasses a large number of discrete areas of work . . . but social work still represents an inwardly unified, unitary whole, because it is defined in relation to the total complex of social distress."[54]

Although leading social work educators had argued since the early 1920s that the universities were not the appropriate place to educate social workers and welfare administrators, they were nevertheless keenly aware that the existing social work schools did not provide their students with either the academic training in such fields as economics and law or the knowledge of administration comparable to that acquired by men at the universities. This deficiency was often used by municipal officials as a reason for disqualifying women social workers from responsible administrative positions. In an attempt to solve this problem, in 1925 Salomon founded the *Akademie für soziale und pädagogische Frauenarbeit* (Academy for Women's Social and Pedagogical Activity) in Berlin in conjunction with both such prominent bourgeois feminists as Bäumer and Baum and the major organizations of female teachers and social workers. The

---

Jürgen Habermas, *Knowledge and Human Interests*, trans. Jeremy Shapiro (Beacon Press, 1971), pp. 140–86. The term "therapeutic-pedagogical prejudgment" (*heilpädagogische Vorentscheidung*) is taken from Käthe Truhel, *Sozialbeamte. Ein Beitrag zur Sozioanalyse der Bürokratie* (dissertation, Frankfurt, 1934), pp. 59–61. For an excellent, but uncritical description of this mode of social-pedagogical knowledge, see Scherpner, "Methoden individualisierender Fürsorge in den Vereinigten Staaten," *FW* 1:11 (February 1927), pp. 509–22, 2:1–3 (April/June 1927), pp. 26–34, 69–81, 120–30.

[54] Preußisches Ministerium für Volkswohlfahrt, ed., *Richtlinien für die Lehrpläne der Wohlfahrtsschulen*, p. 3, and Preußisches Ministerium für Volkswohlfahrt, ed., *Beiträge zur Methodenfrage der Wohlfahrtsschulen*, as well as Sachße, *Mütterlichkeit als Beruf*, pp. 250–71. Salomon, Wronsky, and Muthesius also played a leading role in popularizing the idea of "social diagnosis" and the case-work method. On the reception of case work in Germany, see Salomon, *Soziale Diagnose* (Berlin, 1925), Salomon/Wronsky, *Soziale Therapie. Ausgewählte Akten aus der Fürsorgearbeit* (Berlin, 1926), Wronsky/Muthesius, "Methoden deutscher Fürsorgearbeit," *DZW* 4:3 (June 1928), pp. 113–25, and Wronsky, *Methoden der Fürsorge* (Berlin 1930). Salomon's pamphlet, which originally appeared in *DZW* 1:3 (June 1925), was, as she admitted, a free adaptation of the work of Mary Richmond, the leading American proponent of social case work.

inclusion of higher education for both social work and the teaching professions within a single institution reflected the heritage of the women's movement and Salomon's conviction that they were both essentially pedagogical vocations. The *Akademie* was primarily designed to provide women who had attended the social work schools and who had extensive practical experience with the opportunity to reflect more systematically upon the ethical and cultural significance of their work and its relevance to the women's movement.[55] The *Akademie* also contained a social scientific research department to systematize the insights and experiences of women active in social and pedagogical fields and investigate the issues of women, the family, and the young.[56] Salomon was so deeply embedded in the tradition of the women's movement and still held so tightly to the prewar vision of social work as spiritual motherhood that she was unable to understand the forces which lay behind the demand for greater training for women in administration. Since the universities were devoted to the pursuit of goals which were incompatible with the practical orientation of the social work schools, Salomon argued, it was necessary to create separate educational institutions to cultivate the ethos of selfless service and carry on the tradition of spiritual motherhood. Conversely, the existence of a separate women's academy would have no justification if it did not serve these goals.[57]

Although most social work educators agreed on the need for some form of higher education for the profession, many of them feared that the creation of a separate institution to train women for positions of authority would create an alternative educational route, which would circumvent the social work schools and destroy the unity of the profession. While Salomon maintained that selection to such positions was a matter of personal aptitude which could not be completely supplanted by formal education, she nevertheless hoped that the *Akademie* would attract those ambitious and intellectually gifted women who otherwise might abandon social work schools for universities.[58] Salomon hoped to convince state and municipal officials that the combination of an academic degree and the practical experience which academically trained women received at the *Akademie* provided sufficient preparation to qualify these women for responsible administrative positions in the welfare offices and that women who had attended the *Akademie* should not be required to have state certifica-

[55] Salomon, *Die Ausbildung zum sozialen Beruf*, pp. 233–34, Charlotte Dietrich, "Die Akademie für soziale und pädagogische Frauenarbeit," *DZW* 1:7 (October 1925), pp. 302–7, and Salomon, "Die deutsche Akademie für soziale und pädagogische Frauenarbeit im Gesamtaufbau . . ."

[56] The *Akademie*'s publications included monographs by Bäumer, Hilde Lion, and Marianne Weber, and the research series *Bestand und Erschütterung der Familie in der Gegenwart*, which included 13 volumes up to 1933. See *Alice Salomon. Die Begründerin des sozialen Frauenberufs in Deutschland. Ihr Leben und Werk* (Schriften des Deutschen Vereins, 1958), p. 305.

[57] Salomon, "Die deutsche Akademie für soziale und pädagogische Frauenarbeit im Gesamtaufbau . . . ," and Salomon, "Die Deutsche Akademie für soziale und pädagogische Frauenarbeit und die Geistesschulung der Wohlfahrtspflegerinnen," *SBA* 8:11–12 (November/December 1928), pp. 2–6.

[58] Salomon to Treuge (September 14, 1925), and "Protokoll der 9. Tagung der Konferenz der Sozialen Frauenschulen" (November 16, 1925), AFHSS.

tion as social workers as well.[59] Despite the reservations of many member schools, the Conference recognized the importance of securing access for women to administrative positions and ultimately accepted Salomon's vision of the role of the *Akademie* in training future administrators.[60]

THE FAILURE OF SOCIAL MOTHERHOOD AND THE ABANDONMENT OF THE REPUBLIC

The leaders of the social work profession hoped that the growing number of well-trained, paid women social workers would provide the leverage necessary to realize the political and cultural goals of the women's movement and reform from within what they regarded as the distinctly masculine logic of bureaucratic authority. However, Maria Laarmann warned that women had to be careful not to betray their mission by adopting male modes of thinking and thus become "merely female administrative bureaucrats (*Nur-Verwaltungsbeamte*). That would be nothing but wasted activity, an unfaithfulness of women to their social calling." The key to fulfilling their historical mission, she suggested, was instead to integrate these women into the bureaucracy in a way which corresponded to their feminine nature. Although Laarmann conceded that social work also required those qualities which could only be provided by men, she concluded, citing Helene Lange, that the task was to "transform the world of men into a world which bears the stamp of both sexes."[61]

The infrastructure of the Weimar welfare system was erected around two major organizational innovations: public welfare offices and family welfare (*Familien-* or *Einheitsfürsorge*). Their purpose was to make possible both a more rational and efficient division of labor and an integrated approach to the many aspects of the social problem.[62] Although the establishment of welfare offices was often delayed by competency conflicts with the public health and youth welfare offices which were being established at the same time, these centrifugal forces were nevertheless held in check by the belief that it was impossible to separate completely the different facets of need. As Düsseldorf municipal councilor Josef Wilden explained, "Persons must not be treated as

---

[59] Minutes of the board of directors meeting (March 2, 1928), AFHSS.

[60] "Protokoll über die Sitzung der Konferenz Sozialer Frauenschulen Deutschlands" (October 28, 1927), ADCV 142 F 31. Several Catholic writers criticized the excessively liberal character of the *Akademie* and what they regarded as the intrinsic inadequacies of all interconfessional social work schools.

[61] Laarmann, "Eingliederung der Sozialbeamtin in die Organe der öffentlichen und privaten Wohlfahrtspflege," *SBA* 3:1–5 (January–May 1923), pp. 1–4, 9–14, and Helene Krieger, "Die Aufgaben der beamteten Frau in der öffentlichen Wohlfahrtspflege und ihre Stellung im Beruf," *Die Frau* 32:7 (April 1925), pp. 204–9.

[62] Gerhard Albrecht, *Städtische Wohlfahrtsämter* (= *Flugschriften der Zentralstelle für Volkswohlfahrt*, no. 13, 1920), Christian J. Klumker and Benedikt Schmittmann, eds., *Wohlfahrtsämter* (= *Schriften der Deutschen Gesellschaft für Soziales Recht*, no. 6, 1920), Franz Memelsdorf, *Der Aufbau des Wohlfahrtsamtes in einer größeren Stadt* (1926).

isolated individuals, but rather only as a link in a social chain; [they must not be treated] by one office as someone who is physically or mentally ill, and by another one, in contrast, as a person in need of economic assistance or as someone who is socially uprooted. . . . This can only be achieved when social, economic, and health programs—as the essence of social work—flow together in a single office, the welfare office."[63]

However, the practical implementation of this unitary principle required a certain degree of decentralization, and the end product of this evolution was the creation of a district family welfare system in the first half of the decade.[64] It spread so rapidly because its underlying assumption that the family, rather than the discrete individual, was the proper focus of social assistance provided the foundation for a more holistic approach to the problem of poverty.[65] In Frankfurt and Nuremberg, where the district family social work system was introduced early in the decade, family welfare was conceived in the broadest possible terms. In these cities, social workers were responsible for maternal advising, welfare programs for infants and small children, school health services, statutory guardianship, youth welfare, correctional education, juvenile court assistance, social housing programs, and general applications for monetary relief, as well as welfare for war survivors, *Klein-* and *Sozialrentner*. Family social work was more efficient because, the organizers of the Nuremberg welfare office wrote,

> in social welfare, it is not a question of momentarily relieving an individual person from his or her cares and burdens; it is a question of seeing this person as part of a complex and insuring that all other persons who are connected with the life of this individual are brought within the scope of treatment, that is, that the entire family becomes the object of social work. It is pointless to find a child a place in a kindergarten, where it can learn cleanliness and order, if, at the home to which the child returns in the evening, the child sees a tubercular mother living in an unsuitable apartment—possibly with an alcoholic husband—in the greatest filth and disorder. . . . Thoroughgoing help can only be achieved through social work which begins with the infant and extends through early childhood, school age, and adulthood until the point where the grey-haired grandfather or grandmother takes over the care for the entire family.[66]

Although family social workers were often subordinated at first to that branch of the welfare office which had taken the initiative in the development

---

[63] Josef Wilden, "Hie Wohlfahrtsamt! Hie Gesundheitsamt!" *SPr* 30:35 (1921), cols. 910–12.

[64] The authoritative account of district family social work is Marie Baum, *Familienfürsorge*, SDV N.F. 12, 2d ed. (1928).

[65] Wronsky/Muthesius, "Methoden deutscher Fürsorgearbeit," especially p. 122.

[66] "Vorschlag zur Gründung einer Zentrale für private Fürsorge" (October 10, 1918), StAN C 25/I F Reg Nr. 2. On the creation of the Nüremberg welfare office, see Hermann Hanschel, *Oberbürgermeister Hermann Luppe* (Verein für Geschichte der Stadt Nürnberg, 1977), pp. 94ff. and Susanne Krauß, *Kommunale Wohlfahrtspolitik in der frühen Weimarer Republik* (Magisterarbeit, Erlangen-Nürnberg, 1986), pp. 84ff.

of family social work, the trend was toward the establishment of a separate field work department under the authority of a social work supervisor (*Oberfürsorgerin*). In turn, the social work supervisor was directly subordinated to the director of the welfare office and was responsible for mediating between the pedagogical work of the social workers and the professional administrators employed by the municipal welfare bureaucracy. Although the development of family social work was slowed in the immediate postwar period by the availability of trained social workers, by the middle of the decade the idea had achieved widespread acceptance and had been implemented to some extent in many cities.[67]

The task of achieving this integration into the welfare bureaucracy in a manner which corresponded to their peculiarly feminine nature revolved around two issues: wages and working conditions and the relation of woman field workers to the male bureaucrats who continued to occupy most responsible administrative positions in the municipal welfare offices. In the first half of the decade, the employment and working conditions of most social workers could not easily be reconciled with the generally accepted understanding of the importance of social motherhood to the welfare of the nation.[68] The crux of the problem was the fact that few social workers were actually civil servants (*Beamten*) who were appointed for life and who had a right to salaries and retirement benefits as defined by the Reich civil service regulations.

The job market for social workers remained depressed through the summer of 1924, except for social workers who specialized in social hygiene, who were eagerly sought by cities making the transition to family social work.[69] Paradoxically, though, this short-term crisis helped consolidate the status of the profession because the imbalance in the labor market permitted local government to be more selective in its hiring, while the shortage of certified social workers was leading to a perceptible improvement in compensation. At the end of 1924 the Prussian Ministry for Public Welfare adopted a pay scale which was graduated according to education and experience and which remunerated experienced, certified social workers according to Grade VII of the Reich civil service salary scale, thus placing them on the same level with elementary school teachers. The umbrella association of social worker organizations regarded this decision as a major victory.[70] Although wages and working conditions for social workers as a whole had improved substantially by the middle of the decade, on the whole they still fell far short of both the demands of the social worker associations and the recommendations of the Prussian Ministry for Public Wel-

---

[67] *Mitteilungen des Deutschen Städtetags* (1926), Nr. 7, pp. 163–82.

[68] Zeller, *Volksmütter*, and Sachße, *Mütterlichkeit als Beruf*, pp. 250ff.

[69] "Arbeitsmarktbericht Oktober 1924," *SBA* 4:9/10 (September/October 1924), p. 5.

[70] "Mitteilungen der Arbeitsgemeinschaft," *SBA* 4:9–10 (September/October 1924), p. 5, "Erlaß vom 16. Dezember 1924, betr. Besoldung der staatlich anerkannten Wohfahrtspflegerinnen," *Volkswohlfahrt* 6 (1925), p. 21, and "Arbeitsmarktbericht 1925," *SBA* 5:3–4 (March/April 1925), pp. 5–6.

fare.[71] Moreover, despite these improvements, working conditions remained poor and seriously affected the health of these women. The leaders of the profession were especially concerned about the contagious diseases to which social workers were constantly exposed and the nervous exhaustion—which presented as real a threat to their well-being as these diseases—resulting from the constant confrontation with distress, poverty, and illness.[72]

While the problem of relatively poor pay and working conditions continued to plague the profession, these problems were compounded by the contradiction between the juridification and bureaucratization of social work, on the one hand, and the requirements of personal help, on the other. However, the problems resulting from this contradiction were themselves further accentuated by the fact that most responsible administrative positions were filled by male administrators who remained bound to what women social workers regarded as the masculine, unsocial logic of bureaucratic authority, while women were employed almost exclusively as field workers. To the extent that this contradiction between bureaucracy and personal help, that is, the relation between administration and field work (*Innen-* and *Außendienst*), was interpreted as a conflict between the antithetical principles of masculine rationalism and spiritual motherhood, it gave the debate over the relation between administration and field work a distinctly gendered dimension.[73]

In practice, this gendered division of labor meant that female field workers were responsible for investigating the circumstances of each applicant for assistance and recommending the appropriate measures to be taken in each case. They would then present the details of the case to the appropriate administrator, who would fill out the necessary forms and handle the correspondence with other institutions or government agencies. Although administrators without social work training were, at least in theory, expected to adhere to the recommendations of the social workers regarding the actual treatment of a case, the process seldom worked so smoothly in practice. These administrators often ignored the recommendations made by these women, who, in turn, felt that they were being degraded to mere investigators and thus deprived of the autonomy necessary to realize their vocation. Baum argued that, in principle, social workers should not be subordinated to bureaucrats, and she insisted that the recommen-

---

[71] *Die Arbeitsbedingungen der Sozialbeamtinnen* (= *Schriften des DVS*, Nr. 7, n.d. [1925]) ADCV 142.

[72] All of these complaints were confirmed by a survey conducted in 1924 by the DV and the Prussian Ministry for Public Welfare. See Martha Heynacher, *Die Berufslage der Fürsorgerinnen*, SDV N.F. 6 (1925), and *Verhandlungen des Deutschen Vereins*, SDV N.F. 7 (1925), pp. 125–66. See also Beerensson, "Wohlfahrtspflegerin und Staatsidee," *SBA* 5:5–6 (May/June 1925), pp. 3–5, "Die Ueberlastung der Fürsorgerin," *SBA* 5:7–8 (July/August 1925), p. 7, Idamarie Solltmann, "Zum 'Tagebuch einer Fürsorgerin,'" *SBA* 6:1–2 (January/February 1926), pp. 3–4, and Dr. Kappes, "Untersuchungen über den Gesundheitszustand badischer Sozialbeamtinnen," *SBA* 9:1–2 (January/February 1929), pp. 7–9.

[73] Kempf, "Lehrplankonferenz der Wohlfahrtsschulen . . . ," *SPr* 38:7 (1929), cols. 160–70, and Hertha Kraus, "Gedanken zur sozialen Frauen-Arbeit," *Die Frau* 40:6 (March 1933), pp. 370–77.

dations of the social workers must be unconditionally accepted by untrained administrators or that administrative positions be filled by persons with social work training, which was the solution she advocated.[74] Bäumer regarded petty regulations concerning when and to whom social workers had to report as a symptom of the "completely false and skewed" position of the social worker in municipal administration.[75] In 1929 all five of the family social workers in the town of Guben, which had long been regarded as a model for the organization of family social work, resigned to protest an administrative reorganization which would have reduced their autonomy and, so they maintained, the influence of their feminine nature by subordinating them to a mid-level bureaucrat, rather than the city councilor in charge of the welfare office. As a show of solidarity, the major social worker associations urged their members not to apply for the vacant positions.[76]

Initially, women social workers were quite anxious to establish their position within the local welfare bureaucracy, and they constructed an elaborate caricature of the formalism and fetishization of rules and hierarchy which, they maintained, made it impossible for these "bureaucrats"—in the pejorative sense of the term—to develop a genuine personal warmth for their clientele.[77] However, the insistence of women social workers upon obeying what they described as the logic of emotion and care often led male administrators to disparage these women's work and underestimate their professionalism.[78] Male bureaucrats also resented the demand that women be appointed to positions of authority simply because these women had discovered social work as "their" natural vocation. The medical establishment was particularly concerned to limit the autonomy of women social workers. As one physician wrote early in the decade, social workers had to recognize "that they . . . do not compete for authority with physicians, but rather facilitate their work. Despite all of the strength and energy required by their vocation, they must also command sufficient flexibility and tractability in order to avoid provoking constant conflicts. They must understand how to fit in and, if necessary, subordinate themselves under the guidance of the directors of the welfare office."[79]

Women social workers maintained that this conflict could best be resolved through a proper division of labor, which would free them from those bureaucratic and clerical tasks which denatured their own intensely personal work. In

---

[74] Baum, *Familienfürsorge*, SDV N.F. 12, 2d ed. (1928), p. 94.

[75] Bäumer, "Die Stellung der Sozialbeamtin und der Sinn der Wohlfahrtspflege," p. 264.

[76] Gierke, "Gemeinsame Kündigung aller Gubener Fürsorgerinnen," *Soziale Arbeit* 6:33 (August 24, 1929), pp. 2–3.

[77] "Ein Beitrag zu der Frage 'Innen- und Außendienst in der Wohlfahrtspflege,'" SBA 7:5–6 (May/June, 1927), pp. 6–7.

[78] Israel, "Die Tagung der Sozialbeamtinnen," *Die Frau* 31:10 (July 1924), pp. 297–301, and Beerensson, "Warum ist die Wohlfahrtspflege nicht volkstümlich?" *Die Fürsorge* 2:12 (June 20, 1925), pp. 180–83.

[79] Dr. Jacobi, "Familienfürsorge in der Amtshauptmannschaft Dresden-Altstadt," SPr 30:52 (1921), col. 1349.

view of the peculiarity of social work as individualized personal help, it was entirely inappropriate, argued Adele Beerensson (the chair of the DVS), to encase women social workers "in the armor of a bureaucratic apparatus."[80] Social workers also constantly complained about having to waste time and energy—which could have best been devoted to helping the needy—doing paperwork.[81]

In the 1920s women made relatively little progress toward capturing responsible administrative positions. For example, nationwide only 20 of the 993 youth welfare office directors were women.[82] By the end of the decade, it appeared that the profession was itself being colonized by the bureaucracy, rather than transforming it from within. Moreover, not only did women fail to reshape the local social bureaucracy, they were even made responsible for its failings. As attacks on the welfare system mounted in the early 1930s, critics charged that women were in fact responsible for overextending the scope of social work and thus undermining the morale of welfare recipients. As Bäumer pointed out, women were being burdened with the worst of both worlds: even though their political emancipation had not yet enabled them to transform the masculine political culture of the nation, they were nevertheless being held responsible for the many symptoms of social decay and decline.[83] Nor were the professional associations able to secure pay and working conditions commensurate with their vision of the importance of spiritual motherhood. Although Beerensson had hoped that the discussion of employment and working conditions for social workers at the 1926 DV conference would mark a turning point in the public recognition of the profession, there was little additional improvement between 1925 and the onset of the depression.[84]

Although the labor market for social workers had improved steadily between 1924 and 1927, the prospects of full employment for social workers were dimmed from 1928 onward by the huge increase in the number of graduates of the social work schools.[85] Between 1919 and 1926, 2,755 women graduated from the social work schools, and another 1,442 qualified to take the state certification exam on the basis of continuing education courses offered by these schools.[86] While 441 students graduated from the schools belonging to the Con-

---

[80] Beerensson, "Der Mann in der sozialen Arbeit," *SPr* 36:10 (1927), cols. 251–53, citation col. 252.

[81] Hedwig Stieve, *Tagebuch einer Fürsorgerin* (Berlin, 1925), p. 123, and Emilie Zadow, *Kinder des Staates* (Hamburg, 1929), p. 17.

[82] *Statistik des Deutschen Reiches*, Bd. 421: *Die öffentliche Fürsorge im Deutschen Reich in den Rechnungsjahren 1927 bis 1931* (Berlin, 1933), p. 237.

[83] Bäumer, *Die Frau im deutschen Staat* (Berlin, 1932), p. 70, and Salomon, "Hat die Frau die Wohlfahrtspflege überspannt und verweichlicht?" *FW* 6:2 (May 1931), pp. 67–71.

[84] Beerensson, "Zehn Jahre soziale Berufsarbeit," *SPr* 35:19 (1926), cols. 481–85, Bäumer, "Die Fürsorgerin in der öffentlichen Meinung," *SBA* 10:3 (March 1930), pp. 1–2, "Zur Besoldungsreform," *SBA* 8:3–4 (March/April 1928), pp. 6–10, and E. R., "Berufsschwierigkeiten der Wohlfahrtspflegerinnen in Bayern," *SBA* 9:1–2 (January/February 1929), pp. 9–10.

[85] Lüdy, "Jahresbericht für das Jahre 1927/1928," *SBA* 8:7–8 (July/August 1928), pp. 5–8.

[86] Salomon, *Die Ausbildung zum sozialen Beruf*, p. 18. Before the Prussian regulation of social work training in 1919, a total of 2,922 women had graduated from the social women's schools.

ference in 1926, by 1928/29 the number of annual graduates had risen to 961, and in 1929/30 it reached 2,492, a figure which was nearly as large as the total number of social workers employed by local government in Prussia in 1925.[87] However, by the time these women reached the job market, most of the positions created in the aftermath of the major Weimar welfare laws had already been filled, and the oversupply was made even worse by the cutbacks in hiring caused by the deepening depression.[88] Citing this oversupply, in January 1930 the Prussian Ministry of Public Welfare issued a decree limiting to 35 the number of students who could be admitted annually to each of the social work schools.[89]

By the end of the decade, it was possible to identify the contours of the new profession. On the one hand, the expansion of the municipal welfare apparatus had created more career opportunities for women than could have been imagined before 1918 and had greatly enhanced the public status of the profession. On the other hand, the historical circumstances which had given birth to the social work profession out of the spirit of the women's movement were rapidly ceasing to exist, and the forces which were shaping the profession were pushing it in a very different direction than that intended by the first generation of bourgeois feminists. Salomon argued that the root of the problem lay in the changing spiritual foundations of the profession. Part of the change was due to the transformation of the social calling of the women of the *Großbürgertum* into a paid occupation for women of the middle and working classes. Although the original impetus to the professionalization of social work had come from bourgeois women who had been catalyzed into action by their new awareness of the injustices of the world around them, Salomon lamented that the revolution had spiritually dispossessed both the bourgeois women's movement and the new profession. However, she failed to recognize that the elimination of the unique space within which the prewar bourgeois reform movements had existed was the price to be paid for integration of the working classes into the new state. Salomon was especially concerned that the expansion of public social services was disrupting the immediate relation between the social worker and her clients, and her analysis of the effects of the bureaucratization of welfare, the growing demand for entitlements to social services, and the juridification of welfare, as well as the emergence of mass poverty during the depression, skillfully wove together the central motifs of the Progressive critique of the contradictions of the republican welfare system (which will be examined in chapter 7). While many people feared—or hoped—that these developments would render personal contact superfluous, Salomon insisted that maternalistic

[87] Salomon, "Die Berufslage der Sozialarbeiterinnen," *Die Frau* 39:3 (December 1931), pp. 140–46.

[88] Lüdy, "Arbeitsmarktbericht," *SBA* 9:7–8 (July/August 1929), pp. 67–68, and Lüdy, "Der Arbeitsmarkt," *SBA* 10:3 (March 1930), pp. 30–32.

[89] Reprinted in *SBA* 10:1 (January 1930), p. 9, and "Einstellung der Wohlfahrtsschulen auf die wirtschaftliche und soziale Notlage der Zeit," *Nachrichtendienst* 12:12 (December 1931), pp. 349–50. On the continued deterioration of the job market, see Lüdy, "Der Arbeitsmarkt," *SBA* 11:6 (June 1931), pp. 100–103.

personal help was a permanent necessity because there were intrinsic limits to these tendencies:

> It is possible to alter the material living conditions of a person, distribute support in a purely schematic manner, and provide an existence minimum through the use of guidelines. . . . However, it is impossible to carry out preventive social hygiene or social pedagogy without the engagement of human, personal forces. If it is a question of character and not simply of external circumstances . . . , it is almost always a question of convincing the clients—under unfavorable circumstances and against numerous obstacles—to do something for which they at first lack not only the knowledge, but also the necessary strength of will and resoluteness.[90]

Salomon's arguments were designed to buttress her claim that social work represented a privileged feminine domain and the belief that, by virtue of their biological nature and spiritual essence, women alone could reverse the self-destruction of the welfare system being brought about by the unchecked action of masculine modes of thought and action.[91] To acquiesce in these negative structural transformations of the welfare system and the social work profession would, Salomon concluded, be to betray the highest values and the historical mission of the bourgeois women's movement:

> It is the historical mission of women to preserve the essence of social work even within the bureaucratic apparatus, because it is no coincidence that their entry into public offices took place at the very moment when these positions assumed—to a heretofore unprecedented extent—direct responsibility for purely human concerns. If women are unfaithful to the peculiarities of this work, then the women's movement has been in vain, *then it has attained its goal, but lost its meaning*, because the goal of the integration of women into public life was justified above all by the claim that women were to fully develop their peculiar powers and employ them for the good of society. . . . It is the immanent mission of women—which persists entirely apart from all historical circumstances—to prevent the reification (*Versachlichung*) of themselves and social work.[92]

Salomon's disillusionment reflected the fact that, in every significant respect, the actual development of the social work profession had failed to fulfill the grand hopes which the women's movement had placed in it because the same long-term processes which were leading to the development of social work as a paid occupation were also eliminating the social foundations of that idealized vision of spiritual motherhood which had animated the first generation of social work educators. As a result, as Christoph Sachße concludes, "The labile tension between women's emancipation, civic responsibility for the welfare of society,

---

[90] Salomon, "Typenwandel der Sozialbeamtinnen und Struktur des sozialen Berufs," *FW* 5:1 (April 1930), pp. 1–8. Salomon still refused to recognize paid labor as one of the distinguishing characteristics of professional social work. *Die Ausbildung zum sozialen Beruf*, p. 16.

[91] Salomon, "Hat die Frau die Wohlfahrtspflege überspannt und verweichlicht?" pp. 69–70.

[92] Salomon, "Typenwandel," p. 7, emphasis added.

and a notion of expertise which was oriented primarily to the development of the feminine personality collapsed completely. . . . Emancipatory female engagement in the social cause had been transformed into a poorly paid social service profession, and educational institutions 'of a peculiar level' had in effect become second-rate professional schools."[93]

Rather than asking whether the revolution, women's suffrage, and the creation of a public welfare system might not require a rethinking of that highly idealized vision of social work as a feminine vocation, the leadership of the profession, especially Salomon, insisted more strongly than ever on the supratemporal validity of these ideals. Salomon's commitment to an essentialist view of women's nature and a gendered division of labor imprisoned her in a world which was increasingly distant from the political realities of the Republic and alienated her from the immediate concerns of many rank-and-file social workers. She gradually withdrew from women's politics and devoted her energies to research on women and the family and to the *Akademie*, which represented for her a haven of maternalist idealism in the rising tide of politics and materialism.

In recent years, there has been much debate over the question of whether the gender essentialism of the German women's movement was progressive and emancipatory or whether it in fact undermined their demands for equality and rendered them more susceptible to antidemocratic ideas. In the case of the social work profession, this radical essentialization of femininity did provide both a critical perspective for a maternalist critique of some of the central features of bourgeois society and a rationale for the implementation of many reforms which had long been resisted by those who objected to such an intrusion into the spheres of individual and familial rights. However, by the end of the decade the radicalization of the maternalist mission of women social workers was leading many of these women to either turn their backs on the Republic or to demonize bureaucracy and politics in general as products of masculine modes of thought. As a result, the social work profession, which had been founded on the belief in the centrality of spiritual motherhood and personal help to the social mission of the new state, could offer no spiritual sustenance to a beleaguered Republic where the realization of their ideals seemed as far away as ever before.

THE RETURN OF THE REPRESSED: THE SOCIAL DEMOCRATIC THEORY OF SOCIAL WORK

In the years after the passage of the RJWG and the proclamation of the RFV, there was a massive surge of organizational energy which led to the creation of a nationwide network of welfare and youth welfare offices. These developments marked the culmination of a modernizing, rationalizing process which had begun in the *Vormärz*. Although the professionalization of social work was an

---

[93] Sachße, *Mütterlichkeit als Beruf*, pp. 306–7.

integral part of this process, the problem was that the same social forces which were leading to the creation of a vast, highly bureaucratized and rationalized welfare system were destroying those traditional patterns of social interaction upon which the idea of social pedagogy as friendly helping was modeled. The dissolution of community and the emergence of a fragmented industrial, mass society meant that, despite the best intentions of social workers, social interaction between the social worker and the client was always already burdened by the suspicion that the act of helping was contaminated by ulterior political motives which degraded such help to a means for the attainment of an ulterior end. This inevitably impaired the ability of the social worker to gain the confidence of the client. However, in the absence of an immediate belief in the authenticity of the social worker's will to help, the idea of helping the needy immediately threatened to dissolve into a series of social-pedagogical paradoxes or contradictions between helping and control, education and discipline, and understanding the psychological needs of the client and the colonization of his or her lifeworld.[94]

As a result, the constitution of the social work profession as a system of organized helping was only possible at the cost of reinscribing within the structure of social pedagogical action all of the different manifestations of the contradiction between the social system and affective social integration provided by the social worker. For the social workers themselves, these problems were perceived primarily as a contradiction between the ideal of personal help and the institutional forms through which this help was provided. The entire debate over whether social work is an "incomplete," "unsuccessful," or "semi" profession, or whether it is in fact "over professionalized," as well as the various strategies for resisting, subverting, or escaping from the effects of these contradictions, all represent attempts to comprehend the problematic of professionalization through one specific moment of the thoroughly self-contradictory logic of social pedagogy. Although social work underwent a period of consolidation in the 1920s and acquired many of the features which have been regarded as characteristic of a "profession," by the second half of the decade the profession was beset by an acute sense of crisis, and the subsequent literature is nearly unanimous in the assertion that it failed to complete the professional project.[95]

In the second half of the decade, the vision of social work as organized helping and a distinctly feminine calling was increasingly called into question, first, by the encroachment of men into what the first generation of social workers had regarded as the privileged domain of women, second, by and the formu-

---

[94] Peter Dudek, *Leitbild: Kamerad und Helfer. Sozialpädagogische Bewegung in der Weimarer Republik am Beispiel der 'Gilde Soziale Arbeit'* (Dipa-Verlag, 1988), p. 30.

[95] Richard Münchmeier, *Zugänge zur Geschichte der sozialen Arbeit* (Juventa Verlag, 1981), and Detlev Peukert, *Grenzen der Sozialdisziplinierung* (Bund-Verlag, 1986). A wide variety of frequently contradictory arguments have been advanced to account for this failure. See Thomas Olk, *Abschied vom Experten. Sozialarbeit auf dem Weg zu einer alternativen Professionalität* (Juventa Verlag, 1986), pp. 16ff., 96ff.

lation of a specifically Social Democratic theory of social work.[96] Workers' Welfare harbored a deep antipathy toward existing social work organizations because it categorically rejected that bracketing of politics through which the bourgeois and church welfare groups had attempted to constitute a purely affective, intensely personal relationship between the social worker and the client, which they regarded as the seed from which a new sense of community could grow. On the other hand, the Social Democrats insisted that the social contradictions which had led to the creation of a vast network of welfare and charity agencies could only be resolved through the transformation of the social system itself. They also criticized the idealized conception of personal help advocated by all of the humanitarian and confessional welfare organizations as a mystification resulting from their affirmative attitude toward the existing social order and its inherent inequalities.

However, the marginalization of the Social Democrats created a political space within which bourgeois feminists, male Progressives, and the confessional welfare and social worker organizations could exclude or repress the possibility of social integration through political action and institutionalize their own conception of social work as a sphere of purely affective social integration which bore no relation to social or economic forces.[97] As a result, the Social Democrats argued, confessional and bourgeois charity could not help but be dysfunctional and patronizing because a gaping chasm separated the values, norms, and expectations of the proletariat from those of the middle classes. The Civil Code, Wachenheim complained, knew only the bourgeois family and its needs, and bourgeois and confessional organizations were completely incapable of understanding either the structure of the proletarian family or the specific problems of urban poverty, much less of devising new methods of combating mass distress.[98] Paula Kurgaß, who served as secretary of the Berlin branch of Workers' Welfare from 1929 until 1933, warned socialist social workers not to

[96] Virtually everything of any importance regarding the entry of men into this female field can be found in Sachße, *Mütterlichkeit als Beruf*, pp. 296–304, and Dudek, *Leitbild: Kamerad und Helfer*, who discusses the crucial influence of the youth movement on male social workers, especially in the field of correctional education.

[97] Niklas Luhmann, "Formen des Helfens im Wandel gesellschaftlicher Bedingungen," in Hans-Uwe Otto and Siegfried Schneider, eds., *Gesellschaftliche Perspektiven der Sozialarbeit* (Luchterhand, 1973), I:21–43, especially pp. 31–33, precisely describes that marginalization of Social Democracy through which social work as a field of organized helping was constituted. In this essay, Luhmann argues that social work as a discipline and a profession failed to acquire the social prestige and systematic unity characteristic of the classical professions because in complex societies the contradictions of the social system are displaced into social subsystems—including the social service professions—which produce personality structures and systems of meaning which are necessary to compensate for the intrinsic limitations on such social steering mechanisms as the market and the legal system, but which do not act back upon and alter the structure of the social system itself.

[98] Wachenheim, "Der Vorrang der öffentlichen Wohlfahrtspflege," *AW* 1:3 (November 1, 1926), pp. 65–72.

accept uncritically the ideas of their bourgeois colleagues because bourgeois notions of "order and *Verwahrlosung*, guilt and contrition, morality and immorality" were the standard against which proletarian life was more or less unconsciously measured—and naturally found wanting. She argued that the impossibility of conforming to these ideals within the existing capitalist order should be evident to any social worker who "was skilled in seeing in any individual case the representative of an entire class, in recognizing the situation of the masses in the distress and struggles and defeats of the individual." Any attempt to bring about class reconciliation without first abolishing classes was doomed to failure.[99]

It has been suggested that Workers' Welfare lacked a distinct conception of social work and that its own intellectual bankruptcy was reflected in an uncritical adherence to the ideas of the bourgeois women's movement.[100] However, although this may have been true at least in part during the first years of the organization's existence, it underwent a process of intellectual maturation and generational change during the second half of the 1920s and, in so doing, articulated a distinctly socialist theory of social work which, its members claimed, illuminated the ideological blindness of bourgeois and confessional organizations and exploded the contradiction between their belief in the importance of helping and their allegiance to an economic and social order based on privilege and exploitation. Although the increasing theoretical self-consciousness of Workers' Welfare led to the relative marginalization of Juchacz and others who regarded the organization primarily as a self-help organization for working-class women, it must nevertheless be borne in mind that, at least in part, the purpose of this theoretical radicalism was to create a sense of collective identity for Social Democratic social workers and help them defend their own work against increasingly frequent attacks from the Communist left. Consequently, there remained a substantial distance between this rhetoric and the realities of social work training, whose substance was determined within broad limits by state regulations and social work practice within the confines of the municipal welfare offices.

The belief in the intimate connection between social work and politics was integral to the Social Democratic approach to social work, and the goal of their theoretical labors was to reverse that repression of politics through which bourgeois social workers had attempted to define social work as individualized personal help. While bourgeois social workers focused on the isolated individual because they believed that personal contact, Christian charity, feminine calling, and selfless service were in fact capable of transfiguring the existing social order, the critical potential of a Social Democratic theory of social work lay in its insistence that individual distress must be understood as representative of

---

[99] Kurgaß, "Die sozialistische Fürsorgerin," *AW* 1:5 (December 1, 1926), pp. 133–36 and "Gegen die Isolierung der Wohlfahrtspflege," *AW* 1:5 (December 1, 1926), pp. 133–36.

[100] Sachße, *Mütterlichkeit als Beruf*, pp. 182–86.

that of an entire social class whose situation could only be fundamentally altered through political action.[101] While this leap from the particular to the general and from personal help to social reform distinguished the Social Democratic approach to social work from that of the bourgeois and confessional organizations, it also gave rise to the constant charges that the Social Democrats were illegitimately politicizing the ostensibly neutral sphere of social work. However, to such charges Wachenheim replied that conflicts of worldview and political beliefs were as natural to the welfare system as to every other sphere of public activity. "Social work," she insisted, "is no more holy than any other area, and, moreover, politics is by no means something unholy. It is frightfully naive to always pretend that politics is in itself something immoral. . . . As a rule, it is simply reactionary to whine about the intrusion of politics."[102]

This opposition between Workers' Welfare and the other welfare *Spitzenverbände* was hardened even further by the fact that, although the Social Democrats did regard social work as a sphere of women's engagement, they increasingly distanced themselves from the gender essentialism which they had originally taken over from the bourgeois feminists. "Is social work a women's question?" Kurgaß asked rhetorically. "No, it is a social question whose basis is not gender, but convictions. What social work needs is not the women's movement, but creative politics."[103] The problems caused by these ideological differences were compounded by the fact that the Social Democrats did not have a social work school of their own and thus were dependent to a large extent upon schools run by confessional and bourgeois groups. Of the thirty social work schools which had been established by 1927, nine were run by Evangelical organizations, five by Catholic organizations, seven by local or provincial government, and nine by interconfessional associations, several of which were supported financially by local government.[104] Although Workers' Welfare did provide financial support to help some women attend the existing social work schools, Wachenheim was extremely wary of the reactionary character of most of these schools; she feared that socialist convictions of the women who attended these schools would be contaminated by bourgeois ideology to which they were exposed and that these women might be tempted to betray their own class mission.[105]

---

[101] Kurgaß, "Der sozialistische Fürsorger, seine Weltanschauung, seine Berufsorganisation, seine Mitarbeit in der Arbeiterwohlfahrt," cited in Wachenheim, "Pfingsttreffen 1928," *AW* 3:12 (June 15, 1928), pp. 373–81. For an account of the epiphany which made possible this shift from the personal to the social, see Erna Magnus (the first full-time teacher at the organization's social work school), "Weiterbildung der Sozialarbeiter," *AW* 4:6 (March 15, 1929), pp. 163–70. The Social Democrats also criticized the individualistic perspective of both the pedagogical and hygiene training provided by bourgeois and confessional schools because this systematically occluded the broader social dimension of individual need.

[102] Wachenheim, "Zeitschriftenschau," *AW* 6:2 (January 15, 1931), p. 57.

[103] Kurgaß, "Dreißig Jahre soziale Berufsausbildung!" *AW* 4:23 (December 1, 1929), pp. 747–49.

[104] Salomon, *Die Ausbildung zum sozialen Beruf*, p. 53.

[105] Wachenheim, "Die Wohlfahrtsschule des Hauptausschusses für Arbeiterwohlfahrt," *AW* 4:1 (January 1, 1929), pp. 24–26, and Starmann-Hunger, "Änderung der sächsischen Verordnung über

Worker's Welfare had long been reluctant to establish its own institutions—including its own social work school—because it continued to regard itself as an auxiliary to public welfare. However, as the decade progressed, it was ultimately forced to rethink its position because municipal welfare officials—even in those towns where the Social Democrats enjoyed a substantial degree of influence in local government—were generally unwilling to hire social workers who did not have state certification. Despite its reservations, Workers' Welfare decided in the fall of 1927 to establish its own social work school. The education of the students, their previous work experience, and the occupation of their fathers all reflected solidly working-class origins, which distinguished these students from those attending the bourgeois and confessional schools.[106]

Workers' Welfare claimed some 114,000 members and 2,250 local branches by the end of the decade. Although Workers' Welfare played only a marginal role in the debates over the curricula of the social work schools (from which it was excluded on the pretext that the organization had no experience with social work training), the constant insistence upon the interrelatedness of politics and social work served as a permanent provocation to the bourgeois and confessional organizations.[107] Despite the attempt by Workers' Welfare to establish closer relations with the other social work schools in order to insure that it would have a voice in future discussions on social work training, it was ultimately impossible to bridge the gap between the vision of social work as personal help espoused by the confessional and humanitarian welfare organizations and its own insistence upon the interdependence of social work and politics. These differences were to be of crucial importance in their diagnoses of the crisis of the welfare state at the end of the decade.

THE CONTRADICTIONS OF SOCIAL PEDAGOGY AND THE POLITICAL CULTURE OF THE REPUBLIC

The problems resulting from the failure of the social work profession to reshape the welfare bureaucracy were increasingly compounded by a growing awareness of the gap between their belief in the power of selfless service to transcend

---

die Aufnahme in die Wohlfahrtsschulen und die Prüfung von Wohlfahrtspflegerinnen," *AW* 5:2 (January 15, 1930), pp. 39–41. In addition, since so many of the hospitals were run by confessional organizations, socialist women often had difficulty finding places to perform their internships.

[106] "Wohlfahrtsschule des Hauptausschusses für Arbeiterwohlfahrt," *AW* 3:16 (August 15, 1928), pp. 497–500, Magnus, "Die Wohlfahrtsschule der Arbeiterwohlfahrt," *AW* 6:8 (April 15, 1931), pp. 241–51, Wachenheim, "Die Wohlfahrtsschule des Hauptausschusses für Arbeiterwohlfahrt," *Jahrbuch der Arbeiterwohlfahrt* 1 (1930), pp. 45–66, and Käthe Buchrucker, "Der Stand der wohlfahrtspflegerischen und sozialpädagogischen Ausbildung," *AW* 4:13–14 (July 1, 1929), pp. 385–89.

[107] One issue on which the Social Democrats did exert a strong influence in the latter part of the decade was the reform of correctional education. See "Richtlinien zur Umgestaltung der Fürsorgeerziehung," *AW* 4:10 (May 15, 1929), pp. 289ff., and, for the work of the leading Social Democratic youth welfare expert, Elizabeth Harvey, *Youth Welfare and Social Democracy in Weimar Germany: The Work of Walter Friedländer* (New Alyth, 1987).

all social antagonisms and both the resistance of their clients to this help and their own inability to permanently sustain a high state of commitment in the face of perpetual disappointment. As Richard Münchmeier has argued, social workers tended to regard these disappointments as the result of motivational deficits which could, in principle, be overcome through the intensification of their commitment to an ethics of selfless service (whose propagation was the primary function of social work schools and professional associations). As a result, the fundamental conflict between social structure and the organized system of helping was reproduced in a myriad of ways within the profession itself.[108] On the other hand, their belief in the centrality of helping also led them to blame the resistance of their clientele and their own disappointments on the bureaucratization of social work, the growing demand for entitlements to public assistance, and the inability of the social worker to fully express her own deepest beliefs within a public welfare system, which was supposed to remain neutral on matters of religion and worldview. However, this commitment to helping blinded them to the fact that these problems could not be eliminated without calling into question the existence of both their own profession and, more importantly, the public welfare system itself. As a result, by the late 1920s the crisis of the social work profession became linked in an increasingly direct manner to the political crisis of the state itself. The systematic inability to understand the causes of this crisis provided the point of departure for a critique of central institutions of the Weimar welfare state and for the search for new forms of political organization within which social work and individualized personal help could again become a vehicle for the creation of a national community.

In the most sophisticated contemporary analysis of the structural contradictions of social pedagogy, Aloys Fischer touched the root of the problem when he pointed out that the most fundamental condition for spiritual or moral help was to awaken in needy persons "the will to let themselves be helped" and to inspire confidence that the social worker was animated by no ulterior motives and that she was both capable and willing to provide such help.[109] Fischer himself was aware of how precarious these preconditions were in the modern world, and he suggested that this confidence could best be understood as a sort of "gift of grace" which, although it was the precondition for successful social work, could never be perfectly replicated by human artifice.[110] Even someone with as impeccably Progressive credentials as Marie Baum could only explain the nature of the authority of the social worker by comparing it with the trust which once prevailed in traditional societies between the lady of the manor and her villagers or between the pastor and his flock.[111]

---

[108] Münchmeier, *Zugänge*, pp. 156–57.

[109] Fischer, "Die Problematik des Sozialbeamtentums," in *Leben und Werk*, Bd. 3/4, pp. 319–49, citation p. 319. Münchmeier, *Zugänge*, has rightly noted the importance of this essay, which originally appeared in *Soziale Praxis* in 1925.

[110] Fischer, "Die Problematik des Sozialbeamtentums," p. 320.

[111] Baum, *Familienfürsorge*, p. 36.

Most social workers believed that the solution to this problem, which defined the "possibilities and limits" of social work as a calling and as a profession, ultimately depended on the purity of the social worker's commitment to the ethos of selfless service and her innate reverence for the individuality of the client. Only through the resulting attitude of "awe and reverence," which accepted the client "as he is with all his flaws and blemishes," could she bridge the social distance which inevitably separated the helper from the beneficiary of social help and dispel any suspicion that the helper was using the authority of her position to impose her beliefs upon the client or to propagandize on behalf of any party or worldview.[112] However, the subjective purity of the motives of the social worker was inherently inadequate as a foundation for social-pedagogical action if and as long as other factors made the client unreceptive to this help. These structural contradictions inherent in the idea of helping were further complicated by the same forces which made possible the emergence of the social work profession.

With the emergence of poverty as the subject of public discourse and political debate since the *Vormärz*, responsibility for aiding the poor had been steadily displaced from the hometown community to the district poor relief authority and ultimately to the Reich. Voluntary welfare had also undergone a similar process of bureaucratization, which had led to the creation of the bureaucratic *Spitzenverbände* in the mid-1920s. Although this division of labor had made possible the emergence of social work as a distinct occupation, the accompanying division of responsibility also made it increasingly difficult to maintain the fiction that such professionals were, in fact, animated solely by their love for the needy. This aspect of professionalization led to a contradiction between the status of social workers paid to carry out the mandates of their employers and the claim that they were immediately transfixed by the suffering of the needy.[113] While the mere existence of a public welfare system staffed by paid social workers deprived the needy of some of the freedom upon which a trusting relationship depended, the freedom of the social worker herself was also limited by the difficulties of institutionalizing charisma within the social welfare bureaucracy. It was only possible to compensate for these losses if the social worker had a certain degree of charismatic authority and appeared neither as the mere mandatory of her employer nor as the servant of an impersonal welfare machine.[114] Bäumer believed that the hybrid status of professional social work-

---

[112] B. Heyne, "Möglichkeiten und Grenzen persönlicher Fürsorge," *FW* 3:2 (May 1928), pp. 68–76, citation p. 74.

[113] Fischer, "Die Problematik des Sozialbeamtentums," p. 320.

[114] Ibid., p. 321. This same conflict recurred at a more mundane level in the debates over whether social workers should adopt the title "*Sozialbeamtin*" or continue to be known as "*Schwester*" and whether or not they should wear a distinct uniform modeled loosely on those worn by members of religious orders. Fischer argued that the idea of professional friendship was a *contradictio in adjectivo* and that all attempts to build a profession on such a shaky foundation were inherently problematic because there remained a degree of artificiality in the relationship between the social worker and the client which inevitably led to a sense of degradation, humiliation, and subordination which was not present in assistance offered from friend to friend. Ibid. pp. 324–28.

ers as paid helpers burdened them with the worst of both worlds; while, as a representative of the state, the social worker did not have sufficient authority to make her wishes prevail, her status as a semiofficial nevertheless impaired her charismatic authority as a social helper.[115]

Even though the social work schools regarded the development of the charismatic potential of their students as their primary goal, by the end of the decade Salomon and others were lamenting the definitive routinization of the charismatic aura of the pioneer generation of social workers that was proceeding in step with the transformation of a calling of the women of the *Großbürgertum* into a paid occupation.[116] However, the very idea of social-pedagogical action was called into question at an even more fundamental level by applicants for public assistance who refused to let themselves be helped because they viewed themselves as victims of an unjust social order who deserved an entitlement to assistance, rather than personal help. Since it was highly unlikely that a client who rejected the existing social order would be willing to trust a particular social worker, the legitimacy of the profession itself depended, Fischer argued, on a general trust in the legitimacy of the social order, or at least on the absence of open mistrust. Whoever regarded the existing public welfare system as nothing more than a clever ruse of the propertied would seldom give to a social worker whom he or she suspected of being the representative or servant of this order that complete trust which was the precondition for social help.[117]

The possibility that politics would return through this ideological gap between the social worker and the client represented a serious threat to the profession, and Rosa Kempf analyzed this problem in depth in her keynote address to the 1925 DVS conference.[118] Kempf argued that the labor of the social worker began precisely at the point of greatest danger to the national community—the point where the effects of economic and social differentiation had begun to force national comrades into a state of helplessness and need. She claimed that the ability to work constructively toward national reconstruction could only grow "out of a deep, overpowering sense of the bonds of community," which did not permit the withdrawal or expulsion of individual members. The affirmation of this organic vision of the national community was, Kempf claimed, the precondition for effective personal help. Kempf maintained that this represented the only viable alternative to the temptations of politics, which sought to recreate community through radical social change, but which in practice was socially sterile because it set citizen against citizen instead of emphasizing their common membership in a larger whole. Although Kempf did not explain how this attitude could "unconsciously" influence the client, her ideas were eagerly taken

---

[115] Bäumer, "Die Fürsorgerin in der öffentlichen Meinung," p. 1.

[116] Salomon, *Die Ausbildung zum sozialen Beruf*, p. 203.

[117] Fischer, "Die Problematik des Sozialbeamtentums," pp. 322–23.

[118] Kempf, "Die Wohlfahrtspflegerin und der innere Aufbau," *Die Frau* 33:1 (October 1925), pp. 19–25.

up by all nonsocialist social workers. However, it seems unlikely that they found the same resonance among their clientele.

In their everyday activity, social workers experienced the limits of their work less as objective contradictions than as subjective problems to be mastered, and their attempts to construct a framework which would preserve the meaningfulness of their work in spite of their constant disappointments reveal a great deal about the self-understanding of these women. The most serious problem faced by the profession was the fact that the rejection of politics through which the social field was constituted placed the profession as a whole before the Sisyphean task of combating mass distress on a case by case basis. For Baum, this was "the great problematic" of all social work.[119] According to Kempf, the existence of mass distress posed a serious obstacle to the realization of their ideal of individualized help. "Again and again," she wrote, "the individual runs up against the bars of her cage, the boundaries of her competence, the walls with which all of those who have to protect the fiscal and economic interests of the national economy and public administration surround themselves." It was impossible, she argued, for social workers to compensate for the inequalities and injustices of the existing social order and thus eliminate that mass distress which weighed so heavily upon them and their clients. (She even suggested that such power would be of dubious benefit because it would remove the strongest spur to individual initiative and responsibility.) In view of these limitations, social workers could only maintain their sense of purpose by resigning themselves to either a certain degree of superficiality or indifference with regard to the fortunes of their clients or to "a great inner modesty and humility." Since the powers of the individual social worker did not, beyond a certain limit, increase in proportion to her willingness to serve others, the social worker had to seek the resolution of this conflict within herself by finding those limits which corresponded to her capabilities and which would permit the complete expression of the personality in every aspect of their work. However, such an intellectual position could only be satisfying if the social workers were convinced that these limitations on her activity had been imposed "not by herself, but by that power which brought her to life with all her human limitations."[120]

As Kempf suggested, the attempt to sublimate the contradictions of the profession through religious faith and the aestheticization of the ethics of selfless service had to be linked to a religious interpretation of these problems and a faith that the significance of her own work was not exhausted in the drudgery of her daily duties or negated by the hostility or thanklessness of the people she worked to help. The precise way in which such an interpretive schema functioned can be seen by comparing the widely read fictionalized accounts of the profession written by Hedwig Stieve and Emilie Zadow. Stieve began her narrative with the contradiction between the idealist ethos cultivated by the social work schools and the reality of the assistance they actually provided, and she

[119] Baum, *Familienfürsorge*, p. 30.
[120] Kempf, "Massennot und Wohlfahrtsarbeit," *SBA* 5:5–6 (May/June 1925), pp. 1–2.

then described how these women were overwhelmed by the scope of the mass distress and gradually worn down by the weight of overwork and mental exhaustion. Overwhelmed by the additional work imposed by the introduction of the district family welfare system and deprived of any subjective sense of satisfaction, the social worker described by Stieve became increasingly depressed and desperate before finally succumbing to nervous and physical exhaustion which necessitated a three months' disability leave.[121] Stieve's book was widely criticized, though the criticisms were directed less at her portrayal of the everyday life of the social worker than at her failure to comprehend fully the tragic nature of the profession. Her critics argued that she lacked the inner strength to persevere in the face of all these disappointments and frustrations because she sought subjective, personal satisfaction in the profession rather than selflessly placing herself in the service of a higher ideal.[122]

Zadow approached the problem from a Lutheran perspective and arrived at very different conclusions. Zadow's calling grew out of a consciousness that she was indissolubly bound to the dark world of poverty because both she and her clients were all members of the community of the sinful; the social worker was not morally superior to her clients, but was distinguished from them only by the fact that she had glimpsed a higher world, which she hoped to reveal to her clients through her own active love for them and her utterly selfless devotion. However, while Stieve's social worker suffered a nervous breakdown because she was unable to attribute any higher meaning to those experiences which clashed so sharply with her own expectations, Zadow insisted that her tribulations and disappointments did contain a deeper significance which could only be revealed through faith: "Life goes on in its richness and complexity. She [i.e., the religious social worker or *Schwester*] is not responsible for this. She is only responsible for one thing: to give what she can. Whether she suffices or whether she fails, she does not decide that. Another has the final word." At least in her fictional account, Zadow displayed a surprisingly firm commitment to the principles of Christian charity which helped her successfully navigate the many dangers which she encountered. She depicted the socialist block leader of the working-class settlement to which she was assigned as member of the loyal opposition. In response to an antagonist who argued that charity and welfare were only a modern version of bread and circuses which weakened the self-responsibility of the poor and transformed them into "children of the state," she replied that, for those social workers who were inspired by genuine love for their fellow human beings, there were no hopeless cases. Even though the path was long and winding, she continued to believe in the possibility of opening the eyes of her clients to a higher world: "I believe, and therefore I know. The power of the Crucified will always rise above the unholy tribulations of our existence when there is a living faith in this power. . . . Thought is the enemy

---

[121] Stieve, *Tagebuch einer Fürsorgerin*, pp. 37, 106–7.

[122] Idamarie Solltmann, "Zum 'Tagebuch einer Fürsorgerin,'" and Margarete Cordemann, "Familienfürsorge," *SBA* 7:11–12 (November/December 1927), pp. 6–8.

of everything living, but the peace of God is the end of all thought." Although true peace could only be attained through an understanding which bridged the existential distance between self and other, efforts at such understanding were often unsuccessful because people failed to display that reverence for the individuality of others which was the ultimate meaning of Christian charity and the foundation of all social work.[123]

Despite their ostensible reverence for the individuality of the persons they were attempting to help, most social work educators appear to have been oblivious to the ambiguous relation between education and discipline, helping and control. They were generally much more concerned with insuring that the encounters with the alien culture of the underclasses did not weaken the convictions of the social worker—which might either lead to moral relativism or the abandonment of helping for politics—than with the resistance of the needy to what they perceived as the unwanted imposition of bourgeois and religious norms. Social work educators generally attempted to resolve these problems either by displacing the problem into the transcendent realm, where failure could be sublimated through religious faith, or by attempting to show how it could be overcome through the moral virtuosity of the committed social worker.[124] Mahling, however, went even further and argued that, for the social worker firm in her convictions, the problem of the relation between education and discipline was a pseudo-problem. Since all education consisted in traversing the path from heteronomy to autonomy, he argued that it was impossible to help a child overcome moral waywardness without explaining the proper principles for the formation of a strong character and without awakening in him the desire to fill every aspect of his life with a new significance, and there was no doubt in his mind that the only source of this new spiritual strength was Christianity.[125]

All of those interpretations which maintained that the limitations of helping were, in fact, problems of motivation found their most comprehensive expression in the claim that these limits could in principle be overcome to the extent to which the activity of the social worker was inspired by a transcendent worldview which communicated its positive force in such an immediate, involuntary manner that the social worker would be able to escape from the paradoxes of helping. As Salomon explained, social work required a suggestive power which could not be created through artificial methods, but could only be cultivated and

---

[123] Zadow, *Kinder des Staates*, pp. 70–72, 78, 112–13.

[124] Jakob Bappert, "Die seelische Beanspruchung der Fürsorger und Fürsorgerinnen," *FW* 1:3 (June 1926), pp. 97–103 and "Vom tieferen Sinn der seelischen Beanspruchung unserer Fürsorgerinnen," *FW* 1:12 (March 1927), pp. 537–43, Cordemann, "Grundsätzliches zur Fortbildung der Wohlfahrtspflegerinnen," *SBA* 6:11–12 (November/December 1926), pp. 1–4, Solltmann, "Die Wohlfahrtspflege als Beruf und die Frau," *FW* 1:6–7 (September/October 1926), pp. 253–59, 306–10, and Ernst Jahn, "Die Krisis in der modernen Seelenführung," in Friedrich Ulrich, ed., *Fürsorge und Seelsorge* (Berlin, 1928), pp. 49–85.

[125] Mahling, "Die Zielsetzung bei der Ausbildung der freien, religiös-begründeten Wohlfahrtspflege," *FW* 1:6 (September 1926), pp. 241–46. For the Catholic variant of this professional ethos, see Zillken, "Berufsideal und Berufsschwierigkeiten der Wohlfahrtspflegerin," in Helene Weber, ed., *Ungelöste Fragen der Wohlfahrtspflege*, pp. 39–77.

brought to fruition in the social work schools. "Whoever hopes to transmit strength to another," she argued,

> must draw from the wellsprings of her own strength. The social worker can not do justice to her office when she can not in some way give expression to the foundations of her own worldview, her own faith, her own strength. . . . It is the radiant power of faith, of love, of truth, of the strength of character which allows a spark to leap over to another person. Fire is ignited through contact with fire, life [arises through contact with] living forces.[126]

Elizabeth Zillken, the general secretary of the *Katholischer Fürsorgeverein*, maintained that this peculiar form of social communication would preclude any suspicion that social workers were instrumentalizing their position to propagandize on behalf of any political party or proselytize on behalf of any religion or worldview: "Thanks to my deeply rooted view of life and my vocation, strong moral forces are at work which always seek to affect the person whom I am trying to help without it being necessary to speak of them. From a personality formed in a truly Christian manner something radiates which is felt and accepted by a person who encounters [such a personality]." She precisely captured the pathos of this attempt to escape from the contradictions of professional helping in her insistence that "a pedagogical influence is exerted most strongly not primarily through what one does, but through what one is."[127]

Both bourgeois and confessional social workers agreed that social work was always intimately connected to pastoral activity, but they curtly rejected any suggestion that they were exploiting the dependency of their clients to propagandize for their own religious and political beliefs.[128] In fact, both of these groups insisted that the very existence of both the social work profession and the welfare state itself was endangered by the fact that—in view of the absence of binding moral norms acceptable to the entire population—the combination of religious and political divisions and the religious neutrality of public welfare was systematically preventing social workers from fully expressing those highest and most personal beliefs upon which their ability to transcend the contradictions of professionalization depended. As Solltmann pointed out, "If she has a specific worldview, she must not permit the client to observe that from which she draws her own strength, since she must remain neutral. However, if she does not have one, she herself has no firm moral anchor and will in most cases have to overcome inner struggles which will impair her strength for her work."[129]

Solltmann argued that the principle of neutrality should be abandoned because, if it were rigorously adhered to, it would lead to absurd conclusions. She related the story of a Catholic social worker who visited a household where a

[126] Salomon, "Der Einfluß des Fürsorgers auf den 'Klienten,'" *FW* 1:3 (June 1926), pp. 105–9, citation pp. 107–8.

[127] Zillken, "Berufsideal und Berufsschwierigkeiten der Wohlfahrtspflegerin," pp. 51–55.

[128] Ulrich, "Fürsorge und Seelsorge," in Ulrich, ed., *Fürsorge und Seelsorge*, pp. 86–94; see also Steinweg, "Fürsorge und Seelsorge," *IM* 22:1 (January 1927), pp. 1–5.

[129] Solltmann, "Die Wohfahrtspflege als Beruf und die Frau," p. 255.

sick person had just died. Finding the family in prayer, she knelt, crossed herself, and began to pray with them. Although the woman was later reprimanded by her Protestant superior because her display of her own Catholic beliefs violated the religious neutrality imposed upon municipal employees, Solltmann pointed out that, if the woman had prayed without crossing herself, she would have identified herself as a Protestant, and that, if she had refused to pray, she would have been guilty of an equally ostentatious display of a nonreligious worldview. Such absurdities, she argued, were unavoidable in a pluralistic society in which the competing confessional and political groups all claimed to represent all-encompassing worldviews. However, since the state did have a positive interest in social work which was informed by a commitment to a system of ultimate ends, Solltmann argued that the call for the *neutrality* of public welfare should in fact be interpreted as a demand for the *parity* of all worldviews within public welfare. Such an approach would, she hoped, make it possible to enrich the activity of public welfare, which was increasingly deprived of spiritual sustenance, and, at the same time, bridge the gap between the dictates of morality and the constraints imposed by the religious neutrality of the sovereign state, which was the cause of so much pain and frustration for the social worker.[130]

Unfortunately, the preconditions for such a "positive neutrality" of public welfare were entirely absent,[131] and the chances of reaching a stable corporatist compromise were steadily diminishing as the confessional organizations exploited the fiscal and political crisis of the Republican welfare system to call for the break-up of the entire public welfare system. From the end of the decade onward, the crisis of the social work profession was linked in an increasingly direct manner to the general crisis of the republican welfare state. Progressives, bourgeois feminists, and confessional welfare organizations all argued in different ways that all of those phenomena which were associated with the emergence of the welfare state in the pejorative sense of the word—the general weakening of the moral fiber of welfare recipients, the growth of welfare dependency, and the corresponding politicization of the welfare system—were attributable to the failure of social workers to establish that intimate, trusting, and intensely personal relationship with their clients which was believed to be the indispensable precondition for strengthening their character and integrating them into the national community. They argued that the massive expansion of need during the depression, the bureaucratization and juridification of the welfare system, the neutrality of public welfare, and the penetration of parliamentary politics into the welfare and youth welfare offices had all contributed to this crisis. However, their failure to realize that the development of the profession was itself an integral dimension of this modernizing process misled them

[130] Solltmann, "Sollen und können weltanschauliche Kräfte und Überzeugungen in der Familienfürsorge wirksam werden?" in Weber, ed., *Ungelöste Fragen*, pp. 14–38.
[131] Leo Baeck, "Neutralität," *Blätter des Deutschen Roten Kreuzes* 8:12 (December 1929), pp. 1–6.

into believing that their idea of helping and the quest for national community could in fact be realized if they succeeded in freeing social work from these external impediments. The ensuing search for alternative forms of political and social organization provided the impetus for a wholesale critique of the republican welfare state from 1928 to 1933 and beyond.

Corporatism, *Weltanschauungskampf,* and the Demise of Parliamentary Democracy in the Welfare Sector

ORGANIZING CORPORATE INTERESTS

The groundwork for the corporatization of the social welfare sector had been laid by the RJWG and the RFV. These laws codified the subsidiarity of public welfare with respect to "voluntary welfare" while guaranteeing the latter direct influence on welfare and youth welfare policy at the local level and providing them with substantial public funds free from direct public oversight and control (within the broad framework established by these laws). The semipublic role of voluntary welfare was further reinforced by the implementation regulations drafted by the Labor Ministry in accordance with the 1923 Public Finance Law. These regulations identified the seven *Spitzenverbände* as "peak associations," which were regarded as representatives of both their member organizations and the needy persons they helped.[1] As Paul Frank, a welfare organizer at the Berlin *Zentrale für private Fürsorge*, wrote, the most important trend in the welfare sector was neither the improvement in the level of benefits, nor the acceptance of a preventive, therapeutic approach to need, nor even the codification of certain rights to assistance, but rather the fusion of public and voluntary welfare and the recognition that voluntary welfare had rights and responsibilities which were equal to those of municipal welfare.[2]

In theory at least, the relation between public and private welfare within the youth welfare offices had been defined by the RJWG. However, §5 RFV had specified that the district welfare offices were to serve as a "link" between public and private welfare, and it empowered the government to issue guidelines regulating the precise nature of this cooperation. In response to a Labor Ministry inquiry regarding the position of voluntary welfare on the proposed

---

[1] *RGBl.*, 1923, I, pp. 494–506, especially p. 505, and "Entwurf vorläufiger Richtlinien für die Verwendung der Vorschüsse zur Unterstützung von Anstalten und Einrichtungen der Wohlfahrtspflege auf Grund des §61 des Finanzausgleichsgesetzes" (n.d.), ADCV CA XX 49. Although it does not appear that these guidelines were ever officially promulgated, they nevertheless accurately reflect the actual practice of the Labor Ministry. The special status of these peak associations was finally officially sanctioned by the decree issued on December 11, 1926 (*RGBl.*, 1926, I, pp. 494–97), which laid out the procedures for allocating those funds (the so-called *soziale Wohlfahrtsrente*) which were to be distributed to charitable institutions in accordance with §27 of the law on the commutation of public debt.

[2] Frank, "Struktur und Konstruktion in der Wohlfahrtspflege," *FW* 2:6 (September 1927), pp. 259–65, especially p. 262.

guidelines, the Caritasverband, which took the initiative in drafting a response, argued that the participation of voluntary welfare should be modeled on the RJWG, but with certain modifications.[3] First, the Caritasverband argued that it would be best if, within each district, the various voluntary welfare associations were to thrash out all major differences among themselves in private in order to present a single list of candidates for the positions reserved to them, which local government should be required to accept. Second, the Caritasverband maintained that voluntary welfare could only be truly effective if the district welfare offices were self-governing bodies which were independent of what they regarded as the illegitimate party-political influence of local officials and if they had complete authority to determine how the monies placed at their disposal were used. Such a proposal would have drastically abridged the authority of local government in this important area of municipal activity, and the opposition of municipal officials was the main reason why it proved so difficult to reach agreement on these guidelines. The confessional welfare organizations were also concerned because many of the state drafts of the implementation regulations for the RFV either ignored voluntary welfare or relegated it to a secondary role. At one extreme, such as in Hesse, the welfare offices were to a large extent merely bureaucratic appendages to local government without any substantial participation of voluntary welfare. In Bavaria, which represented the other extreme, the welfare offices were constructed as self-governing bodies which were largely independent of local government. In most states, including Prussia, responsibility for welfare administration was delegated to local government, and the governing committee of the welfare office was constructed as a deputation whose composition mirrored the balance of political forces in local government. The confessional welfare organizations were extremely reluctant to allow the doors which had been so laboriously opened at the Reich level by the RJWG and the RFV to be closed on them at the state level, and ultimately their strategy was to obtain national regulations establishing their minimal goals and then attempt to gain better position wherever possible at the state level.[4]

Although the Caritasverband recognized that the immediate danger of the communalization of voluntary welfare had passed, its deliberations on the guidelines for implementing §5 RFV were overshadowed by the fear that the rapid expansion of the public welfare bureaucracy would inundate confessional welfare and accelerate the secularization of this all-important sphere of public life. What was once given willingly as an expression of religious faith in the form of charity was, the Caritasverband lamented, being transformed into a burdensome public obligation which abridged their religious freedom. It was, therefore, more necessary than ever before to reassert the centrality of positive Christianity as the foundation of charity and welfare, though the Caritasverband

---

[3] This discussion draws on the material in ADCV R 307 I.

[4] See the memorandum to Benedikt Kreutz (who succeeded Lorenz Werthmann as president of the Caritasverband in 1922), "Präsidiumssitzung vom 8.6.26. Material . . . betr. Reichsgrundsätze zu §5 RFV" (June 1926), ADCV 460.040.

also recognized that this spiritual counterattack had to be accompanied at the organizational level by the establishment of local Caritas offices headed by trained professionals and by the expansion of training for Catholic social workers.[5]

The draft guidelines, which were presented to the Labor Ministry and the other voluntary welfare organizations in February 1925, clearly reflected the concerns of the confessional welfare organizations.[6] The preamble denied that the authority of voluntary welfare was delegated or derived from the state, maintaining instead that it was justified independently from the "standpoint of society," and it blithely dismissed both the idea that there could be any conflict between public and voluntary welfare and the possibility that local officials could view the presence of the representatives of voluntary welfare as a foreign body within local self-government. Voluntary welfare hoped to resolve the ambiguities in the relation between public and voluntary welfare contained in the RJWG and firmly establish the subsidiarity of public welfare by *requiring* the welfare offices to delegate the direct provision of services as far as possible to voluntary organizations and *prohibiting* municipal government from establishing its own institutions or programs if the district's needs could be provided for by existing voluntary organizations.[7]

The regulations were also carefully drafted to insure the prerogatives of confession in the delegation of specific cases and the freedom of confessional welfare from what they regarded as undue political influence. The confessional and humanitarian organizations were obsessed with the possibility that the purely neutral and self-sacrificing character of their charitable work would be sullied by the intrusion of considerations of politics or interest. They sought instead to portray themselves as the natural advocates of all the needy and opposed— unsuccessfully—the representation of welfare recipients themselves in the welfare offices.[8] By stipulating that only those organizations which were recognized as legal personalities (i.e., which were registered associations, *eingetragene Vereine* [e.V.]) and which were engaged in practical welfare work could be

---

[5] "Die Einstellung unserer Caritasarbeit entsprechend den sehr veränderten Verhältnissen" (February 20, 1925), ADCV 107.

[6] "Reichsgründsätze über die Zusammenarbeit der öffentlichen und der freien Wohlfahrtspflege" (February 25, 1925), ADCV R 307 I. The basis for their deliberations was a lengthy memorandum prepared by the former Westphalian Oberpräsident Bernhard Würmerling (September 9 and October 28, 1924), ADCV R 307 I. See also Otto Ohl, "Vom Eigenwert der freien Wohlfahrtspflege," *FW* 1:1 (April 1926), pp. 3–8.

[7] In contrast to the Caritasverband, the Inner Mission was generally satisfied with the delegation of welfare programs to Evangelical organizations in the Rhineland, Westphalia, and Hanover. Inner Mission representatives in these areas pointed out that the demand for welfare services so far exceeded the capabilities of municipal officials that there was little danger of their being excluded. The real problem was recruiting enough trained social workers for their own organizations. See the correspondence with Ohl in ADWRh 24.6 and 24.10. These contrasting views are not as incompatible as they may seem at first glance. While the situation was certainly not as dire as the Caritasverband painted it, the Inner Mission could afford to be more conciliatory because it enjoyed the benefits of being a free rider on the aggressive politicking by the Caritasverband.

[8] See the report of the Caritas commission on the draft guidelines for the implementation of §5 RFV (January 16, 1925), and the summary of the various state regulations, both in ADCV R 307 I.

represented in the welfare offices, they hoped to exclude not only Workers' Welfare, which they continued to regard as a proletarian agitation group masquerading under the guise of a welfare organization, but also numerous other left-wing organizations. In view of the intransigence with which this draft promoted the views of the confessional organizations and the cavalier manner in which it ignored the interests of municipal officials, it is hardly surprising that these recommendations were not immediately adopted by the Labor Ministry.

Since the early 1920s, the major voluntary welfare organizations had regarded cooperation amongst themselves as the only way to acquire the political clout necessary to establish a satisfactory working relationship with public welfare, and the need for such an organization had become even more obvious during the debates over the guidelines for §5 RFV. However, since the *Reichsgemeinschaft* had been unable to perform such a role, it was only natural that the parties involved should look for another way to satisfy this need. Such an organization was also important for the Labor Ministry, and in September 1924 Ritter and Julia Dünner, another Catholic who played an important role in shaping welfare policy within the Labor Ministry, proposed that the voluntary welfare *Spitzenverbände* form their own organization. Negotiations were held throughout the fall, and in December 1924 the German League for Voluntary Welfare (*Deutsche Liga der freien Wohlfahrtspflege*) was formally founded by the Caritasverband, the Inner Mission, the Central Welfare Bureau for German Jewry, the Fifth Welfare League, and the Central Welfare Committee of Christian Workers.[9] Membership was restricted to those *Spitzenverbände* which had national organizations, were engaged in practical welfare work, and accepted the necessity of voluntary welfare and its parity with public welfare; public welfare and political organizations were excluded. The League was not to infringe upon the autonomy of its member organizations, and all decisions were to be made on a collegial basis, rather than through majority decisions.[10]

As had been the case with the proposed 1920 Red Cross Association, frictions arose between the Red Cross and the confessional and humanitarian organizations because its claim to be a neutral representative of the *Volksgemeinschaft* and the whole of voluntary charity conflicted with the understanding of the purpose of the League held by the other organizations. Nevertheless, after some initial reservations, the Red Cross soon joined the League.[11] On the other hand, although the confessional welfare organizations had serious reservations

---

[9] Minutes of the founding meeting (December 9, 1924), ADW CA 1195. See also van Acken to Kreutz (December 9, 1924), ADCV 460.1. In fact, Ritter and Dünner were so interested in the establishment of such an organization that they even provided a draft of the statutes. Van Acken to Kreutz (September 6, 1924), ADCV 460.1.

[10] Minutes of the founding meeting (December 9, 1924). After the creation of the League, the *Reichsgemeinschaft* concluded that its role was played out and, against the opposition of the DV, was dissolved. See Jochen-Christoph Kaiser, *Sozialer Protestantismus im 20. Jahrhundert* (Munich, 1989), pp. 112–24.

[11] See the correspondence in ADCV 460.1 and Kaiser, *Sozialer Protestantismus im 20. Jahrhundert*, pp. 158–59.

about inviting Workers' Welfare to join, Ritter regarded such an offer as a political necessity to protect the Labor Ministry against attacks from the left. Moreover, Johannes van Acken, the director of the Berlin office of the Caritasverband, hoped that participation in the League would help split the Social Democratic party, undermine its allegiance to the revolutionary Erfurth Program, and accelerate its transformation into a *Kleinbürgerpartei*.[12] However, despite its increasing reformism, the leadership of Workers' Welfare refused to join the League.

The League itself engaged in relatively little practical work. However, it did enable voluntary welfare to speak with a single voice against both public welfare and Workers' Welfare. The real importance of the League lay in the fact that it affirmed the principle that conflicts within the welfare sector should be resolved among the *Spitzenverbände* themselves, and its members hoped that the organization would serve as the first step toward the creation of a corporatist body which would remove the welfare sector from the sphere of parliamentary control at both the national and district levels. The real question was whether this idea could be successfully translated into practice. Ironically, though, the discussion of this question within the League during the middle of the decade only served to heighten the awareness of the religious, cultural, and political differences which divided the major confessional and humanitarian welfare organizations from each other (and which divided them collectively from both public welfare and Workers' Welfare) and of the problems they faced as long as welfare and social work remained subject to the political oversight of parliamentary bodies at the local and national levels. This growing awareness of the differences dividing them, as well as the intensification of the cultural struggle among these organizations resulting from the creation of a network of welfare and youth welfare offices after 1924, gave rise to a complex debate about the relation of church, state, and society which gave systematic form to all of the paradoxes and conflicts generated by the expansion of the sovereign state into the welfare sector.[13]

KULTURKAMPF IN THE WELFARE SECTOR

Since the vast majority of the working classes belonged at least nominally—by virtue of baptism and the reluctance (or indifference) to officially leave the

---

[12] Van Acken to Kreutz (December 15, 1924), ADCV 460.1. Although Workers' Welfare had emphasized its connections with the SPD and refused to become a legally recognized association, the organization reversed its position after Ritter declared in 1924 that, unless Workers' Welfare established an independent legal identity as a registered association, the Ministry could no longer provide funds to the organization because it could not distribute public funds to a political party. Van Acken to Kreutz (December 15, 1924), ADCV 460.1.

[13] In many ways, the *Weltanschauungskampf* within the welfare sector in the 1920s was symptomatic of the broader structural transformation of Weimar politics and illustrative of the problems examined by Karl Mannheim in *Ideology and Utopia*, trans. Louis Wirth and Edward Shils (Harcourt Brace Jovanovich, 1936).

church—to one of the two Christian confessions, it was inevitable that the claim advanced by Workers' Welfare to represent the welfare of all members of the working classes would lead to conflict with the confessional organizations, who claimed the exclusive right to represent the material and spiritual welfare of all members of their respective churches. Workers' Welfare and the confessional welfare organizations had been engaged in polemical exchanges since 1919, but the problem of practical cooperation at the local level did not become urgent and unavoidable until the middle of the decade, when the growing number of local Workers' Welfare organizations confronted the confessional organizations within the new welfare and youth welfare offices. Although the 2/5 representation had guaranteed the influence of voluntary welfare in the youth welfare offices, it did not specify which organizations were to be represented or how they were to work together, and the potential for conflict grew steadily between 1924 and 1926 with the establishment of the youth welfare offices as required by the RJWG.

According to 1926 Prussian statistics, the Inner Mission and other Evangelical youth welfare organizations were represented in 38% of the 717 youth welfare offices which had been established by that date, a figure which fell far below the percentage of Protestants in the general population in many areas. The Caritasverband was represented in 35% of these offices, the Red Cross and/ or the Patriotic Women's Association (*Vaterländischer Frauenverein*) in 32%, Workers' Welfare in 24% (and in nearly 50% of the big-city youth welfare offices), union organizations in only 6%, and other organizations (including Jewish welfare organizations) in 22%. However, the nature and extent of the cooperation between public and voluntary organizations varied according to the political loyalties and degree of urbanization of the different areas. Voluntary welfare organizations played a proportionately larger role both in Westphalia, where the Caritasverband was particularly active, and in many conservative, rural areas of Protestant Prussia. On the other hand, in Berlin itself public welfare played a much more active role.[14]

The potential conflicts latent in the widespread overlap between confession and party membership finally led to open conflict in the Rhineland and Silesia in 1925–26. The first blow in this new round of conflict was struck in Cologne. There, the Catholic members of the governing committee of the youth welfare office insisted that, since confession and (socialist) worldview were incompatible and since confession clearly enjoyed a primacy over all other factors, the activity of Workers' Welfare had to be restricted to those dissidents who had officially left the church and declared their loyalty to a socialist worldview. In addition, the Catholics also argued that Workers' Welfare should be excluded

[14] "Die Jugendämter in Preußen nach der Statistik des Preußischen Ministeriums für Volkswohlfahrt," *Volkswohlfahrt* 9:24 (1928), Sonderbeilage, Table 1. As of 1928, there were 1,251 youth welfare offices in the entire country, 31% of which were independent; the remainder were attached to the welfare office or some other branch of local government. *Statistik des deutschen Reiches*, Band 421: *Die öffentliche Fürsorge im deutschen Reich in den Rechnungsjahren 1927 bis 1931*, pp. 237ff.

from all youth welfare work because it was not an officially recognized public body constituted for the purpose of the common cultivation of a shared
outlook on life and was not, therefore, qualified to carry out the educational
mission defined in §1 RJWG.[15] These flames were further fanned by the governing committee of the youth welfare office in the Silesian town of Reichenbach, which in February 1926 passed a resolution stating that Workers' Welfare would be assigned responsibility only for those children whose mothers
did not belong to either of the Christian confessions. The resolution also
stated that the mothers of these children should not be allowed to choose
which organization they wished to care for their children; the committee
feared that this freedom of choice would open the door to wholesale agitation
and competition among these groups, even though such a position clearly
conflicted with the rights of parents to determine in which, if any, religion
their children were to be raised.[16]

Workers' Welfare regarded these decisions as the first skirmishes in a confessional "*Kulturkampf* against socialism," and, in response to these aggressive
actions, the socialist organization sought to reaffirm both the primacy of public
over voluntary welfare and the right of parental choice.[17] In response to a com-
plaint filed by Workers' Welfare in the Reichenbach case, the Prussian Ministry
for Public Welfare agreed with Workers' Welfare that the youth welfare office
could not delegate its responsibilities to voluntary welfare organizations solely
on the basis of confessional membership; this would have also excluded the
Red Cross and the Fifth Welfare League. However, the Ministry refused to rule
that Workers' Welfare had rights equal to those of the two confessional organizations because it was not clear whether or not Workers' Welfare represented a
distinct worldview. The Ministry also denied that membership in a political
party could be considered as an expression of a worldview in the sense of the
law; this decision undermined the claim by Workers' Welfare that it was the

---

[15] "Erklärung abgegeben in der Sitzung des städt. Jugendamtes Köln" (December 1925, signed
by Albert Lenné, the Caritas director for the archdiocese of Cologne and the official advisor to the
Katholischer Fürsorgeverein für Mädchen, Frauen und Kinder), ADW CA G 77. For the substantial public controversy generated by the events in Cologne and Reichenbach, see the series of
articles by Karl Vossen (a Catholic Landrat with close ties to the Caritasverband), Robert Görlinger
(the director of Workers' Welfare in Cologne), and Lenné under the title "Die Zuständigkeit der
freien Organisationen in der praktischen Jugendfürsorge," *Wohlfahrtspflege in der Rheinprovinz*
2:5,7, and 8 (1926), respectively, Vossen, "Die Berücksichtigung des Bekenntnisses bei der Jugendfürsorge," *Jugendwohl* 31:3 (1926), pp. 95–98, Görlinger, "Die Krise in der rheinischen Jugendwohlfahrtspflege," *AW* 1:2 (October 15, 1926), pp. 33–40, and Wachenheim, "Der Vorrang der
öffentlichen Wohlfahrtspflege. Grundsätzliches zur Krise in der Rheinischen Jugendwohlfahrtspflege," *AW* 1:3 (November 1, 1926), pp. 65–72.

[16] Streckenbach, Teubner, and Lengsfeld (of the youth welfare office) to the Reichenbach city
magistrate (February 14, 1926) and the related correspondence in ADW CA G 77. The Caritasverband also shared this desire to limit parental choice. See Günther Braekling, "Die Arbeiterwohlfahrt
und die Caritas," *Caritas* 31:5 (May 1926), pp. 129–34, and the correspondence of the *Katholischer
Fürsorgeverein* in ADCV 319.4 E II 15.

[17] Wachenheim, "Kulturkampf gegen den Sozialismus," *Die Gemeinde* 3 (1926), pp. 546–51.

legitimate representative, if not of all of the working classes, then at least of the members of the SPD and their children.[18]

The confessional welfare organizations were well aware of the origins of this cultural conflict and its implications. As Joachim Beckmann, a leading youth welfare activist in the Inner Mission, wrote in dramatic yet accurate terms a few years later,

> Social work has become the great, decisive area of a cultural conflict, a violent struggle for hegemony and dominance between the Christian confessions and irreligious, antiecclesiastical worldviews. . . . [This battle] is fought from year to year with increasing bitterness. . . . What can be the only possible explanation? Only the fact that here it is a question of truly ultimate things—upon which the existence or nonexistence, the life or death of communities depends—which are here locked in combat with each other. The time when everyone believed that welfare could confidently be left to the state is at an end. . . . Welfare is not technique or a trade and can not be made the object of administration. . . . Rather, it is a social work of a distinctly personal, confessional, *weltanschaulich*, cultural-political nature whose preconditions, methods, and strategies are rooted in ultimate beliefs.[19]

The debate between the confessional organizations and Workers' Welfare revolved, at the polemical level, around the rather abstruse question of the metaphysical status of socialism as a distinct worldview and, therefore, of the moral foundations of the social work undertaken by Workers' Welfare. The confessional and humanitarian organizations had frequently asked whether Workers' Welfare considered itself to be the representative of a specific political party (the Social Democrats), a specific social group (the working classes), or a distinct worldview (historical materialism); they were particularly distressed that Workers' Welfare appeared to deny the existence of all "transcendent" values, which all of the other voluntary welfare organizations viewed as the foundation of their ethics of selfless service. In the first two cases, they could argue that, as a self-help or interest group, Workers' Welfare was not entitled to representation in the youth welfare offices; in the latter case, they insisted on the incompatibility of worldview and confession and the primacy of the latter over the former. Before 1918, the SPD's declaration of religion to be a matter of individual conscience expressed the visceral opposition of the working classes to the established churches and had been an unavoidable political tactic. However, since the revolution had given the Social Democrats the opportunity to participate constructively in political life, many people had attempted to define the

---

[18] See the decision (January 6, 1927) in ADCV CA XX 49. The question of choice was not easily resolved. In February 1930, the Prussian Ministry of Public Welfare prohibited welfare officials from inquiring of all juveniles committed to correctional education whether or not they wished to be assigned to an institution run by the confession to which they nominally belonged, but insisted that a considered decision by juveniles who had reached the age of majority in religious affairs had to be respected, *Zentralblatt* 22:11 (February 1931), pp. 398–400.

[19] Joachim Beckmann, "Wohlfahrtspflege und Kirche im Weltanschauungskampf der Gegenwart," *Gesundheitsfürsorge* 5:10 (October 1931), pp. 255–62, citation pp. 255–56.

positive cultural and/or religious content of socialism, and the relegation of religion to the sphere of individual conscience had even been dropped from the party platform in 1925. Workers' Welfare increasingly began to insist that its own work was, in fact, motivated by higher, ethical and cultural ends. This challenged the confessional welfare organizations on their own territory and set off a lengthy, heated, and ultimately rather casuistic debate over whether or not socialism represented a worldview in the sense of the RJWG.

By the mid-1920s the politicization and the organizational transformation of the social welfare sector had proceeded far enough, the new political and organizational issues had become clear enough, and the practical problems involved in such cooperation had become pressing enough that in 1925–26, immediately after the founding of the League, the DV sponsored a series of confidential conferences to address the conflicts of principle which had arisen among the major organizations in implementing the RJWG and the RFV.[20]

In the early 1920s, Salomon had tried to provide a spiritual foundation for cooperation by identifying those aspects of welfare work which were common to all of the different organizations working in the field. However, at the first of these conferences, Paul Erfurth, the director of the Inner Mission social work school in Elberfeld, declared that cooperation on such an interconfessional basis was impossible because the *Spitzenverbände* had evolved into "complex entities which encompass, permeate, and administer all of the relevant areas of activity with their worldview." Although such activities as vocational advising and the operation of labor exchanges, where the moral education of the clients played no significant role, represented the limit of the fundamentally pastoral nature of social work, "however, in almost all other areas this complexity of the welfare organizations always makes itself felt in the demand to encompass all spheres of social work." This link between social work and pastoral activity was especially true in the area of hygiene, where religious beliefs cast the social problem in an entirely new light:

> It can be demonstrated and proven that [confessional social work] early on recognized and called attention to the connection between hygiene and morality, between sin, guilt and social abuses. . . . That hygiene is only a shadow image of the divine idea of purity and that, therefore, for example, sexually transmitted diseases can not be combated with any success through hygienic or economic assistance and can only be decisively combated through religious-ethical measures—the state, science and socialism have been blind to this insight until quite recently.[21]

[20] See the "Kommission zur Vorbereitung einer Konferenz über das Zusammenarbeiten der öffentlichen und der freien Wohlfahrtspflege," ADCV 461.055. Commission meetings were held on February 12, April 22, and August 6–7, 1925, and June 11–12, 1926. They generally consisted of several introductory talks followed by extensive discussion. In the following, the reports will be cited by author and date, and the discussion will be cited by date and page number. The only other person to exploit this material is Edward Ross Dickinson, *The Politics of German Child Welfare from the Empire to the Federal Republic* (Harvard University Press, 1996), pp. 183ff.

[21] Erfurth, "Die evangelisch orientierte Wohlfahrtspflege" (February, 12, 1925), pp. 3–4, reprinted

Erfurth's colleague Otto Ohl, the Inner Mission director in the Rhineland, maintained that even these limitations, and consequently any attempt to devise a schema for the division of labor among the major welfare organizations, would be problematic because, "in the strict sense, there are no neutral areas in which we can completely exclude worldview. Even help which is apparently purely monetary remains incomplete when it works on a strictly neutral basis."[22] Franz Keller, professor of *Caritaswissenschaft* in Freiburg, made an even stronger case for the centrality of religion and the pastoral mission of the church in all facets of social work. According to Keller,

> Since the Catholic ideal is essentially supernatural, . . . there is, according to the Catholic perspective, no distress which can be viewed—subjectively or objectively—apart from this ideal. Rather, all distress ultimately appears as religious distress, insofar as even economic or cultural-ethical distress is always seen only as an obstacle to the realization of the highest religious goals.

This perspective did not make the work of Catholic charities any less professional, Keller insisted, "but rather allows every type of distress to appear all the more urgent and every emergency aid all the more significant, the more that both are seen in the light of a higher religious world."[23]

From the mid-1920s onward, the efforts to resolve the fundamental conflicts which had arisen since the revolution focused increasingly on two issues: 1) the question of the extent to which it would be possible for these organizations to reach a *modus vivendi* among themselves and with public welfare (and thereby pave the way for the reprivatization of the public, political domain of social work within a corporatist framework); and 2) the question of the extent to which an ethics of selfless service would permit social workers to express those religious and moral values upon which their ability to influence the character of the needy was believed to depend, though in a way which would preclude the possibility of instrumentalizing their work to advance particular religious or political ends. The solution to these two problems depended on preserving the fiction of the strict separation of state and society and the existence of a sphere of purely affective social integration. However, these conditions were undermined from the mid-1920s onward, first, by this multidimensional cultural struggle and, second, by the dual recognition that, while control over state power was necessary to institutionalize a particular welfare reform strategy within a self-enclosed segment of the public sphere, in a democratic society, the propagation of these values was itself the precondition for securing control over a limited amount of state power. However, although the purpose of these conferences was to promote greater understanding and cooperation between these

---

in *IM* 24:10–11 (October/November 1929), pp. 429–39, citation p. 437. For a systematic statement of the new position of the Inner Mission in a confessionally and politically divided country, see Erfurth, "Ecclesia ancilla: Kirche, Innere Mission," in Hans Ehrenberg, ed., *Credo ecclesiam. Festgabe Wilhelm Zoellner* (Gütersloh, 1930), pp. 117–52.

[22] Discussion (February, 12, 1925), p. 15.

[23] Keller, "Caritas als Notwendigkeit," *FW* 2:1 (1927–28), pp. 1ff., citation p. 3.

groups, in fact they accelerated the fragmentation of the welfare sector along religious-political lines and the corporatist hollowing-out of the state and the public sphere.

In his address to the DV commission, Adolf Stahl, the director of the research department of the Inner Mission, explained that, from the point of view of the Inner Mission, the realization of the educational goals defined in §1 RJWG required that responsibility for youth education be fully delegated to confessional welfare organizations.[24] The starting point for Stahl's argument was a highly idealized vision of education, which was shared by all of the confessional and humanitarian welfare organizations. According to Stahl, education was

the greatest creative act of which the individual is capable, a creative act flowing forth from the deepest irrational depths of his essence (and for this reason always individually colored to the highest degree), completely permeated by the stream of personal spiritual life, in its goal thoroughly determined through the nature of his own being, whose primordial force alone is capable of bringing about the miracle of influencing the spiritual life of another. Educational labor is self-revelation, is the self-communication of the personality of the educator.

Since individuals in the employ of the state could never fully express their own ineffable individuality, the state could never undertake this pedagogical mission directly and could only establish minimal requirements and protect the free expression of those unique and autonomous individuals who alone could be the agents of genuine social pedagogy. This was the true significance of §1 RJWG as a framework law.

However, perfection of the individual personality was, Stahl continued, only possible on the basis of a positive confession of faith. "There is no such thing as generic religious education," he insisted, "only religious education within a confession." Consequently, religious education had to be carried out in an integral manner which would encompass every aspect of the unformed personality of the child. Since there were no religiously neutral spheres of social life, simple religious instruction in the school or the mere attendance of catechism classes—which before the war had satisfied the legal requirements for religious education and for the observation of the principle of confessionality in youth welfare work—was no longer considered adequate.

In opposition to the Social Democrats, Stahl maintained that the act of baptism had to be regarded as an unambiguous parental declaration regarding the religious education of their children and that the state should be required to adhere rigidly to this original choice. However, Stahl pushed even further the principle of confessional control over religious education. He regarded the legal requirement that confession "be taken into account" in youth welfare as an admission that the state did not feel itself competent to determine the content

---

[24] This and the following paragraph are based on Stahl, "Was verstehen die Religionsgesellschaften unter 'religiöser Erziehung' . . . ?" (June 11–12, 1926).

and method of religious education and that it had, therefore, simply limited itself to securing the right to such education. This requirement could only be satisfied, he argued, if the entire education of the child were entrusted to "consciously evangelical personalities" who were to have authority over every pedagogically significant decision taken on behalf of the child, including the determination of the institutions and persons who were to be directly responsible for the religious education of the child. Since the youth welfare offices were interconfessional and neither they nor organizations representing other confessions possessed any standard by which to determine which persons or institutions were competent to provide a proper Evangelical education, Stahl concluded that this decision ultimately had to rest with the institutional church and with those voluntary welfare organizations officially recognized by the church. The arguments presented by Albert Lenné on behalf of the Caritasverband were pithier and more legalistic, but came to the same conclusion: for the purpose of religious education, the milieu itself must be "of the same confession."[25] The rights of the church in this respect were, explained Joseph Beeking, the general secretary of the Caritasverband, based upon the sacramental nature of baptism, which imposed upon the community the obligation to insure that the baptized child actually enjoyed the supernatural benefits promised by the church.[26]

The realization of the conception of religious education shared by the Inner Mission and the Caritasverband would have so attenuated the public substance of and public control over youth welfare that the very idea would have become entirely illusory. However, the Social Democrats concentrated not so much on defending the idea of public education as on establishing the status of socialism as a worldview with rights equal to those of the Christian confessions. According to Chemnitz Workers' Welfare director Rudolf Schlosser, although the center of gravity of the hopes and aspirations of the working classes was secular and had a distinctly materialist tone, the new vision of human beings and community upon which these hopes centered was nevertheless a "summons from the absolute."[27] Schlosser argued that the idea of community had been lost to Christianity because its connections with a social order based on private property had led to an obsessive, mystified faith that the salvation of the individual soul could only be achieved in a transcendent realm beyond the reality of class society. Although material things could never be ends in themselves, in a society based upon private property and a fundamentally egoistic struggle of all against all, only a radical transformation of the mode of production could make possible the realization of this Christian idea of community. For these reasons,

[25] Lenné, "Forderungen, die wir Katholiken vom Standpunkt des katholischen Bekenntnisses aus hinsichtlich der 'Rücksichtnahme auf das Bekenntnis' . . ." (June 11–12, 1926).

[26] Discussion (June 11–12, 1926), p. 57.

[27] Schlosser, "Sozialistische Erziehung" (June 11–12, 1926), and his "Über sozialistische Erziehung," *AW* 1:6 (December 15, 1926), pp. 161–69. Heimerich, *Jugendwohlfahrt und sozialistische Weltanschauung. Referat gehalten auf der Tagung der Arbeiterwohlfahrt in Kiel Mai 1927* (Kiel, 1927), p. 12, was even more radical in his insistence that the socialist worldview was "a new, absolute principle and the only antithesis of capitalist-bourgeois beliefs."

Schlosser maintained, education could only be considered as a manifestation of a socialist worldview if it regarded the child as the bearer of a new society. Workers' Welfare, he concluded, should have the responsibility for the care of all working-class children because they would never acquire a true consciousness of the historical mission of the proletariat if they were placed in the care of confessional organizations: "The child of a consciously proletarian-socialist family belongs for the sake of spiritual bonds in the sphere of consciously socialist education, that is, to Workers' Welfare, even if the family does not have a party membership book, because our goal is not party membership, but the new person."[28]

Not surprisingly, the debates over the status of socialism as a worldview were inconclusive because the question of the respective rights of Workers' Welfare and the confessional welfare organizations could not be settled through the interpretation of existing legislation. Although Stahl and Ohl conceded the Christian roots of the idea of community espoused by the Social Democrats, they differed as to whether the professedly secular orientation of Workers' Welfare contradicted the Christian concern for the transcendent or whether it simply failed to address the issue. While the Protestants were at least willing to engage in a dialogue with the socialists as to the bases of their claim to the right to represent the welfare of Christian industrial workers, Lenné continued to insist that there was nothing to debate.[29] The only member of the DV commission to seriously oppose this tendency to subordinate the rights of the state to those of the churches and their welfare organizations was Gertrud Bäumer of the Interior Ministry. Bäumer argued against Constantin Noppel, the Caritas director for Bavaria and one of the most intransigent defenders of an integralist opposition to the modern state, that, despite the moral obligation felt by the church, the youth welfare offices ultimately had to bear full legal responsibility for juvenile education. Therefore, the youth welfare offices could not completely delegate their responsibilities and simply limit themselves to distributing cases and subsidies in accordance with the wishes of voluntary welfare groups. Since neither confession nor any other single dimension of social life encompassed the totality of education, she argued that the youth welfare offices had to mediate and transcend these conflicting views, but that they had to learn to do so in a way which was very different from the forced cooperation currently imposed by the state upon the *Spitzenverbände*. To achieve this goal, the youth welfare offices had to have their own pedagogical "substance," mission, and ethos which would enable them to serve as vehicles for the type of "national education" advocated by Fichte; only in this way could they represent, from the point of

---

[28] Schlosser (Chemnitz), "Sozialistische Erziehung" (June 11–12, 1926). In the 1920s, the most important socialist pedagogical movement in Germany was the *Kinderfreundbewegung*, whose guiding spirit was Reichstag deputy Kurt Löwenstein. See Löwenstein, *Sozialismus und Erziehung. Eine Auswahl aus den Schriften 1919–1933*, neu herausgegeben von Ferdinand Brandecker und Hildegard Feidel-Mertz (Berlin, 1976) and *Wie das Leben lernen . . . Kurt Löwensteins Entwurf einer sozialistischen Erziehung* (Berlin, 1985).

[29] Discussion (June 11–12, 1926), pp. 1–54.

view of the child's right to education, "a unitary pedagogical approach on the basis of a unifying national idea."[30]

THE *VÖLKISCH* SEARCH FOR ORGANIC UNITY
BETWEEN STATE AND SOCIETY

One of the issues which wound its way through all of the commission meetings was the question of whether the idea of the *Volk* might provide a basis for constructive cooperation in the deeply divided welfare sector. This issue was of crucial importance to all of the participants. Although the confessional organizations insisted that the religious neutrality of the sovereign state rendered it *a priori* incapable of exerting a positive moral influence upon the needy, they also maintained that all attempts to endow public welfare with a positive spiritual content conflicted with the priority of revealed religious truths and that, therefore, every attempt by public welfare to coordinate the activity of the voluntary welfare organizations represented an illegitimate infringement upon their freedom to witness these truths in their charitable work. The implication was that public welfare should limit itself to administrative tasks and those hygienic programs which did not possess any direct influence upon the character of the needy and support without reservation the work of voluntary welfare, which was to enjoy unquestioned supremacy.

Naturally, such a position was unacceptable to both the Social Democrats and the representatives of public welfare. Barmen municipal councilor and later Heidelberg mayor Carl Neinhaus lamented the fact that the idea of the state was undergoing a severe crisis.[31] Recent literature, he noted, read "like one long obituary for the state." In the economic sphere, organized capital and labor were increasingly attempting to put themselves in the place of the state, and a similar process was taking place in the welfare sector, where it was possible to observe "the many, if only tentative attempts of organizations representing a specific worldview . . . to spiritually dispossess the state." The crisis of confidence between public and private welfare was attributable, Neinhaus suggested, to the "atrophication of the idea of the state and the will of the state," or at least the atrophication of a specifically Germanic conception of the state. In contrast to rationalist individualism which had evolved in western Europe and the associated conception of society and nationality as voluntary associations, Neinhaus maintained that the most distinctive trait of German political thought was the belief in the natural rootedness of the individual in a *Volkstum* which was (onto)logically prior to the individual and, by implication, to all of those social groups which were eating away at the substance of the state. Neinhaus conceived of the *Volkstum* as "a supraindividual, autonomous entity, a *corpus mys-*

---

[30] Ibid., pp. 58–60.

[31] Neinhaus, "Versuch zu einer ideellen Grundlegung der öffentlichen Wohlfahrtspflege" (April 22, 1925).

ticum, from whose invisible bonds we can not disengage ourselves without destroying all possibility of spiritual and moral life. . . . It is the single real, natural community which, like the family, encompasses contemporary man, despite all of the corrosive tendencies of the day." For Neinhaus, public welfare was an expression of the common commitment to helping needy "national comrades" (*Volksgenossen*) for the sake of the *Volkstum*. The only way to overcome the antagonisms among voluntary welfare organizations and avoid despiritualizing the state and public welfare, he concluded, was to reawaken a consciousness of this primordial *Volkstum* and establish its primacy over both church and society.

Neinhaus hoped that this notion of *Volkstum* would be accepted as a higher ideal which would embrace the special values of the different voluntary welfare organizations, a position which was seconded by Ohl. The relativity of all secular institutions, Ohl argued, mitigated in favor of both a certain degree of pluralism within the welfare sector and an attitude of benevolent neutrality among the different voluntary welfare organizations.[32] Like Neinhaus, Ohl also regarded the *Volk* as the primary reality of social life. While some drew skeptical conclusions from the fact that the *Volk* meant something very different to each group, Ohl maintained instead that these differences supported the Protestant idea of the relativity of all different beliefs in the welfare field, "as long as they are inspired from the pure will to help." Moreover, the representatives of the Inner Mission also had—potentially—a much more positive attitude toward the state and public welfare than did the representatives of the Caritasverband, who tended to demonize the state as a creature of naked force devoid of all higher values. Ohl sought to find a middle ground between a position which reduced the state to "substanceless" (*blutleere*) neutrality and one in which voluntary welfare was directly controlled by an established state church, and he argued that the greatest good could be achieved by permitting the unfettered activity of all voluntary associations because it was impossible to fully encompass all of these creative forces in any single organization, either the state or the church.

The idea of the *Volk* proposed by Neinhaus and Ohl enjoyed a mixed reception from the other members of the commission. While, for the Lutherans, this new position entailed the abandonment of their hopes to again become an established *Volkskirche*, the key question in these conferences was whether the Caritasverband would be willing to accept this relativity for itself. Neundörfer conceded that there were many aspects of the Catholic church which were not necessarily determined by church doctrine, including its strong national dimension, and he hoped to chart a course between the sacrifice of what was essential to the Catholic church and opportunistic compromise. However, he nevertheless warned that "one can not and must not sacrifice something essential, because to do so is to give up one's self." In particular, he refused to accept Erfurth's claim that both confessions represented partial revelations of the truths of the Chris-

---

[32] Ohl, "Grundlagen und Ziele" (April 22, 1925).

tian religion.[33] In view of these differences, it seemed unlikely that the confessional and humanitarian organizations would be able to reach a *modus vivendi* among themselves, much less settle their equally divisive differences with Workers' Welfare and public welfare.

Bäumer argued that the imposition—in the form of state recognition of the semipublic status of the *Spitzenverbände*—of a system of forced cooperation represented an acute danger to the autonomy of voluntary welfare. However, she also rightly pointed out that the mere mutual toleration by the various voluntary welfare organizations could never provide a basis for constructive cooperation.[34] Her own ideal was an "organic democracy" which balanced between that freedom which was necessary to sustain the vitality of voluntary welfare and the guidance and coordination which could only be supplied by public authorities. However, she provided no suggestions as to how this lapidary formulation might be translated into concrete practice.[35]

Although Stahl agreed in theory with the conclusions drawn by Neinhaus and Ohl regarding the importance of the *Volkstum* as a potential basis for cooperation, he pointed out that the root of the problem lay in the fact that the *Volk* "did not form a national community," that is, that the empirical *Volk* did not correspond to its ideal form. Under such circumstances, the formation of the German League for Voluntary Welfare marked the limit of what could be achieved regarding the rationalization of the welfare sector. Recent conflicts and these conferences themselves had, he concluded, "condensed the many oppositions and tension into a few fundamental conflicts, which are simpler, but more obtrusive." Since the spiritual energies of the various organizations grew directly out of their conviction of the absolute validity of their respective worldviews, there were strict limits on the extent to which any organization could moderate its position without compromising its fundamental beliefs.[36] However, Polligkeit warned that this insistence on the absoluteness of their respective beliefs, and the resulting unwillingness to make the necessary concessions, might make it necessary to solve these problems through methods "which are thoroughly alien to social work, through parliamentary means and the mechanical balancing of numerical participation."[37]

While the Protestant representatives of both public and voluntary welfare had attempted to build a bridge between their two spheres, the Catholics—especially Lenné—insisted on drawing the line between them as sharply as possible. Although Noppel admitted that, with the possible exception of Workers' Welfare, all of the welfare organizations represented at the conference shared the intermediate goal of selfless service, he warned that such an admission did not preclude "that we consider ourselves absolute in other areas. The mission-

[33] Discussion (April 22, 1925), pp. 3, 12, 18–19, 28–29.

[34] Ibid., p. 6. See also Bäumer, "Strukturfragen der Wohlfahrtspflege," *Blätter des Deutschen Roten Kreuzes* 5:12 (December 1926), pp. 3–13, and Frank, "Struktur und Konstruktion."

[35] Bäumer, "Strukturfragen der Wohlfahrtspflege," p. 8.

[36] Discussion (April 22, 1925), pp. 7–9.

[37] Ibid., pp. 1, 11.

ary force of the individual movements should not and can not be constrained."
Nor did it imply that public welfare represented a neutral basis for cooperation.
Rather, he argued, the goal of public welfare should be to render itself super-
fluous by stimulating the development of free societal forces.[38]

The Catholic members of the commission were uniformly hostile to this notion of the *Volkstum* and to the role of public welfare which it implied. Neundörfer's hostility toward the state—even such a manifestly conservative one as
that envisioned by Neinhaus—represented an attempt to defend the traditional
rights of family, parish, and church against the claims of the sovereign state; it
anticipated the new, distinctly Catholic definition of the principle of subsidiarity, which would find its first doctrinally binding pronouncement in the 1931
encyclical "Quadragesimo Anno." This new definition differed markedly from
the original usage, which simply meant that the individual and/or family had to
exhaust their own resources before public authorities would intervene, in that it
assigned a positive value to these smaller, more "natural" communities in the
order of creation. This meant that the activity of these communities had an
ontological priority over larger, more artificial communities, such as the state,
whose rights could only be subsidiary, and that, therefore, the state should refrain from intervening in any sphere where its action was not required by the
demonstrated incapacity of smaller communities to satisfy their own needs.[39]

In this tug of war between those Protestants, such as Neinhaus and Ohl, who
believed that the *Volkstum* could provide a positive foundation for the corporatization of the welfare sector, and the Catholic and Protestant opponents of this
idea, the Fifth Welfare League and the Red Cross found themselves in a difficult position. Bäumer frequently expressed her discomfort with the term "humanitarian" because it implied a concern merely with this-worldly, material
values. In fact, those members of the Fifth Welfare League who were active in
the youth welfare field were advocates of a *Kulturprotestantismus* which owed
more to Kant, Fichte, and Humboldt than to Luther and whose religious motivation was found more in the perfection of the personality than in the expiation of
sin. The Protestants who were represented in the Fifth Welfare League did not
participate in these conferences, and they failed to present themselves as a
distinct alternative to the two conservative confessional organizations. The Red
Cross also found itself in a peculiar situation. As Felix Grüneisen, the chair of
the German Red Cross, pointed out, it made all of the confessional welfare
organizations uncomfortable: "We stand in the midst of the centrifugal forces of
the time, that pull toward political, religious and other forms of one-sidedness.
There are, however, very few which today recognize the need for synthesis."
Although Grüneisen opposed the depoliticization of welfare and its isolation

---

[38] Ibid., pp. 16–23.

[39] Ibid., pp. 11–12, 28 and (August 6–7), pp. 19–20. On this distinctly Catholic doctrine of
subsidiarity and its influence on welfare legislation in the Federal Republic, see Joachim Matthes,
Gesellschaftspolitische Konzeptionen im Sozialhilferecht (Ferdinand Enke, 1964), pp. 17–66, 85ff.,
and "Quadragesimo Anno," in *Five Great Encyclicals* (Paulist Press, 1939), pp. 146–47.

from the broader concerns of public life as "almost a denial of the state," he was unable to present a coherent alternative. Instead, the Red Cross had to content itself with proposing a weak version of its own social hygiene program as the missing synthesis.[40]

As the different positions became clearer in the course of these discussions, the lines of cleavage became more visible. Although Neundörfer agreed with the Protestant representatives of voluntary and public welfare that the work of public welfare should in principle be made deeper and more spiritual, he and Beeking were not at all clear as to how Neinhaus could hope to give public welfare a sense of spiritual mission without at the same time transforming the idea of the *Volkstum* into a secular religion.[41] Although Neinhaus had earlier argued that *Volkstum* was primarily an ethical-cultural category, these Catholic criticisms forced him to claim that the *Volkstum* did in fact have a distinctive "metaphysical" value, which Neundörfer immediately condemned as a "new paganism."[42] Although Ohl denied the religious nature of the *Volkstum*, it was not clear how else he could hope to square the circle and guarantee the necessary autonomy to voluntary welfare without at the same time despiritualizing public welfare.[43] By pushing to the fore the conflict between church and state, this exchange revealed the basic contradiction running through all of these conferences: a positive conception of state sovereignty, which appeared to be the only possible basis for constructive cooperation, also destroyed the possibility of such cooperation for those organizations which insisted that their transcendent, religious values took priority over the claims of the sovereign state. Every attempt to resolve this paradox by presenting the state as a neutral authority further denatured the state in the eyes of those who condemned its neutrality in moral and religious matters, while this neutrality simply displaced the unresolved cultural conflicts back into the societal sphere while making them seem all the more intractable. Despite the obvious appeal of the myth of the *Volk* for many of the participants in these meetings, its attraction was not strong enough to overcome the traditional loyalties to church and class. As a result, voluntary welfare continued to insist that democratic control of the welfare sector was incompatible with voluntarist social engagement. As Bäumer told the commission, although it was pointless to press these divisive arguments to their logical conclusion, it was no more productive to paper over the real differences dividing the various organizations.[44]

In view of the seeming impossibility of finding a basis for constructive cooperation which would not contradict the absolute claims made by each organiza-

---

[40] See Grüneisen's comments in discussion (April 22, 1925), pp. 4–6, 25–27.

[41] Discussion (August 6–7, 1925), pp. 74, 76, 84, 88. Neinhaus also accused voluntary welfare of displaying a "very refined egoism," because these organizations only had the freedom to insist upon their special mission because public welfare bore primary responsibility for alleviating mass distress.

[42] Discussion (August 6–7, 1925), pp. 78, 94–95.

[43] Ibid., p. 89.

[44] Discussion (April 22, 1925), p. 6.

tion for their respective worldviews, the focus of these commission debates shifted toward the question of the relative autonomy of social work from religion and politics and the possibility of cooperation based on a common commitment to an ethics of selfless service.[45] Writing in another context, Ohl summed up the sentiments of all of the participants, with the exception of the Social Democrats. "To these fundamental considerations," he wrote,

> must be added the deep concern for the future of our polarized German social work system. In all social work, it must be a question of selfless service to other persons. This service can not tolerate being degraded to a means to any political end, rather than taking place solely for the sake of helping. . . . What makes the needy so inwardly hopeless, desperate and bitter is not merely their external distress, but the feeling that people do not have any understanding of their situation, the hardness and absence of love of the national "community" which has thrust them into the depths. For us all, it is a question of the purity of service, because we are all of the conviction that all of the need in our people can not be alleviated through any type of will to power, but only through the will to serve.[46]

Statements of such sentiment could be multiplied *ad infinitum*. This problem was so complicated because, to the extent that the elimination of personal distress was believed to depend upon giving the indigent individual a new moral center, it was impossible to categorically distinguish selfless service from proselytizing or social work from social discipline. Moreover, this issue cut two ways, affecting both the relations among the various voluntary welfare organizations and the relation between the social worker and her clientele.

In his commission report, Neundörfer pointed out that the political struggles of the recent past had bound both the Caritasverband and the Inner Mission more closely than ever before to the institutional church. These developments, he continued, had increased the danger that this ideal of selfless service would be subordinated to the missionary and pastoral activity of the church. The same was true for Workers' Welfare, which distinguished its own activity from that of the SPD, but which nevertheless insisted that its own work would serve the Social Democratic worldview in the same way as the other welfare *Spitzenverbände* promoted their own worldviews. Neundörfer argued that both the churches and the political parties had to recognize the relative autonomy of social work because both would violate their own vocations if they subordinated social work to particular ends. Although the institutional church represented a closed body within which social work had to be subordinated to pastoral activity, the commandments of Christian love, Neundörfer maintained, knew no such limits and the religious character of its work did not entail any restriction of its activity to the members of the religious community. It was,

---

[45] Erfurth, "Die evangelisch orientierte Wohlfahrtspflege," Ohl, "Grundlagen und Ziele des Zusammenwirkens . . ." (April 22 and August 6–7, 1925), and Ohl, "Die Innere Mission im Kampf der politischen Parteien" (1929, unpublished; original typescript can be found in the library of the Diakonisches Werk).

[46] Ohl, "Die Innere Mission im Kampf der politischen Parteien."

therefore, possible to relativize Catholic charity without relativizing the Catholic faith.[47]

However, since church doctrine imposed upon the faithful the obligation to insure a proper Catholic education for all Catholic children, they could not be indifferent to the education of the members of their own confession. In such cases, Neundörfer maintained, it would be wrong to dismiss the pastoral dimension of social work as the manifestation of an illegitimate craving for power on the part of the church. Although Neundörfer conceded in the abstract the possibility that the education of Catholic children could be entrusted to nonconfessional organizations if the fulfillment of their religious needs could be insured, in practice this requirement could seldom be met:

> When Social Democratic Workers' Welfare limits its social work in principle "to earthly concerns" and quite often in fact adopts an expressly anti-religious attitude, when public officials send Catholic children for months at a time to rural convalescent homes without any consideration of religious factors or consent to adoptions in which the inherited faith of these children is lost with almost complete certainty, when educational and correctional education institutions run by those of different faiths . . . make obvious attempts to convert [Catholic children], our consciousness of our religious obligations forbids us to leave social work to others, and we must demand that [these children] be left to the care of our own institutions.[48]

This meant that the religious requirements of social work could only be satisfied by educating Catholic children in a thoroughly Catholic milieu, and Neundörfer suggested that the principle of individualization would have to be reinterpreted in this direction.

Bäumer appeared to endorse Neundörfer's affirmation of the relative autonomy of social work without, however, following his confessional reasoning.[49] She argued that it was inevitable—indeed, desirable—that the work of municipal social workers would be influenced by their religious beliefs, but she condemned the conscious attempt to use social work to influence the client in favor of one worldview or another. However, she insisted that this conscious self-limitation did not undermine the ethic of selfless service or deprive public welfare of all spiritual sustenance. She argued instead that involuntary membership in the national community represented the primary social reality which bound together the social worker and her clientele and provided an autonomous foundation for both an ethics of selfless service and the positive cooperation of public and voluntary welfare.[50] The problem was that, for the integralists in the

---

[47] Neundörfer, "Eigenständigkeit der Wohlfahrtspflege und Absolutheit der Kirche" (August 6–7, 1925), pp. 38–58, Neundörfer, "Die Eigenständigkeit der Wohlfahrtspflege gegenüber Kirche und Staat," *Hochland* 23:7 (April 1926), pp. 69–76, and Juchacz/Heymann, *Die Arbeiterwohlfahrt* (Berlin, 1924), p. 8.

[48] Neundörfer, "Eigenständigkeit der Wohlfahrtspflege und Absolutheit der Kirche," p. 49.

[49] Discussion (August 6–7, 1925), pp. 60, 71.

[50] Ibid., pp. 85–87, and Bäumer, "Gedanken über den Sinn der Fürsorge," in Friedrich Ulrich, ed., *Fürsorge und Seelsorge* (Berlin, 1928), pp. 5–17, especially p. 10.

Caritasverband, these national values conflicted with confessional loyalties, and this conflict posed from a different perspective the central question of the political parameters within which it would be possible for this ethics of selfless service to transcend these cultural antagonisms.[51]

The efforts by Neundörfer and Bäumer to establish a basis for corporatist cooperation by either sublimating the very real political and religious conflicts into the idea of national education or displacing them into the nonpolitical realm of an ethics of selfless service were attacked from critics who well understood the logic of cultural struggle, but who drew different conclusions from this insight. In contrast to Neundörfer, Noppel insisted upon the subordination of social work to the pastoral mission of the church and emphasized the religious foundations and meaning of social work. He dismissed Neundörfer's distinction between charity and pastoral activity because he did not believe that it was possible to sufficiently separate material support from spiritual welfare. He also maintained that, because of the essentially interconfessional character of public welfare offices and the absolute priority of pastoral work over social work, a Catholic social worker could not, in good conscience, attempt to express her own deepest convictions through her work within such an office and that it would be necessary to make a personal choice between confessionality and interconfessionality.[52]

On the other hand, Heimerich, the representative of Workers' Welfare, insisted that all attempts to depoliticize welfare through a corporatist system were futile because there was no such thing as a "neutral" (*gesinnungsfreier*) state. The separation of welfare and politics was, he argued, "a chimera":

> It is impossible to divide the wholeness of life. It will always remain only an illusory separation. This demand would also turn upside down the entire basis of our public life. In addition, the new state is still young and weak, and one takes no pleasure in the present form of parliamentary government. As a result, a kitchen cabinet government of interest groups (*Nebenregierung der Verbände*) has emerged, of confessional and economic interest groups. This is leading to a new type of corporate state and to the renewed subjugation of the working classes to the ruling estates.[53]

Any attempt to remove the welfare and youth welfare office from the sphere of competence of municipal government would, he maintained, unleash other demands and lead to the complete dismemberment of municipal government and, ultimately, the state itself.

Neither side appears to have been much swayed by the arguments advanced

---

[51] While Klumker also supported the religious neutrality of youth welfare, in a 1930 article Hans Achinger suggested that all such arguments were self-deceptive because all education necessarily entailed influencing youth in the sense of a specific worldview. Klumker, "Hochschule und soziale Ausbildung," *ASS* 62 (1929), pp. 589–601, and Achinger, "Fürsorge und Weltanschauung," *Zentralblatt* 22:6–7 (September/October 1930), pp. 181–90, 223–32.

[52] Discussion (August 6–7, 1925), p. 75.

[53] Ibid., pp. 35–36, 70–71.

by their opponents. In the end, these meetings accelerated the confessionalization of youth welfare and the tendency on all sides to insist that religious and/or *weltanschaulich* education could only be guaranteed within a culturally homogeneous, self-enclosed, self-governing milieu which could protect these children from the unsettling influences of a pluralistic society. By 1926, a workable corporatist solution to cultural struggle in the welfare sector seemed further away than ever, and whatever doubts may have remained in the minds of German Catholics about the status of a socialist worldview and whatever tenuous hopes they may have harbored for cooperation between the Caritasverband and Workers' Welfare were dashed by *Quadragesimo anno*, which declared socialism to be incompatible with Catholicism.[54]

Although the representatives of the Inner Mission repeatedly stressed that their attitude toward Workers' Welfare was different from that of their Catholic counterparts because their respect for individual freedom of conscience prohibited the Lutheran church from placing upon its members the same demands for external conformity as did the Catholic church, their conclusions about the possibility of cooperation were no less pessimistic. According to Beckmann, all efforts to establish the conditions under which these conflicts could be resolved was in fact rendering them more intractable, and he feared that any attempt to definitively resolve these conflicts would force Workers' Welfare to take an irrevocable stand against the confessional welfare organizations and thus precipitate a political confrontation with potentially perilous implications for the nation:

> In this case, the entire issue becomes a question of political power. All of the necessary legislative judgments can not be settled at the theoretical level, but fall into the sphere of parliamentary party struggles. But this will never yield a solution to the problem (the principle of majority rule!), but rather the opposite: unprecedented heightening of conflict to the point of a *Kulturkampf* (and, depending on the outcome, religious war).[55]

For the sake of the Gospels, Beckmann urged, the Inner Mission should not follow the aggressive course pursued by the Caritasverband because he feared that this would lead to a definitive rupture between Social Democracy and Christianity. The only alternative was to work to overcome socialism from within through the force of the Gospels. Nevertheless, he despaired, "every solution is only an illusory one."[56]

---

[54] "Quadragesimo anno," pp. 157ff.

[55] Beckmann, "Arbeiterwohlfahrt und Jugendfürsorge," pp. 10–11, and "Nachschrift. Ausschuss für offene Jugendfürsorge in Neuwied a.Rh." (November 21–23, 1927), both in ADW CA-G 78.

[56] Beckmann, "Arbeiterwohlfahrt und Jugendfürsorge," p. 12.

The Contradictions of the Republican Welfare State, 1928–1933

THE WEIMAR welfare system represented the culmination of a century-long attempt to solve the problems of poverty and social insecurity in an acquisitive society through the rationalization of the sphere of social reproduction and the extension of both social rights and social obligations. The telos of this rationalizing, modernizing process was the idea of a "risk-free existence," or what contemporaries called "*der risikofreie Mensch,*" in which the existential uncertainties of working-class life would be socialized and, to as great an extent as possible, prevented or remedied through public intervention. As Hans Muthesius argued at the 1930 conference commemorating the fiftieth anniversary of the DV's founding, the welfare system represented

> the most immense attempt at rationalization. . . . We have conceived of the plan to exclude chance from human life and attempt in advance to consciously guide the life of both the individual and society. A grandiose attempt, when we see the progress of culture—at least in theory and when observed from a certain distance—in the repression and exclusion of chance.[1]

While the perfection of the risk-free existence by subjecting the existential risks of everyday life to scientific analysis and rational control accelerated the secularization of providence and the disenchantment of the world, this process was itself propelled by both the confidence in the ability to improve the human condition and a nagging metaphysical need for certainty which was increasing in direct proportion to the disenchantment of the world by this calculus of social utility.[2]

Although the relief residence system, the Elberfeld system, and the voluntary associations for the prevention of poverty and vagrancy represented the first stage in the modernization of poor relief and charity, the conceptual innovation which ultimately made possible the creation of the system of preventive, therapeutic programs established in the 1920s was the emergence of a sociological perspective on the social problem in the 1880s and 1890s. In contrast to the limitations imposed by Christian-bourgeois individualism, this new understanding of the causes of poverty made possible the transition from the relief of the poor, who had previously been regarded as a permanent estate existing on the

---

[1] Muthesius, "Kollektivverantwortung und Einzelverantwortung in der Wohlfahrtspflege," in *Die Stellung der Wohlfahrtspflege zur Wirtschaft, zum Staat und zum Menschen, SDV,* N.F. 15 (1930), pp. 43–55, citation p. 50.

[2] Hans Achinger, "Fürsorge und Rationalismus," *FW* 6:5 (August 1931), pp. 194–99.

margins of civil society, to systematic efforts to eliminate the general, social causes of poverty, illness, and deviance.

However, as the contours of the welfare system became increasingly clear in the second half of the 1920s, there was a growing awareness in many quarters that those same forces which were driving the evolution of the social welfare system were also making it difficult, if not impossible, for these highly bureaucratized institutions to achieve their goal. The bureaucratization and juridification of the welfare system, the resulting politicization of public assistance, and the associated professionalization of social work were all integral dimensions of this modernizing, rationalizing process. By the second half of the decade, though, many observers were coming to feel that the institutional forms through which public assistance was provided were themselves part of the problem because they were interfering with the ability of social workers to establish that I-thou relationship from which that consciousness of the greater social obligations entailed by the new republican conception of social citizenship was expected to grow. In the absence of a sense of correspondingly greater social obligations, it was argued, the extension of preventive, therapeutic programs was leading to the hypertrophy of individual rights, which in turn was causing a decline of public morality and an increase in class conflict as the various groups of public assistance recipients competed with one another to secure legal entitlements to higher benefit levels without developing any sense of obligation to the society which provided this support. While politicians of all parties had originally insisted that the expansion of state social programs had been necessary for postwar reconstruction and the creation of a more social, democratic state, in the second half of the decade they increasingly began to argue that these programs were becoming dysfunctional and transforming their social state into a welfare state in the pejorative sense of the word, or what contemporaries called a *Fürsorgestaat*. Although the sense of crisis was certainly intensified by the Great Depression, its roots lay much deeper, and the depression only brought the contradictions of the welfare state to the surface in their harshest form without adding anything fundamentally new.

In the final years of the Republic, welfare reform debates focused on the structural changes in the public assistance system which were believed to be the cause of this hypertrophy of individual rights, and they explored from this structural, systematic perspective the same set of contradictions which we examined in the concluding section of chapter 5 from the perspective of the individual social worker. Since the Social Democrats maintained that poverty, illness, and deviance were primarily caused by an exploitative social order, not by individual moral failings, they called for the further expansion of both social policy legislation and the social welfare system, and they increasingly ascribed to these measures a pivotal role in the creation of a socialist society. Both the Social Democrats and the Progressives continued to affirm the existence of a broad public responsibility for combating the social problem. This alliance was one of the two pillars of the republican welfare system.

The second pillar was the alliance between the Progressives and the confessional welfare organizations concerning the centrality of personal help provided on a voluntary basis.[3] However, the Progressives were themselves deeply ambivalent about the rationalizing process which they had helped set in motion. Although they never abandoned their belief in the importance of a sociological perspective on the social problem or their insistence upon the crucial role of preventive, therapeutic programs, their efforts to discover the conditions under which social work could again become genuine personal help increasingly turned them into opponents of the public welfare system which they had done so much to create. All of their criticisms of the effects of rationalization, bureaucratization, juridification, and professionalization were echoed by the confessional welfare organizations, which had long maintained that Progressivism itself, and not its bureaucratic distortion, was the cause of the looming crisis of the republican welfare system. Reinforced by the trend toward political reaction at the end of the decade, these criticisms of the republican welfare system by both the Progressives and the confessional welfare organizations gradually came together to give new impetus to the idea of a corporatist organization of the welfare sector in which the endemic problems of parliamentary government in a pluralistic society would be avoided by reprivatizing and reconfessionalizing public welfare within the broad framework of an authoritarian, Christian state.

The Progressives and the confessional welfare organizations greeted the Nazi seizure of power with varying degrees of equanimity and enthusiasm because they hoped that the overthrow of the Republic and the exclusion of the Social Democrats would make it possible to solve the problems which had been revealed in such a glaring manner at the 1925–26 DV conferences and in the *Kulturkampf* over youth welfare. Paradoxically, though, the political dynamism of the Nazis flowed from sources which were very different from those which had fed Progressivism and Christian conservativism during the later years of the Republic. Their goal was not the reprivatization and reconfessionalization of public welfare, but rather the total mobilization of society and the exclusion of confessional charity from the field of voluntary societal activity, and the attempts by the Nazis in 1933/34 to establish their predominance in the welfare sector set in motion another round of cultural struggles whose unexpected outcome demonstrated the intrinsic instability of the authoritarian corporatism envisioned by the confessional welfare organizations.

VOLUNTARY WELFARE STRIKES BACK: THE DISMANTLING OF UNEMPLOYMENT INSURANCE AND THE CRISIS OF MUNICIPAL WELFARE

In the years after the promulgation of the RGr, welfare reformers had called for the extension of the social insurance system and the expansion of old-age security programs in order to relieve the burdens placed on municipal welfare by the

---

[3] This is not to say that the confessional welfare organizations necessarily opposed the social intentions embodied in the republican welfare system; they simply felt that these intentions could best be realized through personal help. See, for example, Johannes Horion, "Die Zukunft der Wohlfahrtspflege," *Wohlfahrtspflege in der Rheinprovinz* 7 (1931), pp. 1–4.

emergence of the new poor and restore the integrity of its subsidiary, individualizing method. The most significant achievement in this direction was the 1927
Unemployment Insurance Law which, in theory at least, shifted responsibility
for supporting the able-bodied unemployed from municipal welfare to the Unemployment Insurance Administration. However, the unemployment insurance
system immediately became the object of intense conflict between organized
labor and big business before being overwhelmed at the end of the decade by a
level of long-term, structural unemployment which far exceeded the capacity of
the system. Between 1930 and 1932, chancellor Heinrich Brüning (Center)
availed himself of the growing state fiscal crisis to pursue a specific political
agenda: the elimination of reparations, the reform of public finances and the
reduction of what he regarded as excessive social spending, conservative constitutional reform, and a rigorous deflationary program designed to restore the
international competitiveness of German products by reducing domestic wage
and price levels. However, Brüning's deflationary policies initially had a pro-
cyclical effect which intensified both the preexisting structural weaknesses of
the domestic economy and the effects of the international conjunctural downturn. Constructive measures to combat unemployment were at the bottom of
Brüning's list of priorities, and he was only willing to contemplate such steps
after attaining all of these other goals.[4]

Between 1929 and the spring of 1932, there was a complex debate over the
reform of unemployment assistance which pivoted around the relation between
the unemployment insurance system, the fiscal, economic, and social policies of
the Brüning administration, and the mounting crisis of municipal welfare. The
1927 law had originally made the Reich responsible for guaranteeing the sol-
vency of the unemployment insurance system, and the cost of supporting the
rapidly growing number of unemployed created by Brüning's policies was initially shifted to the Reich in a way which made the reform of the unemployment insurance system the precondition for both balancing the Reich budget
and achieving Brüning's broader goals. Even though the original purpose of the
unemployment insurance system was to keep the unemployed from having to
turn to municipal welfare, Brüning, and later Papen, chose to solve the fiscal
problems of the Reich—and, in the process, dismantle one of the pillars of the
republican welfare state—by employing emergency powers to progressively reduce the level and duration of unemployment insurance benefits and restrict the
sphere of persons eligible for such benefits. Although these measures eventually
balanced the finances of the unemployment insurance system and the Reich
government, they did so only at the cost of hollowing out the unemployment
insurance system and thereby displacing onto municipal welfare the burden of
supporting those persons who were not (or were no longer) covered by the
vestiges of the unemployment insurance system. The emergency decree which

[4] Young-Sun Hong, "The Political Economy of Unemployment Assistance in the Great Depression: Unemployment Insurance, Municipal Welfare and the Dismantling of the Republican Welfare
State, 1930-1933" (unpublished manuscript).

had been planned by Brüning, but which was promulgated by the Papen administration in June 1932, altered the principles of the unemployment insurance system and reduced benefit levels and eligibility criteria to such an extent that it destroyed in all but name the unemployment insurance system created in 1927.

As Brüning's deflationary policies pushed unemployment up from 3 million in March 1930 to a peak of more than 6.1 million in February 1932, the cost of supporting the unemployed cascaded downwards and created a fiscal crisis of immense proportions for municipal welfare, and, as a result, public assistance levels were increasingly determined by fiscal considerations, rather than by the individualized, need-based approach codified since the war. Not only did this carefully orchestrated crisis of municipal finances force municipal welfare to retreat from the ambitious network of preventive, therapeutic programs which formed the backbone of the republican welfare system which had been constructed since the war. In fact, the mounting fiscal crisis made it difficult for municipal welfare to satisfy even the most basic material needs of the unemployed, much less pursue the more ambitious goals advocated by welfare reformers, and by the end of 1932 the extensive and ambitious public welfare system which had been constructed through the 1920s had been decimated to such an extent that it was little more than the organized distribution of public alms.

Although municipal politicians and welfare reformers called for reforms which would halt this cascade and shift the mushrooming cost of unemployment assistance back to the Reich, their concerns were brushed aside by a Brüning administration intent upon pursuing its deflationary policies. This focus on domestic finances and the revision of the reparations settlement committed Brüning to policies which further destabilized a political system which had already lost its center of gravity and led him to fatally underestimate the political implications of the mass distress entailed by these policies. Equally important, by reducing the standard of living of the unemployed, the reductions imposed by Brüning eliminated the braking influence which unemployment insurance and municipal welfare had upon the downward movement of wages. In this way, the simultaneous dismantling of municipal welfare and the unemployment insurance system served as the mechanism through which Brüning's deflationary policies were implemented and the vehicle through which these cuts in social spending were transmitted to the working classes. While the growing awareness among welfare reformers that the reconstruction of the Weimar welfare system depended directly on political and economic forces over which they had no control left municipal welfare officials in a state of desperation and intellectual disarray, voluntary welfare took advantage of this unexpected opportunity to wage an all-out counterattack on the very principles of public welfare in an attempt to reestablish its traditional predominance in the field.

While Brüning had pursued an increasingly stringent and destabilizing policy of fiscal austerity and conservative retrenchment, the Papen administration which came to power in June 1932 was openly reactionary in politics, economic policy, and social affairs, and the policy statement issued by the new administration on June 4, 1932, contained both an unambiguous defense of "free enterprise" and one of the most famous attacks on the republican welfare state:

> The postwar governments believed that, through a constantly expanding state socialism, it was possible to largely eliminate the material concerns of both workers and employers. They attempted to make the state into a sort of welfare state and, in this way, weakened the moral forces of the nation. They assigned to the state tasks which, by its very nature, it can never fulfill. Unemployment was increased even further through these programs. The inevitably resulting moral corrosion of the German people—heightened even further through an unholy, community-destroying class struggle and increased through cultural Bolshevism, which, like a corrosive poison, threatens to annihilate the best moral foundations of the nation—must at last be checked.[5]

The Social Democrats argued that, since an effective welfare system was only possible as long as social insurance and labor protection legislation insured that the basic needs of the masses were met, the immediate task was to defend democracy against the rising tide of social reaction; if social insurance were further undermined, welfare would again sink to the level of prewar poor relief.[6] In contrast to Papen's denunciation of the welfare state, the Social Democrats defended the moral value of social insurance and social welfare as forms of cooperative self-help. As Hans Maier told the Central Association of German Invalids and Widows shortly before the election which saw the Nazis reach the peak of their parliamentary influence,

> To the mean-spirited depiction of the state as a welfare institution we oppose the idea that the state should be an organization for mutual aid, that the state should be imbued with a cooperative spirit, a state which protects the weak, cares for the poor, and provides for the elderly. We want a state which will relieve the unpropertied of their concern for their very existence and which give working persons the certainty that in time of disability and old age they can rely upon this community which benefited from their labor in better days. We want to insure that the victims of this labor, which they undertook for the community, do not remain helpless. It is not mutual assistance which weakens moral forces; rather, it is distress, misery, and *Angst* which threaten to corrode public morality.[7]

The emergency decree issued on June 14, 1932, was the first major social policy and social welfare measure of the new Papen government.[8] It gave the Reich government a vast degree of discretionary authority in the area of unemployment assistance, and this authority was employed to implement all of the cuts which had been previously proposed by the Brüning administration. The

[5] *AdR. Das Kabinett von Papen*, 2 vols., ed. Karl-Heinz Minuth (Boppard, 1989), pp. 13–14.

[6] Wachenheim, "Für den Wohlfahrtsstaat!" *AW* 7:12 (June 15, 1932), pp. 353–57.

[7] Cited in Albert Hoffmann, "Finanznot und öffentliche Fürsorge," *AW* 7:15 (August 1, 1932), pp. 467–70, citation p. 469.

[8] *RGBl.*, 1932, I, pp. 273–96, as well as the decrees from June 16, July 16, and August 2.

level of insurance benefits was reduced by 23%. Moreover, although the twenty-week duration of unemployment insurance benefits remained unchanged, the decree stipulated that the unemployed only had an entitlement to such benefits for six weeks. Beyond this period, eligibility for unemployment "insurance" benefits was predicated on demonstrated need as determined by a means test which differed little if at all from that applied by municipal welfare. The wage class system, which was the conceptual foundation of unemployment insurance, was further weakened by pegging the basic benefit to geographical location, that is, to cost of living and estimated need, rather than previous earnings and contributions. Benefits for the higher wage classes were also sharply leveled downward, benefits for unmarried persons were lowered disproportionately, and supplements for dependent family members were increased, a decision which brought insurance benefits further into line with the principles of municipal welfare. The decree also permitted the government to use these funds to defray the cost of other forms of unemployment assistance; this covertly transformed insurance contributions into another form of general tax revenue and insurance benefits into another form of public assistance. With regard to local welfare, although the decree could not directly impose the desired 15% reduction on local welfare rates, the Finance Minister explained that the budget for all forms of unemployment assistance was based on the assumption that such a reduction would be achieved, and he implied that it was the responsibility of state and provincial authorities to see that local rates were adjusted so as to achieve the expected reduction in average per capita benefits.

As the Great Depression bottomed out through 1932, industry and social conservatives such as Papen appeared to have achieved their goal of breaking up the republican welfare system. In an increasingly reactionary manner, Brüning and Papen employed emergency decrees to undermine crisis relief (which had been established in 1926/27 for persons whose eligibility for unemployment relief and, later, insurance benefits had expired) and the Reich obligation to provide loans to subsidize the deficits of the Unemployment Insurance Administration—the two flanking measures upon which the insurance system had to depend in time of crisis—and thereby hollow out unemployment insurance from within without incurring the odium of a direct attack on the unemployment insurance system itself. Unemployment insurance, properly speaking, no longer existed; crisis relief benefits lay below the level of municipal welfare; and municipal welfare directly bore the burden of supporting more than 2 million welfare unemployed. As Helene Simon complained with bitter sarcasm, "How low must our level of social-policy thinking have sunk for people to believe that it is still possible to speak of the existence of an insurance system when the payment of benefits depends on whether or not the needy person is poor enough to need these benefits."[9]

The dismantling of municipal welfare directly affected the standard of living of a huge portion of the population and indirectly affected even more persons

---

[9] Simon, "Die Armut der Nation," *AW* 7:14 (July 15, 1932), pp. 439–43.

through the downward pressure on wages exerted by falling welfare rates and insurance benefits. In September 1932, some 4.3 million heads of household— including dependent family members, 8.7 million persons—were supported by municipal welfare; another 1.8 million persons plus their dependents were receiving unemployment insurance and crisis relief benefits whose level hardly differed from that of municipal welfare. As a result, the rise and decline of municipal welfare became a barometer of the standard of living of 20% of the population—one out of every five persons—not counting the recipients of disability or military pensions, whose benefits were also reduced substantially during these years.

Since early 1931, municipal welfare authorities had warned that the Reich could only solve its financial problems by cutting back on unemployment assistance because it could depend on municipal welfare to step in on a subsidiary basis and fill the gap. By the end of 1931, at the very latest, municipal welfare was no longer able to perform this function. Instead, municipal officials were increasingly forced to lower their own welfare rates and gradually dismantle the far-reaching preventive, therapeutic programs which they had established during the 1920s. While the effect of the 1926 Labor Ministry decree requiring local welfare authorities to publish their rates had been to nudge up local welfare rates between 1926 and 1930, from late 1930 onward Reich and state influence over local rates began to operate in the opposite direction to compel local welfare officials to lower their benefits. In September 1931, Prussia had mandated the reduction of municipal rates in accordance with the decline in the cost of living since the spring of 1929, and other states took similar measures before November 1932, when the Reich government issued a decree requiring the head of the local government to set local welfare rates under the supervision of state or provincial authorities. In the larger cities, where rates had increased the most between 1926 and 1930, general welfare rates were reduced 19–21% between 1930 and 1932 and enhanced welfare rates were reduced 28%. The rate levels established by the fall of 1932 generally remained unchanged through the fall of 1936.[10]

Increasingly, welfare rates were determined less by individual need than by the financial resources available to local welfare authorities, and, by the second half of 1932, there was a very real danger that financial constraints would push these rates below the existence minimum.[11] The general reductions in the level

[10] These figures are calculated from *Statistik des Deutschen Reiches*, Bd. 512/I: *Die öffentliche Fürsorge im Deutschen Reich in den Rechnungsjahren 1932 bis 1936*, p. 58; they correspond only approximately to the figures given in *Statistik des Deutschen Reiches*, Bd. 421: *Die öffentliche Fürsorge im Deutschen Reich in den Rechnungsjahren 1927 bis 1931* (1933), p. 26. See also "Senkung der Richtsätze und der Unterstützungshöhe," *Nachrichtendienst* 12:5 (May 1931), pp. 130–34 and the article by the same title in *Nachrichtendienst* 12:9 (September 1931), pp. 271–74.

[11] Polligkeit, "Grundsätzliches zur Richtsatzpolitik in der öffentlichen Fürsorge," *SPr* 41:44 (November 3, 1932), cols. 1385–95, and "Die Bedeutung der Richtsätze für das Existenzminimum, den Fürsorgeaufwand und den Finanzausgleich," *Nachrichtendienst* 13:9 (September 1932), pp. 231–33.

of unemployment insurance and crisis relief benefits, together with the leveling downward of the benefits provided in the higher wage classes, meant that a substantial proportion of the benefits provided by the Unemployment Insurance Administration was below the local existence minimum in those larger cities where the unemployment problem was most serious. For the lower wage classes, the reductions in unemployment insurance and crisis relief benefits imposed in June 1931 and the reductions in municipal welfare rates in May 1931 and May 1932 basically reduced welfare rates in proportion to the decline in the cost of living and did not entail a reduction in real purchasing power below the level which obtained at the beginning of 1930. The real decline in the level of insurance and crisis relief benefits for the higher wage classes began earlier and was far more precipitous than for the lower wage classes. However, the reductions in welfare benefits in May 1932 and the reductions in unemployment insurance and crisis relief in July pushed the real value of all forms of unemployment assistance substantially below their 1930 peak.

By mid-1932, municipal welfare found itself caught in a painful dilemma; no additional social burdens could be imposed upon those persons who still had jobs without pushing these persons below the poverty line. As a result, in working-class areas poverty and distress rose to levels which had not been seen for decades while, at the same time, the distress of the individual increasingly receded behind the gigantic number of needy persons and the enormous sums which were being spent to support them. However, since it was impossible to either raise additional revenue or further reduce welfare expenditures, in early 1933 the DV announced with resignation that the conditions of the unemployed could not be improved any further through social policy or welfare reforms; any substantial improvement could only be expected from changes in the domestic and international political and economic situation.[12]

Reich officials apparently agreed with the dire predictions by municipal welfare authorities that the insurance benefits and welfare rates established in July 1932 were simply too low for the unemployed to make it through the coming winter. Although the government had apparently expected unemployment to worsen through the second half of 1932, the conjunctural depression had already bottomed out, and in October the Reich decided to use part of the anticipated budget surplus to provide supplements to unemployment insurance and crisis relief recipients for the winter months.[13] In November, the cabinet suspended the time limit on crisis relief for the period between December through March 1933, at which point this suspension was extended indefinitely.[14] This decision to halt both the displacement of the costs of unemployment assistance from the Reich to local government and the forced reduction of insurance and

---

[12] "Unsichtbare Not," *Nachrichtendienst* 13:7 (July 1932), pp. 178–80, and "Die Gefahr unzureichender Fürsorgeleistungen," *Nachrichtendienst* 14:2–3 (February/March 1933), pp. 35–37.

[13] *RGBl.*, 1932, I, pp. 499–501, and *AdR. Das Kabinett von Papen*, pp. 742–43, 765–67, 774–75.

[14] "Minderung der Erwerbslosenlasten der Gemeinden," *SPr* 41:45 (1932), cols. 1445–46, *AdR. Das Kabinett von Papen*, pp. 844–49, 892ff., and *AdR. Das Kabinett von Schleicher* (Boppard, 1986), pp. 4–15.

welfare benefits signaled the completion of the process of social and economic reaction begun under Brüning, and the new regulations and political institutions which had been drafted during this period served as the basis for the conservative stabilization of the insurance and welfare programs which continued through the mid-1930s.

The growing primacy of fiscal concerns left little room for individualized personal help and the preventive, need-based approach to social work which had together provided the framework for welfare reform since the war. In fact, the mounting fiscal crisis made it difficult for municipal welfare to satisfy even the most basic material needs of the unemployed, much less pursue the more ambitious goals advocated by welfare reformers. The long lines of the unemployed who besieged the welfare offices on a daily basis rendered increasingly illusionary the idea of individualized personal help. As the state fiscal crisis deepened through 1931/32, the first items to be struck from municipal welfare budgets were discretionary preventive programs in the areas of infant, maternal, and youth welfare, social hygiene programs, and medical treatment for the poor, as well as subsidies for voluntary welfare. Although these programs had been the most important accomplishment of progressive welfare reformers from 1900 to the late 1920s, they were becoming increasingly difficult to defend. "What, for example, is the purpose of spending a substantial amount of money for a sanitarium stay for a child," asked Hertha Kraus, the Social Democratic director of the Cologne welfare office, "if at the same time the parents and siblings of this same child sit around without any income at all because we have to close our doors?"[15] As Heimerich lamented, these cutbacks were reducing municipal welfare "to the level of the most primitive poor relief of the prewar era."[16]

This dismantling of preventive, therapeutic welfare also had a debilitating impact on the social work profession. As means testing and local welfare rates were increasingly used to reduce assistance levels and exclude people altogether, rather than to insure provision of adequate and appropriate support, this inverted the original vision of the profession and, to a greater extent than ever before, social workers became inquisitors rather than helpers.[17] Under the influence of American casework, the social work profession had developed a highly rationalized methodology which was oriented toward the provision of need-based help determined on the basis of social diagnosis. However, the massive displacement of the unemployed from the insurance system onto municipal welfare upset all of the presuppositions upon which modern social work was based and created a contradictory situation in which the attempt to provide individualized personal help on a mass basis frustrated

---

[15] Kraus, "Gegenwartsfragen der kommunalen Fürsorge," *Die Frau* 39:7 (April 1932), pp. 436–39.

[16] Minutes of the DV executive committee (March 10, 1932), IfG 228.

[17] Bäumer, "Die Jugendwohlfahrtspflege in der Krisis," *Blätter des deutschen Roten Kreuzes* 11 (1932), pp. 388–91.

the aims of social workers without putting them in a position to provide for the needs of the unemployed.[18]

Although social workers had always regarded the routinization of charisma within the expanding social bureaucracy as a direct threat to their vision of individualized personal help, this vision was called into question by both the masses of unemployed who surged into the public welfare offices and by the vast bureaucracy created to hold back this flood. In the words of Frieda Wunderlich,

> The exhaustion of the helper, who must discharge his assigned task, who has to dispatch a specific number of endangered persons, physical and psychological over-burdening, judgments solely on the basis of documents, uneconomical dismantling endangering the most profound effect of helping, that strength which flows from within. Faced with this attack, the question arises: will the tragic interaction between bureaucracy and massification permit the demonic force of the apparatus to prevail over charismatic powers?[19]

In addition to this bureaucratic submersion of personal help, the self-understanding of the profession was also shaken by the fact that most of the unemployed did not belong to the traditional clientele of municipal welfare. They were able-bodied persons who had not only become unemployed due to forces beyond their control, but who also had been slowly deprived of the right to unemployment insurance benefits. They resented the intrusion and tutelage of inquisitive social workers, and their belief that they were entitled to assistance directly contradicted the subsidiarity of municipal welfare and the self-understanding of social workers as the providers of personal help. No coherent solution to the problems of the social work profession was possible without a solution to the problem of unemployment.

During the depths of the depression, welfare reformers were increasingly obsessed with the apparent irreconcilability of bureaucracy and personal help. A separate publication was even founded to redirect attention toward "the human dimension of social work" and bring about "the reconciliation between organization and humanity."[20] Karl Fischer, Nuremberg city councilor and the editor of this journal, feared that social workers, or at least social work administrators, were growing increasingly blind to the fact that the needy could not be treated in an instrumental, bureaucratic manner without fundamentally distorting the nature of social work: "We have recognized, investigated and registered imperfections in our human existence, pondered how things could be changed; then we passed laws, and now we are administering the matter. But we have forgotten how the human being, who would be the victim of this process, would feel and how he would develop. . . . *a human being should never be treated,*

---

[18] Achinger, *Falsche Fürsorge verschuldet Arbeitslosigkeit* (Berlin, 1932), pp. 29–30.

[19] Wunderlich, "Bürokratie und Gemeinschaftsordnung," *SPr* 40:21 (1931), cols. 654–58, citation col. 658.

[20] Karl Fischer, "Zuvor," *Der Mensch in der sozialen Arbeit* 1:1 (1932), col. 2, and Polligkeit, "Versöhnung zwischen Organisation und Menschentum," ibid., 2:1 (1933), cols. 1–2.

but only served."[21] In placing infinite faith in the power of instrumental reason, humankind had lost its soul, and social work as personal help would remain an unrealizable ideal as long as "organization" continued to be regarded as an end in itself.[22] Despite the critical situation, Polligkeit argued that the great challenge was for those social workers who were constantly being ground down by the unceasing operation of the municipal welfare machine to overcome their own perpetual experience of disappointment and disillusion.[23]

Although Polligkeit valiantly attempted to hold up the flag of individualized personal help, the surrounding battlefield was in complete disarray. The social workers who had fought behind this flag were increasingly alienated by the bureaucratization, juridification, and politicization of welfare; the conflicts between the major voluntary welfare organizations were again intensifying and were beginning to upset the corporatist stalemate reached in 1925/26; and violent political antagonisms toward welfare officials, social workers, and the Weimar system itself often came to a boil in the long lines which every day stretched before the welfare offices and labor exchanges. Nevertheless, Polligkeit and most other welfare reformers perceived the crisis of municipal welfare to a large degree as an external crisis precipitated by national economic and social policies, and the depression primarily affected welfare reform debates by accentuating problems which had become visible before the end of the decade.

As had been the case with the privileged groups of welfare recipients, municipal assistance to the unemployed found itself under attack from all sides as it was forced to step in to compensate for the problems resulting from political decisions regarding the distribution of the costs of war, inflation, and, later, Brüning's depression, a mission for which its subsidiary, individualizing methods were ill-suited. As a result, municipal welfare became a lens which focused and condensed all of the resentments arising out of the postwar and poststabilization settlements and all of the unresolved conflicts regarding the social foundations of the Republic. As one commentator wrote in 1932,

> The state—no matter under which administration—has in front of it almost no one but disillusioned critics and opponents and only lukewarm supporters behind it. War victims, to whom the fatherland still owes a debt of gratitude, pensioners and savers expropriated by the inflation, unemployed persons who, in place of the constitutionally-guaranteed right to work and employment, find themselves forced to settle for a barely-fulfilled substitute right to relief, employers whose commercial existence is endangered or destroyed through the intervention of public power into trade and fiscal policies—all of these groups today place a large question mark behind the question of the meaning and justice of the state.[24]

---

[21] "Briefe aus der sozialen Arbeit," ibid., 1:1 (1932), col. 5.

[22] Ibid., 1:3 (1932), col. 44, and Theodor Marx, "Vom Wesen der sozialen Arbeit. Gesinnungswandel ohne Umbau der Organisation?" Ibid., 1:5 (1932), cols. 65–72.

[23] Polligkeit, "Der soziologische und seelische Strukturwandel der Hilfsbedürftigen," *Die Frau* 39:7 (April 1932), pp. 399–404.

[24] Reimar Hobbing, "Sozialarbeiter und Staatsgesinnung," *Der Mensch in der sozialen Arbeit* 1:12 (1932), col. 196.

The Social Democratic and the confessional welfare organizations reacted to these developments in different ways. Since the beginning of 1932, the Social Democrats had repeatedly emphasized that the fate of the welfare system would be determined by political and economic developments because the entire system of subsidiary, individualized assistance was based on the presumption that the working classes as a whole were capable of satisfying their basic needs through their own labor.[25] By the end of that year, they had become extremely apprehensive about the future of the welfare system. As Juchacz wrote, in terms which summed up all of the socialist antipathies toward bourgeois society,

> The government of the barons has successfully striven to redeem the mean-spirited intentions of the chancellor's [Papen] inaugural speech. . . . The pauperization of a broad stratum of the laboring population is part of the development desired by the economically and politically dominant classes. The reserve army of the unemployed, who are no longer protected by social policy legislation, who are forced to rely on begging, is quite welcome to them as a social phenomenon. They believe that this is necessary in order to again become the "master of their own house" (*Herr im eigenen Haus*). . . . The welfare offices . . . are in a situation . . . like those poor mothers who have no bread for their starving children, whose sheer impotence hardens them against their own maternal love, and who as a defense mechanism clothe their bleeding maternal love in hard words. But in the end the progress of reaction transforms the spirit of the welfare offices. The old spirit of poor relief again celebrates its triumphal entry.[26]

The Social Democrats continued to argue that confessional charity of the old style was a hopelessly reactionary and inherently contradictory undertaking which sought to supplement public welfare without being able to eliminate distress, even though it was funded largely through public subsidies. The confessional welfare organizations, on the other hand, sensed that the intellectual disarray of the Progressives, the fiscal crisis of public welfare, and the marginalization of the Social Democrats presented a unique and unhoped-for opportunity to roll back the clock to the prerevolutionary period and strike back against both the republican welfare system and the politicization of social work by a clientele which had lost all respect for family, authority, discipline, sacrifice, and God. In December 1930, Johannes Sunder, the secretary of the German League for Voluntary Welfare, published a widely read article in which he argued that public welfare should be further dismantled because the service performed by voluntary welfare was of greater intrinsic value and because the mere existence of voluntary welfare existence spared the public purse an estimated 250 million marks annually.[27]

Sunder's claims aroused considerable controversy, especially among the Social Democrats, who pointed out the extent to which voluntary welfare lived

---

[25] Wachenheim, "1932. Krisensturm," *AW* 7:1 (January 1, 1932), pp. 6–7.

[26] Juchacz, "Absinken der Fürsorge," *AW* 7:21 (November 1, 1932), pp. 641–43.

[27] Sunder, "Was erspart die freie Wohlfahrtspflege der öffentlichen Wirtschaft und was könnte sie ihr ersparen?" *FW* 5 (1930/31), pp. 385–402, 521–24.

from public subsidies and the meager wages of their workers in comparison to those employed by public welfare. However, Sunder's provocation failed to hit its mark because fiscal arguments such as these could never provide a compelling ideological justification for the existence of voluntary welfare. Nevertheless, the church charities were convinced that liberal individualism and Marxist collectivism had exhausted their spiritual energies, and they sensed that they were witnessing a resurgence of faith in God and a renewed longing for those irrational, primordial forms of communal life which could only be sustained through religious faith.[28] A 1932 essay by Elizabeth Zillken captured the mood of anticipation among the confessional welfare groups and spelled out their vision of what a reformed, reprivatized, and reconfessionalized welfare system would look like:

It appears that the hour has come for voluntary welfare, for a voluntary welfare which truly represents the will of the people to help each other, which awakens and cultivates authentic brotherly love among all strata, which brings flocks of helpers to all who need help, which leads person to person, Christian to Christian, brother to brother, sister to sister, which, in a word, does everything which public welfare is not, or is no longer, capable of doing. It is a task of miraculous beauty, a field whose extent and limits can not be seen, a task whose correct fulfillment would also have the power to change the face of the earth: brotherly love in action . . . in which many problems—whose solution often fails in the present situation—could be solved.[29]

Between 1931 and 1933, confessional welfare reformers focused on three areas: the family, which they argued was being undermined by moral laxity, material need, and the communalization of family life by an expanding secular welfare system; voluntary labor service; and the *Winterhilfe*, which was established in the winter of 1930/31 by the German League for Voluntary Welfare, whose members regarded it as a school for conservative, patriotic virtues and as the antithesis to the form of self-help and class solidarity preached by the Social Democrats.[30] Confessional welfare feared that unemployment was leading to the dissolution of existing social ties and thereby setting in motion a decline toward destitution, *Verwahrlosung*, criminality, and ultimately atheism and political radicalism. However, since there was no way that voluntary welfare could compensate for the massive reductions in public social spending, these organization sought to counteract the social consequences of unemployment by intensifying their efforts to integrate the unemployed—especially the young—into the local religious community and thereby keep them away from the street, the *Kneipe*

[28] Steinweg, "Zeitenwende?" *FW* 7:7 (October 1932), pp. 285–92.
[29] Zillken, "Notzeit und freie Wohlfahrtspflege," *Mitteilungen des Vereins katholischer Sozialbeamtinnen Deutschlands* (January/March 1932), pp. 3–9, citation p. 3.
[30] Although the history of the *Winterhilfe*, which was the one major collective undertaking by the members of the German League for Voluntary Welfare, is usually written as a prehistory of the program in the Nazi period, for the Weimar context and the implications of the program for the relation of voluntary and public welfare, see Jochen-Christoph Kaiser, *Sozialer Protestantismus im 20. Jahrhundert* (Oldenbourg, 1989), pp. 159–85.

(pub), and the welfare office, which were the most potent symbols of the moral dangers of unemployment. In the hands of Catholic social critics, the idea of mutual support by local occupational groups was presented as an alternative to both the schematic, impersonal insurance system and public welfare. Such self-help organizations could easily be interpreted as the basic building block for the corporatist reconstruction of civil society which these Catholic social theorists hoped would arise out of the ashes of the republican welfare state.[31]

SOCIAL DEMOCRACY, "*DER RISIKOFREIE MENSCH*," AND THE CONTRADICTIONS OF THE PROGRESSIVE PROJECT

The most articulate advocate of a specifically Social Democratic theory of the welfare state in the final years of the Republic was Hans Maier. Drawing on the Webbs, Maier argued that the historical mission of the welfare state was to insure that all citizens shared the material and cultural progress of the nation by reducing the risks of working-class life, including disability, illness, old age, and unemployment. This risk-free existence was necessary if labor were to become a vehicle for the self-realization of the personality, rather than remain the alienated and alienating experience which it had historically been for both the working classes and the bourgeois political economists working in the Malthusian tradition. For Maier, the perfection of the welfare state required, as Helene Simon had argued in the early 1920s, the rationalization of both production and consumption to limit the commodification of labor and free the masses—whose only wealth was their labor power—from the compulsion to sell their labor at any price and under any conditions: "The term 'welfare state,' which has been employed with cynical connotations against the tendency of recent legislation, is of programmatic importance for us and the target of the neo-Malthusians, Manchesterians, and those who oppose a risk-free existence." Although such a risk-free existence could only be definitively achieved in a socialist society, Maier believed that the Weimar welfare state had taken important steps toward securing the rights to work, health, and education for the unpropertied classes and that the most pressing task was to prevent the confessional and bourgeois parties from using the depression to roll back the achievements of the Republic.[32]

In contrast, although the Progressives affirmed both the social *causes* of dis-

---

[31] Doris Kaufmann, *Katholisches Milieu in Münster 1928–1933. Politische Aktionsformen und geschlechts-spezifische Verhaltensräume* (Düsseldorf, 1984), pp. 138–48, and Franz Keller, "Arbeitsdienst als Mittel der Entproletarisierung und Standwerdung," *Jahrbuch für Caritaswissenschaft* (1933), pp. 115–27.

[32] Maier, "Der Pauperismus und seine Überwindung. Zum 50. Todestag von Karl Marx," *AW* 8:5 (March 1, 1933), pp. 129–36, "Der risikofreie Mensch. Zum 50jährigen Bestehen des Deutschen Vereins," *AW* 5:22 (November 15, 1930), pp. 673–78, "Politik und Wohlfahrtspflege," *AW* 4:20, 22 (October/November 1929), pp. 609–14, 673–77, citation p. 611, and "Der Grundsatz der individuellen und gesellschaftlichen Verantwortlichkeit in der neuzeitlichen Wohlfahrtspflege," *Archiv für soziale Hygiene und Demographie*, N.F. 5 (1929), pp. 369–73.

tress and the responsibility of society for helping its needy members, their be-lief—which they shared with the confessional welfare organizations—in the crucial role of personal help in *solving* the social problem made them much more ambivalent about the public welfare system than the Social Democrats (as can be seen in the statement by Muthesius cited at the beginning of this chap-ter).[33] Between 1928 and the end of the Republic, the Progressives articulated a complex genealogy of the contradictions of this rationalized, bureaucratized system. However, despite the acuity of their historical vision, their commitment to personal help transformed their genealogy of the republican welfare system into a history of the corruption of helping. Consequently, the growing convic-tion on the part of both the Progressives and the confessional welfare organiza-tions that genuine helping could not be carried out within either the highly rationalized, bureaucratic framework of public welfare or the equally ratio-nalized voluntary welfare *Spitzenverbände* increasingly led both groups to call for the break-up of the public welfare system and the devolution of its respon-sibilities onto voluntary organizations.

Already in his address to the 1928 International Conference of Social Work, Polligkeit had told the audience that the root of the manifold problems of the republican welfare system could be traced to the same event which had made possible their greatest accomplishments: the emergence of a social conception of poverty. This had had such far-reaching consequences because the resulting expansion of environmental reforms increasingly made "organization"—that is, the creation of the most rational, economical social relief programs and the mobilization and coordination of the work of persons engaged in providing this help—into an end in itself. At the same time, the recognition of the social origins of poverty promoted the juridification and politicization of public assis-tance as both the propertied and the poor mobilized and began to make political demands against that social order which they believed to be responsible for the social problem. As Polligkeit argued,

> We bring specific forms of need which we wish to meliorate into an inner relation
> with the prevailing social and economic order, to questions of national economy,
> national health and national culture. The suffering individual is seen only as the
> representative of a category of persons of similar fate. . . . Help for the poor is
> transformed into a struggle against poverty, welfare for infants, tubercular persons,
> and juvenile offenders is transformed into a struggle against infant mortality, tuber-
> culosis and criminality. But at the very moment when we move from the poor

---

[33] Some Progressives, such as Hilde Eiserhardt, the secretary of the DV, attacked the very idea of the welfare state, and even Social Democrats worried aloud that the *"Fürsorgestaat"* was creating persons whose *"Fürsorgeversorgtheit"* was making them more unsuited than ever for the arduous task of creating a socialist society. Eiserhardt, "Wohlfahrtsstaat?" *Blätter des deutschen Roten Kreuzes* 10:5 (May 1931), pp. 267–76, and Robert Wilbrandt, "Kampf gegen den Fürsorgestaat," *Die neue Rundschau* 41, Bd. 2 (July–December 1930), pp. 289–301.

person to poverty, from the criminal to criminality, we perform an abstraction which reduces the importance and the treatment for the individual personality.[34]

Under such circumstances, personal help and the bonds it was believed to forge between indigent individuals and the community inevitably receded in importance behind these tasks. For the Progressives and the confessional welfare organizations, the many specific problems of the republican welfare system were simply particular aspects of this single, fundamental contradiction.

Bureaucracy was the master trope in the Progressive analysis of the contradictions of the welfare system, though the term had three distinct meanings within the Progressive discourse of the time. First of all, the term bureaucracy was used to refer to all of the problems which stemmed from this shift from help for the individual poor to the struggle against poverty and all of the motivational problems associated with the idea of a risk-free existence. As Muthesius told the 1930 DV conference, "We have been entangled in the erroneous belief that if we create the organizational—that is, bureaucratic, official, institutional—structure for the welfare state, then the appropriate beliefs will follow automatically."[35]

The expansion of preventive, therapeutic programs had two important consequences. On the one hand, for welfare reformers themselves there was a tendency for the desire to meliorate the distress of the suffering individual to recede completely behind the perceived need to construct a comprehensive, rationalized system to compensate for every conceivable source of social insecurity. The logical end product of this trend was the creation of "a state in which there is available to every individual for all possible contingencies . . . and for every stage in life" a network of social programs and social workers to turn aside all of these contingencies, and they feared that this rationalization of existential risk was taking on a life of its own and becoming an end in itself.[36] On the other hand, welfare reformers believed that the creation of a comprehensive welfare system to socialize risk and systematically combat social insecurity was furthering the hypertrophy of individual rights and undermining individual responsibility because of the particular manner in which the needy comprehended the function of the welfare bureaucracy. If people knew that society would care for all of the different manifestations of distress, argued these reformers, then they would begin to rely upon the existence of an all-encompassing public welfare system; this, they argued, could make people more improvi-

---

[34] Polligkeit, "Scope and Relations of Public and Private Agencies of Social Work," in *First International Conference of Social Work*, 3 vols. (Paris, 1929), I:668–99 and his comments in I:705–12. The central passages of this address appeared in German under the title "Entwicklungstendenzen in der öffentlichen und freien Wohlfahrtspflege," *SPr* 37:26–27 (1928), cols. 601–5, 625–28. This speech and Aloys Fischer, "Die Problematik des Sozialbeamtentums," in *Leben und Werk*, intro. Karl Kreitmair (Munich, n.d.), pp. 319–49 are far and away the two most important contributions to this Progressive analysis of the contradictions of the welfare system.

[35] Muthesius, "Kollektivverantwortung und Einzelverantwortung," p. 51.

[36] Fischer, "Die Problematik des Sozialbeamtentums," p. 332.

dent than they would normally otherwise have been in the absence of this public safety net. However, these deleterious side effects could be avoided if assistance was provided in a personal manner and did not exhaust itself in the provision of monetary assistance or the struggle against the general social causes of need. From this perspective, Progressive welfare reformers regarded the social question primarily as one of popular education, and Aloys Fischer believed that it would be possible to escape at least in part from these paradoxes by transforming the tutelary, social *welfarist* approach to social work into a constructive social *pedagogical* one.[37]

At the 1928 International Social Work Conference, Polligkeit had noted that, since the 1890s, the social perspective on poverty had tempted public welfare to assume an increasing degree of primary responsibility for the welfare of the individual and that these developments were giving rise to a false, socialistic conception of justice, which postulated that all individuals should be entitled to identical benefits from the state, regardless of the precise nature and scope of their individual needs. This temptation to assign a greater weight to the rights of the individual than to his or her obligations, and the resulting politicization of social work, were, Polligkeit concluded, the unavoidable consequence of institutional rationalization of social work which neglected the human dimension and which failed to insure that the development of a new social ethic kept pace with the expansion of public responsibility for the welfare of the individual. A reaction against the weakening of the principles of subsidiarity and individualization was unavoidable, Polligkeit concluded, and he correctly prophesied that the coming confrontation over the future of the welfare state would pivot around the relation of individual rights and the social obligations of welfare recipients.[38]

The concept of bureaucracy functioned in a second distinct way in this Progressive analysis of the contradictions of the republican welfare system. Since the *Vormärz*, the provision of public assistance and charitable giving had been altered in fundamental ways by the evolution of more rational forms of organization to insure the adequate, economical provision of support to the needy and combat the criminal abuse of public assistance. The first stages in this process had been the creation of district poor relief authorities to assume the public responsibilities of hometown communities and the establishment of associations for the prevention of poverty and begging to rationalize individual philanthropy and voluntary social engagement. This process had culminated in the 1920s with the creation of both a vast public welfare bureaucracy and a network of hierarchic, increasingly rationalized voluntary welfare *Spitzenverbände*. The mere existence of such organizations meant that the assistance they provided

---

[37] Ibid., pp. 330–34.

[38] Polligkeit, "Scope and Relations," pp. 674–75, as well as Klumker's comments in *Die Berufslage der Fürsorgerinnen*, SDV N.F. 7 (1926), p. 140. Salomon advanced very similar arguments in "Die Familie in der privaten Fürsorge," *Zweite Internationale Konferenz für soziale Arbeit/Second International Conference of Social Work* (Karlsruhe, 1933), pp. 386–94.

would always be mediated by rational calculations concerning the intended effect of such help and would never be simply an expression of the immediate concern of one individual for another. As Käthe Truhel explained in the first systematic study of the impact of bureaucratization on social work, with the discovery of the general, social causes of poverty and the creation of bureaucratized organizations to combat the various dimensions of the social problem, social assistance was "no longer the self-evident expression of human proximity and community, which already contains within itself the latent impulse to help. Rather, it is cooler, above all more rational. . . . The individual act of help is no longer precipitated through the sight of a suffering person, through the sympathy with the suffering of an individual, but is already [mediated] through the concept of poverty."[39]

The interposition of a formal organization between the helper and the needy—that is, the division of authority and labor between raising funds and the actual provision of help—tended to transform the social worker into the mandatory of the organization. This process had, the Progressives argued, deleterious effects on both the client and the social worker. On the one hand, this division of labor made the relation between the social worker and the client increasingly anonymous, and the personal act of helping was increasingly supplanted by the mere provision of material assistance. The loss of personal warmth and the social bonds which this was believed to forge was the unavoidable price which had to be paid for the rationalization of helping.[40] On the other hand, this division of labor and the resulting professionalization of helping also had, as we saw in chapter 5, important consequences for the motivation of social workers, who were bound by the goals of the agencies employing them and whose commitment to selfless service was, consequently, always mediated through the aims of her employer in such a way that it was impossible, these Progressives feared, for the social workers to fully express their own personal concern for the persons they assisted.[41] Polligkeit went so far as to question whether or not the idea of a personal relation between the social worker and the client could still be regarded as the basis for social work in a world where charity had been largely supplanted by organized welfare, where public agencies and private associations had taken over the role of the individual benefactor, and where the receipt of public assistance was increasingly regarded as an entitlement rather than as a source of social obligations. In view of this dual hollowing out of personal help, it was hardly surprising that social work was, to a greater extent than ever before, being transformed into social work administration.[42]

---

[39] Truhel, *Sozialbeamte. Ein Beitrag zur Sozioanalyse der Bürokratie* (dissertation, Frankfurt, 1934), pp. 76–77.

[40] Truhel, *Sozialbeamte*, p. 81.

[41] Polligkeit, "Die Bedeutung der Persönlichkeit in der Wohlfahrtspflege," *Die Stellung der Wohlfahrtspflege zur Wirtschaft, zum Staat und zum Menschen,* SDV, N.F. 15 (1930), pp. 55–73, citation p. 57.

[42] Ibid., pp. 60–61.

The concept of bureaucratization was also employed in a third distinct sense to describe the effects of the politicization and juridification of public assistance and the deleterious consequences of these developments upon the voluntaristic impulse. The discovery of a sociological perspective on poverty had increasingly led social workers to view the applicant for public assistance as a representative of an abstract category of persons; this had undermined the subsidiarity and individualizing nature of public welfare and simultaneously burdened it with responsibility for combating mass, social problems through environmental programs and monetary assistance, rather than providing personal help to the suffering individual. On the one hand, this inevitably entailed an increasing juridification and bureaucratic regulation of social work in order to compensate for this growing distance from the needs of the welfare recipients by promulgating laws and regulations to cover every imaginable situation and spell out the specific rights of all of the various groups of welfare recipients. This process had severe deleterious consequences, Klumker argued, because, "increasingly, the activity of both public and voluntary welfare is limited almost exclusively to complying with those regulations; it is forced into the most hopeless schematism, and precisely for this reason in many cases it can not but damage or destroy those living relations with which it comes into contact."[43] On the other hand, the recognition of the social character of need also led to the politicization of welfare, that is, to what Polligkeit and other Progressives called the emergence of a group mentality and the demand for entitlements to specified levels of public assistance for legally defined groups, such as had been codified in the RGr. However, the Progressives and the confessional welfare groups all believed that this politicization of welfare and the resulting struggle of organized interest groups against the common good had to be halted at all costs because they were having disastrous consequences not only for public finances and public morality, but also, and more importantly, for the voluntaristic dimension of social work. As Polligkeit noted, "In the popular mind, this is apt to lead to the belittling of the intrinsic value and significance of the benevolent work of voluntary welfare, which is disparaged as charity and rejected. . . . A nation is inwardly impoverished if it does not constantly foster and stimulate this will to help. And even if the institutions of voluntary welfare could be replaced by those of public welfare, the instrument necessary to foster the social spirit would still be lacking, without which no state and no nation can prosper."[44]

Polligkeit did not disparage the sociological perspective on the social question or deny the achievements of public welfare, but he did argue that the very real problems resulting from the juridification and politicization of public assistance and the focus on the external milieu could only be solved through the proper division of labor. If public welfare were responsible for promoting the human capital of the nation and insuring that no necessitous persons remained

---

[43] Klumker, "Staat, Volk, soziale Fürsorge," *Caritas* 36:3 (March 1931), pp. 104–7, citation p. 105.

[44] Polligkeit, "Scope and Relations," p. 678.

without assistance, then voluntary welfare would be free to pursue its own unique mission of aiding needy individuals solely for their own sake and provide a greater degree of personal help to their charges than permitted by the bureaucratic structure of public welfare. "It is our duty," he concluded,

> nay from the point of view of social work, our chief task, to help individuals in their personal need and in a personal way. It seems to me that we have now come to a turning point in our evolution at which we must not throw away the advantages which we have obtained by our sociological way of thinking and acting, but rather increase their value by directing our relief activities to a greater extent than formerly toward the personality of the sufferer.[45]

This analysis of the contradictions of the republican welfare system shaped Progressive proposals for welfare reform during this period. The only person to suggest that this contradiction between bureaucracy and personal help could be overcome was Truhel, who viewed it as one manifestation of the broader contradiction between, on the one hand, the abstract, formalistic conception of justice characteristic of the rule of law and, on the other hand, the new social conception of justice, which sought to compensate for the concrete social inequalities in capitalist society. She believed that the experience of this contradiction served as both a permanent corrective to the self-reifying logic of bureaucratic reason and a permanent stimulus to the individual social worker.[46]

However, most Progressives were far more pessimistic about the consequences of bureaucratization, and Klumker was the most vocal Progressive critic of public welfare in the last years of the Republic. Klumker argued that the crisis of the welfare system was caused by the colonization of voluntary welfare by public, bureaucratic organizations. Although the immediate sense of community, from which both public and voluntary welfare drew their spiritual sustenance, was constantly being renewed in spontaneous mutual aid in face-to-face communities, Klumker warned that this sense of solidarity was being smothered by an irrational mania for organization. While the mass distress of the postwar period had provided the initial stimulus for the creation of a vast public social bureaucracy, its subsequent expansion was, Klumker argued, "sustained by the peculiar belief—imported from other areas into social work—that the state is capable of carrying out all possible tasks. This is the origin of the great dangers that threaten social work today."[47]

The growth of an immense welfare bureaucracy created an equally large chasm—which had not existed as long as public welfare had been provided primarily by voluntary and honorary workers—between the logic of bureaucratic authority and organization and the existential concerns of the recipients of public assistance.[48] Klumker was especially critical of what he regarded as the

---

[45] *First International Conference of Social Work*, I:708.

[46] Truhel, *Sozialbeamte*, pp. 129ff.

[47] Klumker, "Woran krankt die deutsche Fürsorge der Gegenwart?" *FW* 5:8 (November 1930), pp. 337–43.

[48] Klumker, "Staat, Volk, soziale Fürsorge."

fiscal irresponsibility of the public and the obsession of social insurance and welfare authorities with external trappings of bureaucratic authority. This led to the erection at the local, state, and national levels of a vast, costly social service bureaucracy, the proliferation of organizations, publications, and conferences, and the construction of the most modern, best equipped, and best staffed institutions and luxurious administrative "palaces" whose cost were entirely out of proportion to the far more modest needs of their beneficiaries.[49] The unavoidable conclusion to be drawn from these arguments was that the only way to escape from these contradictions was to break up public welfare and return its responsibilities to voluntary organizations. However, the break-up of public welfare would have been equivalent to the break-up of the Republic itself and could only have been achieved through an authoritarian counterrevolution against the parliamentary system. Both Social Democrats and welfare reformers on the radical right believed that Klumker's attacks on public welfare in fact provided much support for such a course of action, and his jeremiads prompted Maier, a former student, to argue that Klumker was throwing the baby out with the bath water by failing to distinguish between the valid political goals of public welfare and the organizational problems which were preventing it from realizing these goals.[50]

The most powerful depiction of the underside of the welfare bureaucracy was Justus Erhardt's *Straßen ohne Ende*, which bears many stylistic similarities to Alfred Döblin's *Berlin Alexanderplatz*. The novel describes the fate of both a young boy from an impoverished home who is sentenced to correctional education and a well-meaning social worker who were both caught up in the irresistible yet self-defeating movement of a completely impersonal welfare machine which, with sovereign disregard for the feelings of all involved, was incessantly working to churn out the justice promised by the RJWG:

> The machine is running now and no one can escape from its action. The youngster embezzled and knocked about and thus landed in the welfare system. He has escaped [from correctional education] and is being sought. He is sought, therefore, he will be caught and locked up. He can't go back, he stands outside. Whoever stands outside can never come back in again. All of the doors are locked up tight. Life follows its own course. Whoever gets caught in the machine will be threshed through until he comes out again in back or down below. And whoever moves around inside the machine will be crushed to death. Lie still and be silent. A wheel spins. Many gears mesh with each other in order for there to be justice and order in the world. Herr Schulze [the father of the young offender] . . . comes again and

---

[49] Klumker, "Fürsorge und Almosen," *FW* 6:9 (December 1931), pp. 385–93, and "Die Zukunft der Fürsorge," *FW* 7:1 (April 1932), pp. 1–7.

[50] Wachenheim, "Zeitschriftenschau," *AW* 6:2 (January 15, 1931), pp. 56–57, Wachenheim, "Apparat in der Fürsorge? Rechtsanspruch?" *AW* 6:7 (April 1, 1931), pp. 197–200, Gottlieb Friedrich Storck, "Jugendwohlfahrt im neuen Staat," *Zentralblatt* 25:1 (April 1933), pp. 1–7, and Maier, "Fürsorge, Almosen und Entwicklung der Wohlfahrtspflege," *AW* 7:3 (February 1, 1932), pp. 70–76.

again to the conclusion that this justice must be absurd. He tries to be objective about things; you can't expect more from bourgeois-capitalist society than it offers—but here the veil is lifted from the entire rotten system. As if you didn't know that already? You get to know an arrangement best when you try it out on yourself. And we live in a social *Volksstaat.* . . .[51]

The intellectual roots of many Progressive members of the DV reached back to Friedrich Naumann's national, social movement, and some of them—including Polligkeit and Hilde Eiserhardt (Polligkeit's assistant at the DV)—welcomed the Nazi seizure of power. In a programmatic statement published in May 1933, Polligkeit blamed the crisis of the republican welfare state on the politicization of welfare and the hypertrophy of individual rights. While the DV had long insisted that the establishment of a comprehensive preventive, therapeutic welfare system was possible only in conjunction with a popular consciousness of the greater obligations imposed upon the citizenry by such a system, Polligkeit complained that

> the predominant political attitude of the postwar period favored the *rights* of the citizen against the state, but completely neglected his *duties*. A movement which considered the 'risk-free existence' to be the ideal of the citizen within the state wanted to foist off onto society responsibility for all of the dangers in the life of the individual. Under the influence of these trends, group egoism and party squabbling in the parliaments have led to the most grievous abuses in the regulation of the welfare system.[52]

Polligkeit noted with satisfaction that "what was impossible for many a year is now attainable," and he expressed his hope that a strong, authoritarian government would finally make it possible to implement those reforms which had been blocked by the divisions among the Weimar parties.

Polligkeit's attack on parliamentary government was one facet of an authoritarian mentality which increasingly subordinated the rights of the individual to those of the community, and he suggested that, in opposition to both the group egoism and the overextension of social rights in the Republic, "the demand for greater self-help and self-responsibility is rightly making itself felt" in the widespread popular support for the Nazis.[53] Polligkeit argued that what was necessary was a fundamental reorientation of the welfare system which would push the pendulum back in the direction of a greater emphasis upon the social duties of the individual, and his efforts to define the political preconditions for both effective social work—as personal help—and fruitful cooperation among voluntary welfare soon turned into a litany of complaints which blamed the Repub-

---

[51] Erhardt, *Straßen ohne Ende* (Berlin, 1931), pp. 176–77. Erhardt was the director of the Berlin Landesjugendamt.

[52] Polligkeit, "Das Fürsorgewesen im Aufbauprogramm der Reichsregierung," *Nachrichtendienst* 14:4–5 (April/May 1933), pp. 66–70, citation p. 67.

[53] Ibid.

lic itself for virtually all of the undesirable consequences of the rationalization of public assistance since the early 1800s.[54]

THE CHURCH CHARITIES, NATIONAL SOCIALISM, AND THE FAILURE OF AUTHORITARIAN CORPORATISM

While the confessional organizations subscribed fully to the Progressive analysis of the problems resulting from the bureaucratization of social work, they argued that the crisis of the republican welfare system was caused by Progressivism itself, not by its bureaucratic distortion. The influential Protestant theologian and pedagogue Helmuth Schreiner attributed the crisis of the republican welfare system to its secularism and the combination of a eudemonistic conception of welfare, which knew no higher aim than the satisfaction of material needs, and a public welfare system, which, as a creation of the sovereign state, excluded those religious forces from which social work ultimately had to draw its spiritual sustenance. As Schreiner argued in an attack on the liberal anthropology which underlay the idea of social pedagogy,

> The aim of social work "through faith" (*aus Glauben*) is not a happy society, but rather a moral community, not a sum of rescued individuals, but the kingdom of God. This thesis expresses the rejection of the individualist and eudemonist misunderstanding of social work. As long as they do not take seriously the knowledge that the meaning of all life of the individual and the community is only revealed through obedience to a supraindividual task, they always and inevitably disintegrate. . . . Evangelical social work is the worship of God or it is nothing at all.[55]

Echoing Schreiner, Joachim Beckmann insisted that social work required the combination of pedagogical and pastoral work, "because for social work it is ultimately a question of strengthening and creating spiritual-moral realities: labor, family, marriage, humanity, national community." Since the provision of social services without the simultaneous emphasis on the religiously sanctioned obligations of the recipient toward self and society undermined personal responsibility, Beckmann argued that the personal, moral causes of social distress could only be eliminated if social workers were free to witness and proclaim their religious beliefs through their charitable work.[56]

Part of the problem was that massive expansion of the confessional *Spitzenverbände* since the early 1920s and the recognition of their semipublic status

---

[54] "Öffentliche und freie Wohlfahrtspflege als Bundesgenossen im Kampf gegen die Volksnot," *Nachrichtendienst* 14:7 (July 1933), pp. 138–40.

[55] Schreiner, *Pädagogik aus Glauben*, 2d ed. (Schwerin, 1931), pp. 44–63, 118–37, citation pp. 130–31.

[56] Beckmann, "Wohlfahrtspflege und Kirche im Weltanschauungskampf der Gegenwart," *Gesundheitsfürsorge* 10:5 (October 1931), pp. 255–62, citation p. 258. See also Stahl, "Volksnot, Fürsorge und Außenpolitik," *IM* 26 (1931), pp. 321–27 and "Evangelische Liebestätigkeit im Wandel der Wohlfahrtspflege," *IM* 27 (1932), pp. 297–305.

had implicated these organizations in the same dynamic of bureaucratization which they believed had exerted such a baneful influence on public welfare. The mediation of personal help through ulterior considerations was, Schreiner argued, corrupting both the ethos of giving and the ethos of receiving; in view of these problems, he insisted that the "essential," purely selfless devotion to the needs of others could only be achieved through Christian charity undertaken on a strictly voluntary basis. He predicted that there would be an inevitable tendency to break up the compulsory cooperation within the parliamentary framework of the youth welfare offices and move toward a more complete devolution of public responsibility onto societal groups. Schreiner urged the confessional welfare organizations to have the courage to break free from the constraints imposed by their corporatist integration into public welfare, subordinate considerations of economy and efficiency to the laws of charity, and "waste" their resources in an unrestricted economy of love. Schreiner was skeptical as to whether fundamental change would be possible as long as the semipublic activity of the welfare *Spitzenverbände* were linked directly to the state.[57]

There was an intrinsic affinity between the antiliberalism of the Nazis, their anti-Bolshevism, and their call for an authoritarian moral renewal and the antipathy of both confessional welfare organizations to the ideas of 1789 and 1918. Consequently, most members of the Inner Mission enthusiastically greeted the Nazi seizure of power. However, although the Inner Mission welcomed the exclusion of the Communists and the Social Democrats from public life by the Nazis, the emotional appeal of an authoritarian state went much deeper. Many conservative Protestants interpreted the history of the modern age as a process of corruption and decline which had begun with the turning away from God in the name of individualism and rationalism and which, in the absence of absolute truths, had inevitably degenerated into atheism, communism, materialism, and revolution, first in 1848 and again in 1918. Consequently, they interpreted the Nazi seizure of power as a sign of a religious reawakening and a categorical break with the entire liberal era which would ultimately bring about a return to the virtues of service and obedience within an organic community. These attitudes toward individualism, liberalism, and modernity led these conservative Protestants to endow the authoritarian state and the *Volk* which figured so prominently in Nazi rhetoric with eschatological significance and thus bring about a partial fusion of Protestantism and National Socialism.

Although Catholic charity organizations sympathized with the antiliberal, anticommunist rhetoric of both the Nazis and conservative Protestants, in the period leading up to the Nazi seizure of power and in the first months of 1933, these organizations remained as skeptical about the place of Catholic charity in

---

[57] Schreiner, *Pädagogik aus Glauben*, pp. 137–47, Beckmann, "Wohlfahrtspflege und Kirche im Weltanschauungskampf der Gegenwart," and Kurt Lücken, "Grundsätzliches und Kritisches zur Caritasarbeit der Gegenwart," *Caritas* 38:1–2 (January/February 1933), pp. 6–12, 57–59, as well as Schreiner's earlier philippic, *Der Ruin der freien Wohlfahrtspflege durch ihre Freunde* (Schwerin, 1925).

a Nazi state as they had originally been about its place in the Republic. They initially refused to cooperate with the Nazis, whom they regarded as unchristian idolaters of Darwin and as Bolsheviks in nationalist clothing, and in many places Nazi party members were excluded from the sacraments by local clergy. Instead, the Catholic charities devoted their energies to defending "natural" communities—family, neighborhood, occupational organization, and church— against attacks by those Nazis who wished to limit the influence of the churches, especially the Catholic church, on public life. As Helene Weber told a meeting of the Association of Catholic German Social Workers in May 1933, in the coming era they would be faced with the choice of embracing either Bolshevism or Christianity. While Weber criticized "fascist" attempts by the state to impose a corporatist social order upon society from above, she regarded societal corporatism from below as the authentic realization of Catholic social doctrine.[58]

The establishment of a stable corporatist system in the welfare sector depended, as we have seen, on the repression of politics, the constitution of a sphere of affective social integration through organized helping, and a benevolent neutrality of the *Spitzenverbände* toward each other. Although these conditions had never been anywhere near satisfied, the political stability of the middle years of the 1920s had placed limits upon the political polarization of the welfare sector, and this state of affairs was reflected in the stalemate between the confessional charities, public welfare, and Workers' Welfare. However, by the end of the decade the conditions of corporatist stability had become completely illusory.

In his November 1932 inaugural lecture at the University of Frankfurt, Hans Scherpner, Klumker's assistant and later successor as professor of social welfare, analyzed the effects of the reemergence of politics within the social work sector.[59] Building on the ideas of Carl Schmitt, Scherpner argued here that the belief in the incompatibility of politics and social work reflected simply the social worker's subjective understanding of the conditions of personal help and failed to understand either that social work was a mechanism—which was no less essential than the socialization of the young or national defense—for the selfpreservation of every society or that the parameters of such help were already defined through the same political process through which the polity itself was constituted. The more intense the political life of the society in its struggle to resolve internal conflicts and fend off external enemies, the more direct became the relation between social work and politics. While stable societies succumbed much more easily to the illusion of the separation of state and society and the belief in the autonomy of helping, Scherpner argued that the connection between social work and politics was much more direct in other cases, such as self-help

---

[58] "Tagung des Provinzialausschusses Westfalen des Vereins Kath. Deutscher Sozialbeamtinnen" (May 21, 1933), ADCV 319.4 F III 3, and Benedikt Kreutz, "Vom Sinn und Wert konfessioneller Liebestätigkeit," *SPr* 41:19 (May 11, 1933), cols. 569–75.

[59] Scherpner, *Fürsorge und Politik* (Berlin, 1933).

organizations of German minorities outside the Reich, the Hitler Youth, and the Communist Red Aid (*Rote Hilfe*). Since social work was essentially implicated in the political structure of every society, it was, therefore, incorrect to argue that state intervention denatured the prepolitical act of helping.

There was nevertheless a real danger that, if the natural cleavages within any society grew too large, social work would be instrumentalized for directly political ends. According to Scherpner, this line was crossed at the moment when welfare organizations reached beyond the limits of their own traditional group—whose shared beliefs had helped sustain the illusion of nonpolitical helping—and attempted to convert persons who did not historically share these values. This intrusion into what had been regarded as the privileged spheres of the other welfare organizations revealed the political dimension implicit in all social work and blurred the ostensibly clear separation of state and society.[60] However, the absence of a set of binding social norms and political values prevented public welfare from resolving the resulting conflicts among the organizations competing for hegemony within the welfare sector. Instead, public welfare—and the state itself—was drawn into the conflict of societal forces. As a result of this disintegration of state sovereignty, the decisions of public welfare offices became "nothing other than compromises resulting from the relative strength of those groups which are in momentary possession of the state means of coercion. . . . Because the consciousness of values which are binding upon all was too weak to assert itself against the particular value systems of the competing groups, *public welfare had to become both the object of contention and the site of conflict.*"[61]

For Schmitt, this fusion of interventionist state and politicized societal sphere described by Scherpner represented the terminal crisis of parliamentary government in bourgeois society, and Schmitt himself believed that this failure had led to the creation of a permanently unstable and inauthentic pluralistic party state which could—though it need not necessarily do so—give birth to a more stable authoritarian state whose legitimacy would be based on plebiscitary, rather than representative, democracy. By reestablishing the distinction between state and society, such an authoritarian state would clearly define the relative spheres of competence between the various voluntary welfare organizations and reprivatize their activity, thereby emptying the societal sphere of that general, political dimension which it had possessed through the liberal era and concentrating this representative function instead in a sovereign "guardian of the constitution" who would virtually represent the political will of the nation.

---

[60] In a passage from a later book, Scherpner described the *Winterhilfswerk* as the archetypical form of politicized helping. Scherpner, *Theorie der Fürsorge* (Vandenhoeck & Ruprecht, 1962), pp. 128–33. Ernst-Wolfgang Böckenförde has argued in very similar terms that this is precisely the point at which state welfarist intervention to promote social justice begins to assume a totalitarian character. Böckenförde, "The Significance of the Distinction between State and Society in the Democratic Welfare State of Today," in his *State, Society and Liberty: Studies in Political Theory and Constitutional Law* (Berg, 1991), pp. 146–74.

[61] Scherpner, *Fürsorge und Politik*, pp. 16–17, emphasis added.

The Inner Mission and the Caritasverband gradually closed ranks as they became aware of their common opposition to those anti-Christian dimensions of Nazism which they had overlooked or played down in their eagerness to overthrow the Republic, and from mid-1933 onward they were both faced with a more immediate problem: the emergence of a new organization, the National Socialist People's Welfare (*Nationalsozialistische Volkswohlfahrt*, NSV), claiming to be the authoritative representative of the Nazi Party in the field of public and voluntary welfare.[62] Since the winter of 1931/32, the many local Nazi self-help organizations had begun to condense into a recognizable central organization with the founding of a Berlin association National Socialist *Volkswohlfahrt*. In March 1933, Erich Hilgenfeldt, a longtime party member, was appointed head of the Berlin NSV. Hilgenfeldt aspired to make the Berlin organization the cornerstone of a nationwide Nazi welfare organization. In May 1933 Hilgenfeldt was, with Goebbels's support, able to obtain Hitler's recognition of the NSV as the party organ responsible for all aspects of the area of welfare and social work, and in the following months he succeeded in building up a nationwide organization while at the same time defending this new organization against encroachment by the German Labor Front and the Hitler Youth, which were also vying for control over Nazi welfare activity. Hilgenfeldt eventually built the NSV into a mass organization, whose nominal membership reached 3.7 million in 1934 and exceeded 17 million in 1943. The ability of the NSV and the *Winterhilfswerke* to bring about the mobilization of substantial portions of the population and the real benefits which they provided to those persons whom they regarded as productive, racially valuable members of the national community enabled these organizations to create a broad level of passive loyalty, if not active support, for the Nazi regime until the end of the war.

The activity of the NSV can not be fully understood without examining the ideological bases of Nazi welfare and the relationship of these programs to the other social and racial policies pursued by the Nazis, whose origins will be discussed in chapter 8, and the present discussion will focus on the growing influence of the NSV and its implications for the corporatist self-government of the welfare sector, which the German League for Voluntary Welfare hoped would follow upon the overthrow of the Republic.

Within the welfare sector, the Nazi *Gleichschaltung* proceeded apace. Although Workers' Welfare had hoped to forestall the worst consequences of a Nazi seizure of power by breaking its formal affiliation with the SPD, the Nazis showed little respect for such legal niceties, and its property was taken over by

---

[62] On the NSV, see Christoph Sachße/Florian Tennstedt, *Geschichte der Armenfürsorge in Deutschland* (Kohlhammer, 1980–92), III:110ff., Eckard Hansen, *Wohlfahrtspolitik im NS-Staat. Motivationen, Konflikte und Machtstrukturen im 'Sozialismus der Tat' des Dritten Reiches* (Maro-Verlag, 1991), Herwart Vorländer, *Die NSV. Darstellung und Dokumentation einer nationalsozialistischen Organization (Schriften des Bundesarchivs*, Bd. 35, 1988), Peter Zolling, *Zwischen Integration und Segregation. Sozialpolitik im "Dritten Reich" am Beispiel der "Nationalsozialistischen Volkswohlfahrt" (NSV) in Hamburg* (Peter Lang, 1986), and Thomas E. J. de Witt, *The Nazi Party and Social Welfare 1919–1939* (dissertation, Virginia, 1972).

the NSV on the basis of the July 14, 1933, law on the expropriation of the property of organizations hostile to the *Volk* and state. With the disappearance of Workers' Welfare, the Central Welfare Committee for Christian Workers no longer served any distinct purpose, and its organizations and properties were divided among the Inner Mission and the Caritasverband. The NSV also swallowed up the Fifth Welfare League in July of that year. Although the Red Cross retained its independent existence, it was again limited to serving as an auxiliary medical service for the armed forces. The Central Welfare Bureau for German Jewry was quietly excluded from the German League and continued its work within the increasingly ghettoized Jewish community. Although the DV executive committee was reorganized on the basis of the *Führer*-principle in May 1933, the organization initially retained its independence because Hilgenfeldt hoped to make it into an umbrella organization where voluntary and public welfare could come together with the various functional *Verbände* to discuss common practical problems. However, his plans floundered on the resistance of local government, which was unwilling to surrender this important area of municipal activity to the NSV, and in late 1935 the DV was finally nazified when Hilgenfeldt appointed Hermann Althaus, who had left the Inner Mission to become deputy director of the NSV, to replace Polligkeit as chair.[63]

Although the first meeting between the NSV and the German League for Voluntary Welfare in May 1933 was cordial enough in outward appearance, the Caritasverband was uncertain whether the NSV was interested in joining or absorbing the League. However, the Nazis were initially reluctant to take any radical steps which might have alienated the churches. Already in March 1933 the Nazis had attempted to dispel the anxiety of the Catholic Church by declaring that the Christian churches were the most important factors in the preservation of the *Volkstum* and that they regarded Christianity as "the unshakable foundation of the ethical and moral life of our people."[64] As part of their attempt to win the loyalty of the churches, on June 1, 1933, the Interior Ministry denounced the expansion of public welfare during the Republic, especially the exclusion of confessional welfare, as a grievous error and emphasized that welfare and youth welfare could never dispense with the Christian charity.[65]

Fearing that German Catholics would again be excluded from the mainstream

---

[63] Hansen, *Wohlfahrtspolitik im NS-Staat*, pp. 86–93, "An die Mitglieder unseres Vereins," *Nachrichtendienst* 14:4/5 (April/May 1933), p. 66, and "Bericht über die Mitgliederversammlung des Vereins," *Nachrichtendienst* 16:8 (August 1935), pp. 246–49. The political fortunes of the DV leadership diverged after 1933. Klumker was removed from his teaching position at the University of Frankfurt in the summer of 1933, and the Nazis continued to persecute him until his death in 1942. However, while Hans Maier was hounded by the Nazis until his death in the late 1930s, Heimerich—although removed from his position as mayor of Mannheim—was permitted to practice law unmolested in Berlin until 1944. Most of the leadership of Workers' Welfare—especially those of Jewish descent—emigrated.

[64] Lothar Kettenacker, "Hitler und die Kirchen," in Günther Heydemann and Lothar Kettenacker, eds., *Kirchen in der Diktatur. Drittes Reich und SED-Staat* (Vandenhoeck & Ruprecht, 1993), pp. 67–87, citation p. 72.

[65] Vorländer, *Die NSV. Darstellung und Dokumentation*, pp. 204–5.

of political life, on June 11 the Fulda bishops' conference issued a pastoral letter which endorsed the new regime, praised the accomplishments of the Nazis in combating communism and atheism, and predicted that Christianity would be a vital force in the national revolution.[66] This move from opposition to collaboration was ratified by the Concordat, which opened up the possibility of securing those special privileges for which the Center Party had fought for since the *Kulturkampf*. The devaluation of the political institutions of the Weimar Republic by the tendency to measure real social and political institutions through the ahistorical standards of Thomist natural law and a radical opposition to liberalism and modernity blinded the Church hierarchy and the increasingly clericalized leadership of the Center Party to the realities of modern political life. In turn, this blindness reinforced the illusion that the Concordat would make possible the creation of a separate Catholic sphere within the authoritarian state. This political illusion represented the Catholic counterpart to the eschatological role assigned to the state and *Volk* by conservative Protestants.[67]

Although these hopes helped cement the initial support of German Catholics for the Nazi regime, they also provided the basis for subsequent Catholic opposition to the expansive tendencies of the NSV in the welfare sector. On July 25, 1933, the Interior Ministry issued a decree which stated that, henceforth, only four organizations would be recognized as welfare *Spitzenverbände* and thus be eligible for Reich subsidies: the NSV, the Caritasverband, the Inner Mission, and the Red Cross. Two days later the German League for Voluntary Welfare was dissolved and a new organization, the Reich Association of German Voluntary Welfare (*Reichsgemeinschaft der freien Wohlfahrtspflege Deutschlands*), which was comprised of the four *Spitzenverbände*, was established to replace the League. Although many members of the Inner Mission were eager for a closer association with the Nazis, the Caritasverband was much more cautious. Despite the insistence by Hilgenfeldt that the NSV be permitted to name the president of the new organization and assume sole responsibility for the *Winterhilfe*, the two confessional organizations acceded to this inevitable reorganization in the hope that the government would adhere to its previous declarations regarding the importance of voluntary welfare.

Through the second half of 1933, the Inner Mission and the Caritasverband were caught between increasingly aggressive attacks on their work at the local level and formal protestations of amity and respect for the other members of the Reich Association by the Reich leadership of the NSV. But it was clear by early fall that the NSV only regarded the Reich Association as a way station in its efforts to establish party control over the entire welfare sector, either by coopting the other *Spitzenverbände* or slowly freezing them out of their traditional fields of activity.[68] In October 1933, Hilgenfeldt declared that the Nazi organiza-

---

[66] Kaufmann, *Katholisches Milieu in Münster 1928–1933*, pp. 160ff.

[67] Böckenförde, "Der deutsche Katholizismus im Jahre 1933," *Hochland* 53 (1960–61), pp. 215–39.

[68] In late August, Gustav von Mann, the director of the Caritasverband's child welfare section,

tion had taken over the leadership of voluntary welfare and that, in the long run, responsibility for voluntary welfare would have to be consolidated in a single organization. Hilgenfeldt claimed for the NSV responsibility for the care of all healthy members of the national community, who were to be the special object of Nazi welfare. He relegated to the confessional organizations responsibility for caring—under the leadership of the NSV—only for those sick persons "whom we can not help any more." Such a pronouncement implied that the Christian charities would become superfluous as the number of such persons was systematically reduced through Nazi health and racial programs.[69]

Despite its increasingly official status, the NSV was not integrated into the official Nazi Party organization until January 1934. In conjunction with this administrative reorganization, Hilgenfeldt and Althaus took a further step toward consolidating Nazi control over the confessional welfare organizations by insisting that the privileged status of the NSV had rendered obsolete the principle of parity, which had been the basic principle of both the German League and the Reich Association. Hilgenfeldt and Althaus demanded that the Reich Association be reorganized in order to explicitly recognize the leading role of the NSV and its right to represent all voluntary welfare organizations. During the ensuing negotiations, the all-encompassing claims of the Nazi Party in the area of political pedagogy clashed with increasing directness with the insistence by the confessional welfare organizations that the pastoral activity upon which they had long based their arguments for the unique, autonomous value of voluntary welfare was prior to the rights of the state. However, both the Inner Mission and the Caritasverband were fighting a battle which was already lost. In March 1934 a new Working Committee of Voluntary Welfare Peak Organizations (*Arbeitsgemeinschaft der Spitzenverbände der freien Wohlfahrtspflege*) was established; this effectively deprived the confessional organizations of their own corporate identity and subordinated their work in those fields claimed by the NSV to the leadership of the Nazi organization.

All of the affinities and conflicts between the NSV and the confessional welfare organizations manifested themselves with all desirable clarity in the unsuccessful efforts in 1933/34 to reform that law which was regarded as the archetype of all republican welfare legislation: the RJWG.

Adolf Stahl, one of the leading figures in the Inner Mission and the editor of its official organ, had begun the conservative attack on the RJWG in April 1933 with an essay which revealed the extent to which conservative Protestantism of the Inner Mission had fused with the authoritarian racial nationalism of the Nazis. Although the socialization of the young was an essential task of every

---

reported that, according to his sources, the ambitions of the NSV extended far beyond the areas claimed in its July guidelines. According to this source, the NSV ultimately hoped to limit confessional welfare to pastoral activity in the narrowest sense of the word and to eliminate the confessional social work schools. Mann, "Besprechung über Fragen der Jugendfürsorge" (August 25, 1933), ADCV 319.4 E II 6, Fasz. 4.

[69] Hilgenfeldt, "Aufgaben der NS.-Volkswohlfahrt," *Nationalsozialistischer Volksdienst* 1 (1933/34), pp. 1–6.

society, Stahl argued that the strength and vitality of the national revolution reflected the fact that "we have rediscovered the soil created by the Lord and permeated with his power in which alone a healthy youth policy can take root: the soil of the *Volkstum*! *Volkstum and Gospels, faith and Volk*. In the unification of this couplet we see the origin and end of successful service to the young." Stahl argued that the RJWG had for two reasons failed to become the foundation for an integral system of surrogate public education for endangered and wayward youth. While the excessively individualist right to education guaranteed by §1 RJWG was, he argued, at best a half-truth, the moral content of public youth welfare had been further hollowed out by the neutrality of the republican state in matters of religion and the conscious disavowal of Christianity as the binding, normative foundation for public education. This had turned public welfare into a moral free-for-all in which Christianity, atheism, humanism, pacifism, and Bolshevism had all been permitted to compete on equal terms for the hearts and minds of the nation's youth. The result was an individualist conception of state and society which had been emptied of that substantive content which could only be provided by the idea of a Christian *Volkstum*. He envisioned the transformation of the Weimar *"Fürsorgestaat"* into the "educational state" (*Erziehungsstaat*) which had been held up by the Nazi pedagogue Ernst Krieck as the goal of Nazi pedagogy. The reconstruction of both youth cultivation and youth welfare on the basis of this Christian ideal of service and subordination was possible, Stahl argued, because of the virtual identity between Germanic customs, the racial traits of the German *Volk*, and Christian faith. Wichern's response to the communist, atheist revolution of 1848 and Hitler's response to the revolution of 1918 represented, Stahl concluded, two manifestations of the same moral impulse.[70]

Arguing from more secular premises, Polligkeit arrived at a position whose practical implications were largely identical with those of Stahl's position. Polligkeit complained that the "distorted image of parliamentary government which we experienced in every area of public life since the war" and the construction of welfare and youth welfare offices on "flawed" parliamentary principles had continuously disrupted the nonpolitical *Facharbeit* of welfare reformers and undermined the trust among the many organizations active in the youth welfare field, trust which was necessary if these social workers were to exert a positive moral influence on the recipients of public assistance.[71] Polligkeit maintained that social work was difficult, if not impossible, within a parliamentary system because the very existence of a plurality of antithetical worldviews and the constant struggle between the proponents of these systems precluded the establishment of a "unitary educational goal which has been

---

[70] Stahl, "Oeffentliche und freie Jugendwohlfahrtspflege im neuen Staat," *IM* 28 (1933), pp. 128–38. See also Stahl, "Das Reichsgesetz für Jugendwohlfahrt im alten und im neuen Staat," *FW* 8:1 (April 1933), pp. 1–14.

[71] Polligkeit, "Grundfragen zur Reform des RJWG," *Nachrichtendienst* 14:10 (October 1933), pp. 249–51. Polligkeit's name is on the typewritten draft in ADCV 319.4 E II 6, Fasz. 4.

shaped by a national, social will" and led directly to a divisive "struggle for the young." While previous efforts to overcome these oppositions had failed because of the irreconcilable differences—especially between the confessional welfare organizations and Workers' Welfare—concerning those values which the *Volk* was ideally supposed to embody, Polligkeit hoped that the spiritual revolution begun by the Nazis would finally establish "a unitary goal for our youth welfare that is capable of transcending all oppositions."[72]

The Interior Ministry had originally hoped to distribute a draft of the revised RJWG in August 1933. However, this goal quickly proved to be hopelessly unrealistic because the solution to the problems of the existing RJWG depended on the resolution of a number of fundamental political issues, including the definition of the substantive goal of public youth welfare, the regulation of the relation between public and voluntary welfare, and the elimination of the parliamentary structure of the youth welfare offices. Since there would be no place for religious neutrality in the field of youth welfare in this authoritarian, Christian state, both the Inner Mission and the Caritasverband insisted that the new youth welfare law would have to clearly guarantee that the ward and guardian belonged to the same confession and, more important, that these confessional principles would permeate the entire milieu in which the child was raised. Such regulations would have perfected that reconfessionalization toward which the church charities had been striving since the 1925/26 conferences, and they would have precluded in principle that equation of religion and worldview which had been the source of so much friction in the 1920s. Moreover, the exclusion of both the Progressives and the Social Democrats from public welfare made the Caritasverband much more willing to make statutory guardianship the focal point of the activity of the youth welfare offices and the foundation for a systematic, integrated system—which had been advocated by Progressive youth welfare reformers such as Klumker and Polligkeit since the turn of the century—designed to protect, supervise, and reeducate endangered and wayward youth. In addition, the Reich Association also wanted to restore those obligations which had been suspended by the February 1924 decree implementing the RJWG, especially preventive programs in the area of maternal and infant welfare, which were of special importance to the NSV.[73]

Initially, the Caritasverband suggested that the law state that public youth

---

[72] Polligkeit, "Jugendwohlfahrtspflege im künftigen Gesamtsystem der Jugenderziehung" (June 24, 1933), ADCV 319.4 E II 6, Fasz. 4. One area in which this affinity between increasingly authoritarian Progressive reformers and the confessional welfare organizations was especially clear was the voluntary labor service. See Peter Dudek, *Erziehung durch Arbeit. Arbeitslagerbewegung und Freiwilliger Arbeitsdienst 1920–1935* (Opladen, 1988).

[73] Polligkeit, "Grundfragen zur Reform des RJWG," Polligkeit, "Vorläufige Stellungnahme zu dem Entwurf eines Reichsjugendgesetzes" (October 19, 1933), and "Vorschläge der Spitzenverbände der freien Jugendwohlfahrtspflege zur Reform des Reichsgesetzes für Jugendwohlfahrt" (September 12, 1933), ADCV 319.4 E II 6, Fasz. 3, "Stellungnahme des Deutschen Caritasverbandes . . ." (September 18, 1933), ibid., Fasz. 4, and Klumker, "Die Zukunft des Jugendamtes," *SPr* 42:18, 20, 21 (1933), cols. 540–44, 601–6, 633–37.

welfare was to educate wayward youth in a Christian, national spirit. However, the reluctance of the Interior Ministry to recognize the subsidiarity of public welfare to an extent which satisfied the Caritasverband led the Catholic organization to emphasize in an increasingly explicit manner the need for a specifically confessional education and to insist more strongly that *by their very nature* the Christian churches had the right to play a decisive role in every stage of the religious and moral education of those children who had been baptized into these churches. The responsibility of the state was simply to watch over the family, to insure that it fulfilled its educational obligations, and see that help was provided to families which were unable to adequately perform these duties.[74]

Although the second half of 1933 represented the high point in the collaboration between the Catholic Church and the Nazis, both of the confessional welfare organizations experienced a rude awakening in September when the NSV argued not only that the Nazi worldview stood firmly on the ground of Christianity, but also that it encompassed both of the Christian confessions and realized their goals. This nonconfessional yet vaguely Christian education had, the NSV argued, a very different meaning than the religious neutrality of welfare during the Weimar Republic because it would be based on *völkisch* or nationalist principles. In the ensuing debate, the all-encompassing claims of the Nazi worldview clashed sharply with those of the confessional welfare organizations. While the Nazis claimed that religious education was an essential element of their own pedagogical principles and not something distinct which could only be provided by the churches, the Caritasverband replied that religious education was itself a "total education" which was of greater importance than political education, which was itself encompassed within the former because religious education invariably produced valuable members of the national community.[75]

In the following weeks, the Caritasverband sought to delimit more precisely the goal of public education, the rights of parents, and the limits of state activity. The revised draft prepared in November contained the most systematic expression of the Catholic doctrine of subsidiarity and its conception of the relation of family, church, and state. The revised version stated explicitly that religious education had to take place within the framework of one of the two Christian confessions and could not simply be based on a vague Christian spirit, such as that which the Nazis claimed to represent.[76] However, before the Asso-

[74] "Vorschläge der Spitzenverbände . . . zur Reform des Reichsgesetzes für Jugendwohlfahrt," Polligkeit, "Vorläufige Stellungnahme . . . ," and "Niederschrift über die Sitzung der Sachverständigenkommission zur Beratung der Neugestaltung der Jugendwohlfahrtspflege" (August 12–13, 1933), ADCV 319.4 E II 6, Fasz. 4.

[75] "Niederschrift der Sitzung der Kommission zum RJWG" (September 15, 1933), ADCV 319.4 E II 6, Fasz. 3.

[76] "Entwurf eines Reichsjugendgrundgesetzes" (November 14, 1933), ADCV 319.4 E II 6, Fasz. 3. See also the programmatic essay by Anna Zillken, "Die Familie als Träger der Erziehung und die Grenzen ihrer Rechte und Pflichten," *Jugendwohl* 22:10–11 (October/November 1933), pp. 241–53. Zillken argued that the contradictions of Nazi educational policy resulted from the fact that the Nazis were simultaneously attempting to achieve two goals which could not be easily reconciled—

ciation could give final approval to this draft, the NSV submitted a new proposal which differed in important ways from this preliminary draft, and a new
draft, which closely followed the NSV proposal, was prepared in the name of
the Association. In that tortuously turgid, pleonasm-filled style characteristic of
all Nazi prose, the NSV draft declared that the goal of education in the new
state was to cultivate a "bodily and psychically healthy, morally firm, spiritually
developed, vocationally skilled German person, who is rooted in blood and soil
in a racially conscious manner and, borne by the living forces of Christianity,
committed and bound to *Volk* and state."[77] Although the NSV draft gave the
Christian churches the right and duty to collaborate in the realization of this
educational goal, it refused to either concede that this right grew out of the
nature of the Christian religion—and thus preceded the rights of the state—or
require that this religious education take place on a specifically confessional
basis. In this way it challenged the Catholic doctrine of subsidiarity without
openly attacking Christianity as such.[78]

The final draft approved by the Reich Association in January 1934 did not
differ in any essential respects from the NSV draft which had been presented in
December. Despite their failure to bring about any substantive changes, the
Caritasverband was, within limits, quite satisfied with the law, whose Catholic
intent was deflected only by the unlimited competence claimed by the Nazi
Party in this area of social life. As Zillken wrote, "If we were not facing a total
state, a state which, together with its official organizations, again and again
claims to encompass Christianity within itself, then we would probably not
have any serious reservations."[79] The problem, as Zillken and other figures in

---

restoring to the family the significance it had long had within Christianity and insuring that children
were raised in accordance with the values of the new state—without, however, socializing the
family itself, as the republican welfare system had threatened to do. She concluded that the supranatural claims of the church and the family had to take precedence over the merely earthly rights of
the state, but denied that this entailed a genuine conflict with the claims of the state because
Christian education necessarily produced good citizens. Catholic pedagogues also attacked the natu-
ralistic monism of the Nazis because it denied the existence of the individual personality, a sphere
of inalienable natural rights, and free will. See Hans-Josef Wollash, "Erziehung in der Wende zur
Nation," *Jugendwohl* 22:7–8, 12 (July/August, December 1933), pp. 169–76, 294–306, and Zillken, "Staatsbürgerliche Erziehung," *Jugendwohl* 22:9–10 (September/October 1933), pp. 229–34.

[77] This NSV draft was apparently prepared with the consent of the Inner Mission, but without the
knowledge of the Caritasverband. Gustav von Mann, "Bericht über die Sitzungen über das Reichs-
jugendgesetz in Berlin, Dezember 1930," "Niederschrift der Sitzung der Kommission zum RJWG"
(December 18–20, 1933), an unsigned memorandum "Die Lage," and Zillken to Schröteler (December 23, 1933), all in ADCV 319.4 E II 6, Fasz. 3.

[78] The NSV representatives at these meetings were personally sympathetic to the desire of the
Caritasverband to anchor the principle of confessional education in the new law. (Two of them—
Althaus and Bertha Finck, who later married Stahl—had left the Inner Mission for the NSV.)
However, they were unwilling to make any concessions on this point because they feared that this
would alienate the *Deutsche Glaubensbewegung* and the more radical Nazis, who adamantly op-
posed compromising the all-encompassing claims of the state in any respect.

[79] Zillken to Schröteler and von Mann to Schröteler (January 8 and 11, 1934), ADCV 319.4 E II
6, Fasz. 3.

the Caritasverband recognized, was that the political situation offered very little reassurance that the safeguards for confessional education contained in the law would be respected in practice.

Although the Nazis never succeeded in entirely excluding the confessional welfare and youth organizations, this was due primarily to a reluctance to alienate the churches, especially during the war, and it seems clear that there would have been little room for the churches or their welfare organizations if Nazi Germany had emerged victorious from World War II.[80] What voluntary welfare failed to recognize was that the goal of a corporatist reconstruction of the welfare system within the framework of an authoritarian, Christian state was being threatened by totalitarian claims advanced by the same Party whose radical opposition to parliamentary government and the rule of law had originally appeared as the indispensable precondition for overcoming the political mechanisms which had been created by the RJWG.[81] The conservative opponents of the Nazis who hoped for a corporatist reconstruction of every sphere of German society were the true utopian antimodernists. Their inward focus upon the institutional church and its societal organizations blinded them to the fact that the scale of social change and the growing radicalization of politics had already long since made it impossible to reprivatize important spheres of public life and thus establish a stable corporatist system in a deeply divided, pluralistic society. The confessional welfare organizations only gradually began to realize—and even then only partially—that the authoritarian alternative to parliamentary democracy which they themselves envisioned was intrinsically unstable and that the totalitarian state of the Nazis was the only alternative to the parliamentary system from which they had fled with such eagerness in 1933. The thorough discrediting of this authoritarian alternative by its implication in the Nazi regime finally opened up the way to the partial modernization of the politics of welfare reform after 1945. The institutional continuities between the corporatist system of the Weimar years and that of the Federal Republic are striking. Although the Catholic principle of subsidiarity came to play a central role in postwar welfare legislation, this was only possible because it shed the antidemocratic thrust which it had in the 1920s and was integrated into a pluralistic, antitotalitarian political consensus which dominated West German politics after 1945.[82] For this reason, the corporatist mechanisms which emerged after World War II were much more firmly rooted in democratic ideas than those envisioned in the 1920s by the German League for Voluntary Welfare, whose goal was to reverse the development of parliamentary democracy, not perfect it.

---

[80] Kettenacker, "Hitler und die Kirchen," and Hansen, *Wohlfahrtspolitik im NS-Staat*, pp. 105–18.

[81] These initial efforts to reform the RJWG were blocked from early 1934 onward by power struggles among the various Nazi organizations interested in youth welfare. While the administrative structure was reformed by decree in 1939, the substantive provisions remained formally in force through the Third Reich.

[82] Joachim Matthes, *Gesellschaftspolitische Konzeptionen im Sozialhilferecht* (Ferdinand Enke, 1964), pp. 16–66, and Edward Ross Dickinson, *The Politics of German Child Welfare from the Empire to the Federal Republic* (Harvard University Press, 1996).

From the Welfare State to the Racial State

EUGENICS AND WELFARE REFORM, 1928–1934

YOUTH WELFARE was also drawn into the political maelstrom during the final years of the Republic, and, for many people, all of the contradictions of the republican welfare system appeared to be condensed in the increasingly bitter debate over correctional education.[1] In his pioneering study of the development of youth welfare in Germany, Detlev Peukert argued that the development of correctional education exemplified the rejection of the ambitious, optimistic goals of the pedagogical movement, which by the end of the 1920s had become aware of the limits and contradictions of its ambitious project. According to Peukert's Habermasian argument, the efforts of pedagogical reformers to rationalize and normalize the behavior of proletarian youth in order to insure the reproduction of bourgeois society were perceived by these children as unwelcome attempts to colonize their life-world, and the inevitable resistance to these programs overtaxed the integrative capacities of bourgeois and confessional social pedagogy. In the context of a deepening economic crisis which made it imperative to avoid all unnecessary expenditures, Peukert argues that the growing willingness to employ repressive, discriminatory measures to eliminate that resistance by "incorrigible" youth which could not be overcome through the symbolic resources available to them reflected the same pathologies of the Progressive project which—tinged with a dose of Nordic racism—underlay the Nazi goal of the racial reconstruction of civil society and that this symbolized the emergence of a distinctly fascist approach to the problems of poverty, delinquency, and criminality.[2]

---

[1] See the literature cited in chapter 2.

[2] Peukert, *Grenzen der Sozialdisziplinierung* (Bund-Verlag, 1986), *Inside Nazi Germany. Conformity, Opposition, and Racism in Everyday Life*, trans. Richard Deveson (Yale University Press, 1987), and "The Genesis of the 'Final Solution' from the Spirit of Science," in Thomas Childers and Jane Caplan, eds., *Reevaluating the Third Reich* (Holmes & Meier, 1993), pp. 234–52. Although Peukert's analysis of this transformation of social pedagogy concentrated on Progressives such as Polligkeit and Eiserhardt, this represents a significant but unrecognized narrowing of his account of the pedagogical orientation of youth welfare during the mid-1920s. In fact, his arguments focus on the entire "pedagogical movement," a much broader and more diffuse group whose membership spanned the entire political spectrum. Their ideas were inspired by the youth movement, but the movement itself was held together only by a common "pedagogical attitude" which was defined in opposition to the doctrinal orthodoxy and pedagogical authoritarianism of the confessional charities. See Peukert, *Grenzen der Sozialdisziplinierung*, pp. 195ff., 240ff., and Peter Dudek, *Leitbild: Kamerad und Helfer* (Dipa-Verlag, 1988). Polligkeit is indisputably the chief villain in Peukert's story. *Grenzen der Sozialdisziplinierung*, pp. 131–33, 259.

The saddle point at which Progressivism was transformed into its patholog-ical, inhumane *Doppelgänger* was the emergence of a new conception of cor-rectional custody (*Bewahrung*) which was increasingly conceived as a form of preventive detention designed to segregate those incorrigible offenders—both juvenile and adult—who formed a more or less permanent, self-perpetuating group within society and who placed the greatest burdens on the welfare and criminal justice systems. According to Peukert, this treatment was justified—in a manner which established the pattern for subsequent Nazi racial policy—by attributing their incorrigibility to their ostensible hereditary inferiority. "The comprehensive, systematic creation of pedagogical institutions ran up against its fiscal limits," Peukert argued, "and in the transition of political systems from the democratic social state to the fascist national community the element of coercion latent in the pedagogical paradigm as an immanent structural possi-bility developed into the social-racist alternative of positive selection for supe-rior types and eradication for degenerate types."[3] The logodicy of the human sciences, Peukert maintains, propelled the dynamic radicalization of that logic of segregation and exclusion which was latent in the same Progressive ideas which had provided the spiritual foundation for the creation of the republican welfare system. Here lay the continuity between the Weimar Republic and the Nazi death camps. "When the Nazis came to power in 1933, the paradigm of selection and elimination, already dominant, is made absolute. What is new is not the paradigm *per se*, but the fact that its critics are forced into silence."[4]

Without disputing the insightfulness of Peukert's interpretation of crisis of the pedagogical paradigm, much of the subsequent literature has edged away from his analysis of the continuity between the Weimar Republic and the Third Reich and the birth of Nazism out of the spirit of Progressive social engineer-ing. By the early 1930s, the very foundations of the social work profession had been severely shaken by an economic crisis which undermined in advance all efforts to socialize proletarian youth into a culture based on work and middle-class notions of order, and the initial optimism of the pedagogical movement was severely dampened by its own reflections on the immanent limits of social pedagogy, by the seemingly endless series of disturbances in correctional education institutions run by both reformers and their critics, and by the in-creasingly violent attacks by conservative opponents upon the ideals of the pedagogical movement. However, the crisis of the pedagogical movement cul-minated in a state of resignation and intellectual disarray which entailed, at worst, a return to the deterrent, disciplinary practices of the nineteenth century, but did not generate the spiritual impulses which could have provided a founda-tion for the racial reconstruction of the European order envisioned by the Nazis.

These new impulses were provided by the eugenic critics who played an increasingly vocal role in welfare reform debates from about 1928 onward.[5]

---

[3] Peukert, *Grenzen der Sozialdisziplinierung*, p. 299.

[4] Peukert, "The Genesis of the 'Final Solution' from the Spirit of Science," p. 244.

[5] There is now a substantial literature on eugenics and such related issues as morality legislation,

Despite the undeniable affinity between the criticisms of the Weimar welfare system which were advanced, on the one hand, by the small coterie of academic eugenicists and the Nazis who provided the mass support for their policies and, on the other hand, those advanced by both Progressives and Christian conservatives, there was an important qualitative difference between their respective positions. The discourse of these eugenic welfare reformers was a new one which was neither latent in nor compatible with the intellectual traditions upon which the republican welfare system had been erected. By depicting this process as the radicalization of pathological possibilities latent in Progressivism, Peukert's genealogy of the "Final Solution" obscures the historicity of the eugenic project and the novelty of the eugenic critique of the welfare state, despite his own intentions.

Eugenic reformers rejected both the individualist, humanist premises which underlay the ideal of social citizenship shared by Progressives and Christian conservatives and the preventive, therapeutic programs which had been created to secure the realization of this ideal. Like Progressives and Christian conservatives, these eugenic critics argued that, in comparison with the declining standard of living of the general populace and the increasingly inadequate support provided to the able-bodied unemployed, excessive amounts were being spent on the care of those whom they regarded as unproductive, asocial, and otherwise parasitic groups. Although this argument was based on the spurious assumption that the fiscal crisis of the republican welfare state could be solved by eliminating the inefficiencies and ostensible extravagances in the system of institutional care, the eugenic attack on state social spending could only have acquired the intense positive resonance which it in fact attained because these

population policy, the regulation of sexuality, and euthanasia in the transition from the Weimar Republic to the Third Reich. See Atina Grossmann, *Reforming Sex: The German Movement for Birth Control and Abortion Reform, 1920–1950* (Oxford University Press, 1995), Peter Weingart, Jürgen Kroll, and Kurt Bayertz, *Rasse, Blut und Gene. Geschichte der Eugenik und Rassenhygiene in Deutschland* (Frankfurt, 1988), Robert Proctor, *Racial Hygiene: Medicine under the Nazis* (Harvard University Press, 1988), Paul Weindling, *Health, Race and German Politics Between National Unification and Nazism, 1870–1945* (Cambridge University Press, 1989), Michael Schwartz, "Sozialismus und Eugenik. Zur fälligen Revision eines Geschichtsbildes," *Internationale Wissenschaftliche Korrespondenz zur Geschichte der deutschen Arbeiterbewegung* 25:4 (December 1989), pp. 465–89, Sheila Weiss, "The Race Hygiene Movement in Germany, 1904–1945," in Mark Adams, ed., *The Wellborn Science: Eugenics in Germany, France, Brazil and Russia* (New York, 1990), pp. 8–68, Gisela Bock, *Zwangssterilisation im Nationalsozialismus. Studien zur Rassenpolitik und Frauenpolitik* (Westdeutscher Verlag, 1986), and Hans-Walter Schmuhl, *Rassenhygiene, Nationalsozialismus, Euthanasie. Von der Verhütung zur Vernichtung 'lebensunwerten Lebens', 1890–1945* (Vandenhoeck & Ruprecht, 1987), Kurt Nowack, *"Euthanasie" und Sterilisierung im "Dritten Reich". Die Konfrontation der evangelischen und katholischen Kirche mit dem Gesetz zur Verhütung erbkranken Nachwuchses und der "Euthanasie"-Aktion,* 2d ed. (Göttingen, 1980), and Angelika Ebbinghaus, Heidrun Kaupen-Haas and Karl-Heinz Roth, eds., *Heilen und Vernichten im Mustergau Hamburg. Bevölkerungs- und Gesundheitspolitik im Dritten Reich* (Hamburg, 1984). The only study to focus specifically on eugenics and welfare is Jürgen Reyer, *Alte Eugenik und Wohlfahrtspflege. Entwertung und Funktionalisierung der Fürsorge vom Ende des 19. Jahrhunderts bis zur Gegenwart* (Freiburg, 1991).

demands were integrated into a worldview which interpreted preventive, therapeutic programs in an entirely different manner than did the architects of the republican welfare system. Progressive welfare reformers believed that society had an obligation to provide the greatest assistance to those who deviated the furthest from prevailing social norms and that social pedagogy and environmental reform were capable of eliminating poverty, deviance, and criminality (though by the early 1930s they maintained that the pendulum had swung too far in this direction).[6] Confessional welfare reformers arrived at similar conclusions based on their understanding of the dictates of Christian charity.

However, while both the Progressive and confessional architects of the republican welfare system sought ways to reverse the hypertrophy of individual rights without abandoning their underlying principles, eugenic reformers and their Nazi supporters viewed the contradictions of the republican welfare system as a biological, rather than an environmental or pedagogical, problem which had to be solved in very different ways than those proposed by Progressive and confessional reformers. Consequently, even though both groups attributed the crisis of the republican welfare system to the hypertrophy of individual rights, the Progressive-confessional analysis of the way the bureaucratization of the welfare system was leading to the decay of helping, the politicization of social work, and the decline of public morality was *not identical* with the eugenic-National Socialist claim that therapeutic programs were facilitating, if not contributing to, the overly rapid procreation of the underclasses and thus leading to the degeneration of the race.

Eugenic welfare reformers argued that social *Fürsorge* was futile, wasteful and, in fact, positively harmful because it ignored the natural, hereditary inequality of all individuals which could neither be eliminated through environmental reform nor transcended through social pedagogy. They criticized over-extended, excessively individualistic *Fürsorge*, which followed the logic of preventive welfare and social rights *ad absurdum* and defended the rights of the sick, weak, and deviant even where these rights worked to the detriment of society. Instead, these eugenic critics demanded that this system of *Fürsorge* be replaced by a new collective *Vorsorge*, which focused instead upon the rights of such supraindividual entities as the *Volk* and the race. As Hermann Muckermann, the director of the eugenics section of the Kaiser Wilhelm Institute for Anthropology, Human Heredity and Eugenics in Berlin and leading Catholic proponent of eugenic reforms, argued in 1929, "Eugenics has been called—and is suited to the task—to free mankind so to speak from an individualist conception of life by directing attention toward the supraindividual continuity of hereditary substance and thereby to the totality of the *Volk* and its smallest biological component, which is precisely not the individual being, but the family."[7]

Eugenic reformers argued that, since the unrestricted procreation of persons

---

[6] Hans Achinger, *Falsche Fürsorge verschuldet Arbeitslosigkeit* (Berlin, 1932), p. 27.
[7] Muckermann, "Wesen der Eugenik und Aufgaben der Gegenwart," *Das kommende Geschlecht* 5:1/2 (1929), p. 48.

who were "unfit" to prevail in the struggle for survival simply perpetuated from generation to generation their inferiority and the suffering it entailed, these persons had the duty to subordinate their procreative rights to those of the *Volk* and race. This sacrifice would, they argued, reduce the total amount of suffering in the world, protect the community from the asocial, criminally deviant behavior of the inferior offspring of these persons, and eliminate the cost of institutionalizing them, while at the same time increasing the genetic quality and general well-being of the race. This biological reinterpretation of Christian theology was part of a broader Social Darwinist worldview, which ascribed value only to those beings which prevailed in the struggle for existence and had no room for the Christian-humanist belief in the infinite value of the individual personality. The resulting elevation of work to the measure of biological, economic, and moral value transformed the right to existence into a question of social utility and laid the foundation for welfare reform and population policies whose *ratio ultima* was the abolition of social spending for those regarded as inferior, unproductive, and asocial and, eventually, the elimination of these persons as well.

THE AMBIGUITIES OF SOCIAL CITIZENSHIP: THE DEBATE OVER CORRECTIONAL CUSTODY, 1921–1928

The codification of the principles of preventive, therapeutic care in the RGr raised important questions about the nature of state welfarist intervention, especially regarding the treatment of that residual stratum of persons—prostitutes, the work-shy, migrant casual laborers, beggars, drunkards, and endangered youth—who resisted the assistance proffered by social workers (or were unwilling to accept the terms upon which such help was offered), but who persisted in forms of conduct which were generally regarded as harmful both to themselves and society at large. Although social workers hoped to make these persons into productive, independent members of the community, they were immediately faced with the difficult question of the extent to which state coercive power could legitimately be employed to place these persons in a position where they could enjoy the social rights available to all citizens. The decade-long debate over a correctional custody (*Bewahrung*) law explored from a variety of perspectives both the justification for, and the limits of, the use of state power to promote the welfare of these individuals and the relationship between the emancipatory and disciplinary dimensions of therapeutic practices.[8]

---

[8] There are two conflicting interpretations of correctional custody legislation in the Weimar Republic: Peukert, *Grenzen der Sozialdisziplinierung*, pp. 263ff., and Andreas Wollash, *Der Katholische Fürsorgeverein für Mädchen, Frauen und Kinder, 1899–1945* (Lambertus Verlag, 1991), pp. 194–225. The most important contemporary source is Hilde Eiserhardt, *Ziele eines Bewahrungsgesetzes* (*Aufbau und Ausbau der Fürsorge*, no. 15, 1929), which reprints many of the key documents from the 1920s and has an extensive bibliography, which she extended into the early 1930s in "Das 'gemeinschädliche Verhalten', ein Grenzproblem von Strafrecht und Fürsorge," *Zeitschrift für die gesamte Strafrechtwissenschaft* 52 (1932), pp. 14–34.

The proponents of a correctional custody law, which was endorsed by all parties except the Communists, argued in various ways that the asocial or antisocial behavior of these persons could be attributed either to a pathological inability to control their own baser urges or an inadequately developed moral conscience. According to Agnes Neuhaus, most of the women cared for by the *Katholischer Fürsorgeverein* "displayed such an unusual weakness of the intellect or will—usually both—that they are on their own completely incapable of leading an orderly manner of life. They have within themselves no moral center, no inhibitions, no possibility of understanding the consequences of their action. They hopelessly succumb to every obstacle, every mood, every temptation. Without protection and without a source of support they are in the long run destined to fall victim to complete *Verwahrlosung*."[9] For this reason, Helene Simon wrote, the aim of correctional custody was "to protect from themselves persons who can not prevail economically, spiritually or morally in free society or who can not adapt to its rules and *thereby* [protect] society from them." She envisaged it not as punishment or retribution, but rather as "education to sociality" or "education to work."[10] The faith that society would automatically benefit from programs which were properly designed to secure the rights of the endangered individual and that the apparent contradiction between the interests of the individual and those of society was in fact only an apparent one both reflected and reinforced their underlying optimism about the effectiveness of the therapeutic, pedagogical measures they envisioned.[11] As Simon explained, "It is impossible to limit a freedom which, in the deeper sense of the word, does not exist at all. The persons with whom we are concerned are slaves to their pathological urges and their environment. . . . In fact it can be said that in the struggle of the spiritually or morally weak against their own powerlessness and the challenges of society it is freedom which enslaves and correctional custody which can emancipate from internal and external compulsion."[12]

In the first years after the war, the idea of a correctional custody law was championed by organizations working in the field of *Gefährdetenfürsorge* to save or rehabilitate endangered or fallen women and girls, and the problems faced by these organizations were very similar to those which had long been faced by organizations dealing with itinerant male workers, vagrants, and the homeless. The initial attempts to draft a correctional custody law in the early 1920s were hampered by a lack of clarity regarding the purpose and scope of the proposed law. While some persons wanted a law which would facilitate the institutionalization of criminal recidivists and the criminally insane, as well as

---

[9] Neuhaus, "Bewahrungsgesetz," in Julia Dünner, et al., eds., *Handwörterbuch der Wohlfahrtspflege* (Berlin, 1929), pp. 136–38.

[10] Simon, "Das Problem der Bewahrung," *SPr* 35:19, 21–22 (1926), cols. 456–60, 518–21, 551–55, citation col. 458, emphasis added.

[11] Neuhaus, "Entstehung und Bedeutung eines Bewahrungsgesetzes," *Jugendwohl* 22:10–11 (October/November 1933), pp. 258–62, 23:1–2 (January/February 1934), pp. 10–13, 31–35.

[12] Simon, "Das Problem der Bewahrung," col. 554.

endangered girls and vagrants, others argued that, if the law were to be conceived primarily as a welfare measure, then its scope would have to be limited to those persons who were the proper object of therapeutic pedagogy. This latter approach would have required a much more careful definition of the relationship of correctional custody to the criminal code and mental health legislation, as well as existing welfare legislation.[13] While the 1923 DV draft of a correctional custody law made little progress toward resolving these key questions, the second draft circulated by the DV in 1924/25 approached the problem from a different perspective. It suggested that all of the offenses which were to be brought within the scope of the proposed law could be understood as different manifestations of the psychopathological dispositions of these asocial persons. This implied that the task of correctional custody was to provide pedagogical services on the basis of an individualized determination of the nature and scope of need, which was itself defined in terms of an incapacity to lead an orderly life and care for one's personal affairs. In contrast to existing legislation, this definition provided an alternative rationale for the institutionalization of adults which did not predicate such action upon the declaration of legal incapacity by the courts, but rather on the general ability of the person to meet the demands of social citizenship imposed upon him or her by the state. To protect the rights of the concerned persons, the authority to order the institutionalization of these persons would be left in the hands of the courts, rather than transferred to the welfare bureaucracy, and the legal protections afforded to these persons were strengthened in other ways.[14]

While §20 RFV and §13 RGr had permitted authorities to sentence to a workhouse persons who failed to support themselves and their families and to reduce assistance to these persons to an absolute minimum, Simon was the first person to clearly show that the logic of prevention embodied in the RGr demanded the abandonment of the deterrent approach which underpinned both these disciplinary provisions and the debate over correctional custody. According to Simon, the preventive thrust of the RGr, which required welfare authorities to undertake "thoroughgoing" (*nachhaltig*) measures to prevent distress, rather than simply meliorating its external manifestations, meant that therapeutic services provided to these persons should be expanded in proportion to their needs, rather than reduced in proportion to their perceived danger to society. These ideas, which represented the logical culmination of the Progressive critique of nineteenth-century poor relief, eliminated the contradiction between the

---

[13] Deutscher Verein, ed., *Die Versorgung asozialer Personen* (Frankfurt, 1922). At this meeting, the Social Democrat Max Quark suggested that, in order to highlight the pedagogical purpose of the institutionalization of asocial persons, the law be termed a *Bewahrungs-*, rather than a *Verwahrungsgesetz*, a term which carried more distinctly disciplinary, penal connotations. This distinction quickly achieved general acceptance.

[14] Deutscher Verein, ed., *Kommissionsberatungen zum Entwurf eines Gesetzes, betreffend Ueberweisung zur Verwahrung* (Frankfurt, 1923), and *Das Bewahrungsgesetz im System der Fürsorge. Zusammenfassender Bericht der Kommissionsverhandlungen im Deutschen Verein* (*Aufbau und Ausbau der Fürsorge*, no. 3, 1925).

general preventive, therapeutic thrust of the RFV and the RGr and the deterrent spirit of those provisions regulating assistance for asocial persons. In this way, Simon made it possible to incorporate a correctional custody law in an integral manner into the broader framework of Progressive welfare legislation.[15] Although Christian conservatives contested Simon's account of the moral weaknesses of these asocial persons, Christian piety had always demanded that the greatest sacrifices be made for those whose distress was greatest, and the general economy of brotherly love easily led confessional welfare reformers to conclusions similar to those of Simon.[16]

Despite the formal submission of two different correctional custody bills by the SPD and jointly by the DNVP and the Center Party, further legislative action remained blocked between 1925 and 1927 by the parliamentary consideration of two other pieces of closely related legislation: the Law for the Prevention of Venereal Disease and the revision of the Criminal Code.[17] The former, which was finally passed in February 1927, reflected the concerns of medical authorities to a much greater degree than those of morality reformers. It placed prostitutes under the supervision of medical authorities, rather than the police, and morality organizations regarded the proposed correctional custody law as a vital means for filling the legislative gap created by the de facto decriminalization of prostitution.

The relationship of correctional custody to the reform of the Criminal Code was substantially more complicated. The 1871 Criminal Code had classified "antisocial behavior" (*gemeinschädliches Verhalten*), which included begging, vagrancy, work-shyness, and prostitution, as a petty offense which could be punished by imprisonment for up to six weeks, after which the convicted person could be sentenced to up to two years in a workhouse. The revised code published by the Reichsrat in 1925 no longer classified antisocial behavior as a petty offense, but proposed a set of "measures for improvement and safeguard," which permitted the courts to sentence persons found guilty of such behavior to up to three years' detention in workhouses or other institutions, such as sanatoria. However, this proposal to abolish criminal penalties for these offenses was criticized by both jurists, who felt that this endangered public safety, and welfare reformers, who insisted that this made workhouses into tacit penal institutions. As a result, these proposals were reversed by the May 1927 government

---

[15] Simon, "Das Problem der Bewahrung."

[16] For example, see Paul Erfurth's comments in *Verhandlungen des Deutschen Vereins*, SDV N.F. 3 (1924), p. 46. Not everyone agreed with these arguments. For example, Georg Steigerthal, the director of the Hamburg workhouse, argued that the optimism upon which both Progressive and confessional proposals for correctional custody were based was entirely unjustified and that, therefore, there was no need for special institutions or special forms of therapeutic practice. Steigerthal, *Zwangsfürsorgerische Maßnahmen gegenüber erwachsenen Personen. Ein Beitrag zur Geschichte des Arbeitshauswesens und zum Problem der Bewahrung* (Berlin, 1926).

[17] III. Wahlperiode, Anlagen 926 and 1067, pp. 1–2. The bill presented by the DNVP and the Center Party took over the DV wording verbatim, while the SPD version was, surprisingly, narrower and gave clear priority to the protection of society, rather than the welfare of the individual.

version of the revised code, which reintroduced criminal penalties *and* retained the measures for improvement and safeguard.

Above and beyond their disappointment at the apparent retreat from progressive penal reform between the two drafts of the Criminal Code, welfare reformers were particularly concerned about the implications of the conflation of deterrent and pedagogical principles, especially with regard to those sections dealing with supplementary workhouse detention for persons convicted of antisocial behavior. They criticized both current practice and the proposed revision for failing to distinguish between those persons who were susceptible to pedagogical influence (and therefore the proper objects of correctional custody) and those who were not. They also criticized the government and the Reichstag for proceeding on the dubious assumption that, through the sheer force of habit and routine, workhouse discipline could resocialize all types of offenders. On the one hand, they argued that it was unfair to sentence these petty offenders to deterrent criminal penalties, because the same moral weakness to which their offenses were attributable rendered such punishment ineffective. On the other hand, they complained that, by indiscriminately sentencing all types of offenders to supplementary workhouse detention (regardless of whether this could be expected to contribute to their resocialization), these measures for improvement and safeguard threatened to render workhouses useless as institutions for therapeutic correctional custody.

To escape from these difficulties, Progressive welfare reformers emphasized that, with regard to these petty offenders, it was important to clearly distinguish between those offenders whose actions were symptoms of social distress and *Verwahrlosung* and those whose offenses were manifestations of explicitly antisocial attitudes; the former were to fall under the authority of therapeutic correctional custody, the latter under that of the criminal justice system. Moreover, they hoped that, once it was recognized that workhouse discipline served no rehabilitative purpose for the latter group of offenders and thus had no role to play in the criminal justice system, it would be eliminated from the Criminal Code. The resulting depenalization of the workhouse would open the way for the creation of a new species of therapeutic correctional custody institutions.[18] The preamble to the 1927 government version of the Criminal Code insisted that criminal penalties were still necessary to combat antisocial behavior, and it suggested that the scope of authority of the criminal justice system might be substantially narrowed and hinted that the penal space created by this restriction might eventually be filled by a correctional custody law. However, in the mid-1920s the Reichstag was unwilling to pursue such a policy and, in fact, moved in the opposite direction from that envisioned by the Progressive advocates of a correctional custody law.

Although the DV commission continued through 1927 and 1928 to struggle with the problem of precisely defining which persons were to be covered by the

---

[18] Curt Bondy, "Arbeitshaus und Bewahrungsanstalt," *Zeitschrift für die gesamte Strafrechtswissenschaft* 50 (1929), pp. 524–38.

proposed law, opponents of the law continued to insist that individual rights could only be adequately protected through procedural safeguards, such as linking committal to the criteria for the declaration of legal incapacity by the guardianship courts, rather than through the refinement of social-scientific terminology. This latter position was reinforced by the Interior Ministry which in January 1928 stated that, in order to insure adequate protection for the rights of the affected individuals, persons committed under any future correctional custody would actually have to have been declared legally incapable by the courts.[19]

As Eiserhard pointed out at the September 1928 meeting of the DV commission, the difficulties in delimiting the scope of the law derived to a much greater extent from uncertainty about its purpose than from the problem of finding precise scientific terminology to describe that state of chronic moral weakness which welfare reformers agreed should be the focus of the law. Eiserhardt argued that, since it was impossible to simultaneously pursue the two antithetical goals of providing therapeutic help for the endangered individual and protecting society from all who threatened it from within, further discussion would only be meaningful if a decision were made regarding the primary purpose of the law and the most efficient means for achieving this goal. If its primary goal were to be the protection of society, then a correctional custody law would have to fill all of the gaps in existing legislation in order to facilitate the institutionalization of all criminal or otherwise dangerous or harmful persons (only a small proportion of whom would be susceptible to therapeutic rehabilitation and resocialization). However, she objected to any attempt to disguise a police law in therapeutic clothing and argued that criminal recidivists and the mentally ill should be excluded from the proposed law in order to insure that its primary purpose would be the protection of individuals who were *verwahrlost* or in danger of *Verwahrlosung*. The DV commission ultimately agreed with Eiserhardt and proposed that the mentally ill and criminal recidivists be excluded from the proposed correctional custody law in order to emphasize its therapeutic character.[20] However, the response by the Reich government in February 1929 to the various proposals advanced by the DV, the Center Party, and

---

[19] Interior Minister to state governments (January 26, 1928), BAP RAM 9243, reprinted in Eiserhardt, *Ziele*, pp. 134–37. The Ministry was unwilling to take any further action without a reliable estimate of the potential cost of the law. According to a 1929 Prussian survey, 17,143 persons who would have been committed under a correctional custody law were already being supported in public and private institutions; the passage of such a law would have simply shifted the cost of assisting these persons from the poor relief and criminal justice systems to the Prussian state, which, however, had already stated that it was unwilling to bear any additional costs that such a law might entail. "Die statistiche Erhebung des preußischen Ministeriums für Volkswohlfart zur Vorbereitung eines Bewahrungsgesetzes," *Nachrichtendienst* 11:10 (October 1930), pp. 343–44, and Eiserhardt, *Ziele*, pp. 173–85.

[20] Eiserhardt in "Niederschrift über die Verhandlungen der Kommission zur Vorbereitung eines Bewahrungsgesetzes" (September 26, 1928), BAP RAM 9243, which also contains the formulation—based on the English Mental Deficiency Act—which was ultimately accepted by the commission.

the DNVP simply reiterated its previous reservations, and it was clear by the late 1920s that there was little prospect of the passage of a correctional custody law in the foreseeable future.[21]

In the course of the decade, the advocates of a correctional custody law had been driven beyond liberal-conservative jurisprudence and the rule of law by the logic of preventive care and the shift—exemplified by Simon and the 1924/25 DV draft—from a deterrent, minimalist approach to a social, need-based view of deviance and delinquency. It was this insistence that the criterion for committal should be actual or potential *Verwahrlosung*, not the fact of having committed a particular criminal offense, which gave the clearest expression to the Progressive welfarist conception of correctional custody as a therapeutic measure and which distinguished the Progressive approach to correctional custody from that of criminologists and mental health experts.[22] However, while all of the various types of experts involved in the drafting of the law struggled to define those forms of social deviance which would justify coercive state intervention, liberal-conservative jurists repeatedly stressed the need for procedural guarantees of individual rights. Peukert concedes that until the late 1920s the debate over correctional custody moved toward both a more explicit formulation of both its therapeutic aim and the requisite legal safeguards.[23] It was ultimately the combination of fiscal constraints and reservations with regard to legal safeguards which blocked passage of the law and limited the absorption of the private sphere by the expanding network of preventive, therapeutic social welfare programs. Despite the differences dividing them, throughout the 1920s there was a tacit alliance between Christian conservativism, Progressivism, and Social Democracy regarding the need to move from a deterrent approach to poverty and poor relief and toward an individualizing, need-based approach built upon preventive, therapeutic principles. The debates over a correctional custody law completed this sea change, at least at the level of theory, and the ideas advanced in the course of this debate provided the final building block in the conception of social citizenship erected by the architects of the republican welfare system.

Peukert shows how, at the turn of the decade, youth welfare reformers began to turn away from their previous interest in the broadest possible formulation of their pedagogical program and became increasingly preoccupied with the limits of educability, which had been revealed with unsettling clarity by the growing number of revolts in correctional education institutions and the public furor aroused by these events. With the onset of the depression, he argues, the desire to reestablish the public credibility of the pedagogical project and make the most efficient use of diminishing resources led youth welfare experts to focus

[21] IV. Wahlperiode, Anlage 878, pp. 48–49 (February 25, 1929).

[22] Bondy, "Arbeitshaus und Bewahrungsanstalt," p. 532. Although Eiserhardt conceded that correctional custody could have desirable eugenic side-effects, she insisted that eugenic goals could never justify the passage of a correctional custody law. Eiserhardt, *Ziele*, p. 73.

[23] Peukert, *Grenzen der Sozialdisziplinierung*, p. 272.

increasingly on segregating out incorrigible youth for disciplinary custody, thus abandoning all broader pedagogical interest in these children. While this account may be true in descriptive terms, the disciplinary institutions which these chastened Progressives envisioned bore a far greater resemblance to classical nineteenth-century penal theory, which aimed at deterrence and retribution, than they did to the plans advanced by eugenic reformers and their Nazi supporters. In fact, at the turn of the decade, the Progressive-Christian approach to assistance for the asocial was to become the lightning rod for the criticisms of those eugenic reformers, who rejected both the individualist, humanist premises underlying this ideal of social citizenship and the preventive, therapeutic practices intended to make its realization possible.

FROM *FÜRSORGE* TO *VORSORGE*

The background to eugenic proposals for the reform of population and welfare policy was the near-panic over the birthrate, which had been declining steadily since the 1880s and which by 1927 had already fallen to a level substantially below that which would be necessary to sustain the population at its current level (even taking into account the onetime effects of the war).[24] Although eugenic reformers were worried about the declining birthrate, their approach to the population problem was determined primarily by their belief that the race was steadily degenerating because genetically inferior, economically parasitic and asocial underclasses were reproducing at a far greater rate than the more gifted classes.[25] However, in contrast to traditional pro-natalists, eugenic reformers did not condemn *per se* the declining birthrate or the spread of contraception. Rather, they maintained that the large differences in fertility rates between different social classes were simply the irrational consequences of the incomplete rationalization of reproduction, that is, the limitation of family size based on egoistic concerns, rather than a concern for the well-being of *Volk* and race. The irrationality of this individualist approach was revealed most clearly and dramatically, these eugenicists argued, in the fact that the decision by valuable couples to insure their own social advancement and that of their children by consciously limiting their family size meant that those families which prevailed in the struggle for survival ultimately succumbed in the process of procreative selection (*Fortpflanzungsauslese*) and were thus unable to influence the genetic quality of future generations.[26] The combination of a declining birthrate

---

[24] Friedrich Burgdörfer, *Der Geburtenrückgang und seine Bekämpfung, die Lebensfrage des deutschen Volkes, VGM* 28:2 (1929).

[25] Muckermann, "Wesen der Eugenik und Aufgaben der Gegenwart," pp. 11, 23.

[26] Lenz, *Menschliche Auslese und Rassenhygiene (Eugenik)*, 4th ed. (Munich, 1932), pp. 3ff., 136–75. Lenz's work was the second volume of a collaborative study by Erwin Bauer, Eugen Fischer, and Lenz, which appeared under the collective title *Menschliche Erblichkeitslehre und Rassenhygiene* (Munich, 1st ed., 1920–21), which was the most influential eugenics textbook published in the 1920s.

and the irrational consequences of a population policy based on individualist considerations intensified the fear in eugenic circles that the underclasses were multiplying at such a rapid rate that they were reducing the resources available to the valuable segments of the population, who were thereby forced to further reduce their standard of living and family size at the same time that their shrinking numbers had to bear the burden of constantly rising social spending to support the rapidly procreating underclasses.[27] Consequently, by the end of the decade, there was already a widespread fear among eugenic reformers that the nation's elites would, within the span of two or three generations, be crowded out of existence by a race of degenerates.[28]

To substantiate these beliefs, Helene Wessel, a Center Party delegate to the Prussian Landtag, published in 1931 a controversial study which compared the income of employed, self-supporting individuals and their families with the amount being spent to support "inferior" persons, including the mentally ill, physically handicapped, alcoholics, persons with venereal disease, asocial adults, and delinquent youth. In this work, Wessel made prominent use of the criminal-biological genealogies which had originally been constructed to prove the heritability of asocial and criminal dispositions in order to show how the failure to check the procreation of these groups exponentially increased the costs of supporting the underclasses as they perpetuated their costly inferiorities from generation to generation, and she came to the conclusion that 10% of the income of the wage-earning classes was being siphoned off to support persons who were not contributing to the welfare of society. Although many people questioned the accuracy of her figures and the validity of her assumption that social insurance beneficiaries and welfare recipients were primarily inferior and economically parasitic persons, her study nevertheless provoked such a strong response because it was impossible to overlook the fact that, in many cases, the cost of institutional care for a single asocial or delinquent person cost approximately the same amount as was available after taxes to many families of 3.5–4 persons who were able to support themselves without relying on public assistance. Wessel concluded that social spending for such persons had already exceeded its legitimate bounds because it was consuming resources which were needed to support healthy, productive segments of the population. "[F]or the sake of the future of our people," she pleaded, "it is time to abandon a welfare system which has been shaped and administered by political agitation and a false sense of humanity. Such a type of welfare only preserves itself at the cost of healthy persons. . . . [and] does not correspond to the principles of justice and love for *an entire people in need*."[29]

---

[27] See Muckermann in *Die Eugenik im Dienste der Volkswohlfahrt. Bericht über die Verhandlungen eines zusammengesetzten Ausschusses des Preußischen Landesgesundheitsrats vom 2. July 1932, VGM* 38:5 (1932), p. 17.

[28] These fears were exploited for propaganda purposes from the late 1920s through the Third Reich. See, for example, the illustrations in Proctor, *Racial Hygiene*, interleaved between pages 20 and 21.

[29] Helene Wessel, *Lebenshaltung aus Fürsorge und aus Erwerbstätigkeit. Eine Untersuchung des*

Muckermann warned that it was impossible for the productive, socially valuable classes to escape from this vicious circle simply by limiting their family size. He argued instead that the goal of eugenic reforms should not be "to eliminate welfare for the inferior, but rather, through the preferential treatment of hereditarily healthy families, to overcome inferiority itself and thus the need for welfare, in order to preserve an adequate subsistence margin [*Nahrungsspielraum*] for those who create it."[30] Hans Harmsen, the leading advocate of eugenic reforms in the Inner Mission, was simply expressing a widely held sentiment when he argued in 1931 that both existing "indiscriminate" welfare programs and the increasingly popular neo-Malthusian approach to birth control had to be replaced by *differential* welfare and population policies which would combine positive measures to encourage socially valuable families to have more children with a broad array of negative measures to limit the procreation of the underclasses.[31]

However, as the deepening economic crisis reduced the resources available for positive programs, eugenic reformers began to shift their attention toward negative measures to limit the procreation of the underclasses. Increasingly, eugenic reformers portrayed welfare recipients as psychopaths and asocials, and they constructed elaborate genealogies, modeled on American work, to document these degenerate complexes. There was a broad consensus regarding the scientificity and social importance of eugenics, and differences of opinion tended to run through the middle of the various political camps, rather than between them, at least until the early 1930s.[32] However, this did not necessarily mean that the persons who used these terms had always fully thought through the implications of the underlying worldview or that they accepted these beliefs without question, and many different discourses on the social question coexisted until Nazi racial legislation forced people to draw the practical consequences from these ideas.[33]

Kostenaufwandes für Sozialversicherung, Fürsorge und Versorgung im Vergleich zum Familieneinkommen aus Erwerbstätigkeit (Eberswalde, 1931), citation p. 85.

[30] Muckermann, "Wesen der Eugenik und Aufgaben der Gegenwart," p. 48, and Lenz, *Menschliche Auslese*, pp. 307ff. These measures included "equalization funds" (*Ausgleichskassen*) to redistribute income from unmarried persons or childless couples to large families of the same social class, the differentiation of taxes and/or wages according to family size, and the differentiation of public assistance in favor of genetically healthy families.

[31] Harmsen, *Praktische Bevölkerungspolitik* (Berlin, 1931), pp. 78–80. Harmsen was a student of Alfred Grotjahn, the leading Social Democratic expert on social hygiene and eugenics.

[32] Weindling, *Health, Race and German Politics*, pp. 483ff., and Schwartz, "Sozialismus und Eugenik."

[33] For example, Hermann Drechsler, *Aktenstaub. Aus dem Tagebuch eines Wohlfahrtsdezernenten* (Berlin, 1932) is often cited—rightly—as a prime example of the influence of eugenics on social work. However, his lurid picture of the immorality and fecundity of the genetically defective underclasses and his advocacy of eugenic sterilization obscure the fact that Drechsler, a Social Democrat, attributed poverty, delinquency, and crime as much to economic and social factors as to heredity. In his book, as in so many other contemporary publications, the relationship between environmental reform and social pedagogy, on the one hand, and eugenics, on the other, remained underdetermined. There was no single SPD position on eugenics. See Christiane Eifert, *Frauenpolitik und*

Many eugenic reformers feared that the existing, undifferentiated welfare system was not only disrupting the mechanism of natural selection, but that it was in fact *promoting* the procreation of the unfit, the degeneration of the race, and the decline of individual responsibility. To redress this situation, the state had to have greater control over the procreation of these classes. As one doctor phrased the issue, "If we recognize society's obligation to care for inferior and infirm persons, then we must logically demand that society have the right to intervene into the affairs of the individual. . . . Public welfare should only have to extend as far as the interest of society reaches."[34]

The most obvious place to begin any systematic effort to reduce the fertility of the "hereditarily inferior" and "socially unfit" underclasses was the limitation of marriage.[35] The idea of compulsory medical examinations for all persons wishing to marry had achieved a moderate degree of support from pro-natalist and medical groups during the war, and in the early 1920s both the Reich Health Council and the Prussian Ministry for Public Welfare considered the question. However, in view of the strong legal opposition to such a severe infringement on individual rights, neither Prussia nor the Reich was willing to call for mandatory premarital health examinations or the prohibition of marriage and/or procreation for persons deemed unfit. Consequently, the limited impact of marriage restrictions in the Republic and the ostensibly dysgenic effects of marriage advice clinics enhanced the significance of a correctional custody law for eugenic reformers.[36]

At the end of the decade, the renewed agitation for the passage of a correctional custody law initially came from those persons who believed that such a measure was the precondition for the reform of correctional education because it would permit the release of those older, incorrigible youths whose behavior was bringing the very idea of correctional education into disrepute. However, the idea was increasingly expropriated by eugenic reformers, who regarded some form of preventive custody as the *sine qua non* for welfare reform and a qualitative population policy.[37] In so doing, though, they stripped the idea of the pedagogical dimension which it had possessed through the 1920s and transformed the Progressive-Christian version of *Bewahrung* as a pedagogical measure into a preventive detention law intended simply to protect society from asocial, genetically defective individuals.

Wohlfahrtspflege (Campus Verlag, 1993), pp. 49–52, Schwartz, "Sozialismus und Eugenik," and Daniel Nadav, *Julius Moses und die Politik der Sozialhygiene in Deutschland* (Gerlingen, 1985).

[34] E. Röper, *Unterwertige und Anbrüchige im modernen Daseinskampf, VGM* 35:5 (1931), pp. 24, 26, and Jens Paulsen, "Die Züchtung des risikolosen Massenmenschen durch die soziale Fürsorge in Deutschland," *ARGB* 21 (1928), pp. 393–415.

[35] Cornelie Usborne, *The Politics of the Body in Weimar Germany* (Macmillan, 1992), pp. 142ff., and Weindling, *Health, Race and German Politics*, pp. 424–29.

[36] *Die Eugenik im Dienste der Volkswohlfahrt*, p. 19, Muckermann, "Wesen der Eugenik und Aufgaben der Gegenwart," pp. 36–44, Lenz, *Menschliche Auslese*, pp. 255–67, and Harmsen, *Praktische Bevölkerungspolitik*, pp. 81–83.

[37] Harmsen, *Praktische Bevölkerungspolitik*, p. 83.

In 1930, it was estimated that 300–600,000 persons—between 0.5 and 1% of the total population—were currently institutionalized because they suffered from hereditary physical handicaps or mental illness. However, the more radical eugenicists went even further and insisted that an effective preventive detention law would also have to be applied to millions of vagrants, alcoholics, criminals, prostitutes and pimps, and incorrigible youth, as well as those antisocial persons with criminal inclinations, whom the original advocates of a correctional education law insisted had to be excluded from the scope of such a law precisely because of their incorrigibility.[38] Above and beyond the legal and political obstacles to a preventive detention law on such a vast scale, such proposals suffered from a fatal flaw because the institutionalization of these persons for the entire length of their reproductive lives would have been prohibitively expensive, and it was the need to find a more efficient and economical means of reducing the burden of these "social parasites" (*soziale Ballastexistenzen*) which brought the question of eugenic sterilization to the center of the debate on welfare reform.[39]

During the 1920s, Fritz Lenz—the first professor of racial hygiene in Germany and editor of the *Archiv für Rassen- und Gesellschaftsbiologie*, the leading eugenic journal—was the most systematic academic advocate of eugenic sterilization, and his analysis of the relation between race and sterilization provided the paradigm for the displacement of the boundaries of individual and collective rights in the subsequent discourse on eugenics and welfare reform.[40] Like other eugenicists, Lenz argued that the procreation of the unfit could not be justified as long as available resources did not permit the unhindered procreation of the fit, and he called for the sterilization of a broad strata of persons who were institutionalized due to various forms of mental or physical disability. Lenz implied that eugenic sterilization should be compulsory, but argued that, as a matter of political expediency, eugenic reformers would have to content themselves with the legalization of voluntary sterilization in the hope that vol-

[38] Otmar von Verschuer, "Vom Umfang der erblichen Belastung im deutschen Volke," *ARGB* 24 (1930), pp. 238–68, and Alfred Grotjahn, *Die Hygiene der menschlichen Fortpflanzung. Versuch einer praktischen Eugenik* (Berlin, 1926), pp. 331–35. The Social Democrat Rainer Fetscher estimated that, in addition to those included in Verschuer's figure, 400,000 adult psychopaths and juveniles in correctional education, 200,000 alcoholics, and 1.2 million tubercular persons were also currently being institutionalized at public expense. Fetscher, "Eheberatung und Sozialversicherung," *Eugenik* 1:8 (May 1931), p. 182.

[39] *Die Eugenik im Dienste der Volkswohlfahrt*, p. 30, and "Aus der Gesellschaft für Rassenhygiene (Eugenik)," *ARGB* 26 (1932), pp. 94ff.

[40] Lenz, *Menschliche Auslese*, pp. 267ff., and Grotjahn, *Soziale Pathologie*, 3d ed. (Berlin, 1923), p. 475, cited in Schmuhl, *Rassenhygiene, Nationalsozialismus und Euthanasie*, p. 47. Lenz summarized these demands in "Zur Frage des Sterilisierungsgesetzes," *Eugenik, Erblehre, Erbpflege* 3:4 (April 1933), pp. 73–76. Lenz praised Hitler for recognizing that the restriction of sterilization to extreme cases would substantially diminish the impact of such measures and for supporting the extension of sterilization to all inferior segments of the population. Lenz, "Die Stellung des Nationalsozialismus zur Rassenhygiene," *ARGB* 25 (1931), pp. 300–308, especially p. 304. On the theory and practice of sterilization in the 1920s, see Usborne, *The Politics of the Body*, pp. 148–55, and Weindling, *Health Race and German Politics*, pp. 388–93, 452–57.

untary measures would eventually make public opinion receptive to firmer measures.[41] Lenz could afford to be so aleatory with regard to the problem of compulsion because he hedged in this insistence upon voluntary sterilization with a
number of forms of indirect coercion. He supported the idea of either forcibly
separating married couples who were dependent on public assistance or predi-
cating further assistance on consent to sterilization. He also suggested making
sterilization the condition for release from preventive detention and granting
marriage licenses only to those couples who could demonstrate that they had
the financial resources necessary to support a family.[42]

In fact, Lenz did not regard the restriction of procreative freedom and individual rights as a problem at all. He argued that the Enlightenment idea of the
infinite perfection of the personality was flawed because heredity placed unsur-
passable limits upon this process and that this idea was intrinsically contradictory because the rights of the individual were meaningful only in relation to the
obligations of the individual toward the supraindividual realities of *Volk* and
race.[43] The recognition of this reality would, he argued, make it possible to
transcend the contradictions of the individualist worldview while giving sterilization a new significance. This interpretation of the idea of the race as a biolo-
gized version of the absolute built an important bridge between eugenics and
conservative Christianity. It permitted Lenz to argue that racial hygiene represented an "irrefusable demand" of Christian ethics and that, therefore, true charity did not entail so much a boundless concern for the well-being of all individuals, no matter what their genetic quality, as a willingness to sacrifice individual
rights to insure the welfare of the *Volk* and future generations.[44] Ultimately,
Lenz concluded that eugenic sterilization was the most humane means of reducing the collective misery of mankind, and he insisted that the redistribution of
wealth and the expansion of the welfare and education systems could have only
a limited impact on the social question.[45]

However, already in 1933 the sociologist Theodor Geiger had warned against
the potentially fatal implications of confusing, as Lenz did, the *logical* meta-
subjects of history—the *Volk* and the race—which underlay the eugenic conception of *Vorsorge* with historical realities. As Geiger wrote, "Concern for the
future of the *Volk* must not be expressed at the cost of the present because the
future rests upon the present; the influencing of future life (eugenics) is only
meaningful *in conjunction with* the care of already-existing life (eubiotics). The
species does not have an independent life, but lives in its individual representa-

---

[41] Lenz, *Menschliche Auslese*, pp. 273ff.

[42] Ibid., pp. 282, 291–92, 301.

[43] Ibid., pp. 271, 274, 550–51. Lenz had first advanced this interpretation of race as an immanent,
biological conception of the absolute in a 1917 essay, "Zur Erneuerung der Ethik," *Deutschlands
Erneuerung* 1 (1917). After the Nazi seizure of power, the essay was reprinted under the title *Die
Rasse als Wertprinzip* (Munich, 1933) with a new foreword endorsing the National Socialist worldview.

[44] Ibid., pp. 558ff.

[45] Ibid., pp. 305–6.

tives; concern for the future of the species includes within itself care for the individual being or it is insanity."[46]

THE CHURCH CHARITIES AND EUGENIC WELFARE REFORM

From 1930 onward, the question of the relation between eugenic sterilization and welfare reform—as well as the broader question of the relation of eugenics and Christianity—was the topic of increasingly intense debate within the two major confessional welfare organizations. Eugenic ideas represented a serious challenge to the Christian charities, and the increasingly widespread employment of eugenic topoi presupposed the abandonment, or at least the reinterpretation, of essential aspects of Christian theology. However, the different ways in which the Protestant and Catholic charities reacted to the eugenic challenge were shaped by the basic theological issues which divided the two Christian confessions. While both of these organizations favored positive eugenic measures which could easily be reconciled with their traditional pro-natalist, antifeminist views, the Protestant focus upon the expiation of sin gave negative eugenic measures a far greater eschatological significance for Protestant welfare reformers than for their Catholic counterparts, and their subordination of the rights of the individual to those of the *Volk* and the race on the basis of this logic of *Vorsorge* frequently threatened to carry Protestant eugenicists beyond the bounds of Christian religion. In contrast, although Catholic welfare reformers agreed that persons who were likely to bring forth genetically inferior offspring were morally obligated to refrain from marriage and procreation, they steadfastly rejected those state-mandated negative eugenic measures which conflicted with Thomist natural law.

The Protestant reception of a eugenic welfare reform was made possible through the growing influence of a school of theological thought which maintained that the exclusive emphasis by Protestant charities upon the ethic of brotherly love had led them to overlook the fact that, in addition to the individuals whom he had created in his own image, God had also created supraindividual entities—families, occupational estates, *Völker*, and races—which, as integral elements of the order of creation, enjoyed the same or even higher right to existence as individuals. Although proponents of this position argued that this contradiction between the ethic of brotherly love and respect for the rights of these supraindividual realities could never be definitively resolved, they claimed that the exclusive emphasis upon the former had so unbalanced the order of creation that charitable institutions which had been designed to alleviate suffering had been transformed into their antithesis and that, in practice, they actually favored evil over good and sickness over health. Even though charity and welfare might help a small number of persons, these Protestants

---

[46] Geiger, "Eugenik. Soziologische Betrachtungen," *SPr* 42:2–3 (1933), cols. 35–43, 65–70, citation col. 36.

insisted that, by facilitating the procreation of the physically and morally sick and the perpetuation of their defects in future generations, they nevertheless sinned against God and the *Volk*. Not surprisingly, they concluded that it was necessary to retreat from the ambitious but flawed goals which the confessional charities had set for themselves in the 1920s.[47]

This Protestant susceptibility to eugenic arguments was attributable in part to a tendency to view biological "inferiority" as the product or manifestation of sin. For example, in an attack on the liberal anthropology of the pedagogical movement, Helmuth Schreiner argued that "it is arrogance without precedent to act as if every person is in principle educable. We have completely forgotten the limits placed upon us by nature. No milieu pedagogy is capable of bringing forth anything from devastated hereditary material. We may complain about this, but we can not alter it. Original sin is a pervasive reality in this realm." Although Peukert cited this passage as evidence of the racist tendencies immanent in the pedagogical discourse on the limits of educability, Schreiner's arguments remained firmly rooted in Lutheran theology, and their thrust can be easily read out of the conclusion of the passage, which continues: "The morally autonomous, free personality is a phantom and will remain such for all times. We are corporeal beings and, as such, limited. We are sinful beings and, as such, thoroughly woven in a sinful existence. Reform movements which overlook this do not create, but destroy."[48]

The driving force, but by no means the only actor, behind the eugenic turn by the Inner Mission was Harmsen, the secretary of the association of evangelical hospitals and convalescent institutions and the editor of the leading evangelical publication in the field of social hygiene.[49] Like Lenz, Harmsen emphasized the need to shift from the individual *Fürsorge* of the republican welfare system to a collective *Vorsorge*, and he insisted that "in pursuit of this goal the interests of the individual must retreat further behind those of society."[50] In early 1931, Harmsen called for a reorientation of evangelical charity which would take

[47] Bernhard Bavink, "Eugenik und Protestantismus," in Günter Just, ed., *Eugenik und Weltanschauung* (Berlin, 1932), pp. 85–139. Bavink's views were also shared by influential figures within the Inner Mission. See, for example, Heinrich Wichern (the grandson of the founder of the organization and a leading figure in the *Bekennende Kirche*, a racist, *völkisch* offshoot of the Lutheran church), *Sexualethik und Bevölkerungspolitik* (Schwerin, 1926), cited in Lenz, *Menschliche Auslese*, pp. 559–60.

[48] Schreiner, "Der Kampf um die Fürsorgeerziehung," *IM* 26 (1931), pp. 194–99, citations pp. 198–99, and Peukert, *Grenzen der Sozialdisziplinierung*, p. 250.

[49] On Harmsen and the position of the Inner Mission regarding eugenic sterilization, see Jochen-Christoph Kaiser, *Sozialer Protestantismus im 20. Jahrhundert* (Oldenbourg, 1989), pp. 316–90, Nowack, *"Euthanasie" und Sterilisierung im "Dritten Reich,"* pp. 91ff., Sabine Schleiermacher, "Die Innere Mission zwischen Initiative und Anwendung sozialpolitischer Maßnahmen in den 30er Jahren," in Peter Büttner et al., eds., *Religion und Umwelt* (Bochum, 1990), pp. 225–35, and Schleiermacher, "Der Centralausschuß für die Innere Mission und die Eugenik am Vorabend des 'Dritten Reiches,'" in Theodor Strohm and Jörg Theierfelder, eds., *Diakonie im Dritten Reich* (Heidelberg, 1990), pp. 60–77.

[50] Harmsen, "Organisation und Leistung der Inneren Mission auf dem Gebiete der Gesundheitsfürsorge," *Gesundheitsfürsorge* 4 (1930), p. 1.

account of the "natural inequality of all human beings" and place greater emphasis upon the impact of social programs on the quality of the population.[51]

At its August 1930 meeting, the International League for Inner Mission and Charitable Service had established a committee for family and population policy, and, in conjunction with these developments, the German Inner Mission established committees for sexual ethics and eugenics in January of the following year.[52] At the first conference of the eugenic committee, Harmsen called for a "eugenic reorientation" of the Inner Mission to complement its reorientation toward family and population policy. He complained that excessive social programs for psychopathic, asocial, and otherwise inferior persons were leading to the disproportionate growth of this segment of the population, while the early release and continued support of these persons had virtually eliminated the eugenic benefits which had traditionally resulted from the institutional care provided to them. He questioned whether in the future it would be possible to sustain the rapidly increasing expenditures to support these persons: "The greater the spread of economic impoverishment, the greater the import of radical demands for the elimination of unfit life."[53] Harmsen argued that evangelical charities had to take every possible measure to limit the procreation of those social groups who, despite their asociality and social inferiority, were receiving preferential treatment from the republican welfare system. A differential approach, he insisted, would insure that in the future public assistance would only be provided to those persons who could become productive members of the community, while asocial and genetically inferior persons were to be institutionalized and subjected to "voluntary or also compulsory sterilization."[54]

Despite the fact that the conference discussion dwelled on the ambiguities and limits of eugenic diagnoses and often proceeded at cross-purposes to Harmsen's intentions, the public statement which was ultimately approved by the conference participants largely endorsed his ideas. The participants agreed that substantial expenditures should only be made for those needy persons who could be expected to again become fully productive members of the community and that it was necessary to limit as far as possible the procreation of those persons whose hereditary predispositions were the cause of "social inferiority and the need for assistance." To the extent that certain hereditary pathological dispositions led the individual to sin against self or future generations, the conference endorsed sterilization as a legitimate means for achieving this goal:

God gave to man soul and body; he gave man responsibility for both, but not the right to do with them as he pleases. . . . Nevertheless, the Gospels do not require the unconditional integrity (*Unversehrtheit*) of the body. If the abilities given by

[51] Harmsen, "Bevölkerungspolitische Neuorientierung unserer Gesundheitsfürsorge," *Gesundheitsfürsorge* 5 (1931), pp. 1–6.

[52] Harmsen, "Gegenwartsfragen der Eugenik," *IM* 26:11 (November 1931), pp. 336–39.

[53] Cited in Kaiser, *Sozialer Protestantismus*, p. 316.

[54] Harmsen, "Eugenetische Neuorientierung unserer Wohlfahrtspflege," *Gesundheitsfürsorge* 5 (1931), pp. 127–31.

God lead to evil or the destruction of his kingdom in this or that member of the community, there exists not only a right, but also a *moral obligation to sterilization on the grounds of charity and the responsibility* which has imposed upon us for not only the present generation, but also for future generations.[55]

This theological perspective on the question of sterilization explains at least in part why Protestant welfare reformers could advocate the same eugenic measures as the Nazis, while objecting to the social utilitarianism of the Nazis and their attacks on Christian charity. Although the nature of this religious obligation presumably gave society the right to sterilize persons without their consent, the conference resolutions called only for the decriminalization of eugenic sterilization, and the participants strongly opposed sterilization for social or contraceptive reasons. Although some of the participants spoke in favor of eugenic abortion and had even already quietly performed both abortions and sterilizations, the public statement rejected this idea, arguing that there was a clear distinction between preventing the conception of hereditarily defective life and the destruction of life once it had begun.

In the second half of the 1920s, Catholic welfare reformers were also extremely active in the debate over eugenic sterilization and welfare reform. Catholic discourse on eugenics pivoted around the question of whether or not sterilization rendered the person incapable—according to the dictates of canon law—of entering into marriage and thus fulfilling the commandment that mankind was to go forth and multiply.[56] Josef Mayer, the editor of *Caritas*, argued that eugenic sterilization should be permitted because the purpose of marriage was not only procreation, but also the provision of emotional warmth and the stilling of sexual urges. Since sterilized persons could continue to serve these purposes, they were still capable of entering into marriage. Once this problem was dispatched, it was easy for Mayer to conclude that the state had the right to sterilize defective persons.[57] In addition to Mayer, Muckermann was one of the most tireless Catholic agitators for eugenic welfare reforms, and he always coupled his proposals for relieving the financial burdens on genetically "healthy," child-rich families with the call for the sterilization of the genetically inferior. Since public authorities had the right to execute murderers, Muckermann argued, why should they not have the right to prevent the perpetuation of hereditary illness through a relatively harmless procedure, not as punishment for a specific offense, but simply in order to prevent future suffering and need.[58]

However, the encyclical "On Christian Marriage," which was promulgated

---

[55] The resolutions of the conference are reprinted in "Gegenwartsfragen der Eugenik," *Archiv für Bevölkerungspolitik, Sexualethik und Familienkunde* 1:2 (1931), pp 114–17. At the Treysa conference, Fritz Bodelschwingh, another epigone of the founders of the Inner Mission, expounded these ideas in much sharper terms. See Schleiermacher, "Der Centralausschuß für die Innere Mission und die Eugenik," p. 70.

[56] For a broader discussion of Catholic views on eugenic sterilization, see Nowack, *"Euthanasie" und Sterilisierung im "Dritten Reich,"* pp. 106ff.

[57] Josef Mayer, *Gesetzliche Unfruchtbarmachung Geisteskranker* (Freiburg, 1927).

[58] Muckermann, "Das Wesen der Eugenik und die Aufgaben der Gegenwart," p. 32.

on December 31, 1930, rejected the arguments advanced by Mayer and Muckermann. The encyclical maintained that procreation and the education of children was in fact the primary end of marriage, that eugenic sterilization did impinge upon the natural right of the individual to enter into marriage, and that, in rendering these persons incapable of entering into marriage simply because of the fear that they would bring forth defective offspring, the state was placing eugenic goals before divine commandments and arrogating to itself authority which it could never legitimately possess. Although the encyclical did concede that genetically inferior individuals should be advised against marrying, it nevertheless insisted that such persons should not be branded as criminals simply because they decided to marry, no matter what the consequences. The encyclical drew the logical consequence of these principles in condemning voluntary sterilization as well. Individuals did not have any greater sovereignty over their own bodies than that which was necessary to insure the realization of the ends of human existence, the encyclical insisted, and they were prohibited from mutilating their own bodies in such a way that would render them unable to perform their natural functions, "except when no other provision can be made for the good of the whole body."[59]

Despite the growing enthusiasm for both positive and negative eugenics, many conservatives in both confessions continued to defend the traditional goals of Christian charity against both academic eugenic theory and the increasingly violent attacks by the Nazis. For example, in his *Myth of the 20th Century*, Alfred Rosenberg, the semiofficial party ideologist and one of the leading protagonists of Nordic racism, attacked Roman Christianity and its doctrine of brotherly love for oppressing the concept of personal honor, which he regarded as the distinguishing characteristic of the Nordic soul, and he decried the devastating consequences of liberal and Christian humanism upon the racial quality of the Germanic people:

> Between the enforced belief in boundless love and the equality of all men before God, on the one hand, and the teaching of democratic racelessness and of "human rights" (ones which are not at all rooted in national concepts of honour), on the other, European society has assumed the role of protector of the inferior, sick, crippled, criminal and rotten. "Love" plus "humanity" has become a general rule which destroys all life-rules and life-forms of a people and estate, and this has excited the present revenge of nature. A nation whose centre embodies honour and duty would not suffer laziness or criminality—it would expel it.[60]

In response to arguments such as these, conservative Christians maintained that the utilitarian tendency to equate the value of the individual with biological health and economic productivity represented the logical culmination of liberal, individualist rationalism, and they attempted to again embed the debate over

---

[59] "On Christian Marriage," *Five Great Encyclicals* (Paulist Press, 1939), pp. 77–123, especially pp. 96–97.

[60] Rosenberg, *Race and Race History*, ed. Robert Pois (Harper Torchbooks, 1974), p. 112.

eugenics and welfare reform within a firmly theocentric framework. In a widely read polemical tract against eugenic euthanasia, Schreiner argued that the increasing popularity of eugenics as a panacea for all of the problems of the welfare state was caused by the same corrosion of moral values which rendered such thoroughgoing preventive care impossible. He traced the root of this contradiction to rationalist individualism which, by denying the existence of absolute moral standards, transformed ethical absolutes into considerations of social utility and thus fostered the insane illusion that men were lords and masters of their own existence. A worldview which prays to "his majesty man" from morning to night, Schreiner warned in apocalyptic tones, "is destroying its own goal through the demand for the annihilation of human life." Both rationalist individualism and the social utilitarianism to which it had given birth was, Schreiner argued, "an infinite superficiality" which overlooked the all-important fact that

> we have not given life to ourselves and, therefore, do not have the right to take it from ourselves or others. We have an immediate knowledge that we do not have "absolute," unlimited command, but rather are called into a responsibility which compels us from within and obligates us in our conscience. What has been entrusted to us will some day be demanded from us by the one who alone can bring life. He alone has the right to pull down this 'earthly tent,' because he alone has the power to redeem.[61]

TOWARD THE RACIAL STATE

The differences between Protestant and Catholic welfare reformers, as well as those dividing the Christian charities and the Progressives from the academic eugenicists and their Nazi supporters, became more pronounced between 1932 and 1935, as the first serious efforts were made to draw out the implications of collectivist *Vorsorge* for the reform of sterilization legislation. The root of the problem was the ambiguous legal status of sterilization which, even with the consent of the patient, was considered a grievous bodily injury and, as such, was punishable under the Criminal Code. The advocates of eugenic sterilization were extremely concerned to provide a firm legal basis for a practice which was tolerated despite its technical illegality. The 1925 draft for the revision of the Criminal Code had proposed, without specifically mentioning sterilization, that medical procedures be decriminalized if they were carried out at the instigation of the patient and provided that they did not offend public morality. In the following years, the Reichstag was inundated with requests to modify this 1925 draft to make it easier to perform eugenic sterilizations on women who were

---

[61] Schreiner, *Vom Recht zur Vernichtung unterwertigen Menschenlebens. Eine sozial-ethische Studie zum Verhältnis von Euthanasie und Wohlfahrtspflege* (= *Arzt und Seelsorger*, no. 13, 1928), and Mila Radakovic, "Die Zwiespältigkeit der modernen Fürsorge," *Hochland* 28 (1930/31), pp. 193–203.

deemed genetically inferior while making it more difficult for women to obtain sterilization for contraceptive purposes. Despite these efforts, in January 1932 the Reichstag legal affairs subcommittee voted in favor of the original draft, which, even though it did not legalize sterilization, secured a limited degree of freedom for women seeking contraceptive sterilizations.[62]

Although the encyclical and the failure to secure a legal basis for eugenic sterilization appeared to represent serious setbacks, they helped galvanize and refocus the eugenic movement. By highlighting the fundamental differences dividing radical eugenicists from both liberals and Christian conservatives, these measures convinced these eugenicists that they could only achieve their goals by securing the passage of a law which explicitly sanctioned eugenic sterilization and defined the conditions under which such action was permitted, not by smuggling it in through the back door of criminal law reform. This new perspective provided the background for the important June 1932 conference of the Prussian State Health Council, which, in conjunction with the transition to the open authoritarianism of the Papen regime, was devoted to the problem of "eugenics in the service of public welfare."

In his preliminary remarks, Heinrich Schopohl, the president of the Council, repeated the familiar argument that excessive procreation by genetically inferior elements was causing welfare costs to spiral out of control, while social spending to support these persons was impoverishing the nation's genetically superior families to such an extent that they were being forced to limit their family size even further. The situation, Schopohl argued, had become so critical that it was impossible to formulate health, population, and welfare policies without taking into account eugenic considerations.[63] While Muckermann tried to balance between the conflicting demands of eugenic science and Catholic doctrine by making his stand on the large gray area of the Criminal Code,[64] the jurist Eduard Kohlrausch argued that a special eugenic sterilization law was necessary to achieve these goals for two reasons: 1) because it was impossible to derive a positive sanction for such actions simply through the tacit decriminalization of sterilization; and 2) because the codification of a public right to sterilize inferior persons would have such far-reaching implications for liberal-conservative jurisprudence that such a step would have to obtain explicit legislative sanction. The legal status of sterilization for medical or contraceptive reasons was ambiguous because of the unavoidable conflict between individual rights and public morality. The question of eugenic sterilization was even more complicated, and Kohlrausch argued that every attempt to create a legal loophole for eugenic sterilization by decriminalizing medical procedures performed with the consent of the patient would come to grief on the conflict between individual rights and

---

[62] Bock, *Zwangssterilisierung im Nationalsozialismus*, p. 55, and Lenz, "Die Sterilisierungsfrage im Strafrechtsausschuß des Reichstages," *ARBG* 26 (1932), p. 230.

[63] *Die Eugenik im Dienste der Volkswohlfahrt*, pp. 6–7.

[64] Ibid., pp. 7–26, which recapitulated the ideas he had put forth in "Denkschrift über eugenische Vorschläge zur Erhaltung der erbgesunden Familie," *Eugenik: Erblehre, Erbpflege* 2:4 (1931), pp. 86–91, and Muckermann, *Wohlfahrtspflege und Eugenik* (Freiburg, 1932).

those of the state. Although Kohlrausch admitted that compulsory sterilization would be the logical consequence of such an extension of state authority, he nevertheless argued that it would be unwise politically to force this idea upon an unreceptive public. He was willing to retain the idea of consent on a provisional basis provided that it was clearly established that the legitimacy of compulsory sterilization derived from eugenic science and the priority of the rights of *Volk* and state over those of the individual.[65]

In view of the financial impracticality of preventive detention as a means of limiting the procreation of the underclasses, the commission called for the decriminalization of eugenic sterilization. The commission also endorsed Kohlrausch's suggestion that the concept of severe hereditary inferiority be supplemented by the term "unfit for social life" (*lebensuntüchtig*) in order to explicitly reflect the idea that it was the congenital inability of these persons to adapt to prevailing social norms which justified state action. Although many members opposed compulsory sterilization more for tactical reasons than for reasons of principle, they were willing to content themselves with the decriminalization of eugenic sterilization on a voluntary basis because they were confident that there were numerous means of indirectly coercing the underclasses. The draft of a sterilization law which was ultimately approved by the commission codified these mechanisms by extending the right to apply for the sterilization of specific persons to physicians, medical officials, welfare officials, and the directors of prisons, hospitals, and other institutions for the care of the sick, infirm, and mentally ill.

The draft of the law on eugenic sterilization approved by the Prussian State Health Council broke with liberal-conservative jurisprudence in two key respects. First, the proposed law would have extended state authority to an extent which was incompatible with the liberal and Christian belief in the sovereignty of the individual over his or her own body. Second, by insisting that the consent of genetically inferior persons should not be considered as a necessary condition for *eugenic* sterilization and that the consent of genetically healthy persons should not by itself provide sufficient grounds for *contraceptive* sterilization, the law would have graduated civil rights according to perceived hereditary quality; in so doing, it would have imposed upon women reproductive obligations and restrictions which did not exist for men.[66]

In view of the political implications of the proposed law, Lenz and the members of the commission rightly believed that it would be impossible to pass a sterilization law as long as Germany remained a parliamentary democracy.

---

[65] *Die Eugenik im Dienste der Volkswohlfahrt*, pp. 42–54, and Kohlrausch, "Sterilisation und Strafrecht," *Zeitschrift für die gesamte Strafrechtswissenschaft* 52 (1932), pp. 383–404.

[66] *Die Eugenik im Dienste der Volkswohlfahrt*, pp. 54ff., and Bock, *Zwangssterilisierung im Nationalsozialismus*, pp. 42–58. In November 1932, the eugenics committee of the Inner Mission approved the draft sterilization law and even proposed expanding the scope to include persons who were *verwahrlost* or inclined to asocial behavior and making the sterilization dependent solely on the consent of the legal guardian. Harmsen, "Zum Entwurf eines neuen Sterilisierungsgesetzes," *Gesundheitsfürsorge* 7 (1933), pp. 1–7, and Kaiser, *Sozialer Protestantismus*, pp. 338–39.

They feared that any attempt to secure the passage of a sterilization law would in fact lead to the prohibition of sterilization, rather than its legalization. Progress in this area, Lenz argued, could not be expected through the legislative process, but only from the personal initiative of individual physicians. However, he hoped that a fundamental change in the constellation of political forces, which he believed to be imminent, would clear the way for eugenic legislation.[67] Events proved him right, and the political upheaval of 1933 permitted academic eugenicists to dispense with all of those provisions designed to protect individual rights, with which they had been forced to hedge in their more radical demands by the parliamentary system. In turn, they provided the patina of scientific authority for the *völkisch* ideas and Darwinistic worldview of the Nazis. In his address to the first meeting of the Reich Interior Ministry's Commission for Population and Racial Policy (*Sachverständigenbeirat für Bevölkerungs- und Rassenpolitik*) on June 28, 1933, the Nazi Interior Minister Wilhelm Frick recapitulated all of the arguments which had been advanced by the eugenic critics of the republican welfare state since the late 1920s.[68]

Frick's comments laid the groundwork for the Law for the Prevention of Hereditarily Diseased Offspring (*Gesetz zur Verhütung erbkranken Nachwuchses*). Against the vigorous opposition of the Catholic vice-chancellor Papen, the law was approved by the cabinet on July 14, 1933, the same day as the concordat with the Vatican (though the law was not officially promulgated until two weeks later so as to avoid offending the Catholic church). In a way which exemplified the transformation of the idea of welfare within the eugenic tradition, the preamble argued that sterilization represented "an act of charity and *Vorsorge* for the next generation" and a "truly social deed for the affected hereditarily defective families."[69] The law reflected, noted the official commentary, the intent of the regime to "cleanse the body politic" by preventing the perpetuation of inferior hereditary substance; it was based on the principle that the state had responsibility to insure both that the inferior did not procreate and that healthy families were not permitted to withhold children from the state. According to the commentary, this law definitively established the "primacy and authority of the state in the area of life, marriage and the family."[70]

The law provided for the compulsory sterilization of hereditarily defective persons if there was a strong probability that their children would suffer from serious physical or mental defects of a hereditary nature, including congenital feeble-mindedness, schizophrenia, manic depression, epilepsy, Huntington's chorea, blindness, deafness, and serious physical deformities, as well as severe alcoholism. During the Third Reich, approximately 400,000 persons were ster-

[67] Lenz, "Ist Sterilisierung strafbar?" *ARGB* 25 (1931), pp. 232–34, and "Rassenhygiene und Sterilisierung im Preußischen Landesgesundheitsrat," *ARGB* 27 (1933), pp. 180–85.

[68] "Ansprache des Herrn Reichsministers des Innern Dr. Wilhelm Frick auf der ersten Sitzung des Sachverständigenbeirats für Bevölkerungs- und Rassenpolitik," *ARGB* 27 (1933), pp. 412–19.

[69] Arthur Gütt, Ernst Rüdin, and Falk Ruttke, *Gesetz zur Verhütung erbkranken Nachwuchses vom 14. Juli 1933 nebst Ausführungsverordnungen*, 2d ed. (Munich, 1936), pp. 77–78.

[70] Ibid., p. 5.

ilized on the basis of this law, and an indeterminate but presumably substantial number of persons were, without their knowledge and/or against their will, sterilized outside the framework of the law.[71] Two-thirds of these persons were sterilized because they were believed to be suffering from hereditary feeble-mindedness, and almost all of the other persons sterilized under the law were diagnosed as schizophrenic, epileptic, or manic-depressive.[72]

Although the law was framed in medical terms, eugenic discourse on population and welfare policy was fundamentally a discourse about social behavior, and all of those social categories which the Nazis had attempted to repress through their formal reliance on medical terminology returned through the back door in the commentary on the category of feeble-mindedness. In addition to the results of intelligence tests, whose implicit prejudices have long been recognized, the inability to lead an orderly, independent life in accordance with generally accepted public norms was also regarded as an indication of feeble-mindedness. However, while employment in an occupation which required individual initiative and independent judgment was considered as *prima facie* evidence of genetic health and social normality, the commentary stated that feeble-mindedness was probable in cases where a person only carried out repetitive, menial tasks under the supervision of another; the fact that persons could support themselves and lead orderly lives was not decisive in such cases. However, the commentary also stated that even persons who clearly displayed intelligence and personal initiative could also be considered morally feeble-minded if they refused to adhere to generally accepted social norms.[73]

Despite the provisions for compulsory sterilization, most persons associated with the Inner Mission welcomed the law. Protestant charity workers only began to oppose Nazi legislation to any significant degree after the implementation guidelines obligated the various types of institutions which cared for these persons to notify the authorities of all persons who fell under the provisions of the law and after the Nazi linkage of sterilization to compulsory abortion and euthanasia made it impossible to ignore the differences between their theological justification of sterilization and the more radical consequences of the monistic worldview of the Nazis. However, their own advocacy of eugenic sterilization helped legitimate Nazi policies, and both their deification of the authoritarian state as a bulwark against sin and their apostrophization of the *Volksgemeinschaft* made it difficult for these conservative Protestants to find a firm point from which to criticize Nazi policies. Neither the Inner Mission nor the Lutheran church ever took a firm public stand against these Nazi policies.[74]

On the other hand, Catholic welfare reformers were much more hostile toward the sterilization law than their Protestant counterparts. They reaffirmed

---

[71] Bock, *Zwangssterilisierung im Nationalsozialismus*, p. 8.

[72] Schmuhl, *Rassenhygiene, Nationalsozialismus, Euthanasie*, pp. 156–60.

[73] Gütt/Rüdin/Ruttke, *Gesetz zur Verhütung erbkranken Nachwuchses*, p. 125.

[74] On the attitude of the Protestant charities toward the Law for the Prevention of Hereditarily Diseased Offspring, abortion and euthanasia, see Nowack, *"Euthanasie" und Sterilisierung im "Dritten Reich,"* pp. 91ff., 120ff., and Kaiser, *Sozialer Protestantismus*.

both the unity of humankind and the supranatural ends of Christian charity, and in January 1934 the Catholic clergy publicly reiterated the official position that sterilization was incompatible with Christian morality. Even Muckermann, who had so vigorously promoted voluntary sterilization, was prohibited by the Nazis from further public speaking after he opposed compulsory sterilization in a series of public sermons in December 1935.[75] In a critique of Nazi racial legislation, Franz Keller affirmed the importance of that concern for future generations which lay at the root of the eugenic notion of *Vorsorge*, but rejected the eugenic equation of moral value with biological health. He argued that, even when there was no prospect of healing the physical defects of a person, Christian charity had to look beyond the physical world and concern itself with the full realization of the personality in communion with God. Keller concluded that charitable service to the living—including eugenics—was a Christian duty, as long as it served the construction of life, not its dismantling or annihilation. "For true charity," he wrote, "there is no life which is not worth living. All that lives is God's creation, and it is, therefore, good that we serve the creator in them."[76]

The reaction of Progressive welfare reformers to the Law for the Prevention of Hereditarily Diseased Offspring was more ambivalent, and the interpretation of their motives is complicated by the fact that after April 1933 the Progressives lost what little ideological unity they had retained until that point. In the weeks and months after the Nazi seizure of power, the DV and other welfare reform groups pressed with renewed vigor for the passage of correctional custody and migrant relief (*Wandererfürsorge*) laws, while welfare authorities, the police, and the Nazi party all intensified the persecution of vagrants, beggars, alcoholics, homosexuals, and the asocial in conjunction with the sterilization law and the November 1933 law on the sterilization of habitual criminals and sex offenders.[77] The key question, as Peukert has noted, was whether or not these legislative proposals and the concrete practices during the Third Reich reflected a substantial identity between the logic of Progressive welfare reform and that of Nazi racial theories.[78]

---

[75] Kreutz, "Vom Sinn und Wert konfessioneller Liebestätigkeit," *SPr* 41:19 (May 11, 1933), cols. 569–75, Nowack, *"Euthanasie" und Sterilisierung im "Dritten Reich,"* pp. 106ff., and Wollash, *Der Katholische Fürsorgeverein,* pp. 316ff.

[76] Keller, "Eugenik und Caritas," *Jahrbuch für Caritaswissenschaft* (1935), pp. 73–83.

[77] Michael Burleigh and Wolfgang Wippermann, *The Racial State: Germany 1933–1945* (Cambridge University Press, 1991), pp. 136–97, Wolfgang Ayaß, *'Asoziale' im Nationalsozialismus* (Klett-Cotta, 1995), Ayaß, "Vagrants and Beggars in Hitler's Reich," in Richard Evans, ed., *The German Underworld: Deviants and Outcasts in Geman History* (Routledge, 1988), pp. 210–37, Klaus Scherer, *'Asozial' im Dritten Reich. Die vergessenen Verfolgten* (Votum Verlag, 1990), Carola Kuhlmann, *Erbkrank oder Erziehbar?* (Juventa, 1989), and Ernst Klee, *"Euthanasie" im NS-Staat. Die "Vernichtung lebensunwerten Lebens"* (Fischer-Verlag, 1983), pp. 34–75.

[78] Peukert, *Grenzen der Sozialdisziplinierung,* pp. 274ff. However, Peukert did not distinguish the political loyalties of the various DV members. Of the persons Peukert names, only Polligkeit and Eiserhardt could be considered Progressives, while Steigerthal's unprogressive views were notorious. Moreover, Peukert's own reading of the available material does not convincingly substantiate

Polligkeit and Eiserhardt were clearly pleased by the Nazi seizure of power, which appeared to eliminate the political obstacles which had previously blocked the passage of correctional custody and migrant relief legislation. In a programmatic article published in June 1933, the author—presumably Eiserhardt, who had been one of the most consistent advocates of a pedagogical focus of a correctional custody law—argued that the Reichstag had failed to pass a correctional custody law during the Republic because of the opposition of certain circles, "who, out of a misplaced respect for the freedom of the individual, placed too little value on the public interest and the protection of society." She argued that such restrictions were necessary in the interest of both these "unhindered, weak-willed" persons themselves and the community. She dismissed as a "completely misleading humanism" the idea that such legislation could entail a substantive infringement upon the rights of these persons: "Today the idea is generally accepted that the common good and the interest of the *Volk* must take precedence over the interest of the individual, that personal rights—no matter how high they are to be respected—must stand aside when their unrestrained expression injures the common good." However, Eiserhardt suggested that the proposed *Bewahrungsgesetz* should serve as a pedagogical measure (a *Fürsorgegesetz*), rather than simply a means for the preventive detention of dangerous and recidivist criminals, though it is far from clear how all of these contradictory demands could have been reconciled in theory or practice.[79]

In late June 1933, the DV submitted a petition to the Nazi Party leadership in which it called for the issuance of migrant relief and correctional custody laws. This petition—which could only have been drafted by Polligkeit, probably in conjunction with Eiserhardt—complained that existing legislation was inadequate because, in the absence of a correctional custody law, it was impossible to compel those persons who were in greatest need of help to submit to treatment. However, while Nazi welfare reformers and the Law for the Prevention of Hereditarily Diseased Offspring spoke in vague but ominous terms about the exclusion or eradication of the sick and weak, the DV petition did not, despite a broad endorsement of eugenic measures, follow the same logic of biologistic *Vorsorge*. Instead, the DV and Catholic advocates of correctional custody argued that such a pedagogical measure was necessary to supplement Nazi racial legislation because sterilization would only solve part of the problem unless steps were taken to insure the socialization of persons whose sterilization had

---

the claims he advances. He misleadingly shifts in mid-chapter from the DV and the General Conference on Correctional Education (*Allgemeiner Fürsorgeerziehungstag*) to legislative initiatives sponsored by Himmler and the SS. Many studies of the German welfare system during the Third Reich have focused on Hamburg, and Steigerthal figures as a prominent villain in every account. Evelyn Glensk and Christiane Rothmaler, eds., *Kehrseiten der Wohlfahrt. Die Hamburger Fürsorge auf ihrem Weg von der Weimarer Republik in den Nationalsozialismus* (Ergebnisse, 1992), and Ayaß, "Vagrants and Beggars in Hitler's Reich."

[79] Eiserhardt, "Warum brauchen wir ein Bewahrungsgesetz?" *Nachrichtendienst* 14:6 (June 1933), pp. 102–4. Peukert, *Grenzen der Sozialdisziplinierung*, p. 407, attributes this article to Eiserhardt.

rendered them potentially more asocial by removing the reproductive obstacles to the unhindered pursuit of their instincts. However, in so arguing they clearly implied that correctional custody could also represent a viable *alternative* to sterilization. Since heredity did not place nearly as narrow limits on social pedagogy and environmental reform as eugenic reformers and their Nazi allies had implied, eugenic sterilization was ineffective and unnecessary to the extent that poverty, criminality, and delinquency were in fact social phenomena which could be remedied through correctional custody. As the DV petition stated, "For not a small proportion of those persons in need of *Bewahrung*, a stay in an institution will successfully, through calculated influence and compulsory labor, accustom them to an orderly life."[80] Nevertheless, these leading figures in the DV stopped short of publicly criticizing eugenic sterilization, and, on the basis of available materials, it is impossible to unequivocally characterize the position of the Progressive members of the organization on this important issue.

During the crisis of the republic, Polligkeit and Eiserhardt were anything but vigorous defenders of democracy, and their hostility to the parliamentary system and the hypertrophy of preventive welfare blinded them to the differences between their own hope that a stronger state would insure the proper functioning of a preventive, therapeutic system and the eugenic rejection of the very principles of therapeutic welfare in the name of a biologistic, totalitarian conception of social citizenship. The differences between the Progressives and the Nazis over the function of correctional custody and its relation to sterilization were subtle, though not unimportant, but they do point toward more fundamental differences in worldview. This is not to deny that some prominent Progressives—such as Hans Muthesius—participated in some of the more brutal aspects of Nazi welfare policies. However, there is little evidence to support the claim that, as a group, the Progressives were logically driven toward Nazism to escape from the limits of their own reformist project. Rather, the participation of Progressive welfare reformers and social workers in the implementation of Nazi racial policies seems to have been more a matter of individual character and circumstance than worldview.[81]

---

[80] "Vorarbeiten für den Erlaß eines Reichsgesetzes zur Regelung der Wandererfürsorge und eines Reichsgesetzes zur Bewahrung verwahrloster und gemeinschädlicher Personen," *Nachrichtendienst* 14:7 (July 1933), pp. 134–36, "Nationale Eugenik. Gesetz zur Verhütung erbkranken Nachwuchses," ibid., pp. 136–37, Neuhaus, "Entstehung und Bedeutung eines Bewahrungsgestzes," Wessel, *Bewahrung—nicht Verwahrlosung. Eine eugenische und fürsorgerische Notwendigkeit* (Geilenkirchen, 1934), and Jürgen Blandow, " 'Fürsorgliche Bewahrung'—Kontinuitäten und Diskontinuitäten in der Bewahrung 'Asozialer,' " in Renate Cogoy, Irene Kluke, and Brigitte Meckler, eds., *Erinnerung einer Profession. Erziehungsberatung, Jugendhilfe und Nationalsozialismus* (Votum Verlag, 1989), pp. 125–43.

[81] On Muthesius's activity in the late 1930s and early 1940s, see Christian Schrapper, *Hans Muthesius (1885–1977). Ein deutscher Fürsorgejurist und Sozialpolitiker zwischen Kaiserreich und Bundesrepublik* (Votum Verlag, 1993). Eckard Hansen reports that the Nazi leadership in Frankfurt were surprised and unconvinced by Polligkeit's support for the Nazis in 1933, and in September 1934 one DV member who had been a member of the Nazi Party since 1929 told the Gestapo that he was astonished that Polligkeit still occupied his office and had not been sent to a concentration

Nazi policies against the asocial and inferior became increasingly terroristic as responsibility for these persons shifted from welfare authorities to the police and the courts and ultimately to the SS, while, at the same time, these categories themselves underwent a progressive radicalization.[82] The turning point in this process came in February 1937 when Himmler, who had asserted his authority over the police the previous year, ordered the police to take into preventive custody habitual criminals and other persons who offended public morality.[83] These persons were invariably shipped off to the rapidly expanding network of concentration camps. Moreover, to fend off the objections of judicial authorities, who resented his efforts to annex this important sphere of public activity to the growing SS empire, on December 14, 1937, Himmler issued a decree which permitted the police to detain asocial persons, that is, persons "who demonstrate through behavior toward the community, which may not in itself be criminal, that they will not adapt themselves to the community."[84]

Although welfare authorities had since 1933 ignored or manipulated existing welfare legislation in order to intern those persons whom they deemed asocial or work-shy,[85] from early 1938 onward there was a perceptible slackening of the interest of welfare authorities in preventive detention and vagrant relief laws, which, for all intents and purposes, had been rendered superfluous by the December 1937 decree.[86] For the Nazis, the problem was that, although the 1933

---

camp. Hansen, *Wohlfahrtspolitik im NS-Staat* (MaroVerlag, 1991), pp. 89–90. Polligkeit may well have been spared the necessity of making the choices which Muthesius had to make simply by virtue of the fact that he was never employed in the state bureaucracy.

[82] This radicalization has been explained in different ways. See Peukert, *Inside Nazi Germany*, pp. 233–35, 243ff., Peukert, "The Genesis of the 'Final Solution' from the Spirit of Science," Schmuhl, *Rassenhygiene, Nationalsozialismus, Euthanasie*, pp. 64–65, 355ff., Bock, *Zwangssterilisierung im Nationalsozialismus*, pp. 35–36, 301–2, 347ff., and Bock, "Krankenmord, Judenmord und nationalsozialistische Rassenpolitik: Überlegungen zu einigen neueren Forschungshypothesen," in Frank Bajohr, Werner Johe, and Uwe Lohalm, eds., *Zivilisation und Barbarei. Die widersprüchlichen Potentiale der Moderne* (Hans Christians Verlag, 1991), pp. 285–306.

[83] Patrick Wagner, "Das Gesetz über die Behandlung Gemeinschaftsfremder. Die Kriminalpolizei und die 'Vernichtung des Verbrechertums,'" in *Beiträge zur nationalsozialistischen Gesundheits- und Sozialpolitik*, Bd. 6: *Feinderklärung und Prävention* (1988), pp. 75–100, and Ayaß, *'Asoziale' im Nationalsozialismus*.

[84] Cited in Peukert, *Inside Nazi Germany*, p. 211, and Burleigh/Wippermann, *The Racial State*, pp. 172–73.

[85] Ayaß, *'Asoziale' im Nationalsozialismus*, pp. 57–104.

[86] The last gasp of the correctional custody debate within the Weimar welfare community was the 1938 DV conference. However, by this point, the parameters of the discussion had already been established by Nazi policies. See *Neue familien- und arbeitspolitische Aufgaben der deutschen Wohlfahrtspflege. Bericht über die Tagung des Deutschen Vereins am 23./24. Mai 1938* (Frankfurt, 1938), *Arbeitseinsatz und Arbeitserziehung durch Fürsorge. Festschrift des Deutschen Vereins für öffentliche und private Fürsorge zur Tagung und Mitgliederversammlung am 23. und 24. Mai 1938* (Leipzig, 1938), and Steigerthal, *Fürsorgerische, strafrechtliche und polizeiliche Maßnahmen gegenüber sozial-schwierigen und asozialen Personen* (= *Beiträge des Deutschen Vereins zur Forschung und Praxis der deutschen Wohlfahrtspflege*, no. 2, 1938).

Wagner, "Das Gesetz über die Behandlung Gemeinschaftsfremder," pp. 78–80, dates the definitive irrelevance of welfare authorities to the meeting of the welfare law subcommittee of the *Akademie für*

Law for the Prevention of Hereditarily Diseased Offspring had been supplemented by a number of laws and decrees intended to give the authorities greater control over the asocial, the scope of this law was narrowly defined in medical terms. Consequently, despite the elasticity of the diagnosis of feeble-mindedness, the law did not easily provide a legal basis for the incarceration and/or sterilization of the asocial.

From 1937 onward, there was a broad debate over the precise definition of asociality and its hereditary nature, and in early 1939 work began on the drafting of a law which would provide for the preventive detention and sterilization of "community aliens" (*Gemeinschaftsfremden*), who represented the undifferentiated other against which Nazi ideologues constructed their vision of the national community, but who could not easily be subsumed under the provisions of the Law for the Prevention of Hereditarily Diseased Offspring. The law was to provide the basis for the incarceration of all persons whose failure to comply with Nazi norms of healthy social behavior was attributed to genetic or racial inferiority, but who were not guilty of specifically political offenses. Its express purpose was to definitively block the transmission of that inferior hereditary substance to which the continued existence of an asocial, quasi-criminal underclass was attributed.[87] By 1940, an initial draft of the law had been completed. On the basis of this preliminary work, the Party's Racial Policy Office defined community aliens as "persons who, on the basis of their psychological attitudes—and who, therefore, could not be helped through therapeutic measures—were incapable of satisfying the minimal demands placed by the national community on their personal, social and *völkisch* behavior" were to be considered "incapable of belonging to the community." These included persons whose opposition to the state or querulous natures constantly involved them in conflicts with the state authorities; the work-shy, "pension hunters," and other "freeloaders" (*Schmarotzer*); long-term dependents on charity and public assistance; women who were unable to maintain an orderly household and properly educate their children because of their uneconomical, unrestrained, and irresponsible way of life; alcoholics; and persons who led an immoral way of life, including prostitutes, pimps, sexual criminals, and homosexuals.[88]

The drafting of the law was repeatedly delayed by power struggles between

---

Deutsches Recht in August 1938, where a representative of the Security Police told welfare officials that their proposals would no longer be considered because the police had assumed responsibility for cleansing the national community of asocial persons. The police forces were only willing to leave welfare officials responsibility for those asocial persons who were incapable of work, an offer which was hardly attractive to persons such as Steigerthal. On the general transformation of Nazi social and welfare policies after 1938, see Christoph Sachße/Florian Tennstedt, *Geschichte der Armenfürsorge in Deutschland* (Stuttgart, 1980–92), III: *Der Wohlfahrtsstaat im Nationalsozialismus.*

[87] Scherer, *'Asozial' im Dritten Reich*, Bock, *Zwangssterilisierung im Nationalsozialismus*, pp. 347–68, and Ayaß, *'Asoziale' im Nationalsozialismus*, pp. 202–9. Ayaß argues that the idea of correctional custody (or preventive detention) was qualitatively transformed after 1938 as the authoritarian approach to asociality, which had guided welfare policy since 1933, was displaced by a totalitarian strategy which was rooted in Nazi racial ideas.

[88] Cited in Scherer, *'Asozial' im Dritten Reich*, p. 51.

the Justice Ministry and the police over the respective role of prisons and concentration camps in rehabilitation and punishment. Although an agreement was finally reached in early 1944, the law never went into effect. Nevertheless, the community aliens law represented the negative apotheosis of the measures which had been advocated by eugenic welfare reformers since the late 1920s, and its graduation of rights according to ostensible genetic quality marked the logical terminus of that transformation of the rule of law entailed by a eugenic approach to welfare and population policy.

Conclusion: Nazi "Welfare" and the Rejection of the Republican Welfare System

Over the past decade, the welfare and social policies of the Nazi regime have shifted from the periphery toward the center of scholarly attention as it has become increasingly clear that social and welfare policies to benefit productive, racially valuable, and politically reliable members of the national community can not be separated from either genocidal policies designed to segregate and ultimately annihilate those persons regarded as racially inferior, socially deviant, and politically unreliable community aliens or wars of conquest designed to create the political and economic foundations for their racial reconstruction of civil society.[89]

The Nazi critique of the republican welfare system and their own alternative vision of the role of social services began with the same problem which had been the focus of Progressive critiques: the hypertrophy of individual rights. As Hellmuth Reichert wrote in 1935, the root of the problem was the transformation of a subsidiary right to public assistance into a de facto actionable right of the individual against the state and the resulting tendency of broad sections of the populace to regard themselves simply as usufructuaries of the state who did not feel that the benefits of membership in the *Volk* entailed any reciprocal obligations toward the *Volk*.[90] This crisis was widely attributed to the principles

[89] The most important contributions to this new approach to the Nazi state are Peukert, *Inside Nazi Germany*, and Bock, *Zwangssterilisation im Nationalsozialismus*. More than a decade ago, Tim Mason argued that future research would have to pay greater attention to the social or welfarist pretensions (*fürsorgliche Gehabe*) of the regime. See Mason, "Die Bändigung der Arbeiterklasse im nationalsozialistischen Deutschland," in Carola Sachse, Tilla Siegel, Hasso Spode, and Wolfgang Spohn, *Angst, Belohnung Zucht und Ordnung. Herrschaftsmechanismen im Nationalsozialismus* (Westdeutscher Verlag, 1982), pp. 11–53, Wolfgang Schneider, ed., *"Vernichtunspolitik." Eine Debatte über den Zusammenhang von Sozialpolitik und Genozid im nationalsozialistischen Deutschland* (Junius Verlag, 1991), Ulrich Herbert, "Arbeiterschaft im 'Dritten Reich'. Zwischenbilanz und offene Fragen," *GuG* 15 (1989), pp. 320–60, Martin Geyer, "Soziale Sicherheit und wirtschaftlicher Fortschritt. Überlegungen zum Verhältnis von Arbeitsideologie und Sozialpolitik im 'Dritten Reich,'" *GuG* 15 (1989), pp. 382–406, and Marie-Luise Recker, *Nationalsozialistische Sozialpolitik im Zweiten Weltkrieg* (Oldenbourg, 1985).

[90] Hellmuth Reichert, *Die Neuordnung der Wohlfahrtspflege im nationalsozialistischen Staate* (dissertation, Breslau, 1935), pp. 6–7, 19.

of humanitarian and Christian charity, whose deleterious consequences were compounded by the underlying belief in the equality of all individuals, the insistence upon the determining influence of the milieu, and the "delusion of the universal malleability of mankind, of the omnipotence of education."[91] The effect of these arguments was to invert the basic principles of need-based social services which had been codified during the 1920s and negate their underlying principles. This Nazi inversion of republican *Fürsorge* led to the basic principles of Nazi welfare: that the welfare of the *Volk* took priority over that of the individual and that the rights of the needy individual could never be greater than the obligations toward the community assumed by the individual.[92] From these principles derived the oft-repeated slogan "the common weal before private interest" (*Gemeinnutz geht vor Eigennutz*).[93]

This insistence upon the primacy of community over individual has two implications which are of overriding importance in understanding the nature of Nazi welfare and its relation to republican *Fürsorge*. First, by collapsing the distinction between law and morality, it provided the basis for a totalitarian conception of social citizenship which eliminated the sphere of personal rights and freedom of conscience which had ostensibly made possible the degeneration of republican *Fürsorge*. Both liberals and Christian conservatives recognized a moral obligation to provide at least an existence minimum for those persons who made no positive contribution to society, though they denied that this moral obligation could be transformed into a legal right without endangering the foundations of society. Consequently, the mere fact of indigence was not itself a criminal offense, notwithstanding the quasi-criminalization of vagrancy and begging or the fact that both groups insisted that, in certain cases, this existence minimum should be provided in the form of compulsory institutional care. In the narrow field of welfare, Nazi welfare reformers believed that the direct obligation of the individual to engage his or her energies in the service of the common good held out the potential to overcome the debilitating conflict between the preventive goals and subsidiary, individualizing methods of social welfare by establishing a dynamic relationship between the level of such engagement and the level of social services.[94] This vast extension of social obligations was based on the conviction that the failure to comply with the "obligation to act in a conformist manner and actively engage oneself" (*Pflicht des Wohlverhaltens und des aktiven Einsatzes*) would injure not only the individual, but the entire community, for whose welfare each individual was directly re-

---

[91] Ilse Geibel, *Die Umwertung der Wohlfahrtspflege durch den Nationalsozialismus* (*Pädagogisches Magazin*, no. 1398, 1934), pp. 9, 22.

[92] Hermann Althaus, *Nationalsozialistische Volkswohlfahrt* (Schriften der Deutschen Hochschule für Politik, Abt. II, no. 2, 1935), pp. 9–10.

[93] Herwart Vorländer, *Die NSV. Darstellung und Dokumentation einer nationalsozialistischen Organization* (*Schriften des Bundesarchivs*, Bd. 35, 1988), p. 200.

[94] Oskar Martini, "Die Aufgaben der öffentlichen Fürsorge nach Beendigung der Massenarbeitslosigkeit," *Neue familien- und arbeitspolitische Aufgaben der deutschen Wohlfahrtspflege*, pp. 49ff.

sponsible.[95] The de facto criminalization of asociality and indigence under the Nazi regime meant that welfare officials and the state were no longer limited to appealing to the conscience of the recipient, but could employ the courts and the police to directly impose social norms and obligations upon all citizens.[96] Or, to put the issue in different terms, this potentially infinite extension of the social obligations of the individual reduced the sphere of freedom of conscience and action to such a degree that it was no longer possible for the individual to pursue unmolested activities which conflicted with the norms of the national community.[97]

This dynamic relationship between social rights and social obligations was the basis for the total, permanent mobilization of the nation, the "achievement socialism" (*Leistungssozialismus*) which Althaus envisioned as the successor to the welfare or redistributive socialism of the Weimar era,[98] and the eventual transformation of the welfare state—in the pejorative sense of the word—into an "educational state" (*Erziehungsstaat*) or "labor state" (*Arbeitsstaat*). As Althaus wrote, "Germany has been transformed from a welfare state to a labor state. Collective welfare has been transformed into National Socialist help *by* the community and education *to* community: Welfare is no longer sympathy with the weak, but help to become strong."[99] The NSV and the *Winterhilfswerke* were the vehicles *par excellence* for the realization of this goal, and the other well-known slogan of the NSV—"We're not here to suffer along, but to fight along!" (*Nicht mitzuleiden, sondern mitzukämpfen sind wir da!*)—derived directly from this activist spirit based on the priority of sacrifice over rights.

The second major implication of the Nazi insistence upon the primacy of community over individual was that the eugenic conception of the *Volk* and race opened the way to differential social and welfare policies which could be graduated infinitely in both positive and negative directions now that public policy was no longer constrained by the rule of law. As the Nazi vision of a modern, achievement-oriented society was refracted through the lenses of their racial ideas, the progressive and repressive dimensions of modern social and welfare policies—whose precise relation to one another had always been somewhat ambiguous—were separated from one another and applied in a highly selective manner to different segments of the population. Increasingly, "legitimation through labor" (*Bewährung durch Arbeit*), rather than individual need, became the basic criterion for determining social status and social rights, and asociality and work-shyness became crimes against the community. Those persons who

[95] Hilgenfeldt, *Idee der nationalsozialistischen Wohlfahrtspflege* (Munich, 1937), p. 10, and Hans Achinger, *Sozialpolitik und Fürsorge* (Berlin, 1939), citation p. 194, who criticizes this trend.

[96] Peter Zolling, *Zwischen Integration und Segregation. Sozialpolitik im "Dritten Reich" am Beispiel der "Nationalsozialistischen Volkswohlfahrt" (NSV) in Hamburg* (Peter Lang, 1986), pp. 79ff.

[97] As Michael Kater argues, there was no longer a "right to sickness" or, by implication, indigence. Kater, "Die 'Gesundheitsführung' des Deutschen Volkes," *Medizinhistorisches Journal* 18 (1983), pp. 349–75, especially p. 351.

[98] Althaus, *Nationalsozialistische Volkswohlfahrt*, p. 10.

[99] Althaus, "Zum Geleit," *Arbeitseinsatz und Arbeitserziehung durch Fürsorge.*

were classified as inferior, asocial, or work-shy became the object of repressive measures which were graduated from lower wages and lower levels of social services via measures to discipline and reeducate those persons who could potentially be integrated into the national community, but who failed to conform to the Nazi vision of the *Volksgenosse*, to eugenic sterilization and internment in concentration camps.[100]

As we have seen, the NSV claimed for itself the honor of providing assistance to the vital, healthy members of the *Volk*, while relegating to the confessional charities the duty of caring for the hopelessly sick and infirm, and it placed special emphasis on promoting the welfare of healthy, racially valuable families through "hygienic leadership" (*Gesundheitsführung*).[101] A variety of programs, such as the *Hilfswerk Mutter und Kind*, the expansion of family social work, and rural convalescent trips for urban youth, simply extended some of the more innovative Weimar social hygiene programs within a eugenic framework. Although Nazi welfare reformers increasingly appropriated the rhetoric of prevention, all of these initiatives were colored by a strong desire to move away from the "welfare for the inferior" or "degenerate welfare" (*Minderwertigenfürsorge*) of the republican period. This reorientation of welfare was so important for the Nazis because they believed that, by giving preference to the sick and weak over the strong and healthy, this degenerate welfare had accelerated the process of negative selection and accentuated the dysgenic effects inherent in all individualistic welfare.[102] Instead, in the future the task of welfare had to be "the protection of that life which is worthy of being protected and strengthened and which will itself in the future be capable of serving the greater whole with its strength and productivity."[103] Welfare had to become as Emmy Wagner put it in 1934, "racially conscious," and in this way individualist *Fürsorge* was to be transformed into collectivist racial policy (*Rassenpolitik*).[104]

Exactly where these racial policies might lead was unclear, but the implications were ominous. As Hilgenfeldt wrote in the inaugural number of *Nationalsozialistischer Volksdienst*, "The unfit must be liquidated [*ausgemerzt*] mercilessly and without reservation on the basis of the insight of our National Socialist worldview that the right of the individual is inferior to the right of the community and that the right of the individual must be violated when the right

[100] Hans-Uwe Otto/Heinz Sünker, "Volksgemeinschaft als Formierungsideologie des Nationalsozialismus. Zu Genesis und Geltung von 'Volkspflege,'" in Otto and Sünker, eds., *Politische Formierung und soziale Erziehung im Nationalsozialismus* (Suhrkamp, 1991), pp. 50–77, and Peukert, "Arbeitslager und Jugend-KZ: die 'Behandlung Gemeinschaftsfremder' im Dritten Reich," in Peukert and Jürgen Reulecke, eds., *Die Reihen fast geschlossen. Beiträge zur Geschichte des Alltags unterm Nationalsozialismus* (Peter Hammer Verlag, 1981), pp. 413–34.

[101] "Satzung der NS-Volkswohlfahrt," Vorländer, *Die NSV. Darstellung und Dokumentation*, pp. 201–3.

[102] Althaus, *Nationalsozialistische Volkswohlfahrt*, pp. 11–13.

[103] Geibel, *Die Umwertung der Wohlfahrtspflege*, p. 21.

[104] Wagner, *Grundlagen einer artbewußten Fürsorge* (Berlin, 1935).

of the community demands this."[105] However, few persons were as blunt as Wagner about the implications of this decision to place the welfare of the *Volk* and race above that of the individual members through which these meta-subjects existed. Every person, she wrote, must stand in awe before the greatness of the state and the divine mission of the German *Volk* and, if necessary, be integrated through social work into the national community which he or she had to serve; the only persons who stood outside the national community were those who excluded themselves. Wagner told her readers that welfare authorities had to make their charges aware that they had to make a clear decision: "Whoever constantly and out of their own free will opposes the national community must accept responsibility for this action, up to annihilation." To degenerate welfare which served only the individual, she opposed a racially conscious welfare whose fundamental principle was that the *"welfare, indeed, the life of the individual itself must be sacrificed when the welfare and life of the whole demands this, when state and economy, Volkstum and culture are endangered."*[106]

These were the logical consequences which could be drawn from the eugenic reorientation of welfare in the 1930s. Although some, such as Stahl, might have been willing to identify Christianity and *Volkstum* with very little remainder, these eugenic consequences are hardly compatible with either Progressivism or Christianity, at least in any recognizable sense of these words. The preventive, therapeutic practices pioneered by the Progressives since the 1890s provided a set of disciplinary practices that could be—and were—easily appropriated by the Nazis for their own ends, and the influence of social-scientific discourses on the social question upon Nazi racial and welfare policies demonstrates the existence of a strong, distinctly modern continuity between prewar Progressivism, the republican welfare system, and National Socialism.[107] These developments were facilitated by the continuity of social work personnel and social reformers across the Weimar Republic, the Third Reich, and the Federal Republic.[108] How-

[105] Hilgenfeldt, "Aufgaben der NS-Volkswohlfahrt," *Nationalsozialistischer Volksdienst* 1 (October 1933), pp. 1–6, citation p. 5.

[106] Wagner, *Grundlagen einer artbewußten Fürsorge*, pp. 6, 7.

[107] Despite the undeniable influence of eugenics and other social sciences on Nazi policies, in any attempt to assess the modernity of the Nazi regime it is well to bear in mind Norbert Frei's reminder that, all of these phenomena notwithstanding, Hitler's own worldview and that of many of his followers was little more than a bundle of resentments, prejudices, and hatreds held together by a popular social Darwinism. Norbert Frei, "Wie modern war der Nationalsozialismus?" *GuG* 19 (1993), pp. 367–87.

[108] On the continuities at the level of social work technique and personnel (at least for those persons who were not dismissed on political grounds in 1933), see Helge Knüppel-Dähne and Emilija Mitrovic, "Helfen und Dienen. Die Arbeit von Fürsorgerinnen in Hamburger öffentlichen Dienst während des Nationalsozialismus," in Hans-Uwe Otto and Heinz Sünker, eds., *Soziale Arbeit und Faschismus* (Suhrkamp, 1989), pp. 176–97, Stefan Schnurr, "Die nationalsozialistische Funktionalisierung sozialer Arbeit. Zur Kontinuität und Diskontinuität der Praxis sozialer Berufe," in Otto and Sünker, eds., *Politische Formierung und soziale Erziehung im Nationalsozialismus*, pp. 106–40, and Glensk and Rothmaler, eds., *Kehrseiten der Wohlfahrt*. As Knüppel-Dähne and Mit-

ever, the Nazi project for the racial reconstruction of civil society implied a
fundamental redefinition of the meaning of welfare which stripped the concept
of all liberal-Christian connotations and reduced the value of the individual to
the economic and military productivity of the individual and his or her contribution to the body politic in its unceasing struggle for survival. In this process,
these continuities at the level of technique were themselves refunctioned as they
were subordinated to an antithetical system of substantive ends.[109] This continuity of personnel and technique was facilitated by the apparent identity of the
authoritarianism of both the Progressives and the confessional welfare groups,
on the one hand, and that of the Nazis, whose external forms were similar, but
which ultimately drew on different sources and had very different practical
implications. These differences only came to the surface with the definitive
consolidation of a specifically Nazi state between 1936 and 1938 and with the
adoption of welfare, population, and social policies whose implications could
no longer be overlooked.[110]

---

rovic note, although social workers did not make life and death decisions, they did make the
preliminary determination as to who was to be turned over to the police bureaucracy, p. 190.

[109] For these reasons, it has been argued that the term modernity can be applied to the Third Reich
only if it is stripped of its traditional connotations of improvement, progress, and emancipation to
such an extent that both the concept of modernity and the very idea of Nazi "welfare" become
meaningless. Burleigh and Wippermann, *The Racial State*, pp. 2, 17, and Otto and Sünker, "Volksgemeinschaft als Formierungsideologie," p. 71. For a defense of the use of the term "welfare" state
to describe Nazi policies, see Sachße and Tennstedt, *Geschichte der Armenfürsorge in Deutschland*,
III:11–17, 273–78.

[110] Schnurr, "Die nationalsozialistische Funktionalisierung sozialer Arbeit," especially 137–40,
Sachße and Tennstedt, *Geschichte der Armenfürsorge in Deutschland*, III:81ff., Hansen, *Wohlfahrtspolitik im NS-Staat*, and Recker, *Nationalsozialistische Sozialpolitik im Zweiten Weltkrieg*.

THE EXTENSIVE periodical literature published by the various welfare reform groups is the most important published source on the development of the German welfare system. Unfortunately, a comprehensive list of all of the articles cited in this work would defeat the purpose of a bibliography. However, since these publications are, like the welfare system itself, fragmented along political-religious and functional lines, the following paragraphs provide a brief guide to the most important publications.

The most influential welfare reform group was the Deutscher Verein, and from the 1880s into the early 1930s the *Schriften des Deutschen Vereins* (*SDV*) are the most important single source on welfare reform debates; these volumes contain both the monographic reports which were prepared for the DV annual conferences and the minutes of the conference discussions. From the turn of the century until its demise in 1920, the *Zeitschrift für das Armenwesen* (*ZfA*) was the official organ of the DV. For a brief moment in the early 1920s, *Soziale Praxis* (*SPr*)—the most important Progressive publication in the social policy field since the 1890s—also served as the major forum for welfare-related issues as well. However, in the early 1920s the DV began publishing the *Nachrichtendienst*, which quickly became the leading specialized publication for welfare reformers and municipal welfare officials. In the mid-1920s, the DV also began publishing a second series, *Aufbau und Ausbau der Fürsorge*. In the immediate postwar period, *Concordia*, published by the *Zentralstelle für Volkswohlfahrt*, was also an important publication.

Each of the *Spitzenverbände* also had their own house organ for issues of general interest: *Caritas*; *Die Innere Mission* (IM); *Arbeiterwohlfahrt* (*AW*; in the immediate postwar period, *Die Gleichheit* was the main forum for Social Democratic discussion of welfare reform); *Blätter des Deutschen Roten Kreuzes*; *Proletarische Sozialpolitik*; and *Freie Wohlfahrtspflege* (*FW*), which was the official publication of the German League for Voluntary Welfare. In addition, the *Deutsche Zeitschrift für Wohlfahrtspflege* (*DZW*) was published by the Labor Ministry. It reflected an ecumenical, middle-of-the-road approach on most issues and sought to smooth over conflicts between public and voluntary welfare. *Volkswohlfahrt* was the official journal of record for the Prussian Ministry for Public Welfare.

In the youth welfare field, the leading publications were the *Zentralblatt für Jugendrecht und Jugendwohlfahrt* (published by the General Conference on Correctional Education [*Allgemeiner Fürsorgeerziehungstag*], its contributions spanned the entire political spectrum); *Die Erziehung* (which represented the views of the pedagogical movement); *Jugendwohl* (Catholic); and *Evangelische Jugendhilfe*.

Each of the major social worker associations also had its own publication: *Die Sozialbeamtin* (originally published by the DVS, but was succeeded in 1921 by *Soziale Berufsarbeit* [*SBA*], which was published by the *Arbeitsgemeinschaft der Sozialbeamtinnenvereine Deutschlands*); *Soziale Arbeit* (published by the women active in youth welfare under the auspices of Humanitas); and the *Mitteilungen des Vereins katholischer Sozialbeamtinnen Deutschlands*. In addition, *Die Frau* was also an important forum for the discussion of women and social work.

In the field of social hygiene and eugenics, this study has relied primarily on *Gesundheitsfürsorge. Zeitschrift der evangelischen Kranken- und Pflegeanstalten*, *Archiv für Rassen- und Gesellschaftsbiologie* (*ARGB*, the leading eugenic publication), and Preußisches Ministerium für Volkswohlfahrt, ed., *Veröffentlichungen auf dem Gebiet der Medizinalverwaltung* (*VGM*).

UNPUBLISHED PRIMARY MATERIALS

Archiv des Deutschen Caritasverbandes, Freiburg (ADCV)

B I 3 DV	Kommission zur Überprüfung des materiellen Fürsorgerechts
CA XVII	Sozialfürsorge
CA XX 32	Zusammenarbeit
CA XX 49	Arbeiterwohlfahrt
CA XX 52	Internationale Arbeiterhilfe
R307	I Gesetze über Wohlfahrtspflege
107	Denkschriften, Eingaben, etc. des DCV
142	Soziale Frauenschule
219.3	Berufsverband katholischer Fürsorgerinnen
319.4 E II 1	RJWG. Entwürfe, Auslegung, etc.
319.4 E II 6	RJWG. Caritaskommission
319.4 E II 15	Religiöses Bekenntnis und Weltanschauung in der Jugend- und Gefährdetenfürsorge
319.4 F I 1a	Zentrale des KDF
319.4 F III 1a	Verein katholischer Deutscher Sozialbeamtinnen
319.4 F III 3	Westfälische Provinzialarbeitsgemeinschaft der Berufsverbände der Wohlfahrtspflegerinnen Deutschlands
460	Reichsgemeinschaft von Hauptverbänden der freien Wohlfahrtspflege
460.1	Deutscher Zentralausschuß für die Auslandshilfe
461.055	Deutscher Verein

Archiv des Instituts für Gemeinwohl, Frankfurt (IfG)

225–31	Deutscher Verein für öffentliche und private Fürsorge

Archiv des Diakonischen Werkes der Evangelischen Kirche, Berlin (ADW)

CA G 77	
CA G 78	
CA 480a	
CA 688	Verband der evangelischen Wohlfahrtspflegerinnen Deutschlands
CA 816	Konferenz der Leiter der Frauenschulen
CA 868	Zusammenschluß der Berufsarbeiter(innen) der Inneren Mission aus Anlaß der Revolution
CA 980	Reichsgemeinschaft von Hauptverbänden der freien Wohlfahrtspflege
CA 1165	Spitzenverbände der öffentlichen Wohlfahrtspflege
CA 1184	Humanitas to Labor Ministry (July 4, 1924)
CA 1195	Deutsche Liga der freien Wohlfahrtspflege

Archiv des Diakonischen Werkes der Evangelischen Kirche in Rheinland, Düsseldorf (ADWRh)

10.5.1	Deutsche Liga der freien Wohlfahrtspflege
24.6	Delegation von Aufgaben der öffentlichen Wohlfahrtspflege am Organe der freien Liebestätigkeit (Rundfrage)

24.10   Kurse der Inneren Mission zur Einführung in die Neuregelung der
                 öffentlichen Wohlfahrtspflege

Bundesarchiv Koblenz (BAK)

R43 Reichskanzlei
I/837
I/842

R86 Reichsgesundheitsamt
2318

Bundesarchiv, Abt. Potsdam (BAP)

Reichsarbeitsministerium (RAM)
7000   Frauenfürsorgereferate in RAM
8905   Zuziehung der Kb/Kh Vereinigungen zu Reichsausschuß
8906–7   Niederschriften des Reichsausschusses
9149   Vereinigung der freien gemeinnützigen Kranken- und Wohlfahrt-
                 seinrichtungen Deutschlands
9164   Zusammenarbeit zwischen öffentlichen und privaten Wohlfahrtsp-
                 flege
9184–90   Notstandsmaßnahmen für Rentenempfänger der Invaliden-/Ange-
                 stelltenversicherung
9195   Kapitalkleinrentner
9234   RFV
9238   Einsprüche der Kriegsbehindertenorganisationen
9258–60   Übergang des Armenwesens zu dem Reichsarbeitsministerium
9240   Initiativgesetz
9242   Wandererfürsorge
9243   Verwahrungsgesetz
9244–45   Verordnung zur Änderung der RGr
9246–47   Entwürfe RFV, VO, RGr
8873   Fürsorge für Kriegswitwen und -waisen

Reichsjustizministerium (RJM)
1514–15   Jugendwohlfahrt

Geheimes Staatsarchiv Preußischer Kulturbesitz, Abt. Merseburg (GStAM)

Rep. 151   Finanzministerium
11736   Frauenreferate

Stadtarchiv Düsseldorf (StADf)

III/4051   Chronik der Wohnungspflege
XX 388   Berufsgenossenschaft mit der Humanitas in Berlin
XX 469   Protokolle, Berlin
XX 471   Korrespondenz mit dem Fünften Wohlfahrtsverband

Stadtarchiv Nürnberg (StAN)

C25/I Alte Fürsorgeregistratur
1   Städtisches Wohlfahrtsamt
2   Zentralauskunftsstelle des stätdischen Wohlfahrtsamts
239   Fürsorgewesen

280   • *B I B L I O G R A P H Y* •

Historisches Archiv der Stadt Köln (HAStK)

Abt. 902:   198 Wohlfahrtsangelegenheiten

Stadtarchiv Frankfurt (StAF)

Magistratsakten - Vereine
6/3–4   Wohlfahrtsschule

Stadtarchiv München (StAM)

Schulamt 3518

Bayerisches Hauptstaatsarchiv, München (BayHStaA): MK 42943
Helene-Lange-Archiv (HLA)

1–4/1   Bund Deutscher Frauenvereine
6–29/3   Anna von Gierke

Archiv der Hochschule für Sozialpädagogik und Sozialarbeit (AFHSS)
Evangelisches Zentralarchiv in Berlin (EZA)

YOUNG-SUN HONG is Professor of History at the State University of New York, Stony Brook.

PRINCETON STUDIES IN
CULTURE/POWER/HISTORY